THE ARGUMENT HANDBOOK

THE ARGUMENT HANDBOOK

K.J. PETERS

broadview press

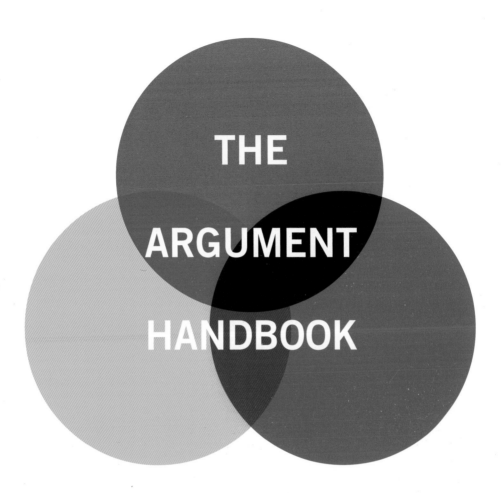

BROADVIEW PRESS – www.broadviewpress.com
Peterborough, Ontario, Canada

Founded in 1985, Broadview Press remains a wholly independent publishing house. Broadview's focus is on academic publishing; our titles are accessible to university and college students as well as scholars and general readers. With over 600 titles in print, Broadview has become a leading international publisher in the humanities, with world-wide distribution. Broadview is committed to environmentally responsible publishing and fair business practices.

Library and Archives Canada Cataloguing in Publication

Peters, K. J. (Kevin J.), author
The argument handbook / K.J. Peters.

Includes bibliographical references and index.
ISBN 978-1-55481-435-0 (softcover)

1. English language—Rhetoric—Handbooks, manuals, etc. I. Title.

PE1408.P467 2018 808'.042 C2018-905035-7

Broadview Press handles its own distribution in North America:
PO Box 1243, Peterborough, Ontario K9J 7H5, Canada
555 Riverwalk Parkway, Tonawanda, NY 14150, USA
Tel: (705) 743-8990; Fax: (705) 743-8353
email: customerservice@broadviewpress.com

Distribution is handled by Eurospan Group in the UK, Europe, Central Asia, Middle East, Africa, India, Southeast Asia, Central America, South America, and the Caribbean. Distribution is handled by Footprint Books in Australia and New Zealand.

Broadview Press acknowledges the financial support of the Government of Canada for our publishing activities.

Canada

Edited by Martin R. Boyne

Book design by Chris Rowat Design

PRINTED IN CANADA

CONTENTS

PART II TYPES OF ARGUMENT

PREFACE

A textbook's preface, like the textbooks themselves, have an odd relationship with their intended readers. It was an editor who made me aware of this when she said, "students buy textbooks, but professors choose them." In other words, professors are the intended audience up to the point that they select a text for their course. Then the primary audience becomes students assigned to read the book.

Surprisingly, what seems approachable, useful, and cool to a professor is not always so for the student. I have been teaching for many years and get to spend a great deal of time with first-year students. When I began to think about writing a textbook, I thought I understood my students' struggles with writing and why they succeeded. I was wrong.

STUDENT EDITORS

It has been a long time since I was a student, and so I don't have a student's perspective and didn't understand their experiences until I asked. The students below were kind enough to share their time and help me understand what I didn't know. These students, drawn from colleges and universities across the country, became the Board of Student Editors. Their insights were indispensable to the development of the examples and features and the selection of models throughout.

Alexa Faye Rhein Aaronson
Alma Acosta
Wenmar Pagulayan Badbada
Sabrina Barreto
Nina Batt
Jamie Battaglia
Dominick Beaudine
Christopher Caruso
Eric Chavoya
Christopher Chien
Cole D. Crawford
Caroline de Bie
Hilda Delgadillo
Mekleit Dix
Elicia Flemming
Sneha Gandhi

Peyton Gajan
Daneil Gherardi
Hannah Gioia
Laurne Glass
Elizabeth Goldhammer
Alvaro Gonzalez
Kelly Hu
Katherine Kennedy
Chrsitin Kilicarslan
Oscar King IV
Alec Lee
Olivia Li
Nicole Lindars
Audrey Liviakis
Sonja Lorance
Hudson Luthringshausen
Zachary Malinski
Tyler Marting
Hannah Maryanski
Kaya McMullen
Laura Miola
Yulissa Nunez
Veronica Pacheco
Alexandra Petosa
Alexia Pineda
Kathleen Porter
Lauren Roknich
Nikolas Romero
Anthony Sasso
Alyssa Smith
Cedar Smith
Jacqueline Smith
Riley Stauffer
John Tavelli
Jenna Thomas
Raven Tukes
Brendan Viloria
Adonis Williams
Nick A. Yim
Vanessa Zavala-Zimmerer

What did they teach me? Well, they helped me realize that those who intentionally plagiarize probably aren't reading assigned chapters. However, good students are worried about mistakes that may lead to an accusation of plagiarism. The student board members also helped me understand their questions and challenges, such as the pressure of managing not one, but multiple research writing assignments in very different courses given by very different professors with very tight deadlines.

Surprisingly, some of my own experiences as a student were mirrored in the student editors. Whenever a new idea was introduced to me in class, my first question was, why do I need to know this? In a similar way, many board members expressed disappointment with professors who cannot justify what they are teaching and with texts that do not bother to describe the value of what they present. For this reason, each chapter begins with a justification of the subject and a brief discussion of its purpose and value.

More to the point, these students helped me understand that at 1:20 a.m., when working on a paper that just isn't coming together, they don't have time to read an entire chapter to remind themselves how to integrate a source or find a sample outline. They need good information built on solid pedagogy, great examples from professional writers, and relevant advice from students who have faced the same problems—and they need it all fast.

MODULAR ORGANIZATION

Informed by the insights of my student editors, I created this modular rhetoric in a handbook format so that students can find what they need quickly and professors can assign the content they want in the order they prefer. Stand alone chapters allow instructors to customize argument course materials to align with their course goals and curriculum. For example, instructors who prefer to cover "Chapter 7. PERSUADING" in the first few weeks of class can assign that chapter. If an instructor does not want to cover "Ch. 11. NARRATING" or "Ch. 14. PROPOSING A SOLUTION," these chapters can be easily skipped and serve as background resources. The modular format also makes it easier for students to zero in on the content they need when they are faced with a blank screen, a hard deadline, and a skeptical audience.

The Argument Handbook is intended to help students in writing, composition, and rhetoric courses. It is also a resource for writers as they navigate courses in all disciplines and deal with everyday situations that call for effective arguments.

APPROACH: THREE LENSES FOR VIEWING ARGUMENTS

Reading the ideas and feedback of the editorial board, it became clear that students attending very different colleges and universities scattered across North America often struggled with similar issues and concepts. For example, students enjoy **invention** exercises, but many don't think it is worth the time when time is tight. **Audience** is a consideration to which many students don't give a second thought, in part because high schools have always provided them with a specific, well-defined audience: the teacher. Colleges and universities, however, confront students with an array of professorial expectations shaped by disciplines, specialties, and individual disposition. Finally, when one member of the board said, "how can I speak with **authority** if I don't have a degree yet?," I was surprised to discover that many students believe an authoritative voice and presence is beyond their grasp.

To help students understand and integrate these concepts into their writing process, *The Argument Handbook* is based on three lenses for viewing argument and focuses on examples that are relevant to today's students.

- **Invention**: From the very beginning, the book expands the sources of invention beyond an individual's memory and experiences to include peers, genres, and the conventions of specific disciplines, as well as libraries and archives. Students learn to see how ideas become evidence, how evidence is understood, and why research is necessary.
- **Audience**: Throughout, the book helps students see persuasion in real-world terms as opposed to a static classroom assignment. The lens of audience teaches

students to look for audience expectations in an email or a lab-report assignment, for example, and it helps students see different genres as ways of meeting the varied expectations of very different audiences.

- **Authority**: To succeed in academic writing as well as in other writing situations, students need to understand genre and disciplinary practices such as sourcing and documentation as ways of building and expressing persuasive power. As they learn the importance of establishing authority in their writing, students will come to see building trust as essential. *The Argument Handbook* also demonstrates how focusing on intentional invention practices (brainstorming, the believing game, etc.) will help students avoid plagiarism as a desperate last resort at the end of a long night of writer's block.

TOOLBOXES

The insights of the student board of editors helped in the development of "Toolboxes": three types of brief, boxed commentaries intended to help students make sense of and apply concepts to their own writing.

- **Breaking the Block** boxes provide step-by-step activities to help students who are at a loss for something to say. Students are often confronted by mental, structural, organizational, tonal, and phrasing blocks that stop invention, drafting, and revision. Additionally, this set of boxes helps students see revision, research, and experimenting with genres and constrictions as forms of invention that can impel greater creativity and clarity of voice.
- **Conventions in Context** boxes focus on how audience expectations can dictate the use of conventions in any given situation. For example, in Chapter 2, the box provides a process for examining an assignment and determining an instructor's expectations by looking at elements of the assignment such as the deadline and the required page count.
- **Responsible Sourcing** boxes help students see documentation and sourcing as means of building trust and authority. These boxes also include practical advice such as strategies researchers use to keep track of their sources.

ACKNOWLEDGEMENTS

My thanks to Charlie and Íñigo López de Loyola, whose spirits animate and inform this work. Carla Samodulski worked very hard on this project. In simple terms, she is magic. Marjorie Mather, Martin Boyne, and their colleagues at Broadview have my undying appreciation and gratitude. Marvin and Elda Peters put me on this path, and I hope I am worthy of their sacrifice. I am thankful that Katie Wiebe and Bev Holmskog tried to teach me writing while I tried to make them laugh. I owe much to Joy Ritche and Kate Ronald, who taught me about the nobility of the profession and how to be a professor. And finally, I am fortunate that my one true love is also my best editor and motivator. Dr. Robin Miskolcze's patience, encouragement, and support made this project possible. A very special thanks to Eliza Peters, whose support, interest in my work, and sense of humor keep me moving forward—I love you, Eliza. I am lucky to have these two women in my life.

PART I

INVENTION AND RESEARCH

CHAPTER 1

ASSEMBLING ARGUMENTS: AN INTRODUCTION

The smartphone revolution began In January 2007 at the Macworld Conference & Expo in San Francisco. At that conference, Steve Jobs, the co-founder of Apple, presented the first rendition of the iPhone. In doing so, he made the argument that traditional phones were obsolete. Back then, most phones lacked the functions of the new iPhone. During the course of Jobs's argument, he presented reasons to support his claim (the different features of the new phone) and evidence to back up those reasons (demonstrations of how the different features worked), as Figure 1.1 below shows.

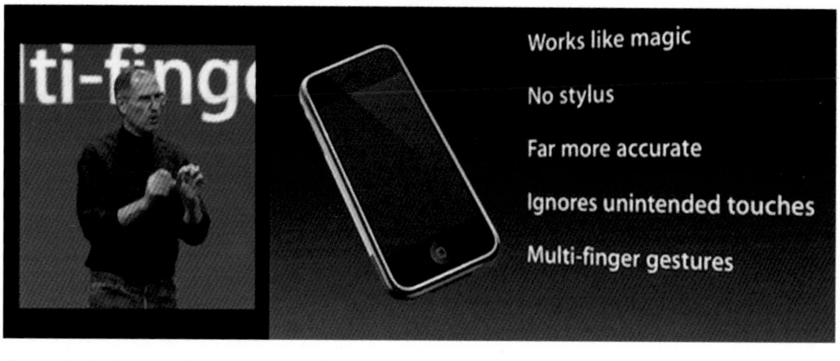

Figure 1.1 Steve Jobs, keynote address at Macworld 2007.

Steve Jobs's arguments persuaded many people of the superiority of this product, inspiring a great deal of devotion and making the first iPhone the highest selling smartphone of the time.

Other device makers have failed to match Apple's dominance, but not simply because of how the competing device worked or how the technology was assembled. When the next new device reinvents the iPhone, or some other product or process we take for granted, that device will be a success or failure in part because of the arguments offered by its creators. Arguments will be offered when the product is first conceptualized and designed. Arguments will be offered to shareholders and investors to fund the product's development. And arguments will be offered on conference stages and in advertisements to customers, to be spread through word of mouth as friends and co-workers persuade one another to buy it. How persuasive arguments are assembled is what this chapter is about.

MODULE I-1

ARGUMENT DEFINED

An **argument** is an attempt to persuade someone to think, believe, or act differently by offering reasons in support of a conclusion. Successful arguments persuade readers or listeners to change an opinion, a belief, or a behavior. In this module, we will examine some of the broadest categories of and reasons for argument and discuss some strategies for writing arguments. We'll also take a look at the type of argument of most immediate concern to students: academic arguments.

Strategies for Argument

Whatever their purpose and subject, writers of effective arguments employ strategies, or tricks of the trade, to persuade audiences. Some basic strategies include appeals to readers' or listeners' tendency to trust authority, appeals to their emotions, and the use of different types of reasoning.

Three ways to appeal to an argument's audience. Arguments are persuasive if they appeal to their intended audience, just as cooking a friend's favorite food for a birthday party is a way of appealing to her appetite and thereby communicating your feelings. The three common rhetorical appeals are described briefly below and in more detail in Chapter 17.

- **An ethical appeal, or *ethos***, involves an author or speaker moving the audience to believe that the source of the message is trustworthy and authoritative. It is an effective strategy because an audience tends to trust writers and speakers who are authorities on the issue at hand. Citing recognized experts in a field, including the academic degrees and publishing record of a source, and carefully documenting your sources using a widely accepted documentation style, such as the system recommended by the Modern Language Association (MLA) or the American Psychological Association (APA), are ways of making an ethical appeal.
- **An emotional appeal, or *pathos***, does just what it says: it appeals to the emotions of the audience in an attempt to move its members to think, believe, or act differently. For example, the SPCA shows images of animals in distress to provoke pity and thereby motivate the audience to send in a donation.
- **A logical appeal, or *logos***, relies upon logical reasoning and solid evidence to persuade. Most logical appeals are based on two types of reasoning: inductive and deductive.

Types of Reasoning or Logic

Reasoning is a means of connecting the evidence you have discovered to your conclusion, using logic. The two types of reasoning described below are commonly used in a wide variety of arguments. They are described in greater detail in Chapter 17.

- **Inductive reasoning** starts with observations about the world or your surroundings; you then use these observations to draw a conclusion that you believe is probably true. Induction is an exploratory form of reasoning because it can lead to previously undiscovered conclusions.
- **Deductive reasoning** uses one or more rules or general truths to come to a conclusion. Unlike induction, deduction involves the application of known truths or undisputed knowledge.

The chapters in Part II describe in detail many different types of arguments and ways to approach your subject and engage your audience. Part II also includes a number of useful strategies that can help you build persuasive arguments. Although you no doubt make many arguments in your daily life and at work, the type of argument you are probably most concerned about is an academic argument.

Characteristics of Academic Arguments

An **academic argument** is a specialized way of persuading an audience to think, believe, or act differently for the vital purpose of advancing knowledge. The goal of an academic argument is not simply to win or persuade. Scholars construct arguments to find, develop, test, and contribute knowledge to the ongoing exploration and discussion among others in a discipline or specialty.

Different disciplines and professors have various specific requirements for a successful academic argument. In general, however, if you are going to join the discussion in a field by making your ideas public in an academic context, you need to know that your audience will expect an argument composed of the elements listed below.

- **A thesis**: Academic arguments are built around a clearly stated thesis, or conclusion, which the reasons and evidence support. The thesis is the assertion to be proved. It typically appears at the beginning of an argument and is often restated and expanded toward the end. For more on the thesis and its role in research and guiding the reader, see Chapters 2 and 17.
- **Evidence**: Academic arguments often include data and other types of information that are used to support the reasons that in turn support the thesis. Evidence must be acceptable, valid, and authoritative in the eyes of the audience if the reasons are to have any persuasive power.
- **Reasoning**: In academic contexts, reasoning is used to connect an argument's reasons (or 'premises') to its conclusion, in order to demonstrate that the conclusion is true. The standards of reasoning and appropriate conclusions may vary from one discipline to another, even when the subject matter is the same. A biologist may reason toward a conclusion about the constitution of the human body, while a dance professor may reason toward a conclusion about the ideal movements of that body. In both cases, the subject is the human body; but the reasoning of the biologist is not likely to look very much like the reasoning of the dance professor.
- **Knowledge of the larger debate**: As stated above, academics argue to contribute to the ongoing exploration and discussion within a particular discipline. To join the conversation, the authors of an academic argument must demonstrate that they know what has already been said (discovered or disputed) by other scholars. Also, they must show why their ideas are relevant and how they contribute to the larger debate.
- **Adherence to conventions**: **Conventions** is another term for the grammar, punctuation, style, format, and tone that adherents of an academic discipline or specialty will expect. Though all disciplines have some conventions in common, such as spelling, different disciplines have different expectations. An argument that does not correctly use the conventions scholars or professors expect will not be persuasive and may suggest that the author or speaker is not ready to join the conversation.

Non-Academic Arguments

Not all arguments are academic. Many discussions in popular media may not be seen as persuasive by an academic audience or welcome in an academic setting. For example, **debates**, in which two people or two teams try to "score points," declare their opinions, or play to the crowd, can be a setting for arguments. However, debates may not be perceived as exploring or contributing to knowledge. **Quarrels**—angry disagreements—happen when people become frustrated with their inability to persuade and either forget to use or give up using reasons and evidence to support their points (see Figure 1.2). One familiar type of quarrel is common to cable TV panel discussions, which are more about the fireworks of clashing personalities than an attempt to discover truth using reasons and evidence. Academics are as passionate as any other profession; however, cool restraint is the expected demeanor of a seeker of truth.

Figure 1.2
Sometimes a quarrel just isn't worth the effort.

Tweets or sound bites, features of media discussions as well as political campaigns, are summaries of positions or short assertions lacking evidence. Tweets or sound bites are closer to bumper stickers than reasoned argument because they lack evidence and reasoning.

Some assertions and disputes are not arguments at all. Self-indulgence and bullying have no place in argument. Self-indulgent speakers talk to hear their own voice and brag about their accomplishments. Though such behavior can seem like an argument, it is rarely persuasive. Bullying or threatening the audience in some way also is not persuasive in an academic setting because the bully is neither using reasons and evidence nor contributing knowledge.

Visual and Multimedia Arguments

Most of the time, academics and others use language to make arguments, but they can also make them using imagery, sound, and technology, as Steve Jobs did when he introduced the first iPhone. You can find videos of Jobs's presentation, titled "Reinvent the Phone," on YouTube. His "keynote" is still a good example of a persuasive multimedia argument.

Visual arguments such as the one in Figure 1.3, which are most frequently encountered outside of the academic world, may look very different from written arguments. Visual, multimedia, and textual arguments, however, are built for the same purpose and all are composed of reasons and evidence.

Figure 1.3
Terry Richardson's Equinox ads are provocative and have proven successful in targeting a specific clientele that understands fitness as fashion.

A **visual argument** makes use of elements such as imagery and text, negative and positive space, layout and color, as well as info-graphics such as charts and graphs to persuade someone to think, believe, or act differently. For example, the advertisement shown in Figure 1.3 makes a cause-and-effect argument. The strength of the man is caused "BY EQUINOX." More prominently, the ad would have you believe that the beauty of the woman demonstrating the same strength as the man is also a product of Equinox gyms.

You do not have to be a graphic designer or an advertiser to develop visual arguments. Each time you update your Facebook profile with photos or graphics, you are using images and text to persuade others of your personality, qualities, likes, and dislikes.

As multimedia capabilities and tools become as common and easy to use as a smartphone, the expectations for persuasive visual arguments will increase. If you can build a strong argument, you can build a strong visual argument. For more on visual arguments, see Chapters 8 and 25.

Invention, Audience, and Authority: Three Lenses for Viewing Argument

Whether you are constructing a written or visual argument, and whatever the argument's context, it is natural to feel overwhelmed by the many decisions you have to make as you move through the process of composing a persuasive argument. However, if you look at your task through these three lenses, a great deal of the noise and confusion will melt away:

Invention: Information retrieval and synthesis. In other words, what you find out about an **issue**—a matter about which people disagree—and how you put this information together.

Audience: The people you are attempting to persuade. Understanding the audience's thoughts and expectations is the key to your persuasive power.

Authority: Traits and qualities that establish your credibility, leading an audience to pay attention to and be persuaded by your argument.

Invention, audience, and authority are the essential perspectives that shape three parts of this text. Each of these parts focuses upon a central task of building a successful argument:

Invention: Part I. Invention and Research
Audience: Part III. Appealing to Your Audience
Authority: Part V. Projecting Authority

Each of these parts will give you practical tools, tricks of the trade, time-saving exercises, and simple solutions to the problems that pop up whenever you try to build an argument.

MODULE I-2

INVENTION AND RESEARCH: HOW WILL YOU FIND IDEAS AND EVIDENCE?

Invention is the process of retrieving and synthesizing information and ideas in order to generate new perspectives, ideas, and arguments. An effective invention process suits an individual's style of composing and helps that writer move from frustration to inspiration and break writer's block. The type of information you seek and where it can typically be found should determine your invention process. When you retrieve the information from within your head, the invention process is called *looking within*. Chapter 3 presents invention strategies that will help you look within, including freewriting and imposing artificial limits on your writing. When you seek information outside your own thoughts and beyond your own experience, you are *looking around* by consulting friends and peers or going into the field to observe. Chapter 3 will also help you look around to invent. *Looking to research* helps you look beyond your immediate experience and the experiences of others that you consult to seek the ideas of scholars and other experts, that is, the authorities in the field. Chapters 4 and 19 will help you locate and gather the ideas of scholars and experts. Chapter 20 will help you analyze and evaluate what you have gathered so you can draw informed conclusions.

How Invention Saves Time and Effort

Whatever your composing task, you usually have only a limited period of time to complete it. Within that time, you must gather ideas and information, organize your material and write a draft, and then revise and proofread your writing. When you use one or more invention strategies to develop some ideas to work with, organizing, drafting, revising, and proofreading become much less daunting tasks.

However, the more time you spend looking at a blank page or procrastinating out of fear that you have nothing to say, the less time you will have for the other stages of the composing process. See the Breaking the Block box entitled "Invention Never Stops" for an invention strategy that can help you in this situation.

Breaking the Block
Invention Never Stops

Everyone experiences writer's block. It is important to remember that writer's block is not necessarily caused by a lack of ideas. Often, writers get stuck because they have too many ideas to choose from and too many potential audiences to talk to.

To overcome writer's block, you can use invention throughout the composing process. In addition, you are surrounded by the most valuable invention tool ever discovered—friends and peers.

INSTRUCTIONS: For one week, record your ideas as Step One describes, and then share them with others. Remember to include the day and time of each recorded thought.

Step One: Record Your Ideas

- Keep some means of recording your ideas near you at all times. It could be a notebook, a scrap of paper, or your smartphone's notes or voice memo app.
- Do not judge or dismiss any idea that comes to mind until you have kept it for a week and thought about it numerous times.
- When you have a great idea or a great question, or when you see something amazing, record your thoughts before they evaporate.

Step Two: Share Your Ideas

- Bounce your ideas off friends and peers.
- Write down or record how others respond to your ideas. Also, don't forget to write down your own thoughts and responses.
- Remember that critical responses are just opportunities to re-see and reshape your thinking.

Step Three: Give Your Ideas the Respect They Deserve

- At the end of the week, review all your notes or listen to the recordings you made.
- Look for connections between your ideas and observations and the responses of friends and peers.
- Categorize and prioritize the ideas and responses using some or all of the following, or other categories that seem appropriate to the task:
    - Big ideas I must develop now
    - Ideas related to big ideas
    - Thoughts that need time to develop
    - Problems to be solved
    - Solutions looking for a problem

How Writers Use Research to Discover Ideas

You may think that research consists simply of finding an assigned number of sources to support a thesis. Finding sources that confirm your existing opinions is not research, however. Instead, research is a process of discovery.

Research is another kind of invention. When you conduct research, you internalize information outside of your own experience so that you can challenge and develop your understanding. Research is necessary because new ideas are built upon existing ideas. When you learn about the ideas of others, observe the world around you, and engage in critical thinking and conversations with knowledgeable sources, you will develop a deeper, more informed perspective on your subject, you will have more to say, and your argument will be more persuasive. In short, you do research to discover what you do not know so that you may know more.

When a student reads a scholarly article or when reporters review court records, they are doing research. Research is not limited to print sources such as scholarly books and papers, however. When a sculptor studies the anatomy of a hand, she is doing research. When the famous scientist, anthropologist, and author Jane Goodall observes chimpanzees in their natural habitat, she is doing research. There is no single way to do research. There are, however, good and bad research methods. Chapter 2 will help you make a research plan and Chapters 4 and 19 will show you the tricks of the trade that researchers use to be thorough and efficient.

Researching How People Think and Talk

Through research, you will also gain an understanding of the expectations of your audience as you discover how your intended audience or those who work in a specific discipline or field think and talk about your subject. Use your understanding of how your audience thinks and what they expect to shape your argument.

Individuals in the film industry, for example, think and talk about *aspect ratios* and *medium shots*, whereas those in the computer industry talk about *LANs* and *bit rates*. If you are writing a paper for a history professor, clues to your professor's expectations will be found in the arguments written by other historians, or in the way that professor formulates her ideas in class.

Knowing how members of your audience think, what they value, and how they will understand you is as important as knowing what you want to say. When the writers of an episode of *CSI* want realism, they ask real crime scene investigators what word they would use to describe a piece of evidence and what procedures they would follow in a given situation. The writers of *CSI* also need to know the words a detective would *never* use to describe evidence. The audience of *CSI* expects realistic dialogue, and the writers do their best to meet this expectation. The same is true of the academic world.

Research helps you determine what you want to say and how to say it. Chapters 15 and 16 explain how to read the situation that you and your audience will share and how to discover audience expectations so that you can shape what you want to say appropriately and persuasively.

Using Invention and Research to Shape Your Voice and Authority

Invention and research provide ideas and ways to talk about those ideas. Research can also help you determine the evidence that an audience trusts, respects, and will listen to. Imagine that you are working on a new app for mobile devices that helps students prioritize their daily activities, and you need to make a pitch for it to three entirely different audiences: your friends, potential investors, and a software engineer.

Investors like those in *The Shark Tank* reality TV show will want to hear about the likelihood of sales and returns on investment. Your friends, on the other hand, might be interested in how the app will help them plan their day. However, if you are trying to describe the app's functions to a software engineer or an app developer, you may need to use technical terms to describe how the app will gather calendar data and then migrate it to an SMS (a Short Message Service on a cell phone).

Research and reading in this area will not only help you understand how app developers talk but also help you join their conversation as a respected voice. Of course, an engineer can understand your app as your friends do, but if you can use the language an engineer uses and the information she respects, you and your ideas will have much more persuasive power and be more appropriate for the intended audience.

MODULE I-3

AUDIENCE: WHO WILL CONSIDER YOUR ARGUMENT?

Any argument you make will most likely sound persuasive to you. Creating an argument that persuades others is a greater challenge, however. The success of an argument depends upon two main things:

1. **The argument itself**—the thesis, reasons, and evidence you assemble.
2. **Your understanding of the audience** you are trying to persuade.

Building an argument without your audience in mind is like packing a bag without knowing where you are going. Should you take a parka or swimsuit, formal or casual clothes? An audience can be a single person across a desk from you, a crowd in an auditorium, or many different people who will read your writing at different times and in different places. If you obtain a good understanding of your audience, you will find that the decisions you must make as you write become easier.

Clarify Your Audience

A friend who knows you well—who is aware of your interests, passions, and needs—will often give you a more appropriate gift than someone who hardly knows you. A coach who studies the strengths, weaknesses, and strategies of an opponent will give her team a greater chance of success. In the same way, a writer who uses invention strategies and does research with a carefully defined audience in mind will be more persuasive than a writer who does not.

Mistakenly, though, writers sometimes limit their invention and research as they build their argument. For some, invention strategies may seem a waste of time as a deadline approaches. For others, the "rightness" of their argument is so clear to them that they feel no need to conduct further research to discover additional evidence that supports their reasons or will help them respond to opposing views. In both cases, writers need to look at their argument from the perspective of a typical audience member, rather than relying on their own judgment of what is persuasive. In the end, your knowledge of your audience's beliefs and ways of reasoning—and how you apply that knowledge—will help determine whether your argument succeeds or fails.

Types of Audiences

Audiences are always complex, but in general there are three different kinds of audience members for an argument:

1. **The Doubters**: those who strongly disagree with you and are unlikely to change their minds despite your reasons and evidence.
2. **The Choir**: those who already agree with you and need no further persuasion.
3. **The Receptive**: those who have not considered your position, are undecided, or are leaning in a different direction but will give you a chance to make your argument.

Remember that your audience's disposition—doubters, members of the choir, or the receptive—depends upon the nuances of your argument. If a person or the members of an audience are doubters and disagree with you, it is usually not because they are irrational or stubborn. It is more likely that the members of your audience have a different perspective on the issue or their values are different from yours. Chapter 18, Using Contemporary Rhetoric, will show you how to use two different ways of understanding arguments—the Toulmin and Rogerian models—to better understand the audience you hope to persuade.

To persuade those who think, believe, and act differently, you must look beyond your own experience to consider the perspective of your audience. Invention and research, described in the previous section, can help you understand and persuade your audience. In addition, the following Conventions in Context box provides some strategies for learning about the audience for an argument.

Conventions in Context
Research Your Audience

Debbie Lyons-Blythe is an Angus cattle rancher from White City, Kansas. What would you need to know before you could try to persuade her to buy a different pickup truck, try yoga, or vote in support of a new oil pipeline? Before you can persuade members of your audience, you must research them. Here's how.

Read the Location

If a place, a region, or even a virtual place such as a specialized discussion board defines your audience, learn as much as you can about that place. You might check the website of the local Chamber of Commerce, for example, or look at community web pages or voter registration statistics.

Read the Culture

If the members of your audience have common cultural traits such as age, career path, membership in a faith community, or a distinct interest, study the magazines, newspapers, and blogs your audience is likely to read.

Read Their Disposition

Once you have a sense of your audience's background, try to think as its members do. Then consider the values and beliefs that inform or shape their opinion.

Draft a Profile

In a brief paragraph, describe one member of your audience and what one person in your audience may think about your position. For example, Debbie Lyons-Blythe would probably agree with a local newspaper editorial that opposed an oil pipeline crossing her cattle pasture. However, like other local landowners, she may feel strongly that she has the right to use her land as she wishes, and so she may have no problem with neighbors choosing to lease their land to the pipeline company.

MODULE I-4

AUTHORITY: WHAT WILL PERSUADE YOUR AUDIENCE?

If you spent all your time with like-minded people who were willing to put your wants and needs before their own, you would have no need to make arguments. In addition, you would hear few arguments and have little opportunity to learn anything new. Few people other than dictators live in such circumstances. If you want to share what you know, make a change, stay on a particular course, help others, or prepare for the future, you need to make an authoritative argument.

A **good argument** is well reasoned and makes use of solid evidence. An **authoritative argument** is a good argument that demonstrates expertise in some way. In rhetorical terms, **authority** consists of the traits and qualities that lead an audience to pay attention to and be persuaded by an argument. Authoritative traits and qualities are displayed by a speaker or demonstrated by a text. However, these traits and qualities have no effect if the listener or reader does not recognize the authority to begin with.

Markers of Authority

Authority must be apparent or visible in an argument to be recognized by an audience. Each audience understands authority differently, and in different situations different markers of authority will be recognized. Strong arguments draw upon markers—indications—of authority that the audience will recognize: the traits and qualities of the writer that demonstrate his or her extensive knowledge, experience, achievement, or scholarship about a specific subject.

For example, the two images in Figure 1.4 portray two very different situations. When Joseph Francis Dunford Jr., four-star Marine Corps General and Chairman of the Joint Chiefs of Staff, gave his inaugural address at the Marine Barracks in Washington, his authority was obvious to a wide audience. The authority of the "godfather of street skating," Rodney Mullen, speaking at TEDxUSC, is obvious to a more specific audience: skateboarders. The markers of authority pictured on the left are very different from those on the right, yet both speakers are authoritative and persuasive.

Figure 1.4 Speeches by Rodney Mullen (left) and General Dunford (right). Watch both on YouTube and notice the different traits and qualities of authority expressed by both.

Gaining Authority by Establishing a Reputation or Representing an Institution

An individual can gain authority in two ways: by building a reputation or by representing an institution. Well-known speakers or writers can draw upon their reputation as a source of authority. Oprah Winfrey, for example, is known to be a brilliant multimedia producer and star who is also generous and empathetic. These traits and qualities shape the way in which readers, listeners, and viewers perceive Winfrey's publications and other activities.

Just as many people recognize the unique markers of authority that Oprah Winfrey possesses, most people can also recognize the medals of distinguished military service worn by General Dunford because two well-known, respected institutions, the Defense Department and the Marine Corps, have recognized his service, expertise, courage, and military mind.

As a result, when Oprah Winfrey speaks about the difficulties faced by orphans in South Africa or the challenges women confront in executive positions, her audience is likely to be receptive to her views because of what they know about her. Similarly, most people who hold a high rank in the military and who wear a uniform decorated with medals, such as General Dunford, will command attention and, at least initially, be seen as credible.

Authority drawn from having a public reputation or representing an institution is not available to most people, however. If the audience for your argument does not know you, and your hard work and brilliance have yet to be recognized by a prestigious institution such as a university, you need to demonstrate your authority by other means.

Demonstrating Authority within an Argument

If you are present to share your ideas, one means of establishing authority is to take control of the traits and qualities you are exhibiting. If you are writing an argument, and may never meet your reader, the path to establishing authority is the same: you need to take control of the textual traits and qualities that are marks of credibility and use them to create authority. To help you build authoritative arguments, Chapters 20 and 21 will help you find and use information and evidence. In addition, authorities you do not personally know yet still trust demonstrate their expertise by sharing their sources and presenting their arguments in the most understandable way possible. Chapters 22 and 25 will help you document your sources and select the medium that best suits your purpose, message, and audience.

CHAPTER 2

PLANNING YOUR WRITING AND RESEARCH

If you're not falling, you are not trying hard enough.

This line, often heard among rock climbers, doesn't mean they want to fall. Rather, seasoned climbers know that taking challenging routes and pushing themselves mean that occasionally they will fall, so when they begin a climb, they plan with that risk in mind. They place their ropes carefully and double-check the carabiners that can save their life if they lose their grip. Being prepared for a fall doesn't just mean a climber will avoid injury if she falls, however; it means she can move more quickly, take more risks, and achieve greater heights than if she had not prepared.

Of course, if a climber drives to a rock wall or mountain and simply starts scrambling, she can probably get some way up the rock face more quickly than if she were to take the time to make a plan and take precautions. However, if the goal is to reach the summit successfully, descend safely, and be able to climb again next weekend, a climber needs a plan and the right tools and techniques.

Likewise, if your goal is to deliver a persuasive argument, a good plan will save time, keep you focused when the going gets tough, and give you the confidence to continue. This chapter shows you how to make a plan, frame your subject, and write a research question.

MODULE I-5

MAKING A WRITING AND RESEARCH PLAN

To plan your work effectively, you first need to consider your assignment or other writing situation in order to prepare a reasonable work schedule.

Using Deadlines, Page Counts, and Real Time

Your writing and research plan will be shaped first and foremost by three variables:

1. The due date of the assignment or project.
2. The project size or page count required by the assignment or task description.
3. The time and energy you can commit to the assignment or project.

In the absence of a good plan, each of these variables can work against you. But they can also work *for* you, helping you to create a powerful argument. Though it may sound odd, deadlines and page limits can help you to allocate your time and energy effectively, once you understand and take control of these variables.

What can a **deadline** do for you?

- A deadline can help you to concentrate on your subject and keep your mind open to new ideas and innovative problem solving.
- Meeting your deadline adds to your authority, as you prove you can get the job done and shows that you have the study skills to handle any assignment.

Page or word limits can also help you to plan your work.

- A 5-page paper cannot do what a 25-page paper can. Page limits tell you how much mental energy you are expected to invest in preparing your argument.
- A 25-page white paper is unlikely to have the same emotional impact or tone as a 400-word editorial. Page or word limits can be clues to the style, structure, and complexity that your audience expects.

If you know the type and complexity of argument your readers expect, you can plan your invention and drafting schedule so that all-nighters become unnecessary.

The Conventions in Context box entitled "Reading Deadlines and Length Requirements" will help you discover the unstated expectations that come with most assignments and writing tasks.

Conventions in Context
Reading Deadlines and Length Requirements

Assignments and writing prompts are as much a part of tradition as are genres. Like genres, assignments and prompts telegraph expectations. However, assignments often include stated and unstated expectations.

Use Questions to Investigate the Assignment

- Look at the due date and consult the course syllabus. What subjects will have been covered between the beginning of class and the deadline? Most likely your professor will read your work to see how you have learned what has been covered in the course so far.
- Consider the word or page length required. A 500-word blog assignment allows you to develop one idea or introduce a few opinions. However, if you are assigned a 20-page argument paper, you cannot develop only one idea or rely solely on your own opinions. Opinions in themselves are not arguments, and researched arguments take a great deal more time and pages to develop than simply writing an opinion.
- Look for indications of the formality and style your instructor expects. A blog post or peer-review comments on a fellow student's draft can be informal. In a research paper, class presentation, or annotated bibliography, however, a casual tone and the use of personal pronouns like *I* or *we* may be unwelcome.
- Consider how much the assignment counts toward your final grade. Instructors will have very different expectations for an argument paper that is worth 15% of the final grade than they will for a researched paper that is worth 50% of your grade.
- Pay attention to clues from your audience. If your professor discussed the suspicious reasoning in an article and then asks you to respond to it, you will want to focus on the article's reasoning. If she asks you to look at an example of the use of emotional appeals in a campaign speech, focusing on the use of logic in the speech may not meet expectations. "Emotional appeals" and "logical appeals" are discussed in Chapters 1 and 17.
- Again, every assignment or writing task will include stated and unstated expectations. If you are confused or don't know what is expected, it is always best to ask your professor.

Making a Real-World Schedule

Neither students nor professional writers can afford to sit around waiting for inspiration to strike. As the great writers and artists quoted below suggest, composing takes time. The more time you commit, the more your work will appear inspired.

Inspiration comes of working every day—Charles Baudelaire

Inspiration exists, but it has to find us working—Pablo Picasso

You can't wait for inspiration. You have to go after it with a club—Jack London

The challenge is to make the most of the time you have through careful planning. Unfortunately, however, sometimes the plans and schedules we create are based on an overly optimistic view of the time available.

To make a **real-world schedule**, start with your real world:

- ✓ Begin with a calendar that includes unavoidable events and obligations, such as classes, work hours, regular meetings, and routine tasks like laundry as well as big events like weddings.
- ✓ Enter events and activities that are not unavoidable but are likely. For example, do you walk the dog every afternoon or is Thursday night movie night? Do not plan to work when you know you will be doing something else.
- ✓ Write down the due date of your assignment or project.
- ✓ Now move your due date forward one day. This is your working due date, to allow for a broken-down printer or other last-minute crisis.
- ✓ Look at the time available between today and your working due date. For each day, write down the amount of time you will be free and likely to commit to the assignment or project. Keep in mind that you will have other, competing projects as well.

Overestimating the time you will be free to work on the project may feel good now, but it will cause stress later when the time you counted on is not there. Do not assume you will have more time without knowing exactly where that time is coming from and when it will occur.

Update your schedule as your due date moves closer. If new obligations get in the way of your progress, make sure to note the changes on your calendar. Your next step is to make time for the three stages of writing.

Making Time for Your Writing Process

Everyone's writing process is different, but a productive process includes three important functions:

1. Invention and research
2. Drafting and revising your argument so it appeals to your audience
3. Editing and polishing your use of conventions to establish authority.

Part I, which you are reading right now, describes how to start the invention and research part of your process. Part II describes modes of argument and provides common genres that will help you draft your argument. Part III will help you understand and engage your audience. Part IV will help you find and integrate sources to build your authority. Part V will help you polish an authoritative voice.

Each writer moves through the writing process in a different way and at a different pace. Because the writing process is *recursive*, each writer will circle back and repeat different parts of this writing process at different times. Finally, each assignment and project will require you to spend different amounts of time on the various parts of your process. Until you know your process and pace and understand what the assignment or project requires, set aside equal time for invention and research, drafting and revising, and editing and polishing. You can then adjust your time as you make progress. The Breaking the Block box entitled "Organize Your Time on Task" will help you set up a writing schedule.

Avoiding Procrastination

Procrastination is seductive. You may know people who always seem to wait to the last minute yet still manage to get good grades. If they can do it, why can't you? After all, most people would rather focus on things they want to do instead of assignments they have to do. Procrastination is even more seductive if an assignment seems unreasonable and you suspect that you will not have enough time to complete it successfully.

To make the most of the time you have and avoid procrastination, you need to know the most common causes of procrastination:

- Fear of deadlines
- Fear of failure
- Excessive perfectionism
- Too many options, subjects, or perspectives
- Too many other activities

It's common for writers to feel overwhelmed sometimes, and even paralyzed. Productive writers fight the urge to procrastinate with a writing and research plan, a working calendar, and a focus on only those subjects they want to or have to explore and write about. Like having a plan and a calendar, framing your subject carefully will save you time and energy.

Breaking the Block
Organize Your Time on Task

Sometimes an assignment seems overwhelming because you can't imagine how to do it. And sometimes a project seems daunting because you know all too well what it will take to do an excellent job. When facing a big task, like a research project, your best strategy is to divide and conquer.

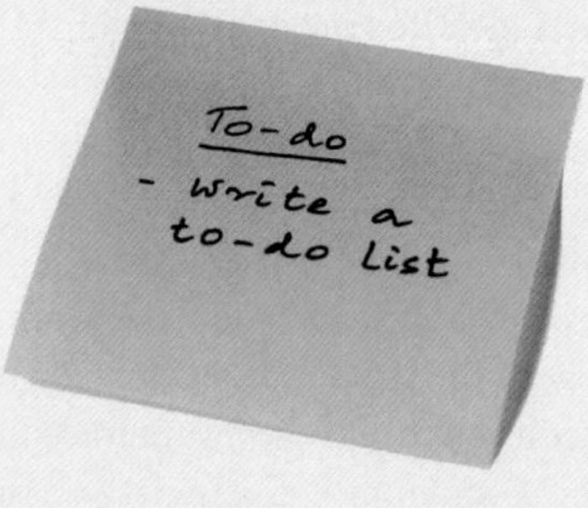

Step One: Describe What You Hope to Accomplish at Each Stage of Your Writing Process

For example, if you can commit roughly 36 hours over the course of six weeks to the assignment, assume you will spend 12 hours on invention, 12 hours drafting and revising, and 12 hours editing and polishing.

Once you have settled on the time you have to work on each stage of the process, make a list of the tasks you will need to accomplish for each stage. For example, if you are writing a researched argument, by the end of the first 12-hour stage, you should have started your research and practiced various invention strategies, resulting in a promising subject that will lead to a research question. Module I-6 will help you develop a research question.

By the end of the second 12-hour stage, you should have drafted your thesis, outlined your argument, and written a solid working draft of your paper. Once you have a draft, if possible, ask a number of people, such as peers or your professor, to review it and provide comments and suggestions.

During the third 12-hour stage, you should rewrite based on both the feedback from your readers and the result of your own careful reading, after having set the paper aside for a while. Then, with the larger parts of your paper set, do quality-control checks for logic, flow, voice, style, documentation, and grammar and punctuation. (These topics are all covered in Part V.) When you are done, you will be able to deliver your argument with confidence.

Step Two: Be Flexible

As you work, you will find you need more or less time for each stage. Sometimes the research falls in your lap and the argument seems to write itself, and sometimes you discover a problem with the structure of your draft during your final polishing stage. Don't panic. You can always adapt your process to what you discover and the challenges you face. If you have organized your time and tasks, you will write a stronger argument and you will have more time to fix big problems than you would have if you had procrastinated, failed to plan, and tried to pull the paper together at the last minute.

MODULE I-6

FRAMING YOUR SUBJECT

When you **frame** your subject, you identify what you need to research and write about and what you do not need to deal with. Having a carefully defined frame has three benefits:

1. It will help you stay focused and prevent you from wasting time and energy.
2. It will keep you on track as you research and draft and will provide a path for your argument.
3. It helps you manage audience expectations.

You might think of framing your argument in terms of an actual frame you place around a collage of words and images. For example, it is hard to imagine a frame that could contain all the important events, locations, and names of the 2016 US presidential campaign. Even if you could frame such a massive collection of events and subjects, the many different elements within the frame would be so overwhelming that it would seem nonsensical. Even a specific subject like the media coverage of campaign rallies offers so many good subjects to explore that it would seem impossible to decide on any one. Yet your professor expects you to pick a subject and get to work (see Figure 2.1).

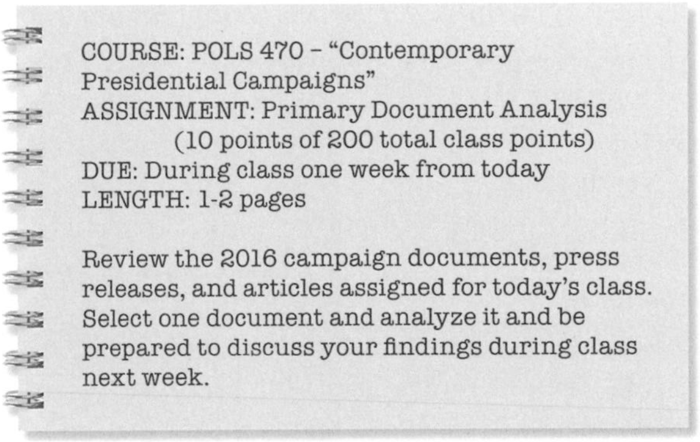

COURSE: POLS 470 - "Contemporary Presidential Campaigns"
ASSIGNMENT: Primary Document Analysis
(10 points of 200 total class points)
DUE: During class one week from today
LENGTH: 1-2 pages

Review the 2016 campaign documents, press releases, and articles assigned for today's class. Select one document and analyze it and be prepared to discuss your findings during class next week.

Figure 2.1 An assignment for a political science course that needs framing.

Assignments like the one in Figure 2.1 may seem overwhelming. However, you can tame tasks like this one by building a frame that helps you find your subject. For example, the word cloud and yellow frame in Figure 2.2 shows how a frame can provide a coherent scope and a clear focus on the topic of the 2016 presidential campaign by defining a set of related events, ideas, and names that you could reasonably research and write about.

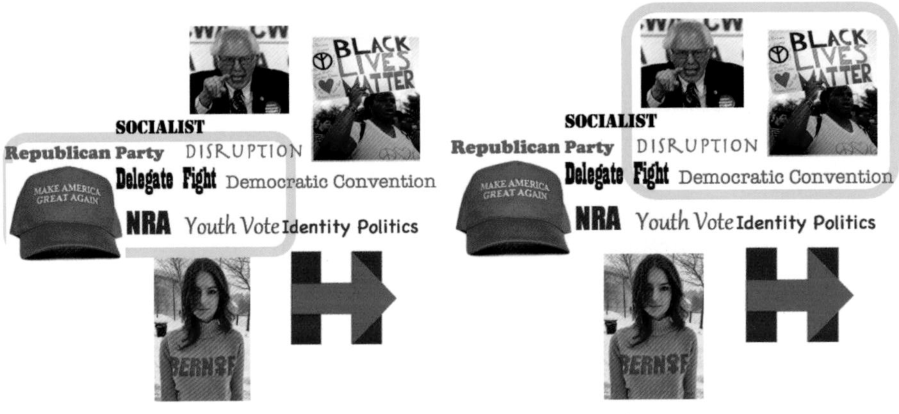

Figure 2.2 A great deal happened during the run up to the 2016 Republican and Democratic Party conventions. A frame can define a context that allows you to focus on a subject. Moving the yellow frame shifts your focus and may allow a topic to come to light.

Frame = Scope + Focus

In a paper or a speech, **scope** is the context or breadth of knowledge that you draw upon to make your argument. Academic disciplines provide the initial scope for much of the work you will do in college. The scope in Figure 2.2 limits the context of all possible subjects to the events, ideas, and names within the yellow frame. Writers or speakers **focus** when they concentrate on a single data point, detail, subject, or image. The focus of an argument will help you develop the position you want your reader or listener to accept and adopt. Within the scope in Figure 2.2, for example, you could focus on the concept of disruption as it relates to candidate Bernie Sanders's pursuit of convention delegates.

Controlling scope and focus helps you manage your audience's expectations. If you indicate your scope and focus early in your argument and stick to both, you will have created an expectation in your reader's mind that you subsequently satisfy. To begin, think about what has been assigned and what is expected, which will guide what you promise your audience.

The scope of your research may already be set by the professor's assignment. Your focus will grow sharper as you research, read, and draft your ideas.

Example: If the professor of your course on "The 19th Century Immigrant Experience" assigns you to write an argument, the context of the class provides the initial frame.

> **Immigration** to
> **the United States** during the
> **19th century** considered from the
> **discipline of history**.

As you research the topic of immigration in the nineteenth century, your *scope* narrows to:

> **Immigrant labor** recruited from
> **China to the United States** between the years
> **1840 and 1890**.

Further research may allow you to refine your *focus* to:

> **Chinese immigrants** pursuing the 1850s gold rush **compared** to **Chinese immigrants** recruited during the 1860s to work on the Central Pacific Railroad.

To frame your subject in an academic context, begin by identifying your needs. Once you understand or have established the frame you need to work within, you can more confidently fill that frame with your creativity and insights.

Understanding the Assignment

If your assignment is not clear, you still need information about these requirements, so to frame your subject, you will need to visit your professor or whoever set you the task. Whether you are asking for clarity or trying to understand the assignment given, you'll want to come away with the following:

- **The assigned subject of the project**. What is the specific focus of the assignment and what is the scope, or range or context, you are expected to draw upon as you do your invention and research? The POLS 470 assignment (Figure 2.1), for example, asks you to focus on a single campaign document from class, and the scope is limited to the 2016 presidential campaign.
- **The forms of thinking you must demonstrate**. For an assignment in a film studies class, for instance, are you expected to review a movie or analyze the camera positions in a movie? (Chapter 16 describes forms of thinking common to different academic disciplines.)
- **The knowledge, competencies, or skills you must apply**. Does your communications professor expect you to write a research paper or create a multimedia, oral presentation? In the POLS 470 assignment (Figure 2.1), you are expected to review or read carefully a specific campaign document and analyze it using the methods and approaches discussed in class.
- **The freedoms and limitations of the assignment**. For example, can you use the first person *I* in your paper? Can you use a document or reading you found outside of class? What are the limits and requirements, such as page length or specific databases and documentation styles you should use?

When you start to work on an assignment, your scope will often be very broad. If you don't have a specific subject in mind, your focus could be as large as your scope. However, as you develop your ideas and refine your subject, your scope will get smaller, allowing you to focus on a very specific subject. In other words, your frame will become clearer as you move through the writing process.

Knowing Audience Expectations

Research audience expectations, both the obvious and the unstated. If you do not have a specific assignment, you must still deal with audience expectations as you decide on your frame. Even if you have written instructions or a prompt, some expectations may be implied. Try to identify the following:

- **Who will read and evaluate your work?** For example, if you are free to choose your subject in a first-year writing course, will your professor be your primary audience, or are you allowed to choose a target audience for your paper? (Chapter 15 gives you the tools to analyze your audience.)

- **The discipline or specialization that should inform your perspective.** When researching, do you have to stay within a specific discipline or does your audience, perhaps your professor, value interdisciplinary approaches (drawing from more than one academic discipline)?

Identify Your Promises

If you told your professor or boss you would do an analysis of the fourth-quarter earnings of the top three competitors of the Mattel toy company, you have created an expectation you must meet in some way. Handing in an analysis of only one competitor will not satisfy that expectation. Other promises include the following:

- If you made a proposal, what did you say you would write about? If you are responding to a call or request for information, what does the request imply about your focus and scope?
- If you have already drafted a research proposal, plan, or bibliography, you have already indicated your scope. Will your professor be alarmed or impressed if you expand your scope to include experts and research from other disciplines or sources from other time periods?
- If you have been discussing your research, thesis, and drafts with your professor during individual meetings, how will he or she respond if you hand in a final essay that has a different focus?

Once you know what has been assigned, what is expected, and what you may have promised, you are ready to draft a research question.

Drafting a Research Question

When you have defined a scope and focus for your argument, you are ready to use your framed subject to write a research question. A good research question helps you and your audience in three main ways:

1. It guides your research and reasoning by giving you a focused question to answer.
2. It helps you evaluate the relevance of your sources, ideas, and evidence.
3. It invites your audience into your search for an answer, so they can more readily accept the answer or argument you propose.

Working backwards from the final argument to the question that started the research, we can see the benefits of a good research question. Great documentaries often begin with a research question. Ken Burn's *The Dust Bowl* is driven by a single question:

What was the social and economic impact of the Dust Bowl that took place during the 1930s? To answer his question, Burns interviewed people who lived through the "Dirty Thirties" and consulted experts who have studied the Dust Bowl's impact. He also researched relevant artifacts and letters. Because he poses his question early in the documentary, the audience's curiosity is aroused, and they adopt the question as their own.

The best time to write a research question is after you have done some initial invention and research. Considering your own thinking on a subject, listening to your peers' opinions, and reviewing the thoughts of scholars and experts will give you access to many conversations around your subject. Your research will reveal the questions that provoked other scholars to search for answers and the questions that still remain to be answered.

Discovering Unanswered Questions

Most assignments contain the makings of a research question. If the assignment is not already in the form of the question, try to convert it into one, using the frame of the assignment.

Look to Research

Academic articles often end with a call for additional research. Although an article usually presents the scholar's or researcher's answer to a research question, often the author will pose more questions that need to be addressed. You may find a compelling research question from that source. (See also Chapter 4 for more on this kind of invention.)

Discussion sites and bulletin boards are other places where you can discover the debates and pressing questions of most interest to groups, specialties, and academic disciplines. Ask your professor for suggestions, or use a discussion board search engine such as *Boardreader*, *Omgili*, or *BoardTracker* to find online conversations about your topic. Pay attention to the debates and questions that consistently pop up.

Look to Peers

If you use the five invention questions in Figure 2.3 to discover and develop a subject, you are well on your way to a research question. (See also Chapter 3 for more on this kind of invention.) Use these general questions as a starting point, and then make them more specific based upon your answers. Note that some questions will be more appropriate for certain disciplines than others.

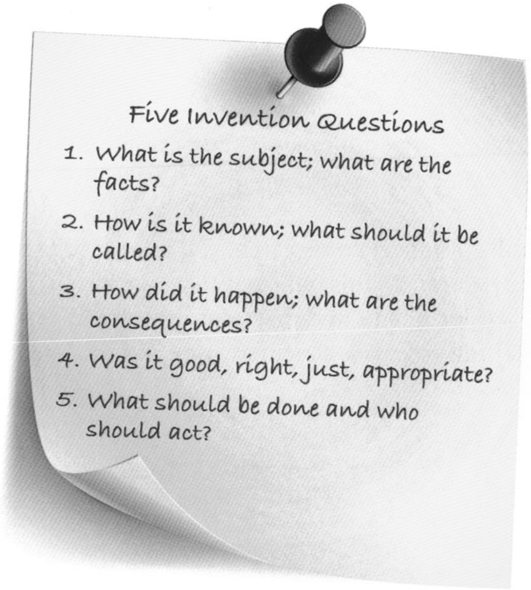

Figure 2.3
These stasis questions have been used for more than 2,000 years to invent ideas, develop authority about subjects, and shape arguments for an audience.

Now share your scope and focus and your answers to the questions in Figure 2.3 with one or more peers, such as a classmate or roommate. Ask your peers,

- what caught their attention,
- what surprised them,
- what they disagree with, and
- what they would like to hear more about.

You may develop a great question from just one of the five invention questions, or your roommate may suggest focusing on answers to two or more. As always, when you are researching a subject or answering a question you really care about, your work and writing will be easier and more engaging.

Finally, write a question that you want to answer. The following checklist will help you formulate a strong research question.

Research Question Checklist

Is my research question…

- **worth answering?** Does it contribute something new or help me demonstrate my skills and understanding?
- **relevant to my audience?** Will my audience want an answer to this question?
- **relevant to the subject?** Does the question define my scope, and is it focused on my intended subject?

- **already answered?** If so, can I add to the existing answer, offer a different answer, or come at the question from a different perspective or with different evidence?
- **overly complicated?** Will my question require more time and energy than is available? Am I going beyond the assignment?

As you draft your ideas and continue your research, you may need to revise your research question. Do not be alarmed! This indicates that you are discovering significant data, information, or documents and that your depth of understanding is growing. Remember, the writing process is a recursive one and you need to be flexible in your approach.

CHAPTER 3

LOOKING WITHIN AND AROUND TO INVENT

They call themselves Jumpsters, and they earn their company, Jump Associates, $200,000 to $500,000 a month depending on the question they have been hired to answer. The Jump Associates (see https://www.application.careers/company/jump-associates-careers) don't sell a product or provide a traditional service like accounting or marketing. In their own words, Jump Associates tackle "highly ambiguous questions that keep great leaders up at night and send the common consultant running for the hills." Their services are based on a simple premise: creativity is an expertise. And yet few companies make time for creativity and many are unaware they need such experts. This is where Jump comes in.

What Jumpsters really sell is the art of **invention**: retrieving and synthesizing ideas through simple yet carefully structured practices in order to spark innovation and generate multiple new perspectives and ideas, free of criticism. Jump Associates can charge so much because companies like General Electric and Harley Davidson understand that invention results in innovation.

MODULE I-7

WHY TAKE TIME TO INVENT?

There are three reasons to use invention strategies thoughtfully:

1. **Your memory is an immense and imperfect filing system**. If you could recall all your memories and ideas and instantly make connections between one thought and another, you would not need to use invention. Using invention strategies helps retrieve old connections and make new ones.
2. **Innovation needs protection**. Do you know a buzzkill? A buzzkill is someone who can suck the air out of a conversation with his or her negative outlook. Criticizing a new idea just as it is coming together has the same dampening effect. Criticism has its place, but when the goal is innovation or invention, we need to sharpen our believing and building skills and save our doubting and criticism skills for later.
3. **Invention strategies save time**. If invention were simply an academic exercise with no practical relevance, companies like Jump Associates would not exist. If a complex question has you stumped, a writing assignment with a deadline is stressing you, or you can't imagine how to persuade a doubtful audience, you must work at it. Invention is the first step, and if you work hard to develop your ideas free of criticism, the rest of your composing task will be much easier.

MODULE I-8

ELEMENTS OF EFFECTIVE INVENTION

Classical rhetoric provides one definition of **invention**—the discovery of the available means of persuasion. This definition and traditional methods of invention were designed to help individuals, working alone, draw upon their own experiences and memories. However, now we see that invention is a social act—new ideas come from groups brainstorming together or individuals engaging and playing with social norms, expectations, and traditions. For example, the musical mashups produced by contemporary DJs are extremely innovative. However, the source of their innovative sound is as much their own minds as it is the variety of songs they sample and arrange for a remix.

If it were not for their brainstorming as they create beats, assemble samples, or play with different genres of music, DJs' distinctive sound would not exist.

Using Invention throughout the Writing Process

Invention isn't just the first stage of your writing process. As you develop an argument, invention provides the tools you need as you move from finding an issue to write about, to developing your ideas about the issue, to deciding on your position or the structure of your argument. As you can see in Figure 3.1, the following elements of an invention process can help writers solve problems and develop their arguments:

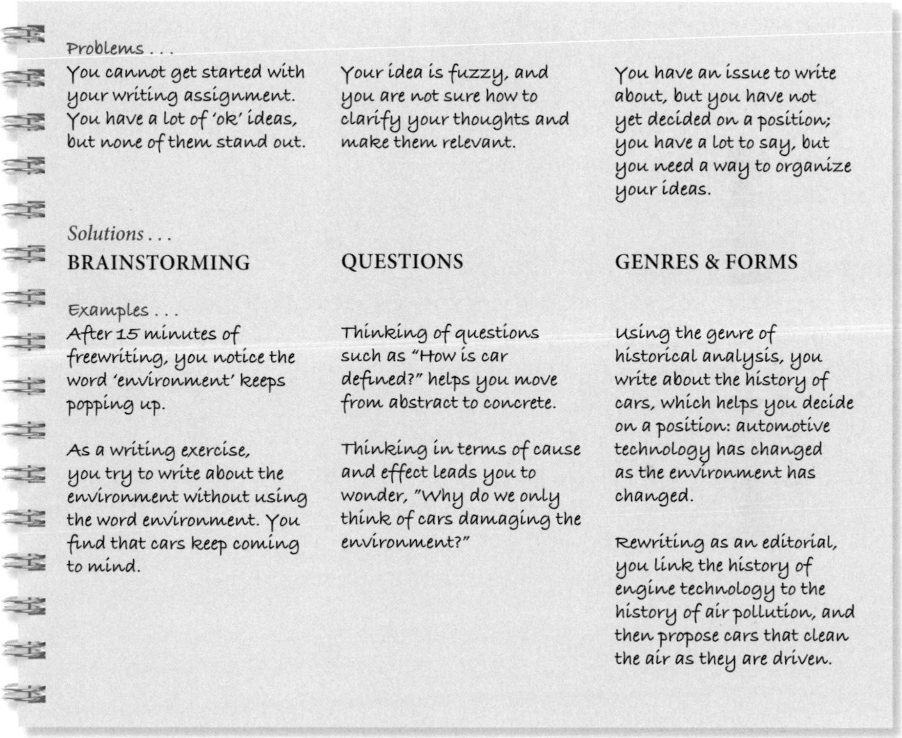
Problems . . .
You cannot get started with your writing assignment. You have a lot of 'ok' ideas, but none of them stand out.
Your idea is fuzzy, and you are not sure how to clarify your thoughts and make them relevant.
You have an issue to write about, but you have not yet decided on a position; you have a lot to say, but you need a way to organize your ideas.
Solutions . . .
BRAINSTORMING
QUESTIONS
GENRES & FORMS
Examples . . .
After 15 minutes of freewriting, you notice the word 'environment' keeps popping up.
As a writing exercise, you try to write about the environment without using the word environment. You find that cars keep coming to mind.
Thinking of questions such as "How is car defined?" helps you move from abstract to concrete.
Thinking in terms of cause and effect leads you to wonder, "Why do we only think of cars damaging the environment?"
Using the genre of historical analysis, you write about the history of cars, which helps you decide on a position: automotive technology has changed as the environment has changed.
Rewriting as an editorial, you link the history of engine technology to the history of air pollution, and then propose cars that clean the air as they are driven.

Figure 3.1 Using invention to develop an argument.

- **Brainstorming** is an umbrella term for a number of strategies that help you look within and around to access memories, to see how others perceive shared experiences, and to use group discussions to develop ideas. Like a data-mining software program, brainstorming strategies help you rediscover what you already know and combine ideas and memories to form new insights and opinions. In Module I-9, you will find seven brainstorming strategies.
- **Questions** can help you clarify your opinions by revealing your assumptions and attitudes. Asking questions about what at first appears to be a simple thought often yields great insight. In addition, if you are confused or unsure

about an assignment, asking your professor can shed light on unstated expectations. More important, simply by asking questions you can turn writer's block into a simple problem-solving activity. Chapters 5 and 6 explain how to use questions to develop the specific genre best suited to your argument. Chapter 6 shows you how to use questions to clarify your argument.

- **Genres** are time-tested ways of structuring arguments. Examples of argument genres include editorials, proposals, and position papers. If you have a jumble of ideas and research notes, trying out various genres can give you different ways of seeing and defining the scope of your subject. For example, you can frame the position that "manned exploration of Mars is practical" as a definition, an analysis, and an editorial to see which genre best suits your purpose for writing and your audience. See Chapters 5 and 7–14 for genres and forms that can help shape your argument.

Getting Comfortable with the Mess

Invention is the messy act of gathering the raw material of ideas so you can start thinking on the page—building and connecting ideas without judgment. If you are worried about neatness or grammatical correctness while using invention strategies, you will limit your creativity.

In fact a mess, like a counter full of ingredients, can lead to new combinations and new perspectives simply because in a mess very different items and ideas will be near each other. Just as a kitchen with a chaotic array of spices, unusual ingredients, and splatters of sauces on the wall and floor is a part of creating a new taste, a mess of ideas is a necessary condition of an effective invention strategy.

No Criticizing during Invention

> *A new idea is delicate. It can be killed by a sneer or a yawn; it can be stabbed to death by a quip and worried to death by a frown on the right man's [woman's] brow*—Ovid

Do not judge an idea before its time. If you have ever spent an hour staring at a blank screen, or writing down a sentence only to erase it, you know the silencing power of self-criticism.

Because new ideas are delicate, they need time to grow. There will be time to criticize and judge later. As you practice the invention strategies in this chapter, remember that the goal is to let the ideas flow, no matter how odd, off-topic, or strange they might be.

For instance, while you are sitting in the library trying to think of something to say about climate change, the thought of going fishing keeps creeping into your thoughts. You could dismiss the thought as a distraction (and a temptation), but if you hold on to it you may find that the best way to talk about atmospheric CO_2 concentrations is to talk about how climate change can affect personal hobbies like fishing.

Giving Yourself Time to Invent

Whether your goal is an innovative statement, a persuasive argument, or just a new answer to an old question, giving yourself time to invent at the beginning of your project is much more efficient and less stressful than trying to develop a new idea or new perspective as the deadline nears.

MODULE I-9

INVENTION STRATEGIES

Here are step-by-step instructions for seven popular, tried-and-true invention strategies:

- freewriting
- listing
- looping
- a picture = 10,000 words
- explosive writing
- constrictive writing
- say it again and again

Different strategies will work better for different tasks. Give yourself time to practice each one and determine which ones work best for you. For most of these strategies, your first step should be to kick everyone out, shut the door, turn off all the noise, and silence your cellphone so that you can concentrate on the task at hand.

Freewriting

Freewriting is writing quickly, without stopping, for at least 500 words or two pages. When done effectively, freewriting produces the raw materials for ideas without self-monitoring or self-criticism. It is an excellent strategy for overcoming writer's block.

Step One: Set Your Task and Goals

- At the very top of the page, write your goal—to write without stopping, correcting, or editing for at least two pages.

- Write your question, subject, or issue on the next line.
- Remind yourself that you will not get up or allow yourself to be distracted until you have written 500 words.

Step Two: Write

- Write 500 words, or two pages, as fast as you can without editing, erasing, or correcting.
- If you are writing on a computer, make the screen dark so you cannot see what you are doing. Make it bright again to save your work when you are done. If you are working on paper, don't look back as you write.
- If your mind wanders, write down the wandering thought and try to link it back to your question, subject, or issue.

Step Three: Reflect and Move Forward

- Save, analyze, and select as described in Module I-10.

Listing

Listing requires you to write for at least 10 minutes, but you can continue for as long as it is productive to do so. It can be especially helpful at the beginning of the writing process. It is also well suited to helping you develop ideas as you write or as you confront writer's block.

Step One: Start Your List

If you are developing your own subject,

- list words or phrases that describe what it is about the subject that interests you, and
- list words or phrases that describe the steps you think you should take as you explore your subject.

If you are responding to an assignment,

- list words or phrases that describe the things you must do or talk about, and
- list words or phrases that describe what you can say or would like to say about the assigned subject.

If you are struggling with a problem,

- list all of the ways you have tried to solve the problem, and
- make a list of all the things that are keeping you from a solution.
- Then review the two lists you have just made, and make a third list of the ways in which a friend, an expert, or your professor might solve the problem.

Step Two: Reflect and Move Forward

- Save, analyze, and select as described in Module I-10.

Looping

Some strategies are designed to generate a subject to write about. **Looping** is a kind of mapping method that helps you explore and expand upon an assigned subject or subject you have in mind.

For example, a common assignment in many nonfiction and journalism courses is to write your own personality profile. Looping would help you map out and bundle the mishmash of experiences, memories, and events that is your life.

Step One: Center Your Question, Issue, or Subject

- At the very top of the page write down your goal—to write without stopping, correcting, erasing, or editing for at least 20 minutes.
- In the center of the page, write a word or brief phrase that represents your question, issue, or assigned subject and draw a circle around it. (See Figure 3.2.)

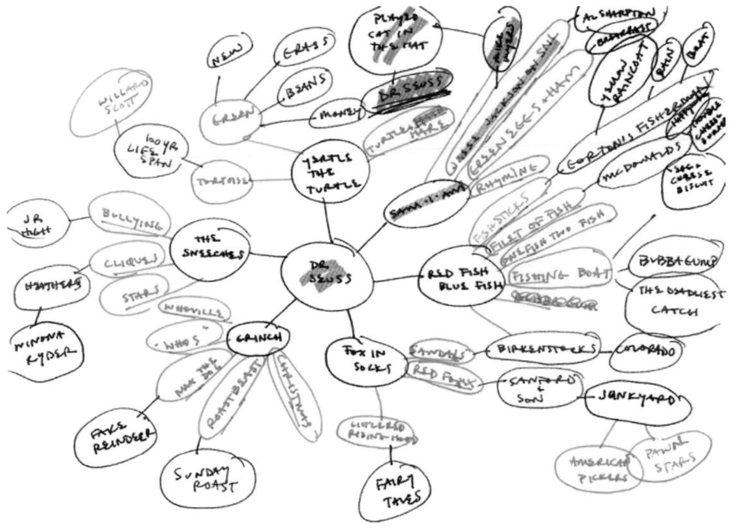

Figure 3.2 Typical results of a looping exercise.

Step Two: Loop

- Think about the word or phrase at the center of your page, write down the next idea that comes to your mind, and then draw a circle around it and draw a line between the first circle and the second. Continue as you think of additional words and ideas.
- As your loops multiply, you will find some of your ideas relate to the center idea and some relate to other loops. Draw lines wherever you see relationships.
- Some ideas are of another kind. If one idea is the opposite of or hostile to another, use a dotted line to express this relationship.
- Feel free to use different colored pens or pencils to express the differences and similarities between the ideas.

Step Three: Reflect and Move Forward

- Save, analyze, and select as described in Module I-10.

A Picture = 10,000 Words

A picture = 10,000 words draws upon thought-provoking images to help you develop a subject or an approach to a subject. It can help you to explore a complex or jumbled scene, mine a dynamic social situation for hidden meaning, or just provoke memories. Freezing the frame, as a photograph does, will help you focus on what would otherwise be a blur of activity.

Step One: Find an Image

If you have been given a subject, describe it in five words or a couple of brief phrases on the top of a blank page or screen.

If you have no subject, type three words or a short phrase that comes to mind.

- Using the words or phrase, search for three images that best represent your initial description. If you need to search for images, try databases and networks such as Pinterest, Flickr, or Picsearch.
- The images can have a theme, such as three images from a county fair, or the images can simply catch your eye, such as a scuba diver, a sunset, and a street sign. They can be positive or negative representations, they can represent the whole of your subject or parts of it, and they can even seem unrelated, but for some reason they just stick with you.
- Select your images. If they are on your phone or camera, print them large or save them and put them on a big screen.

Step Two: Write

- Study the three images and then write about them as fast as you can without stopping, correcting, erasing, or editing for at least 500 words or two pages.
- If your mind wanders, write down the wandering thought and try to link it back to your question, subject, or issue.

Step Three: Reflect and Move Forward

- Save, analyze, and select as described in Module I-10.

Explosive Writing

Explosive writing requires that you write for 10 minutes at least three different times during a single day. This strategy is well suited to creative-writing tasks like developing scenes, settings, and character profiles.

Step One: Light the Fuse

- Explosive writing can happen on the go; therefore, during the day you will need to carry a notebook and pens or pencils, or a mobile device you like to write on. You will also need an alarm like a cellphone alarm.
- At the very top of your paper or screen, write down your goal—when the alarm sounds, you will write without stopping, correcting, or editing for at least ten minutes.
- Set your alarm, or some reminder, so that at least three times during the day, you will begin your explosive writing exercise.

Step Two: Write

- When the alarm goes off, stop wherever you are (if you can), take a deep breath, and look around. Look for at least two minutes, and be sure to look in all directions.
- If something catches your eye, focus on it. If nothing catches your eye, focus on the feel, mood, atmosphere, and tone of the space you are in.
- Then write one page, or around 300 words, about your focus. You can begin with a description, but end with some kind of concluding statement about what you have seen.
- Don't forget to save each entry.

Step Three: Reflect and Move Forward

- Save, analyze, and select as described in Module I-10.

Constrictive Writing

This strategy helps many writers and poets to improve their language skills and create surprising compositions. To use **constrictive writing**, you put an artificial limit on yourself and try to write around that limit. For example, in 1939, Ernest Vincent wrote the novel *Gadsby: A Story of Over 50,000 Words without Using the Letter "E."*

Step One: Create Your Constriction

- Don't be easy on yourself.
- Consider writing two pages composed of sentences that are all exactly five words long. Or write two pages about a subject (such as rattlesnakes) without using any words that describe or represent your subject (words like reptile, snake, slither, and coldblooded would be off-limits, for example).
- Write down your subject and your constraint or limit at the top of your page or screen.

Step Two: Write

- Unlike freewriting, constrictive writing allows you to write very slowly and thoughtfully. Don't edit what you have written, but if you want to take another crack at a sentence to make it better, feel free to try again, and again, and again.
- Do not worry about paragraph structure or internal logic. Simply say as much as you can given the constraint or limit.
- Save and set aside your work for at least two hours.

Step Three: Reflect and Move Forward

- Save, analyze, and select as described in Module I-10.

Say It Again and Again

The **say it again and again** strategy focuses on rewriting and helps you think about how words and ideas are constructed and how ideas develop as people discuss and trade thoughts. Writers have used this technique successfully for hundreds of years. This strategy works best with a specific subject or idea, as it helps you explore different sides of a dispute or different perspectives on a subject.

Step One: Find Your Focus

- Write a brief sentence that describes your subject at the top of the page. Or summarize your thesis or an opposing claim in a single sentence at the top of the page.
- This is not freewriting. You may write slowly and deliberatively. But try not to go back and revise or edit.

Step Two: Write

- Rewrite the subject sentence 30 times.
- You can change the sentence structure or use synonyms to recast the sentence, but your rephrased sentences cannot look or sound exactly like the first one. Also, each sentence must have roughly the same meaning as the first.
- After experimenting with **synonyms**, different words that mean the same thing (like *fast* and *quick*), you will need to look for other ways to rephrase. Try different sentence structures, shift from a positive statement to a negative one, and think about the relationships between the parts of speech (between a verb and noun, for example). For example, the lyric "we are never getting back together" can be recast as "coupling is not in our future." The two sentences are similar, but the noun and verb shift makes a big change.
- It is easy to get distracted during this exercise and lose momentum. Keep in mind that the benefits do not become apparent until after you have rephrased your sentence at least 20 times. Patience is required.

Step Three: Reflect and Move Forward

- Save, analyze, and select as described in Module I-10.

MODULE I-10

MOVING FROM INVENTION TO DRAFTING

Invention never ends. However, you do have to transition your ideas from the free-write or the looping page, for example, to a draft. Your invention activities will generate a number of ideas, and you don't really know which idea or combination of ideas will lead to a promising thesis until you give it a try. For this reason, it is important to save all your invention work and begin to analyze your work to discover new ideas, connections, or perspectives.

Save Your Invention Work

Never throw away or delete your invention work. If you have put serious mental effort into the task, it will continue to provide ideas and new perspectives each time you return to it.

Remember that invention is a cumulative process. You can't simply do it once. Whenever you are stuck, you don't know what to say, or you can't figure out a problem, go back to your invention work and extend what you have already done or try a different strategy.

If you are developing a portfolio—especially if you are required to turn one in—your initial invention work represents your first steps toward a polished essay or speech. To keep the creative momentum going, and to document your work as part of a final portfolio, you need to do more than simply slip a page in a folder or save your work to your computer.

Critiquing and Selecting at the End

Because you won't be critiquing or editing ideas as they come to you, once you've used invention strategies to generate lots of raw material, you will have to decide how best to move forward. The following steps will help you move from invention to evaluating the ideas you have generated.

- Set aside your invention work for at least two hours, and then return to it with fresh eyes. Each invention session is an act of surprise. If you move too quickly to drafting, you will not benefit from the shift in perspective that time can provide.
- When you come back to your work after a pause, be ready to take notes or jot down new ideas as you look for links you had not considered before. Search out new approaches, perspectives, or definitions.
- Prioritize. Make a list of ideas and connections that provoke the most thought and ideas, even if they are negative or critical ideas.
- Make a list of ideas and connections that seem closest to or help you think about your assignment or your subject.
- Organize your ideas into topics. For example, in the looping exercise you might list all the ideas that bridge or link with a single, common bubble or word. Or write all the ideas on separate sticky notes, put them on a wall, and try different clusters of topics.
- Organize your ideas and connections into types:
  - ideas that explain
  - ideas that are examples
  - ideas that prove or challenge
  - ideas that redefine or shift perspective
- Start to think of the ideas and connections you have generated in terms of your assignment, your purpose, and your audience. Chapter 2 guides you through framing your ideas or subject. Chapter 15 helps you understand your audience's expectations, and Chapter 16 discusses the objectives and purposes common to academic contexts.

CHAPTER 4

LOOKING TO RESEARCH TO INVENT

Going with your gut as a strategy for making a public argument can work for poorly informed pundits, real or pretend, as well as other public figures. The most persuasive writers and speakers, however, are the most informed about their subject and their audience's views.

If you wait until you have formed your thesis or written a first draft to begin research, you are likely to look for quotations and statistics that confirm the biases and beliefs you already hold. The result can be an uninformed, overconfident argument with limited persuasive power. Satirist Stephen Colbert (Figure 4.1) coined the term *truthiness* for the type of uninformed and overconfident arguments that use research only to confirm what the arguer feels in his or her gut.

Figure 4.1
Stephen Colbert in his famously uninformed television persona.

Ridiculing *truthiness* is now a staple of contemporary comedy because willful ignorance is funny and because there is no longer a defense for a lack of knowledge. Anyone with access to a public library or the Internet can do research to discover what they need to know to be informed.

Research is invention—it is your means of gathering trusted, relevant information, beyond your own or your peers' experience, and of beginning to internalize what you find. This chapter will show you research tricks of the trade that will save you time and energy as you invent. This chapter will also tell you how to use the information you find to develop your ideas and build a persuasive argument.

MODULE I-11

WHY USE RESEARCH TO INVENT?

Three Reasons to Use Research to Invent

What does research do for you? Here are three reasons to invest in the process.

1. **Research provides you with data and information beyond your own experience**. Research allows you to tap into the hard work already done by thinkers, scholars, and people like yourself trying to figure out difficult problems. For example, you may have heard that Ebola is deadly and untreatable. However, without facts and data all you have is heresay. A quick review of the World Health Organization's website will provide a May 30, 2018 article documenting the successful use of a vaccine to control Ebola in the Democratic Republic of the Congo and a brief history of the development of the vaccine.
2. **Research yields data, information, and knowledge**. Research gives you an understanding of how people talk about your subject and how audiences respond to different types of arguments about your subject. You may not know what "breaking the taper on the ball joint" means if you don't hang around auto technicians. And yet a little research and reading in a "Chilton Auto Repair Manual" will not only explain what it means but also make a case for the best way to do it.
3. **Research can enhance your thinking with solid reasoning and reliable evidence, giving your argument more authority and persuasiveness**. From an audience's perspective, the only way you can persuade others about the Ebola vaccine or use terms like *ball joint taper* correctly is if you know what you are talking about. To be persuasive, you must convince your reader that you are a knowledgeable source on your topic.

Research Defined

The word **research** describes a three-step process, outlined in Figure 4.2, in which you gather and analyze information and then draw conclusions from it.

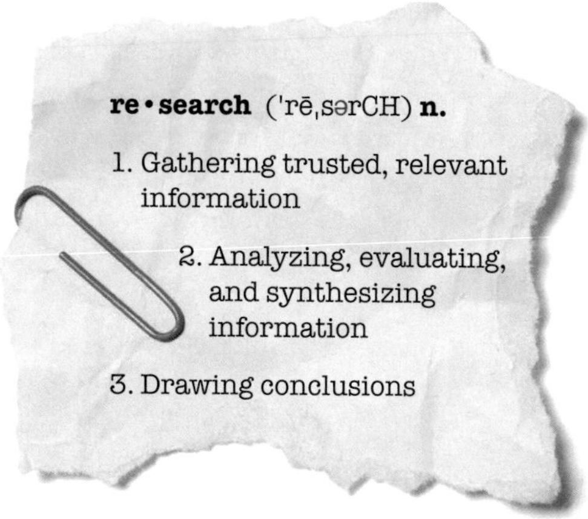
re•search ('rē,sərCH) n.
1. Gathering trusted, relevant information
2. Analyzing, evaluating, and synthesizing information
3. Drawing conclusions

Figure 4.2
The three steps in the research process.

When you conduct research, you are looking beyond your own ideas to discover what you do not know. In the same way that you look around to friends, peers, and your community to gather new ideas and different opinions, when you do research you look to scholars and experts to learn more.

This chapter demonstrates how to use research as a means of invention. Chapter 19 explains how databases and search engines work and how to use them to identify relevant information and data you can trust. Chapter 20 helps you analyze, evaluate, and synthesize what you have found, and Chapter 24 provides tools to make sure your conclusions are sound.

MODULE I-12

USING RESEARCH TO FIND AND DEVELOP IDEAS

During the invention stage, you are not using research to prove or disprove a thesis, or to argue for or against a point of view. The initial purpose of research is to discover information and use your discoveries to provoke and expand your thinking. In fact, research during invention is a bit like a study-abroad program.

The goal of studying abroad is to be exposed to other cultures and perspectives, absorb a different language, and consider other ways of thinking as a means to enhance your own. Just as you need to engage in conversations to get the most from a travel experience, you need to throw yourself into the conversations about your subject to get the most from research.

Each idea, discovery, debate, opinion, and argument about a subject is part of a conversation that has been going on for some time. Research is part of your preparation to join the conversation so that when you do, your ideas will be heard and respected.

Researching to invent requires a different kind of reading from what you will do later in the process. Whether you need a clearly defined subject and approach or you already have them, the goal during invention is to read for ideas that provoke more ideas.

A trick to wringing the most provocative ideas from the research you do at this stage is to play both the believing game and the doubting game.

The Believing Game

When you play the believing game, you suspend your disbelief and put your critical impulse on hold, as you often do when you watch certain types of movie. It is easy to act like you believe in positions you agree with. The challenge and real benefit come when you play the believing game while reading or seeing strange or even disagreeable opinions and expressions. If you play the game well, the benefits of believing are significant.

1. As a research tool, the believing game keeps your eyes open. Rather than dismissing an argument you disagree with, playing the believing game will allow you to consider the points of the argument fairly.
2. If you are preparing an argument, you are often trying to persuade someone who thinks differently than you do. The believing game helps you understand your audience's point of view—what its members think and why they would disagree with you—before you make your argument.
3. The believing game also allows you to test your own argument before you go public. To do this, you need to discover your argument's weakness and anticipate counterarguments opposing your position. If you can believe in counterarguments to your own position, you will be able to anticipate points, questions, reasons, and evidence put forward by future opponents. Your audience may not have these counterarguments in mind, but if you can raise them and then deal with them in your own argument, you have a better chance of persuading your audience.

Breaking the Block
The Believing Game

For this strategy, you will adopt the perspective of the author or creator of a work. Not only must you imagine that you agree with him or her; you must also assume you want to promote the ideas and opinions you have read. Then you will expand the author's idea to see where it leads. The writing component of this exercise will take 15–20 minutes.

Remember that this game is a tool for provoking ideas so you can build persuasive arguments.

Step One: Research

Find an editorial, blog post, image, or any expression of an opinion or idea that you find disagreeable or strange.

At the very top of a blank screen or page, write your goals:

- You will read or observe the text you found.
- You will accept the author's perspective and claim, extend its logic, develop additional supportive reasons, and apply it in different situations.

Start reading or observing and believing.

Step Two: Write

Set your timer for 10 minutes and begin writing without stopping, correcting, or editing for at least that amount of time.

If you are struggling, use each of the lines below to start a new paragraph.

- I believe it, and it affects me...
- I believe it, and that changes my understanding of the past...
- I believe it, and so now I must rethink...
- I believe it, and so in the future...

After at least 10 minutes, write one more paragraph in which you describe the beliefs, values, and thinking of someone who holds the position you just tried to believe.

Step Three: Reflect

Set your work aside for at least two hours.

When you come back to it, look for ideas, lines of thought, or questions that can help you develop your own ideas and perhaps find your subject.

The Doubting Game

The doubting game is a critical approach. Rather than trying to adopt the author's perspective, as in the believing game, you pull back from it and try to identify errors, problems in reasoning, and negative or unforeseen implications that will undermine the argument.

The doubting game can help you understand your own positions more clearly and refine your thinking on a given issue. It is most useful during invention as a way of provoking a "rebound response." For example, you may never have given space exploration much thought until someone close to you mentions that she is studying engineering because she wants to be an astronaut and go to Mars. Listening, you might begin to think of arguments against investing in or even thinking about space travel. Without your friend's comments to react to, however, you would never have built an argument against space travel.

Figure 4.3 René Descartes doubted everything he could not prove, leaving one truth: "I think; therefore I am."

Breaking the Block
The Doubting Game

Examine a brief argument and then build a case against it. The writing component of this exercise will take 15–20 minutes.

Step One: Research

Find a brief journalistic editorial, preferably about an issue in which you have no interest at all. If you have been given an assignment, look for an editorial that takes a position on the assigned issue.

At the top of a blank screen or page, write your goals:

- You will read the editorial once.
- Then you will read through it slowly one more time and underline each individual assertion and each bit of supporting evidence.

Step Two: Write

Start at the beginning of the editorial and write for 10 minutes. For each paragraph of the editorial, write a sentence describing the error, fault, or contradiction you see in the argument. The following tips will help you find fault with and critique what you read.

- Doubt each point and statement.
- Look for contradictions between statements, assumptions the writer is making (for example, that the taxpaying public should approve of how tax money is spent), and parts of the argument.
- Examine the editorial for errors in logic, such as assumptions that will not hold and exaggerations.
- Think of evidence and reasons that would refute the central argument.
- Consider negative consequences if the argument won the day or the proposal were adopted.

Step Three: Reflect
Set your work aside for at least two hours.

When you come back to it, try to string your marginal notes together in the form of a rough outline. As you do, imagine you are writing to the same audience as the author you just critiqued.

MODULE I-13

SEARCHING EFFICIENTLY

Assuming you have little time, how can you use research to gather and develop your ideas quickly and efficiently? Knowing what is available, the types of sources, and how information is organized will save effort and energy as you move your project forward.

Knowing What Is Available

An excellent way to dig into the vast storehouse of information and knowledge available from libraries, archives, and databases is to focus on the types of information you need, whether primary or secondary, analytical, disciplinary, or indexed. Let's look at each type.

Primary sources and data are just that: first sources of information that have not been processed, manipulated, or interpreted. An example of a primary source is a postcard, a novel, or a work of art that is not presented (published) with any analysis, interpretation, or commentary. Primary data are just the raw values or numbers that have been collected. If your parents measured your height every year from age 2 to 20 and recorded the results, or if you gathered answers from a survey you posted or recorded observations of animal behavior during a field study, you have primary data. Other examples include these:

- a primary source: *Moby-Dick*, a novel by Herman Melville published in 1851.
- primary data: 1940 Census raw data (see Figure 4.4).

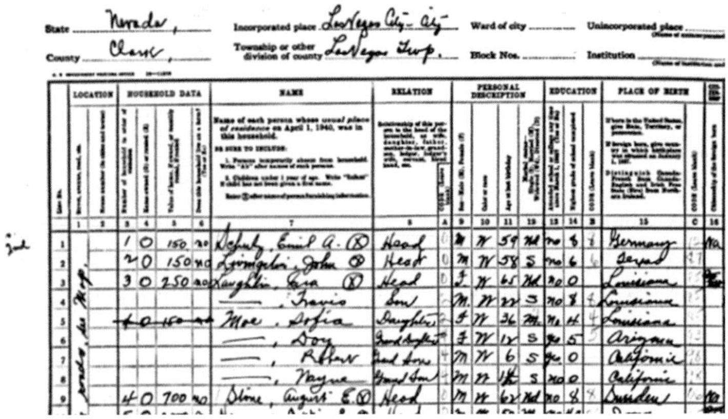

Figure 4.4 Unprocessed data, like this sample from the 1940 US Census, are primary data.

Secondary sources and data analysis are works of analysis, interpretation, or commentary about primary data and primary sources. Examples include the following:

- a secondary source: a book by Nathaniel Philbrick titled *Why Read Moby-Dick?*, published by Viking in 2011.
- data analysis: An article by Robert A. Margo titled "Race, Educational Attainment and the 1940 Census," published in *The Journal of Economic History* in 1986.

Disciplinary knowledge is not a single set of data or a single work. Rather, it is knowledge collected and organized according to the perspective of a specific academic discipline or specialty (such as English literature or theoretical physics). You can identify categories of disciplinary knowledge in libraries by their call numbers. Here are a few examples:

NA1-9428	**Architecture**
NA1-60	General
NA100-130	Architecture and the State

SD1-669.5	**Forestry**
SD119	Voyages, etc.
SD131-247	History of forestry

Disciplinary knowledge is also collected and organized by organizations and institutions such as the University of Chicago, which maintains a collection called *American Film Scripts Online*, and the New Bedford Whaling Museum, which holds the largest collection of handwritten accounts of whaling voyages.

Finding the Knowledge That Is Available

Indexed information is similar to an index found in the back of a book, only much larger. A research index is an alphabetical listing of terms such as subjects or titles that point to or reference articles, books, or other types of documents. We live in a time of "big data" and automated indexing; as a result, many prefer to use search engines rather than indexes of documents. Keep in mind, though, that a search engine will search only where it is pointed; it will search only the content included in its scope and look only for the terms used. Google is pointed at the whole World Wide Web, but indexes list the knowledge of a specific discipline. For example:

- The *Biography and Genealogy Master Index* is a list of biographical information of living and deceased persons from every field of activity and from every country in the world.
- The *Avery Index to Architectural Periodicals*, published by Columbia University, is a list of current architecture and design literature.

Because indexes are narrowly focused, they may save you time and help you stay within your scope as you research.

Choosing Your Approach

As noted earlier, during the invention stage you are looking for interesting and provocative ideas and beginning to integrate what you have found with your own thoughts. Each type of information—primary and secondary sources, disciplinary knowledge, and indexed information—will help you find, gather, develop, and refine ideas in different ways. Here's how.

If you are looking for a subject and you do not have a hard deadline, browsing through raw data may spark some interesting observations. For example, if you are curious about your hometown and what it was like when your grandmother was in high school, raw census data and newspapers of the time may lead you to a subject.

If you are looking for a subject and have only a few weeks before your deadline, you may not have time to browse or analyze raw data. In this instance, you should look to someone else's data analysis and secondary sources.

If you have a subject but are not sure how to approach or define it, you could turn to the indexed information within a specific database. For example, if your subject is the effect of thoroughbred breeding and training practices, *The Daily Racing Form*'s online "Formulator" will give you years of data so that you can compare past training practices and performances against current ones.

If you are trying to meet expectations, such as proving to a graduate school that you are ready for a Master's program, look to disciplinary knowledge—for example, articles in professional journals—to help you learn how scholars think and talk. If you are interviewing for a job at a radio station, you would do well to read the professional journals and magazines that people in the broadcasting industry publish and read.

If you have proposed to write an investigative article for your local alternative newspaper, you can use secondary sources to begin to shape your thinking, and then begin your investigation by reviewing primary sources and examining raw data.

If, for example, you have a tip that cheating is rampant at the local horse-racing track, you could begin by reading a source such as *The Tradition of Cheating at the Sport of Kings* by Glenn Thompson, a trainer with over 30 years of experience, to learn about the sport, its rules, and its sketchy training practices. Then you could turn to newspaper stories about recent cheating scandals to learn how trainers and owners cheated and how it was detected. Finally, you could examine data sets such as equine injury databases, trainer treatment logs, and race results to discover unusual or unexplainable trends.

Once you have thought about and developed your subject, you are ready for more focused research. Chapters 19 and 20 show you search strategies and tricks of the trade used by professional researchers and scholars.

Whether you are researching to learn about a subject area, considering professional opinions and scholarly findings, examining primary sources and data sets, or conducting your own experiments and interviews, you need to protect your hard work and communicate your authority. A lost citation or forgotten name can prevent you from using valuable research in your argument. The Responsible Sourcing box titled "Who, What, Where, When" will help you think about the citation information you will need to ensure your research is usable and authoritative.

Responsible Sourcing
Who, What, Where, When

If you use other people's intellectual work, such as their words, ideas, or images, you will need to give them credit. Crediting sources is not only the right thing to do, but it will also give your voice and your argument greater authority.

Find the Who, What, Where, When.

Although there are many different types of documentation styles, nearly every style requires you to gather four kinds of information in addition to the text or images you are quoting or using:

- **Who** authored or produced the document, idea, or image? There is usually a person or group that authored, produced, or created the material you want to use. If you found your source with the help of a library or database search, the results page probably names the who. If biographical information is also provided, such as the degrees held by the author or what makes her an authority, this kind of information will be useful in your argument, so keep track of it.
- **What** is the document, idea, or image you will use, and what is the title? Since the same document can be reproduced in a number of versions, record that information, too. For example, *Red Badge of Courage* is a print novel, an e-book, an audiobook, and a movie. Documents, ideas, and images can also be contained by something that answers the what question. For example, a poem can be contained in an anthology, an article can be contained in JSTOR, and a movie can be contained by Netflix.
- **Where** was the document, idea, or image published? The location or origin of the document is the where. An article, for example, can be found in a print journal, an online magazine, or an advocacy website.

The where is also answered by providing the name and location of publishers. Finally, information like the version or volume number of a book or the volume and issue number of a magazine explains where in the sequence of volumes or editions of a magazine an article or image is located. The where of an article provides context and indicates the article's authority.

- **When** was the document, idea, or image created or published? The date of a source can communicate context and authority. In some disciplines, an article written in the 1980s is considered contemporary, and in other disciplines a 15-year-old book or article would be old news.

Keep the document information with the document.

Whether you are using paper copies and notes, or you keep all your research on your laptop or an app like Evernote, make and keep copies of your sources until your paper is graded. Make sure to keep copies of the book's title and copyright pages or the magazine's or journal's cover and table of contents, as this is where the who, where, and when info is generally found. Also, copy and keep all notes, lists of works cited, and bibliographies, as they are a great place to find more sources. And keep your notes organized.

Chapters 21 and 22 help you integrate and cite your sources, two crucial parts of a persuasive argument.

PART II

TYPES OF ARGUMENT

CHAPTER 5

UNDERSTANDING ARGUMENT FORMS AND GENRES

How would you describe Adele's music? So far, she has won 15 Grammy awards in nine different categories. In 2012 Billboard named her "Top Pop Artist" and gave her the "Top Rock Song." The Country Music Television Awards recognized her with a "Performance of the Year" award. She has also won awards for "Best Jazz Act" and "Best Neo Soul Act." And in 2016 she won the "Best Female R&B/Pop Artist" at the BET Awards. Does this mean she is a rock/country singer who does a jazz/neo soul/R&B/pop act?

You may ask, why do classifications matter? Do we really need to label something like Adele's music? After all, for some, Adele's brilliance is that she adapts, combines, and reimagines diverse forms and genres, creating her own uniquely new yet old-school sound.

Adele's blending and bending of different forms and genres show how these categories can help readers and writers in two ways: as a way of categorizing expressions and as the building blocks of expression.

To some people, forms and genres are ruts or rigid patterns that limit creativity. However, in both music and argument, they can be a source of invention and creativity, a way to engage and entice an audience, and a way to build and demonstrate a voice of authenticity and authority.

MODULE II-1

WHY DO I NEED TO KNOW FORMS AND GENRES?

Before looking at how forms and genres can help you solve practical problems, let's begin with a definition of each. Because forms are understood in many ways, it is easy to confuse them with genres. One way to keep them straight is to keep in mind how writers and speakers use them:

- forms are purposes and strategies
- genres are practices and plans that use recurring forms

Defining Forms

Forms are successful, time-tested habits of thought that achieve a purpose. In classical rhetoric, forms were also called commonplaces, because they were seen as places or points that people had to have in common if a dispute was to be resolved. Because disputes often have similar qualities, forms reflect the most common types of arguments. For example, if you were an ancient Roman buying wine, you might argue with the wine merchant over how much wine was in an *amphora* or wine jug. An argument over the volume of a *congius* measure of wine (about 0.92 of a gallon) would be in the form of a definition argument. Or if you wanted to explain how a wildfire started, your purpose would be to prove the cause of the fire and your strategy would be a cause-and-effect argument.

Forms are typically divided into two types: common and special.

Common Forms

Tradition has defined a number of common forms (Figure 5.1). Chapters 7 and 9–14 describe the most frequently used of these.

COMMON FORMS:
Persuade
State the Facts
Define
Narrate
Analyze and Evaluate
Determine Cause
Propose a Solution

Figure 5.1
These are only a few of the common forms defined by Aristotle and others.

Forms can guide or determine the content, organization, and even the sentence structure of a piece of writing or a speech. Consider these two sentences.

1. "As I drove home, I saw lightning hit the utility pole, which explains why the TV doesn't work."
2. "I drove home, lightning struck a utility pole, and then the TV stopped working."

The first sentence determines the cause of the broken TV. The second sentence narrates a trip home. Both sentences use the same information in the same order. However, a shift in the phrasing changes the form of the sentence.

Special Forms

The way in which forms shape ideas and meaning is most apparent in special forms, which are habits and conventions of thought used by people dealing with specialized tasks or jobs, such as bull riders, professors, and pilots. Like common forms, special forms shape ideas and meaning. For example, when commercial pilots take off or land, they use the "Sterile Cockpit" form. The purpose of the "Sterile Cockpit" form is to eliminate all distractions during critical flight procedures. The strategy of this form is to strictly limit conversations to the operation of the aircraft.

Within a university, you will find that many professors and other specialists use both common and special forms to focus their research and lectures. As you progress through courses in your major, you will be required to use both common and special forms as habits of your thinking. The best way to understand and learn to use forms is to watch, listen, and read specialists (such as your professors) shape ideas and meaning with forms.

Using Forms in Your Reading and Writing

Professors and writing instructors talk about individual forms in the same way a coach teaches the purpose for and strategy of each type of golf swing or a cooking instructor breaks down different cooking methods. To play a complete game or prepare an excellent meal, you need to put together a number of different strategies. In the same way, if you can understand and use each form individually, you can use several forms together to build a complex argument. In fact, you will rarely use a single form to build an argument. For example, a persuasive research paper often begins with definition, moves to narration, and then analyzes and evaluates or determines a cause, ending with a proposed solution. Readers and writers use common forms in three ways:

1. **Forms guide readers**. Forms help you understand a writer's intention and approach. For example, before you read the book *The Civil War: A Narrative*, you know that the author, Shelby Foote, is going to describe the sequence of events named the Civil War from a specific perspective. In an argument, the

primary form is often indicated or stated in the thesis to let the reader know how the argument will proceed and what to expect. In addition, when forms shift in an argument, such as from a statement of facts to an analysis, the writer is often moving from one point to another.

2. **Forms are invention tools**. Forms help you recast your thoughts in different ways, yielding different perspectives. Recall your last family disagreement, and then consider the following forms and the shift in perspective they provide.
    - How would a reporter *state the facts* of the disagreement?
    - How would a historian *narrate* the dispute?
    - How would a family counselor *determine the cause* of the quarrel or *propose a solution*?

    Sometimes you can resolve a dispute or present an effective argument simply by persuading your audience to look at an issue in a different way.
3. **Forms structure an argument**. When writing or reading, think of forms as editorial guidelines helping you determine what to leave in, what to develop, and what to cut out. For example, you may have a great deal of research and much to say about teaching yoga in elementary schools. Different forms can help you decide which evidence and reasons to use and which to cut. If your education professor routinely emphasizes the critical analysis and evaluation of educational approaches, you can assume she may expect the same of you in the yoga argument. If so, a narrative describing the benefits of the cobra pose may not have a place in your audience's preferred form of argument.

Defining Genres

Genres are well-established ways of using a form or forms to achieve a purpose. More specifically, genres are ways of addressing recurring rhetorical situations and engaging audiences that have proven successful over time. As a result, you can recognize a genre by its repeated forms, such as its structure, style, and idiom. For example, fire marshals use a genre called a "Fire Incident Report" to organize their findings after investigating the cause of a fire. A "Fire Incident Report" written by a professional will use the cause-and-effect and narration forms, it will stick to the facts, and its tone will be objective because that is what is expected of this genre.

Genres can serve very different purposes and use unexpected forms because they are elastic. That flexibility allows you to adapt forms and genres to solve a wide range of rhetorical problems.

- **Forms and genres solve invention problems**. Think of forms and genres as solutions that others have found useful when shaping arguments, expressing emotions, and persuading audiences. Sometimes established forms and genres will suit your needs. But you can also blend and reimagine forms and genres that other writers have used. It is important to keep in mind that the qualities of a given genre are not set in stone. Genres constantly evolve, and new genres appear, because writers and speakers use bits and pieces of different genres, remix old genres, and even use genres in situations where the audience expects something completely different.

- **Forms and genres solve audience problems**. Because forms and genres shape audience expectations, you can use them to satisfy those expectations. For example, if you are giving a valedictorian address or offering the maid of honor a toast at a wedding, investigating some examples of either genre will give you a good idea of what your audience of classmates and proud parents or wedding guests will expect. In fact, genres are a powerful tool of classification people use to find and evaluate information. Imagine opening iTunes or Spotify and finding that all references to genres have disappeared.
- **Forms and genres solve authority problems**. If Adele couldn't capture the essence of soul or didn't understand contemporary country music, the fans of those genres wouldn't give her a second listen. Adele's audience embraces her blending of forms and modification of genres because her deep understanding and appreciation of each genre, obvious in her songwriting and stylistic choices, give her the authority to do so. In the same way, if you show the judge you are familiar with the genre of a courtroom argument, odds are she will listen carefully and not disregard your arguments.

MODULE II-2

USING FORMS AND GENRES TO HELP YOU INVENT AN ARGUMENT

Forms are purposes and strategies, while genres are practices and plans. When you begin thinking about an argument you want to make or an assignment to which you need to respond, you may also be thinking about the different purposes you hope to achieve and the ways to achieve them. Let's say your history professor has assigned you an argument paper about some aspect of the impact of modernism upon contemporary society. However, as you research the topic you find that modernism can describe movements in architecture, art, literature, and music. Clearly, a definition is called for, and as Chapter 10 describes, different types of definitions suit different types of arguments and genres. After some thought, you decide to begin your argument with an etymological definition and then do an analysis and evaluation (see Chapter 8) of modernism's impact upon contemporary music.

As you invent and do research, reading for genre just as you read for evidence and reasoning will help you build your own argument. You will find that many different forms are used in many different combinations. Just as an insightful argument or piece of evidence can advance your thinking, an innovative use of a genre or parts of a genre can help you advance your audience's understanding. You will rarely use just one form to build an argument.

Trying out different genres for your ideas can provide you with new insights and new ways of understanding your subject. The Breaking the Block box entitled "Using Forms to Find a Subject" will show you how to look for the forms and genres of others to gain a new perspective.

For example, imagine you have been assigned to write an editorial. If you have never written one before, the task may seem intimidating. However, a brief analysis of newspaper editorials and a quick online search for editorial outlines should yield something similar to the outline in Figure 5.2.

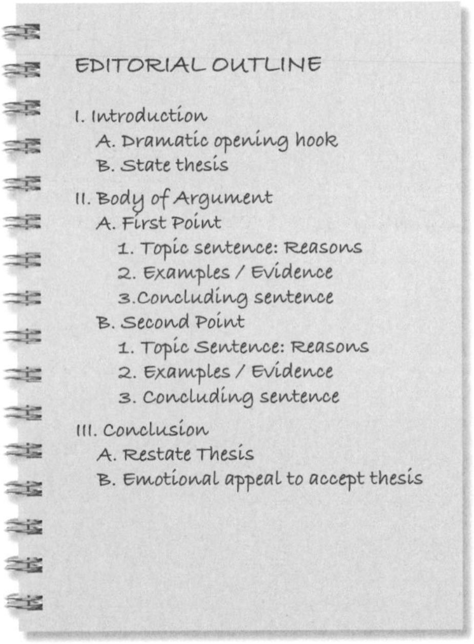
EDITORIAL OUTLINE
I. Introduction
A. Dramatic opening hook
B. State thesis
II. Body of Argument
A. First Point
1. Topic sentence: Reasons
2. Examples / Evidence
3. Concluding sentence
B. Second Point
1. Topic Sentence: Reasons
2. Examples / Evidence
3. Concluding sentence
III. Conclusion
A. Restate Thesis
B. Emotional appeal to accept thesis

Figure 5.2
This is just one example. Your editorial should be organized to fit your purpose and audience.

As you know, editorials are written for different purposes and can have different structures. You are not required to use this particular outline—it is not as if there is some secret society or bureaucracy that sets the rules for genres, but at the same time there are certain accepted and expected practices. If plans and outlines like the one in Figure 5.2 are useful, use them. If not, adapt and reimagine the practices and plans of others to fit your needs and your audience's disposition and expectations.

Breaking the Block
Using Forms to Find a Subject

Looking for a subject for an argument? This activity will help you come up with ideas. It can be done in any public or crowded place, and it includes 10 minutes of writing.

Step One
Sit in a busy public space. Observe and listen to the people around you, looking for repeated actions, behaviors, or expressions (possible forms).

Step Two
Take notes on what you are seeing and hearing, describing in detail what is being repeated and how.

Step Three
Consider what might be causing these repeated behaviors or expressions. For example, when ordering coffee, why do people begin with the size, type of drink, and then special requests? ("A *venti latte* with extra foam, please.") Is the cause location, peer pressure, menu? Why do conversations stop when people enter an elevator? Is there predictability to the conversation between the grocery store checkout clerk and the customer?

Step Four
Define the repeated behaviors you see and expressions you hear. Are they forms or coincidences?

Step Five
Analyze what you have discovered. Why have these repeated behaviors or actions caught on? How do the forms help the people involved? What rules, authorities, or expectations do the forms suggest or reveal?

Step Six
When you explore forms and how they come to be, you are also exploring your culture, a rich source of possible subjects to write about. Pick the form that most interests you and write for 10 minutes on its origin, purpose, value, and meaning.

Forms and Genres Are the Building Blocks of an Argument

You can use any form or combination of forms with nearly any genre or combination of characteristics from different genres to build an argument. Obviously, some combinations are more effective than others. For example, you would not use the genre of a résumé if your purpose was to determine the cause of a fire. If your professor assigns a research paper, she may be surprised if you hand in a long narration. Below is a list of common forms and the genres writers use to shape their argument for different audiences.

Persuade
- advertisements
- editorials
- blogs
- research papers

State the Facts
- résumés
- newspaper articles
- historical accounts
- bibliographies

Define
- definition essays
- Facebook pages
- literature reviews
- profiles

Narrate
- personal narratives
- memoirs
- lab reports
- case studies

Analyze and Evaluate
- text and image reviews
- eulogies
- literary analyses
- consumer reports

Determine Cause
- accident report
- historical analysis
- closing argument
- documentary

Propose a Solution
- proposals
- campaign speeches
- position papers
- conference proposals

As you build your argument, you will also find that you may need to use many different forms, such as a definition and an analysis and evaluation, to achieve your overall purpose. Unless required by your professor or editor, do not get locked into one form or genre. Drafting involves experimenting with words and sentences, but also with forms and genres.

As a set of expectations, or a constriction to work against, a given genre can provoke new perspectives and ideas and provide you with new ways of expressing your views. For example, if you are writing an in-depth article for a journalism class about possible slave-labor practices in US nail salons, think about how the genre of a police report may add drama or help you move through a large number of facts quickly.

MODULE II-3

USING FORMS AND GENRES TO DISCOVER AUDIENCE EXPECTATIONS

When writing in an academic setting, students often make the mistake of trying to write for a general audience. **There is no general audience**, because there is no universal set of expectations that is shared by everyone.

Although a publication such as *USA Today* may seem to be written for a general audience, it is in fact composed of a series of sections and stories organized in very different ways to satisfy very specific audiences. For example, the sports page is written and organized differently than the weather report.

Discovering the expectations, likes and dislikes, and needs of a specific audience can seem like an intimidating task, especially if you have never met the type of person you are trying to persuade or know nothing about your professor. Then again, writers, editors, and producers of all types of media are able to discover a great deal about audiences and individuals they will never meet. How? By researching and understanding the genres and genre elements required, expected, or assigned by a specific audience.

For example, a reader who looks for, opens, and reads with interest the user manual for a NETGEAR RangeMax Dual-Band Router is the intended audience for that manual. The technical writer who composed the manual has no real understanding of the personal characteristics or political views of such a reader, but the writer knows that people looking for technical help expect clear, easy-to-follow technical manuals. The writer of such a manual can refer to other technical manuals for consumer electronics as a guide to the needs and expectations of the intended audience.

In a similar way, because a well-established news magazine such as *Time* has been around for many years, most readers know what kind of writing they will find when they open it. A writer for a news magazine such as *Time* only has to pick up and examine the magazine to understand a great deal about its readers and their expectations.

When you are thinking about your audience, genres help you anticipate audience expectations and use them to achieve your purpose in speaking or writing. If you know your reader is expecting an editorial, for example, your work is half done. To persuade your audience, you need to identify, understand, and then speak directly to their needs and interests. Like the writer of the user manual, you may not know much about your professor, but you can discover a great deal about what professors typically expect of a business case study or a critique of a dance performance by examining the assigned genre.

The following checklist will help you research your audience in an academic setting.

- ✓ **Review the assignment** or writing task. Does your professor have typical expectations, such as a lab report in a lab class, or is the assigned task surprising? Is the assignment intended to teach a form or genre or is the required form or genre simply a way to package your ideas and research?
- ✓ **Ask your professor** for clarification. Ask what kind of common mistakes are made on such an assignment, as well as what advice they have about how to approach, work on, and format your final product. Does she expect a specific form or are you free to use the forms you think best?
- ✓ **Consider other expectations**. If your professor asks for a two-page response to an art installation and gives you a day to write it, odds are she is not looking for a complex argument. If she asks for a business proposal due at the end of the semester, you would do well to ask her for examples and study examples of detailed, well-researched business proposals.
- ✓ **Ask around**. Your professor, the writing assignment, and the syllabus are the best sources of information. However, your classmates' interpretation of the professor's expectations and advice from students who have taken the same class with the same professor can also provide insight.

MODULE II-4

USING FORMS AND GENRES TO ESTABLISH AUTHORITY

Habits create expectations. Just as wedding guests expect some kind of ceremony and patrons of a fancy restaurant expect the staff to treat them in a particular way, the adherents of an academic discipline have expectations based on the habits they have adopted.

Academic disciplines are rigidly structured. When you talk about a sports star such as Tim Howard with your friends, you probably do not worry about how you frame your opinion. However, if your biochemistry professor asks for written observations of an experiment, your options are limited by the situation. Using the style of expression common to a sports bar in a lab report would be a bad move. Your argument may be accurate and entertaining, but it will frustrate the professor expecting a lab report. In addition, it will reveal that you have no authority and are not a member of the biochemistry discipline.

Thus, genres demonstrate an author's authority by placing him or her within a group of experts. Just as you can quickly identify posers or hacks in your area of interest, your audience will be able to tell when you have mastered the expected forms and genres of expression. We know each other—and recognize one another's skills and talents—by how we talk and write.

Doctors, plumbers, engineers, travel writers, and other professionals not only need to learn the concepts and information that are important in their fields. They also need to learn how specialists in their field use forms to shape their thinking and draw upon genres to communicate ideas. When you show you know how to think, talk, and argue like a physician's assistant or a police detective, you demonstrate the authority such specialists have.

Understanding and effectively using the forms and genres expected by a specific audience or group of readers is the fastest way to establish authority and ensure your ideas will be taken seriously.

Used well, genres help you understand a situation and then organize your thoughts and expressions to suit your audience, achieve your purpose, and establish your authority. However, genres are not magic. A writer could use the most traditional and easily recognized editorial outline and yet fail to persuade a single reader. Using a common form or a recognized genre is not enough to make your argument persuasive. You still must offer convincing reasons, backed by solid evidence.

CHAPTER 6

USING STASIS QUESTIONS TO BUILD ARGUMENTS

Detective novels and TV shows like *The Adventures of Sherlock Holmes* are often called "whodunits." Readers or viewers follow the investigator as he or she examines the clues that lead to the criminal. A new genre called police procedurals portrays the crime in the first five minutes and tells you who did it. The question of procedurals is "How do they get caught?"

The drama of this new genre lies in the investigators' skillful use of questions to clarify a complex crime scene, find leads, and discover unseen evidence linking the criminal to the crime. The procedures and questions portrayed on shows such as *CSI: Miami* and *Criminal Minds* are the real ones used by sheriffs, police detectives, and the FBI to investigate crime.

Scientists and journalists investigating complex problems or issues and lawyers and philosophers trying to build persuasive arguments use a different set of questions and procedures called **stasis questions**. These experts use stasis questions because they work, they save time, and they produce persuasive arguments.

MODULE II-5

WHY DO I NEED TO KNOW STASIS QUESTIONS?

When you are confronted with a complex or confounding assignment and a deadline, you have a lot in common with investigators trying to make sense of a confusing crime scene or lawyers trying to persuade a jury. Knowing how to get at the heart of a problem or issue, what to do with the answers you discover, and how to shape a persuasive argument is often a matter of asking the right question at the right time.

The word *stasis* literally means stability or balance, and rhetorical stasis is achieved when two people, or a person and an audience, come to an agreement or a common understanding. Stasis questions will not make your audience agree with you, but they will help you discover the source of a disagreement and then suggest a form of argument that is most likely to persuade your audience to accept your view.

If you have ever been in a quarrel with someone and at some point asked, "What are you talking about?," you have experienced a desire for stasis. For example, imagine your brother has been angry with you all week. You don't know what his problem is or what to say to him.

What Happened: After your brother left for school, you borrowed his sweater and accidently snagged it. Now he is furious.

What the Parties Are Thinking:

> You: I apologized and bought him a new sweater, but he is still angry for no good reason. After all, he never really wore that sweater.
>
> Your brother: She seems to think my stuff is her stuff, and this isn't the first time she took something without asking.

Why You Don't Have Stasis: That an unloved sweater got torn is not in dispute. In fact, the sweater is not the source of the quarrel. This disagreement is about definitions. Your definition of borrowing and your brother's definition of stealing, or taking without permission, are the central issue.

Over time, brother and sister may find their way to stasis if they both come to understand the real source of the dispute. If they used stasis questions, though, they could reach that understanding more quickly.

Stasis questions are a sequence of questions used to examine complex problems or issues. Greek and Roman rhetoric made use of four primary stasis questions. Today, the five primary stasis questions also include a question of value:

1. Questions of fact: What happened? What are the facts?
2. Questions of definition: How is it known? What should it be called?
3. Questions of cause and consequence: How did it happen? What is the consequence?
4. Questions of value: Was it good, right, just, appropriate?
5. Questions of procedure and proposal: What is the best response? Who should act?

Stasis questions are not just some dusty old tool. As we saw in the sweater example, when used in sequence, stasis questions can indicate the type of disagreement and the form of argument best suited to persuading those on the other side of the dispute. In addition to determining the most persuasive form of an argument, these questions help you do a number of important writing tasks:

- **Invent and Understand**—Stasis questions help you invent (discover, research, retrieve, and synthesize information) by clarifying and developing your understanding of complex issues and events.

  For example, if you were asked to write a position paper on a student government resolution requiring trigger warnings, stasis questions can guide your research by breaking down the issue into its most basic elements, such as what is meant by a trigger, before considering more complex issues such as the values or criteria that should be used to evaluate any potential harm that a professor's lecture or discussion could cause.
- **Know Your Audience**—Stasis questions can help you investigate the disposition of your reader or listener, revealing what is unseen or unstated. Without an understanding of the points of agreement and disagreement between you and your audience, persuasion is not possible.

  For example, until you know how your audience understands and defines psychological trauma (embarrassment, social discomfort, or a full blown PTSD flashback), you don't really know if you should write a definition paper, a cause-and-effect paper, or a proposal.
- **Build Authority**—Stasis questions can reveal parts of your argument that need further development, additional research, and more supporting evidence. Stasis questions also direct you to the common form (purpose and strategy) that best suits your argument and audience.

In the following module, each of the five primary questions is expanded into a sequence of secondary questions used to examine a problem or issue more closely.

MODULE II-6

PRIMARY AND SECONDARY STASIS QUESTIONS

Above all, stasis questions are a method of invention. More than simple brainstorming, however, they help you think deeply and systematically about issues and audiences. The Breaking the Block exercise entitled "Think like a Journalist" will help you see the practical value of stasis questions. Stasis questions are organized into primary and secondary questions. Secondary questions probe the same territory as, but at a deeper level than, primary questions.

Defining Primary Stasis Questions

The primary stasis questions are not simply a list but a sequence. The answer to the first makes it possible to find an answer to the second, and so on. So they must be asked in order. The sequence of questions is important because once your questions have identified the areas of agreement, you are left with the question of where the two sides have very different answers. At that point, the real investigation begins.

Returning to the sweater example, brother and sister agree on the facts, but each uses different words and different definitions to describe the event. The question is why: how does each perspective lead to a different definition, and what must happen to move one person to accept the other's definition?

In an academic setting, imagine you have been assigned an analysis of the immigration debate during the most recent election. You discover that for the most part the parties agree on the facts; for instance, the parties agree on the number of legal and illegal immigrants. They also agree on what the terms *legal* and *illegal* or *undocumented* mean. However, they strongly disagree on the cause and consequences of the current immigration policy. The causal question, then, is the point where secondary questions can focus and guide your research.

Defining Secondary Stasis Questions

Each primary stasis question leads to five secondary questions. Answering secondary stasis questions allows you to make a more focused examination once you discover where you and your audience disagree. For example, once brother or sister zero in on definition as their most pressing point of disagreement, secondary questions can help clarify what definitions are in dispute and how they are defining the same points differently.

You will note that many of the secondary stasis questions in the list below are similar to the primary questions. Whether the disagreement is about facts or values, the same sequence of questions can be used to examine the type and the precise source of a dispute.

1. **Facts**: What happened? What are the facts?
    a. Did something happen, or is there an issue?
    b. What are the facts of the event or issue?
    c. Is there a problem concerning the event, issue, or facts?
    d. What cause or change brought about the event or issue?
    e. Can what happened be reversed, changed, or affected?
2. **Definition**: How is it known? What should it be called?
    a. How is the event or issue characterized? Is it a problem, a debate, tension, an impasse, a misunderstanding?
    b. What exactly is the event or issue in question?
    c. Does the event or issue belong to a larger class or category?
    d. Can the event or issue in question be broken into smaller parts?
    e. How is the event or issue related to the larger class or its smaller parts?
3. **Cause/Consequence**: How did it happen? What is the consequence?
    a. Why did it happen?
    b. What might explain what happened?
    c. What possible causes do not make sense or can be eliminated?
    d. What was the immediate or most obvious effect?
    e. Will other consequences become apparent later or in other locations or situations?
4. **Value**: Was it good, right, just, appropriate?
    a. Is the event, issue, or consequence beneficial or detrimental?
    b. How serious is it?
    c. Who has been or will be affected?
    d. If nothing is done, what will happen?
    e. What will it take to change what has happened?
5. **Procedure/Proposal**: What is the best response? Who should act?
    a. Is a response necessary?
    b. Who should respond?
    c. What kind of response is possible?
    d. What kind of response is necessary?
    e. What must be done to respond?

Breaking the Block
Think like a Journalist

Journalists do not have time for writers' block, which is why they use the *who, what, when, where, why*, and *how* questions to quickly gather information. These six questions and the five stasis questions share the same historical source: the invention and analysis of information. This exercise will take only 20 minutes and help you see how often this sequence of questions appears in daily life.

Step One: Look Around

If you have been assigned a subject, skip to step two. If you are free to choose your own subject, watch the news or look through news websites, magazines, and newspapers and read about an ongoing event, issue, or argument. How to prevent violent attacks in schools, how to house the homeless, or the debate about climate change are just three possible issues to explore.

Step Two: Think like a Journalist

Find the heart of the matter. If, for example, you are required to write a sociological analysis of a specific image or ad, the assignment instructions can help. Or you might think about how your professor has demonstrated such an analysis, or ask your professor what one element of the image would lend itself to analysis. In the case of an image or ad, how would advertisers perceive the image and how would consumer activists?

Think about how different groups with different concerns and perspectives on the event, issue, or argument would answer the questions. If possible, interview such people or try to determine how each interested group might answer each question. Make a list of answers representing how each group would answer the primary questions.

Step Three: Dig Deeper with Secondary Questions

Where the groups have similar answers, these answers are the foundation of your argument: the common ground you build on. Where the two groups have very different answers to a primary question, dig deeper. Make a second list of answers to the relevant secondary questions. If you don't know how someone would answer, read a bit more or ask friends or classmates who hold such a perspective.

Step Four: Reflect

Look at your answers. If you were to pick a side or a perspective, how would you persuade those on the other side to change their minds? What points or ideas stand in the way of agreement? Is there a third way, or could the groups meet in the middle?

MODULE II-7

BUILDING AN ARGUMENT USING STASIS QUESTIONS

When you are building an argument, stasis questions can help you invent, develop arguments suited to your audience, and establish authority on complex issues. Let's begin by looking at how the primary and secondary questions can shape your argument. The five questions are linked to common forms of argument, as shown in Figure 6.1.

STASIS QUESTIONS →	COMMON FORMS
What are the facts?	State the Facts
How is it known?	Define
How did it happen?	Narrate/Determine Cause
Was it right?	Analyze and Evaluate
What response is best?	Propose a Solution

Figure 6.1 Arguments are commonly built upon a hierarchy. You must agree on facts if your argument is about definitions. If you are arguing over the best solution, you already agree that there is a problem. The question in dispute points to the appropriate form.

In the following example, you will see how a student used stasis questions to determine the heart of the issue and how to shape the argument with forms.

Inventing with Questions

In her "Advanced Composition" class, Jamie Battaglia was assigned a position paper on any contemporary issue. The subject of medical marijuana caught her attention when her university announced that it would not recognize prescriptions for medical marijuana. Using stasis questions to guide her research, she found answers that helped her develop a deeper understanding of the issue.

Research Notes: Medical Marijuana

1. **Facts**: What are the facts of medical marijuana?
    - The phrase medical marijuana seems to have been coined in the 1990s to distinguish medical from recreational marijuana use.
    - In politics and in the medical community, medical marijuana is very controversial.
    - Alaska, Colorado, Oregon, and Washington legalized recreational use, 24 states recognize the medical use of marijuana, but federal law does not.

2. **Definition**: How is medical marijuana known?
    - Marijuana or cannabis is a plant. Some farmers consider it a weed. Others grow it for its hemp fiber or for medical use.

- The Federal government, directed by the Controlled Substances Act, defines marijuana as a controlled substance similar to cocaine and heroin.
- Some see marijuana as a type of medication that can relieve serious symptoms and treat sickness. Others compare its recreational use to alcohol.

3. **Cause/Consequence**: How did medical marijuana come to be? What is the consequence?
   - After years of debate, some states legalized the medical and recreational use of marijuana.
   - States where the use of medical marijuana is legal have seen an explosion in the number of marijuana dispensaries.
   - The demand for medical marijuana has resulted in more sophisticated farming and crossbreeding methods. Some types of marijuana are much more potent than the marijuana of a few years ago.

4. **Value**: Was it good, right, just, appropriate?
   - Those who oppose legal marijuana say there are no real medical benefits and that marijuana is a gateway drug that leads to serious addiction.
   - Supporters argue that there is medical and anecdotal evidence proving medical marijuana relieves symptoms, cures diseases, and is safe.
   - The pharmaceutical industry claims any medical benefits from marijuana can more safely be found in USDA approved and regulated medications.

5. **Procedure/Proposal**: What is the best response to legalized marijuana and who should act?
   - The federal government and Drug Enforcement Administration promise to enforce all federal laws, close marijuana dispensaries, and arrest drug dealers and users.
   - Supporters argue that citizens should pressure state and federal lawmakers to legalize recreational and medical marijuana and pressure the medical community for more research about its benefits.
   - Some libertarians argue that the government should not regulate any personal freedoms including the use of any drugs for any purpose.

Looking More Closely with Secondary Questions

Looking over the answers to the primary questions, Jamie was surprised to see that nearly all of her sources agreed on the facts of the issue.

However, when it came to how marijuana is defined, she quickly saw that different groups use very different names for the products, and their effects, that come from the marijuana plant. Clearly, the different names (marijuana, medical htc, or hemp) were linked to different definitions.

Once Jamie recognized that the source of the dispute was the conflicting definitions, she moved to the secondary questions of definition.

Secondary Questions: Definition

a. How is the issue of medical marijuana characterized?
As a public health issue, as the difference between medication and drug abuse, as a problem for medical research, as a question of personal rights and freedoms, and as a legislative issue.

b. What exactly is the issue in question?
The issue seems to be the different names people use when talking about marijuana.

c. Does the issue belong to a larger class or category?
It seems like a problem of language, meaning, and legal classification.

d. Can the issue in question be broken into smaller parts?
Different groups who use different words and definitions and their motivation for doing so.

e. How is the issue related to the larger class or its smaller parts?
In terms of language and meaning, the relationship is between culture and law. In terms of smaller parts, the issue is personal motivations and values.

The primary questions helped Jamie identify the type of disagreement at hand. The secondary questions of definition helped her see that the source of the conflict could be found in the cultures that informed the words and definitions used by federal government officials, DEA agents, and state legislators. She could then examine her university's position and the words and definitions used, as opposed to the way in which some students described their use of marijuana.

At this stage, stasis questions helped Jamie understand the issue and helped her make sense of the sources she discovered. In addition, she understands the source of the conflict and the dispositions of potential audiences, such as students with prescriptions or administrators at her university. She can now begin to develop her own position within the ongoing debates.

Questioning Your Audience

In addition to inventing, developing, and clarifying, finding stasis is about finding the common ground you share with your audience. **Common ground** refers to the points that are not in dispute. Common ground is in fact what makes disagreement and persuasion possible. If two parties did not share some common ground, agreeing on some points, they would be talking about completely different things.

Over dinner with her mother, Jamie talked about her research. She described the five questions and the different positions her research revealed. Jamie knew that she and her mother share a great deal of common ground. They agree on the facts, definitions, and consequences of marijuana used as a medication.

When it came to questions of value, ethics, and morals, Jamie was surprised to find that her mother went a different way. Her mother thought marijuana was like alcohol—potentially dangerous, but a matter of personal choice. Jamie, on the other hand, saw marijuana as a powerful medicine, like Percocet or codeine, that must be controlled by the government for the good of society.

If you think of the sequence of stasis questions as a map, it is easier to visualize how two people, like Jamie and her mother, can share some common ground and diverge in other areas (see Figure 6.2).

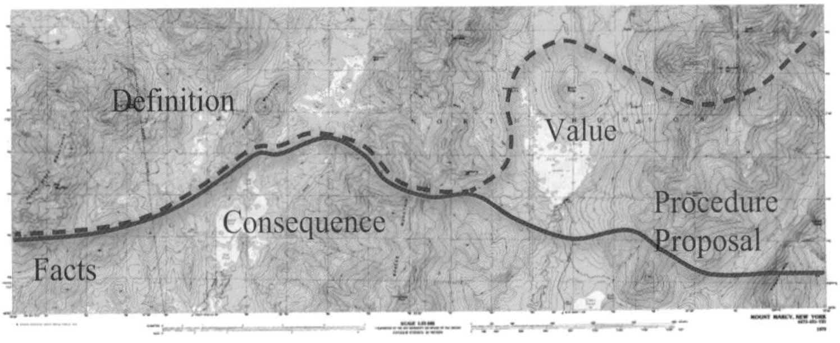

Figure 6.2 In this example, the solid blue path tracks Jamie's answers and the dotted blue represents her mother's answers to the stasis questions.

If Jamie wants to persuade her mother to accept her line of thought, it would be pointless to write a definition argument, as they already agree on definitions. She would need to write an argument focusing on value. If Jamie succeeds and persuades her mother to agree with her view of marijuana as a powerful medicine, the issue of value becomes common ground. Until they agree on values, they will not agree on proposals for controlling marijuana.

Whether you are taking notes, interviewing your audience, or answering the stasis questions for yourself, stay within the scope of the question. For example, when asked about facts, do not define. When considering definition questions, don't answer with opinions about value.

Building Authority: Research and Form

Because different people will answer the stasis questions differently, different audiences will be moved or persuaded by different evidence and different forms. For example, Jamie and her father may agree on the facts but diverge when it comes to consequences. Because he answers the questions differently and they diverge from common ground at a different point than she and her mother do, Jamie would need to research different evidence and use a different form—narration and determination of cause—for her father. Her father may think that a consequence of legalized marijuana is simply increased sales of much more potent marijuana to people who want to get high. However, a narrative that describes a cancer patient who is able to manage nausea and go back to work thanks to professionally grown marijuana may persuade Jamie's father.

In an academic context, things are a bit more complex. For a professor, the goal of an assignment may be to develop a student's research, critical thinking, and writing skills and then to evaluate the resulting argument. The professor's personal views may be irrelevant. Stasis questions, then, may be most useful as an invention tool: a way of exploring the disputed points and terms within an issue assigned by the professor or discovered by the student. For more on writing in academic contexts and understanding academic audiences, see Chapter 16.

Whether you are building an argument to persuade a specific audience with distinct views or demonstrating your understanding of an issue and the points in dispute, answering the stasis questions will lend your argument authority because you will know the ins and outs of an issue, know what is settled or common ground, and know how to shape and form your thesis, reasons, and evidence.

CHAPTER 7

PERSUADING

When a bully pushes a kid out of a favored bus seat, the bully is moving his or her audience with force and fear. When a boss says, "Do it or you're fired," he or she is using power. When a spouse says, "Sweetie, can you rub my feet—I've had a hard day," he or she is using the partner's devotion, sympathy, or sense of guilt to get a foot rub.

Assuming you don't want to bully or pressure anyone, what do you do? You do what the most effective people do: You persuade your audience with arguments. This method is the way things get done in civil society.

MODULE II-8

WHAT AUDIENCES EXPECT OF A PERSUASIVE ARGUMENT

This chapter draws upon classic formulations of persuasive argument, but not because the ancient Greeks and Romans nailed it from the start. Rather, classic rhetorical thought has been reconsidered and refined for over 2,500 years. As a result, classical rhetoric provides the terms and concepts that inform our contemporary understanding of argument. You can find a more detailed description of the classic argument in Chapter 17. In addition, you will find two contemporary approaches to argument in Chapter 18.

Why Would I Need to Persuade?

Persuasion is the act of influencing others. **Persuasion by means of argument** is the attempt to influence people of free will to think, believe, or act differently using reasoning and evidence. Compared to sketchy forms of influence such as force or power, persuasion by means of argument is a more *ethical* means of persuasion.

Necessarily, you cannot define persuasion without defining authority, and you cannot define authority without considering how audiences respond to different types of authority. A position of authority, such as mayor or corporate executive, gives a person the right or power to make decisions for others and determine the activities of employees. Audiences respond to people in positions of authority with obedience or disobedience. **Rhetorical authority**, on the other hand, is an argument that works, or does not, in the mind of the audience. Listeners or readers will grant or recognize rhetorical authority if they are persuaded the speaker or writer has extensive and relevant experience that informs his or her ideas, bases decisions on reasoning and logic, and expresses ideas and arguments clearly. If all of these are true, audience members will defer to the speaker or writer as an authority and are likely to adopt the authority's positions or arguments as their own.

Ethical persuasion is powerful for two reasons:

1. It has the potential to communicate your authority and persuasive force across time and space.
2. When people of free will are persuaded to adopt your argument, they in turn will persuade others.

For example, the ideas in *Magna Carta*, signed by King John of England in 1215, persuaded the founders who drafted the US "Bill of Rights," and those ideas continue to shape the arguments heard in Congress and the Supreme Court.

Professors and instructors ask you to build, write, and deliver a great many arguments. One goal of these assignments is for you to learn how to persuade others ethically. An equally important goal is for you to recognize when others are trying to persuade you to adopt their views, and for you to be able to challenge sketchy arguments. If you use the lenses of invention, audience, and authority, you will better understand what instructors expect of the arguments you build for class.

Using Invention to Discover and Synthesize Knowledge

Effective invention and research will help you not only discover an issue—a subject of debate or problem in need of a solution—that you care about, but also find evidence and reasoning quickly so you can move on to synthesizing what you have discovered.

The ability to synthesize knowledge—reading, gathering information, combining it with your own thinking and knowledge, and then inventing and building arguments that oppose, modify, or add to what you have read—is crucial to many disciplines and specialties. For example, in a philosophy class you may be asked to read an article and then develop opposing arguments. In this type of assignment, your understanding of the original argument may be as important as the persuasive force of your own arguments.

If you begin with a research question you are curious about, you will find that your invention and research are less about doing an assignment than about finding an answer to an interesting question. Research questions are also the foundation of a defensible thesis or claim. The question "Is water wet?" is not worth exploring, but the question "Is the water supply in our town safe to drink?" would have the power to entice your readers and could lead to fruitful research and a compelling thesis. A great research question born of curiosity also has the power to entice your reader and make them look forward to your answer.

Making Your Argument Persuasive for Your Audience

One of the basic goals of education is to be able to share what you have learned and apply your knowledge beyond the classroom. For example, in a marketing class you may be asked to recast the same advertisement for three different audiences. If you can develop reasons that would move a trucker, a stay-at-home father, and a teenager all to buy the same cellphone plan, you have demonstrated that you can read complex audiences and take into account the needs of different groups.

Reasons and evidence that are appealing and persuasive to one audience will not be for a different audience in a different situation. Knowing your audience will make it easier to select and use the most effective appeals. (The three common rhetorical appeals—*ethos*, *pathos*, and *logos*—are described in detail in Chapter 17.) An *ethos* appeal, which demonstrates a speaker's or writer's authority, might involve showing a stay-at-home father that you, as a father, understand the type of plan he needs. A *pathos* appeal, which evokes an emotional response, might mean showing a teenager how the plan will help her connect with her best friends. A *logos* appeal, which involves the use of logic and evidence, could mean comparing different plans for the trucker to show which one will save money.

Making Your Argument Authoritative

If you can defend a position and perhaps even change the minds of your classmates, you are speaking with authority. For example, in a theater arts class, you may need to explain the set you designed and argue that it suits the director's vision of the play. Your ability to compose an argument justifying your artistic choices demonstrates your rhetorical authority as well as your abilities as a set designer.

Dealing fairly with opposing arguments also provides you with the opportunity to demonstrate your authority. If you show that you have seriously considered opposing views and understand them, and if you speak about those who hold such positions with respect, you will also appear to be reasonable and worthy of trust.

When you are asked to make an argument in an academic setting, an understanding of the rhetorical situation will help you recognize just what you are being asked to do and to demonstrate. (See Chapters 15 and 16 for more on academic audiences and writing situations.)

Because thinkers, scholars, and researchers have defined and redefined the elements of persuasive argument, there are a number of different terms for the same basic elements. The terms used in this text are placed within the traditional argument outline shown in Figure 7.1. These elements form the foundation of most academic discussions, as well as debates and arguments in many other areas of life. Mastery of these elements, including the ability to adapt them to your purpose and audience, contributes to an authoritative voice.

Note that contemporary arguments may not make explicit use of each of the elements shown in Figure 7.1. For example, writers of brief newspaper opinion pieces may not provide an outline of their argument in their introduction.

Genres That Persuade

The chapters in this part of the book describe the many forms and genres of argument. Genres of persuasion have a focused objective: to persuade the audience to think, believe, or act differently. Below is a brief list of some of the genres of persuasive writing and speech.

- **Advertisement**: a brief, often visual or audio argument intended to persuade the audience to buy a product or service, or support a person, an idea, or a movement such as a political candidate or cause.
- **Opinion piece/commentary/editorial**: a brief, journalistic argument in which the author tries to persuade the audience of her or his opinion.

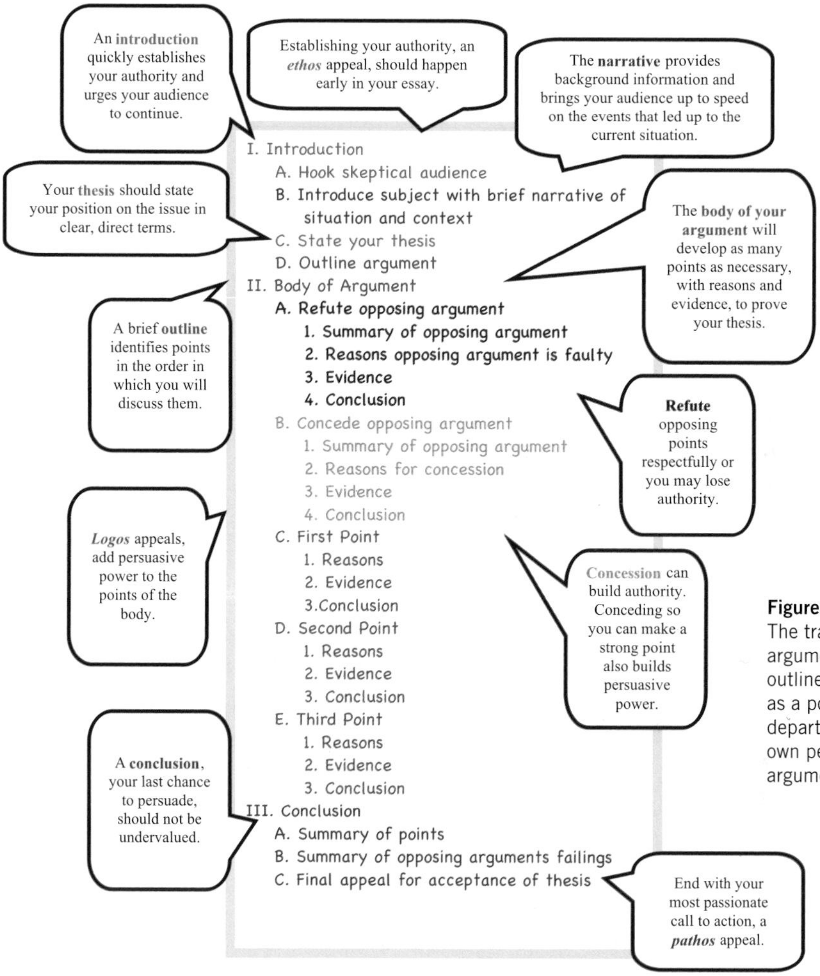

Figure 7.1 The traditional argumentative outline can serve as a point of departure for your own persuasive argument.

[The "body of your argument," "refute," and "concession" bubbles in this figure need to be moved to match the revised outline: IIA and IIB used to be lower down.]

- **Letter to the editor**: a letter, written in response to an article or opinion piece, addressed to an editor of a newspaper, magazine, or news website in which the author expresses her or his opinion in an attempt to persuade the readers of the publication to agree with the writer's point of view.
- **Research paper**: an academic, written argument using evidence drawn from sources to support a claim.
- **Reflective paper**: sometimes called an author's note or a portfolio cover letter, in this genre students reflect on their work and may also assess their achievement of the course's goals and outcomes.

MODULE II-9

A PERSUASIVE GENRE: ADVERTISEMENT

Some arguments are long and use all the elements of persuasion, while other genres of argument are condensed, such as the advertisement below (Figure 7.2).

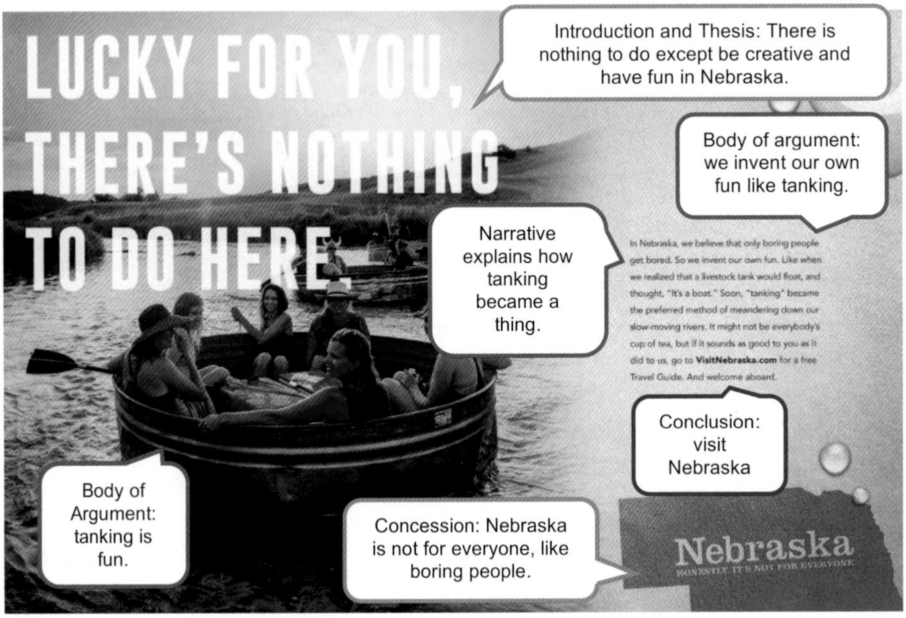

Figure 7.2 In October of 2018, the Nebraska Tourism Commission revealed its new slogan: "Honestly, it's not for everyone."

Questions to Consider

Invention

1. What prompted the creation of this advertisement? What inspired its creators?
2. How do you think the creators of the ad gathered ideas and evidence? How can you tell?
3. What do you think the ad's creators discovered early in the invention and research process?

4. What elements, such as images or type font, contribute to the persuasive power of the argument?

Audience

5. Who is the audience for this advertisement and how do you know?
6. What audience expectations did the ad's creators have to be aware of?
7. How would the argument change if the intended audience were Europeans or tour operators?

Authority

8. How does the ad use color, images, and text to build trust?
9. Which of the elements of a classical persuasive argument have been left out of the ad, and why?
10. What would you do to make the argument more persuasive?

MODULE II-10

A PERSUASIVE GENRE: REFLECTION PAPER

As part of the final portfolio assignment in her first-year College English class, Audrey Liviakis was asked to persuade the professor that she had achieved the course objectives, using evidence from her writing portfolio. As you read these excerpts, note how Liviakis adapted the elements of persuasive argument to her purpose, message, and audience.

> Dear Professor,
>
> As the syllabus states, a student must "submit the final portfolio with a persuasive cover letter summoning evidence and arguments proving the student has achieved the course objectives." *I am pleased to say that I have met and exceeded all your expectations as well as developed a set of writing tools that will help me further my own education. In addition, I have worked to help my classmates achieve the same.*

Narrative is brief, since Professor knows why she is making the argument.

Introduction of Audrey's subject and thesis.

I will begin by showing how I have helped my peers during workshops, and then show my understanding of message, purpose, and audience. Finally, I will prove that I can read and work in distinct rhetorical situations.

Outline of argument also introduces points she will make.

My most important achievement in class was my "critique [of] the work of others and their own drafts based upon the anticipated rhetorical situation" (Outcome 3.c.). For example, this quote from one of my draft responses shows how I applied my knowledge of the interdependence of audience, message, and purpose (AMP). In my response to a peer's draft, I explained that I tried to highlight the AMP. "I had an extremely difficult time identifying your audience ... having conflicting ideas of who your audience might be" (draft response #6). I proceeded to evaluate not only the presence of an AMP, but also the effectiveness of the message. If you review the entire draft response (see Draft Responses folder), you will see that I explained to this student the importance of rhetorical cohesiveness/interdependence and its effects on her piece's success. My suggestion that she rethink the rhetorical situation shows that I know and fully comprehend the proper criteria for critiquing the work of other students. This example also demonstrates that I recognize the interdependence of the message, purpose, and audience (Outcome 1.a.).

The body of the argument is composed of evidence supporting her thesis.

She finishes her first point in the body of the argument with a sentence summarizing the paragraph.

...

A few paragraphs from the body of the argument have been cut for brevity

When reading the book Me Talk Pretty One Day, *I was convinced I understood the intended audience and said so in my reading journal. As you pointed out, I had not really thought about the audience but merely guessed, based on who seemed to like the book and how old the author was. You were right. I didn't really think about the audience of the book as much as I thought about the audience of my peers' papers.* However, after your comment, I changed my idea of the audience. As you will see in the second entry in my reading journal for that book (reading journal #8), my new understanding of the audience of *Me Talk Pretty One Day* is based on the author's voice, word choice, referenced ideas and events, paragraph and sentence length, and even the cover art. As a result, I have a solid understanding of all the parts of the 4th outcome.

She concedes and accepts that she did not understand the audience initially.

The concession allows her to refute the professor's point and argue she learned to better understand the audience and the work.

...

This year, I have clearly exhibited growth as an independent writer, demonstrated dedication to producing excellent work, and expressed my true desire for improvement in both writing and literary comprehension. My final portfolio shows healthy improvement and a progression of skills over time. My improvement shows that I have truly met all the course objectives and benefited from this class. Thank you for an excellent semester and for your guidance.

Sincerely,
Audrey Liviakis

She concludes with her most passionate language, summarizing her argument and restating her thesis.

Questions to Consider

Invention

1. What prompted Liviakis to write her reflection? How do you know?
2. Where did Liviakis go to gather ideas, information, and evidence? How did she retrieve information?
3. What discoveries did she make during research?
4. How does Liviakis communicate her purpose to her audience?

Audience

5. Liviakis's argument is not a typical research paper. In what ways has she shaped this argument differently than she would probably shape a traditional research paper written in response to a prompt?
6. What restrictions or limits did Liviakis have to be aware of?
7. What in the letter communicates Liviakis's attitude toward her audience—her tenor—and her view of her own work—her tone?

Authority

8. How does Liviakis let her instructor know that he or she can or should trust what she has to say?
9. Which of the elements of a classical persuasive argument have been left out of the cover letter, and why?
10. Is her argument, as represented by these excerpts, persuasive? If not, what would you do to make it stronger? If it is, what can you borrow for your own writing?

MODULE II-11

A PERSUASIVE GENRE: OPINION PIECE

An **opinion piece** is a brief argument expressing a specific point of view about a current situation, event, or idea. Sometimes called commentaries or editorials (when they are written by a publication's editorial board), opinion pieces rarely use more than one or two sources. Unlike traditional news stories, opinion pieces do not need to be objective and are often informed by personal experience.

In the following *New York Times* opinion piece, which appeared in 2013, Christina Hoff Sommers argues that boys are being left behind academically as girls rise. As you read, notice how Sommers adapts many of the elements of persuasive argument to her message and audience.

The Boys at the Back

Boys score as well as or better than girls on most standardized tests, yet they are far less likely to get good grades, take advanced classes or attend college. Why? A study coming out this week in *The Journal of Human Resources* gives an important answer. Teachers of classes as early as kindergarten factor good behavior into grades—and girls, as a rule, comport themselves far better than boys.

Introduction begins with a hook—a question that should be answered.

Thesis answers the hook but leads to more questions.

The study's authors analyzed data from more than 5,800 students from kindergarten through fifth grade and found that boys across all racial groups and in all major subject areas received lower grades than their test scores would have predicted.

The narrative provides background information of the study.

The scholars attributed this "misalignment" to differences in "noncognitive skills": attentiveness, persistence, eagerness to learn, the ability to sit still and work independently. As most parents know, girls tend to develop these skills earlier and more naturally than boys.

No previous study, to my knowledge, has demonstrated that the well-known gender gap in school grades begins so early and is almost entirely attributable to differences in behavior. The researchers found that teachers rated boys as less proficient even when the boys did just as well as the girls on tests of reading, math and science. (The teachers

1st point in body of argument—grades biased against boys.

did not know the test scores in advance.) If the teachers had not accounted for classroom behavior, the boys' grades, like the girls', would have matched their test scores.

That boys struggle with school is hardly news. Think of Shakespeare's "whining schoolboy with his satchel and shining morning face, creeping like snail unwillingly to school." Over all, it's likely that girls have long behaved better than boys at school (and earned better grades as a result), but their early academic success was not enough to overcome significant subsequent disadvantages: families' favoring sons over daughters in allocating scarce resources for schooling; cultural norms that de-emphasized girls' education, particularly past high school; an industrial economy that did not require a college degree to earn a living wage; and persistent discrimination toward women in the workplace.

Narrative shows boys have always struggled, and disadvantages holding girls back have disappeared.

Those disadvantages have lessened since about the 1970s. Parents, especially those of education and means, began to value their daughters' human capital as much as their sons'. Universities that had been dominated by affluent white men embraced meritocratic values and diversity of gender, race and class. The shift from a labor-intensive, manufacturing-reliant economy to a knowledge-based service economy significantly increased the relative value of college and postgraduate degrees. And while workplace inequities persisted, changing attitudes, legislation and litigation began to level the occupational playing field.

As these shifts were occurring, girls began their advance in education. In 1985, boys and girls took Advanced Placement exams at nearly the same rate. Around 1990, girls moved ahead of boys, and have never looked back. Women now account for roughly 60 percent of associate's, bachelor's and master's degrees and have begun to outpace men in obtaining Ph.D.'s.

There are some who say, well, too bad for the boys. If they are inattentive, obstreperous and distracting to their teachers and peers, that's their problem. After all, the ability to regulate one's impulses, delay gratification, sit still and pay close attention are the cornerstones of success in school and in the work force. It's long past time for women to claim their

2nd point—biases against boys based on promotion of girls.

rightful share of the economic rewards that redound to those who do well in school.

As one critic told me recently, the classroom is no more rigged against boys than workplaces are rigged against lazy and unfocused workers. But unproductive workers are adults—not 5-year-olds. If boys are restless and unfocused, why not look for ways to help them do better? As a nation, can we afford not to?

Refutes biases and critics with appeal to sense of fairness and duty.

A few decades ago, when we realized that girls languished behind boys in math and science, we mounted a concerted effort to give them more support, with significant success. Shouldn't we do the same for boys?

...

A few paragraphs from the body of the argument have been cut for brevity.

WHAT might we do to help boys improve? For one thing, we can follow the example of the British, the Canadians and the Australians. They have openly addressed the problem of male underachievement. They are not indulging boys' tendency to be inattentive. Instead, they are experimenting with programs to help them become more organized, focused and engaged. These include more boy-friendly reading assignments (science fiction, fantasy, sports, espionage, battles); more recess (where boys can engage in rough-and-tumble as a respite from classroom routine); campaigns to encourage male literacy; more single-sex classes; and more male teachers (and female teachers interested in the pedagogical challenges boys pose).

3rd point—other developed countries have addressed problem.

These efforts should start early, but even high school isn't too late. Consider Aviation High School in New York City. A faded orange brick building with green aluminum trim, it fits comfortably with its gritty neighbors—a steelyard, a tool-supply outlet and a 24-hour gas station and convenience store—in Long Island City, Queens.

On a visit to Aviation I observed a classroom of 14- and 15-year-olds focused on constructing miniaturized, electrically wired airplane wings from mostly raw materials. In another class, students worked in teams—with a student foreman and crew chief—to take apart and then rebuild a small jet engine in just 20 days. In addition to pursuing a standard high school curriculum, Aviation students spend half of the day in hands-on classes on airframes, hydraulics and electrical systems. They put up with demanding English and history classes because unless they do well in them, they cannot spend their afternoons tinkering with the engine of a Cessna 411.

4th point—success also found here in experimental high schools.

The school's 2,200 pupils—mostly students of color, from low-income households—have a 95 percent attendance rate and a 90 percent graduation rate, with 80 percent going on to college. The school is coed; although girls make up only 16 percent of the student population, they appear to be flourishing. The New York City Department of Education has repeatedly awarded Aviation an "A" on its annual school progress reports. *U.S. News & World Report* has cited it as one of the best high schools in the nation.

Evidence of success found in attendance and graduation rates.

"The school is all about structure," an assistant principal, Ralph Santiago, told me. The faculty emphasizes organization, precision, workmanship and attention to detail. The students are kept so busy and are so fascinated with what they are doing that they have neither the time nor the desire for antics.

Success based on skills boys need.

Not everyone of either sex is interested in airplanes. But vocational high schools with serious academic requirements are an important part of the solution to male disengagement from school.

I can sympathize with those who roll their eyes at the relatively recent alarm over boys' achievement. Where was the indignation when men dominated higher education, decade after decade? Isn't it time for women and girls to enjoy the advantages? *The impulse is understandable but misguided. I became a feminist in the 1970s because I did not appreciate male chauvinism. I still don't. But the proper corrective to chauvinism is not to reverse it and practice it against males, but rather basic fairness.* And fairness today requires us to address the serious educational deficits of boys and young men. The rise of women, however long overdue, does not require the fall of men.

She concedes and accepts the audience's sense of historical inconsistency.

Concession sets up passionate refutation.

Conclusion carries on passion in a call to action.

Questions to Consider

Invention

1. What do you think prompted the author to write about this subject?
2. How did Sommers go about gathering ideas, information, and evidence? How can you tell?
3. What evidence appears to contribute to her conclusions?
4. How are the sources available to Sommers different from or similar to sources you might use?

Audience

5. Who is her audience, and how is Sommers's argument shaped by that audience?
6. What expectations, restrictions, or limits did Sommers have to be aware of in making her argument?
7. If Sommers had to compose a billboard advertisement for her ideas, what might it look like?

Authority

8. If you are persuaded by Sommers, why? If not, what in her argument raises doubts or questions?
9. Which of the elements of a classical persuasive argument have been left out of the opinion piece, and why?
10. What is Sommers's strongest point? What is her weakest point? What makes them so?

MODULE II-12

BUILDING A PERSUASIVE ARGUMENT

As with every writing task, the lenses of invention, audience, and authority can help you build a persuasive argument. The checklist below is a guide. Your writing process will be unique and can change with every paper you write.

Invention

A persuasive argument starts with invention, information retrieval, and synthesis.

- Find an issue

✓ If you have been assigned an issue or asked to argue a position, your purpose, focus, and scope will be defined by that assignment and issue. If you are free to choose any issue, find one you care about. Ask yourself:
  - ◎ What do you want to change?
  - ◎ Why do you want to cause such change?
  - ◎ What prevents such change from happening?

✓ Scope is the context or breadth of knowledge that you draw upon to make your argument, such as an academic discipline. Clarifying the scope you will draw on to make your argument will help you avoid wandering off track.

For example, suppose for a history class you are studying medical treatment and disease during the time of American Western expansion. If you start to research disease and medicine during the nineteenth century, your gigantic scope will result in thousands of potential sources and a lack of focus. However, if you limit your scope to the Oregon Trail at its height from 1845 to 1870, you can focus on the medicine that people on the trail carried, and what they died from.

- Find evidence and reasons

✓ A defensible thesis or claim needs to be supported by evidence and reasons in order to persuade an audience. As you research, look for data and information your audience will respect or can be persuaded to trust.

For example, some audience members may be skeptical of your thesis and the political views it suggests. However, if you support your thesis with evidence from *The Lancet*, a highly respected British medical journal, most audiences would have no reason to doubt its credibility. Consider your audience as you do your research, and look for evidence and reasons they are likely to trust.

✓ As you find evidence and reasons, be open to refining your position and changing your argument. Changing your mind as you research is a good sign, because the same reasons and evidence that persuaded you may also change the minds of your audience.

- Draft a working thesis

✓ Your position on the issue you have chosen will evolve as you continue to research and write. Drafting a working thesis, a preliminary statement of your position, can help you by doing the following:
   - Clearly stating an arguable or debatable position on the issue—a position that is easy to understand yet may be disputed by reasonable people. A clear working thesis may look like this:

     The medicine carried by those traveling the Oregon Trail, such as whiskey or vinegar, did not treat illness or cure sickness. Instead, these medicines simply eased symptoms or provided a placebo effect.

   - Indicating the focus and scope of your argument—the subject you are examining and the context or breadth of knowledge that you will draw upon to make your argument.
   - Suggesting what is to come—the outline or the sequence of points that will make up your argument. The working thesis above suggests that the author will first discuss the medicines used on the Oregon Trail and then argue that they were ineffective.

Audience

To persuade the members of your audience to agree with your thesis, you will need to understand their thoughts and expectations.

- Understand the rhetorical situation

✓ Your purpose will determine the audience you address, and your audience will guide you as you shape your argument. For example, if you want to persuade people about medicine on the Oregon Trail, your audience would be those who are curious or have misconceptions about frontier life. If, on the other hand, you are trying to persuade members of your community to accept immigrants from Syria, your audience might be skeptical and some even fearful of your argument.

✓ In an academic setting, you may not be responding to an urgent situation or crisis. However, an instructor will pay as much attention to the passion and energy you commit to an issue or research paper as to your evidence and reasoning.

- Research and reach out to your audience

✓ Your audience is composed of real people who may have good reasons to think or believe differently. Your readers or listeners may be persuaded to share your concern, however, if you provide a compelling yet brief description of what motivated you to write or speak about the issue. In other words, draw your audience in by describing the situation that drew you in.

✓ Seek out friends and family who may disagree with your thesis. Ask them why they think as they do and how they would argue against you. Spar with your professor. Go to office hours and ask your professor to argue against your position. As you research your subject, keep track of counter-arguments or objections raised to the positions you discover.

✓ Look for evidence and reasons that a skeptical audience would accept.

- Organize your argument

✓ The best way to organize your persuasive argument will depend upon your audience's expectations and your evidence and reasoning. The genre you are using can help you to shape your argument. In addition, tradition provides an initial template you can modify to suit your audience, purpose, thesis, and genre (see Figure 7.1).

✓ The structure of your thesis should be reflected in the structure of your argument.

For example, if your thesis includes three reasons to accept your position, the body of your argument must take up all three reasons and provide supporting evidence for each. The Conventions in Context box entitled "Paragraphs Mirror Essays" provides a way to see the structure of your essay.

- Draft your argument

✓ When you draft, you shape and reshape until your argument takes the right form. In other words, you will probably write many drafts before you are satisfied. You will move through the drafting process more quickly, though, if you can get responses and comments from people who play a devil's advocate to your argument. Above all, remember that every part of your draft can benefit from further drafting and reshaping, including your thesis.

✓ Drafting is the process of moving from your own perspective and thinking to that of your audience. As you draft, keep asking yourself what your audience already knows, what they need to know, and what ideas and positions you need to move them to accept.

Conventions in Context
Paragraphs Mirror Essays

Arguments are composed of smaller arguments. As a result, the outline of a persuasive argument often mirrors the outline of a persuasive paragraph.

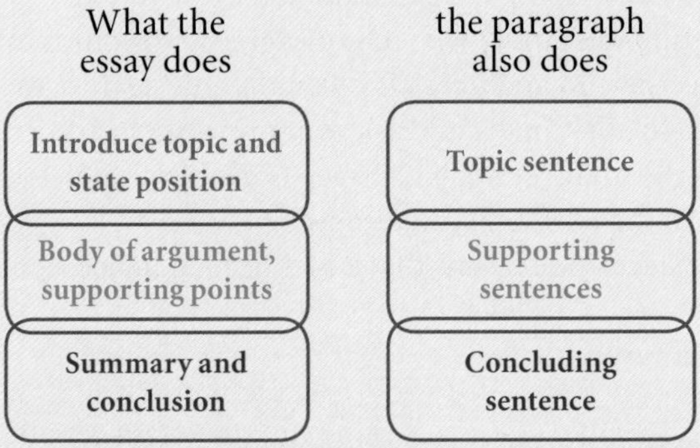

Students sometimes say the basic paragraph, with topic and concluding sentences, is too rigid and boring. Keep in mind, however, that the experience of composing an argument is not the same as the experience of an audience hearing or reading it. Readers and listeners experience clarity, simplicity, and familiar structures as markers of eloquence and authority. In addition, innovation and creativity often begins with basics.

Authority

To persuade your audience, your logic and your sources must be believable and sound. Once you have drafted your argument, you need to pay attention to the aspects of it that will establish your authority for your readers or listeners.

- Check your logic

  In most genres of persuasion, the structure of the argument is established in the introduction. The reader or listener should be able to identify your position on a specific issue and then to describe the situation, context, event, or idea that led you to make your argument. In other words, you want your reader or listener to think, "Tell me more," not "What is she going on about?"

✓ Each point should build on the previous point and support the thesis.

For example, you cannot persuade your audience that changes must be made in school policy that take into account how boys learn and develop without first showing that existing school policies punish how boys behave and learn.

✓ The reasoning must be logical and be supported by the evidence.

For example, in the debate about immigration policy, many people contend that the United States must not admit refugees from Iraq or Syria. The evidence they offer is that the number of violent attacks by terrorists claiming allegiance to the Islamic State in Iraq and Syria (ISIS) is on the rise. However, that evidence does not connect refugees in the United States to that violence. In fact, not one of the 784,000 refugees who have settled in the United States since 1980 has committed a terrorist attack. The Responsible Sourcing box entitled "Fallacies to Avoid" will help you check your logic and reasoning.

Responsible Sourcing
Fallacies to Avoid

All sources are likely to have some bias. However, irrational bias, unthinking bias, and overly emotional bias can damage your argument. When evaluating sources, avoid sources that use the following unfair arguments, or fallacies.

Flattery: Praising an audience may be seen as a suspicious attempt to gain favor. You might hear a politician say, "You are the hard-working soul of America, which is why I hope I can serve as your representative in Congress." Flattery is often used to distract an audience from important or difficult issues.

Populism: Appearing to side with the audience against "them," the "others," or the "elite" that threaten the audience's way of life is an unfounded argument. argument. Like flattery, populism is an attempt to push the audience to see the writer or speaker as a friend and defender who will stand up for "us." Populism is often used to oversimplify complex or difficult issues.

Stacking the deck: A writer who ignores valid opposing arguments or suggests that opposing arguments are wrong or dangerous is stacking the deck. Because no idea is perfect and no one is correct 100% of the time, stacking the deck is a dishonest strategy. Concession is an essential element of classical argument that helps you avoid stacking the deck.

The bandwagon: When a writer suggests that "everyone is doing it," he or she is distracting the audience from important issues and decisions and relying on social coercion or peer pressure to move the audience.

Great women/men, moments, or ideas: Quoting trusted sources is an important part of argument. However, suggesting that a great person would agree with an opinion when that person has never spoken about the issue is dishonest. For example, the legendary lifeguard Eddie Aikau was an amazing big-wave surfer. However, telling a reluctant fellow surfer that "Eddie would go" is an unfair argument. Eddie did go on waves he could handle. But he might not go if he had your skills. Like the bandwagon, this fallacy distracts from the realities of the situation.

Loaded terms: Perhaps the most common fallacy found in persuasive arguments is the use of emotional and derogatory terms to promote a position or create a negative emotional response to opposing arguments. Examples include "the lame stream media" rather than "mainstream media," and "teabagger" for the Tea Party movement. The use of loaded terms is an indication that the writer or speaker has an irrational bias, as are all forms of name-calling.

Just as you will be judged by the company you keep, your argument will be evaluated by the quality of sources you use.

- Make it flow

✓ When an argument is clear, ideas seem to flow effortlessly from the page or speaker's mouth into the mind of the audience. Clarity is also what makes a reader continue to read and a listener pay attention. Significantly, there is not a set of clear words and another set of unclear words. To achieve clarity, you need to pay attention to the language practices and expectations of your audience and the common structures and practices of the genre(s) you use. For a more complete definition of flow, and specific examples of how flow can be disrupted, see Chapter 24.

✓ Move your readers or listeners through your argument by letting them know what is ahead and helping them make the transition between ideas. Marking words such as "next" or "second," or phrases like "in addition to" or "as opposed to," help your reader follow your thinking. Transitional sentences that describe the link between two paragraphs or a shift in topic from one paragraph to the next also give your reader a sense of flow. Chapter 24 describes marking words and transitions.

- Get peer response

✓ Ask your peers to look over your argument and identify the following:
  - Please circle my thesis or claim. If it is not directly stated, please summarize my thesis in the margin.
  - Am I addressing the right audience to achieve my purpose?
  - Which of my points are most persuasive and which may not persuade my intended audience?
  - Please tell me if the evidence I am using supports or does not support my point.
  - Are there counter arguments I need to consider and argue against or concede?
  - What do you think I want my readers to think, believe, or do when they are done reading or hearing my argument?

- Check your voice and style

✓ Voice and style are not *what* you have said or written, but *how* you said or wrote it. Like persuasion, voice and style work, or do not work, in the mind of your audience.

✓ Your voice is a combination of
  - Tone: your attitude toward your subject
  - Tenor: your attitude toward your audience

  Your audience will sense your tone and tenor, so you need to make sure it aligns with your message, purpose, and audience.

✓ Your style is a combination of
  - Level of formality: your word choice and sentence construction
  - Pace: how fast or slow your argument proceeds

  The formality of your voice will depend upon audience expectations, the genre(s) you use, and the rhetorical situation. A research paper will be formal and move at a slower pace than an opinion piece, which can be light or serious and moves up and down the emotional scale depending upon the purpose and audience.

- Revise your argument

✓ When you revise, it's important to see your claim, reasons, and evidence through the eyes of your audience. In your mind, your position is obviously right and persuasive, but how will someone who disagrees see your position? The goal of revision is to close the distance between what you have in your mind and what your audience will understand from your argument.

✓ First drafts should be messy. If yours is not, you may be focusing on tidiness at the expense of effectiveness. As you revise, you will move from refining and reshaping the major aspects of your argument, such as the order of the points you are making, to small matters, such as the punctuation in your citations.

✓ If you have received detailed comments from your peers and are trying out different structures and reasons, you will probably find yourself torn between options for revising. When deciding on what peer advice to take or which sentences to cut or expand, you will find it helpful to focus on your audience and your purpose. Ask yourself, which option will help me persuade my audience so I can achieve my purpose?

CHAPTER 8

ANALYZING ARGUMENTS

MODULE II-13 WHAT AUDIENCES EXPECT OF A RHETORICAL ANALYSIS
MODULE II-14 A RHETORICAL ANALYSIS OF A PHOTOGRAPH
MODULE II-15 A RHETORICAL ANALYSIS OF AN OPINION PIECE
MODULE II-16 BUILDING AN EFFECTIVE RHETORICAL ANALYSIS

Like the tiny pixels that comprise a whole photograph, meaningful messages are composed of small elements and relationships. When small elements of a message contribute to its overall meaning and have their intended effect, they are usually invisible. But when messages break down, as pixels do when an image breaks up on a computer screen, the flawed elements stand out and distract the reader or listener.

When meaning in written communication or speech breaks down, the problem is often relatively easy to point out. Perhaps a speaker has used an unfamiliar term, or the design of a brochure makes it hard to discover the main point of its message. The more useful task, however, is to analyze and understand how the small, subtle elements of a successful argument—such as the elements within the Amazon.com logo or the parts of a powerful photograph—work together.

Amazon's logo, for example, appears to be little more than the company's web address at first glance (Figure 8.1). However, if you take a closer look and ask "what details do I notice in this logo?" you see a mixture of a bold and a regular font in the company's name, as well as an orange line in the shape of a smile. Look a bit closer and you'll see that the orange line also looks like an arrow pointing from "a" to "z," implying that Amazon has everything you could want or need.

amazon.com®

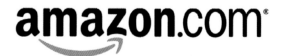

Figure 8.1
In 2000, this third iteration of the Amazon logo was introduced.

Is the argument conveyed by the logo successful? In other words, do the elements of the logo achieve the company's purpose and goals? To answer that question, you first have to determine what the company's goals are, and Amazon's mission statement is a good place to look: "Our vision is to be earth's most customer-centric company; to build a place where people can come to find and discover anything they might want to buy online." According to a 2017 study of global brands by Interbrand Newell and Sorrell, since Amazon adopted this logo in 2000, the company has moved from the 57th to the 5th most valuable brand in the world. Clearly, a growing number of people see Amazon as the first place to look when shopping online. The logo is not the only source of Amazon's success, but evidence suggests that the logo is much more than simply a web address, and it is effective.

This chapter explains how to analyze written and visual texts rhetorically and how to build an authoritative rhetorical analysis argument. Before we can begin to build, however, we must first understand what audiences are looking for in a rhetorical analysis.

MODULE II-13

WHAT AUDIENCES EXPECT OF A RHETORICAL ANALYSIS

Since 2001, a show called "How It's Made" on the Science Channel has focused on how big and small parts are put together to form the common products we often underestimate or overlook, such as a hybrid car or a bag of pasta. Like "How It's Made," a rhetorical analysis promises to give readers a new perspective by examining the parts of a persuasive argument and how they come together to convince, or fail to convince, an audience.

Because rhetorical analyses have been around since Aristotle and are common in and out of the classroom, your audience is likely to have specific expectations. Defining rhetorical analysis—what it is and is not—is an essential first step in understanding an audience's expectations.

Defining Rhetorical Analysis

A **rhetorical analysis** is an argument based upon an analysis and evaluation of a meaningful message or a message that has failed to convey its meaning. Often, we ask what something means. A rhetorical analysis, though, asks *how* something means. To write a successful rhetorical analysis, you need to examine the elements of that message to determine how the parts are organized and work together to achieve, or fail to achieve, a rhetorical purpose such as to instruct, persuade, or delight an audience.

The primary purpose of a rhetorical analysis is to understand how readers or listeners can be persuaded to think differently, believe differently, or act differently as a result of something they read, hear, or see. The *how* question is important. It can explain why and under what conditions an advertisement persuades consumers to buy a soft drink or see a movie, for example. An answer to the *how* question can help you build your own persuasive messages.

When you analyze a message to determine how its elements work together to make a successful argument, you can do the following:

- discover persuasive messages that are hidden or obscured;
- recognize when and how others are using rhetorical elements such as an emotional appeal to persuade you;
- understand how rhetorical elements can work together to form a persuasive strategy and how they can fail;
- evaluate the success or failure of persuasive strategies within different rhetorical situations;
- identify and use rhetorical elements such as an appeal to authority to persuade your audience.

You can learn as much from analyzing failed arguments and miscommunications as you can from examining successful ones. Discovering why an argument failed to achieve its purpose or why an audience came away with a meaning very different from the one its creator intended can provide valuable insights into how arguments connect—or fail to connect—with their audiences. For instance, a campaign manager might analyze the candidate's recent speeches to find out why contributions have suddenly decreased. If the candidate does not know how an audience was turned off, he or she could easily repeat the error.

Composing a Rhetorical Analysis for a Course

Arguments can be written or spoken, or they can be in the form of an image, a series of moving images, a computer program or game, an individual or group performance, and even a physical structure. In an academic situation you may be asked to analyze arguments in many forms.

In an Introduction to Historical Methods course, for example, you may be asked to analyze a presidential address or a president's desk. In a marketing course, you may be asked to analyze a logo as part of a brand analysis assignment. In a political science course, you could analyze a t-shirt worn at a protest. And in a writing or rhetoric course, you may be asked to analyze the effect of various rhetorical appeals in a campaign speech.

Because the range of subjects to analyze is so varied, we will use the term *text* to stand for meaningful messages, events, and artifacts. However, some forms of writing are not rhetorical analyses. These include reviews, summaries, interpretations of meaning, and arguments opposing the analyzed source. A rhetorical analysis may include some or even all of these elements, but its aim is to answer the *how* questions: how an argument is constructed, how a mind is changed, or how an argument failed to persuade an audience.

Using Invention to Prepare for Your Analysis and Evaluation

Your invention process will inform all of the following elements of a rhetorical analysis; however, the foundation of an insightful argument will be the text you select and its rhetorical situation.

- **a text**: As stated above, any meaningful written or spoken text, event, or artifact that makes an argument can be the subject of a rhetorical analysis.
- **the rhetorical situation**: The text you are analyzing comes from a rhetorical situation. Therefore, to analyze the success or failure of a text, you must understand the rhetorical situation that it is responding to. For example, an analysis of "The Gettysburg Address" must consider the situation President Lincoln was responding to on the field near the site of the Battle of Gettysburg on that Thursday in November 1863. The success or failure of a text is determined by the audience's response, and their response is determined by the rhetorical situation, including
    - the author,
    - the author's purpose,
    - the argument,
    - the audience,
    - the setting and relevant events, and
    - the design of the message and the medium in which it is delivered

  Chapter 15 describes the rhetorical situation in detail. The text and rhetorical situation will be the scope of your analysis.

Your Audience's Interests Inform Your Analysis

Once you've determined the text and its rhetorical situation, you need to decide on the rhetorical elements you will use to analyze them. Necessarily, the text, your purpose, and the audience you are addressing should guide your analysis. For example, your purpose may be to analyze an election campaign commercial to fact-check the claims. However, if your audience found the commercial emotionally moving and inspiring, you may need to examine its emotional appeal before you can address its reasoning and logic. Further, in a logic course, your professor may ask who made an argument or what makes that person an authority, but she or he is looking to see your analysis of the argument's structure. In composition and rhetoric courses, you will often be asked to analyze an argument's use of persuasive appeals.

You make an **appeal** whenever you structure an idea or select specific types of information that are attractive and persuasive to a specific audience (see Chapter 17, Module III-13). Tradition defines three types of persuasive appeals, which were briefly introduced earlier:

- ***Ethos***: An *ethos* appeal in an argument points to the writer's or speaker's qualities, experience, values, and knowledge to persuade the audience of his or her authority on an issue. If the writer or speaker is relying on sources, the *ethos* appeal would depend on the demonstrated authority of those sources. To analyze an argument's *ethos*, you would examine the methods its author or speaker uses to convince the audience that his or her claim, reasons, and evidence are authoritative and can be trusted. In other words, you would analyze how the author or speaker moves readers or listeners to believe the source of the message shares their values and experiences.

  For example, during a May of 2018 earnings conference call, Tesla stock dropped 5.5 per cent due to chairman Elon Musk's immature tone and combative tenor. A *Market Watch* headline called Musk a "jerk." During Tesla's June quarter earnings call, Musk worked to regain the confidence many had lost in his leadership with an *ethos* argument. In a humble voice, he apologized for his "bad manners" and explained that he had been "working in the body shop" and on other tasks for 110 to 120 hours a week and had little sleep. Shareholders responded positively to Musk's demonstration of self-awareness, humility, selfless leadership, and self-sacrificing commitment to his company and rewarded him with an 8.5 per cent surge in the value of Tesla stock (Figure 8.2).

Figure 8.2 Musk at work.

- ***Logos***: A *logos* appeal focuses on the reasoning and evidence of an argument by demonstrating the qualities that make the reasons and evidence valid, believable, and true. To analyze an argument's *logos*, you would consider how an author or speaker tries to make the audience believe that the message is true, valid, and beyond doubt.

  For example, if we look at Musk's second-quarter earnings call, we see him making a prediction of future sales growth with a deductive argument:

  > One of the results you're seeing is that the Model 3 market share has surpassed all competitor premium midsized sedans combined. So Model 3 market share is now a majority. In July, it was a majority of all premium sedans. That trend is, we think, likely to continue. We do not think it will stop there.

  You may be thinking, without a source for his sales data, how is his appeal persuasive? Musk knew he was talking to shareholders, market analysts, and consumer-research analysts who could check his data as he spoke. If he fudged the numbers, his next call could be with the Securities and Exchange Commission.
- ***Pathos***: Using emotions, passions, or sentimentality to sway an audience to accept an argument or act in a specific way is a *pathos* appeal. To analyze an argument's *pathos*, you would examine how an author or speaker arouses or uses emotions to move the audience to believe the source, be persuaded by the message, and think or act as the message argues.

  For example, when describing the success of his newest model, Musk described the reaction of buyer who had never sat in or test-driven the Model 3 Tesla he had purchased.

  > I was like, "Wow, OK." I asked him, "Well, how do you feel about the car now that you have it and you've driven it?" He's like, "I love it. It's amazing." So, yes. It seems to be really well-received.

  Portraying the buyer's passion not only demonstrates how well the new model is received but is also an attempt to transfer a car buyer's passion to shareholders—both are pathos appeals.

Whether appeals are effective does not depend solely on the writer's or speaker's words and gestures. Appeals are always situated, which means that their meaning is shaped by the rhetorical situation, including recent events as well as the facts and opinions the audience has in mind.

Other elements from classical or contemporary rhetoric can be the basis of a rhetorical analysis. In analyzing a magazine or Web advertisement, you might consider the format, type font, use of images, and negative space. For an event such as a public official's press conference, you might analyze the staging as well as the tone and tenor of the official's responses. Your audience will expect you to identify the elements that you are focusing on by citing examples drawn from the text you are analyzing. If your focus is a senator's use of the *logos* appeal during a floor speech in the Senate, you will need to identify and examine

- the speaker's purpose or desired outcome,
- the audience's disposition, or prior thinking and beliefs, on the subject of the speech, and
- the strategic use of *logos* by the speaker.

Authority Determines the Persuasive Force of Your Analysis

After your invention and analysis, you will have discovered effective, ineffective, and even curious uses of rhetorical elements. Pointing to an appeal or a mistake is useful, but a thoughtful evaluation of how the writer or creator achieved, or failed to achieve, the overall strategy confirms your authority as someone whose analysis can be trusted. Persuading your audience of what you have found, however, is a product of both your hard work and your ability to explain and evaluate what you have discovered.

After your analysis, your audience will expect you to make a judgment or evaluation—to state how well, or how poorly, the author of the text used the elements strategically to achieve his or her purpose. Returning to Ryan Lochte's apology, you could argue that his *pathos* appeal was effective in persuading a sympathetic audience. However, for those in the audience who consider Olympians to be role models for American children, his *logos* appeal would most likely have been seen as a dodge.

Taken together, the parts of a rhetorical analysis should provide your readers or listeners with a new perspective so they can see the text you have analyzed in a new way and understand aspects of it that they may have overlooked before.

MODULE II-14

A RHETORICAL ANALYSIS OF A PHOTOGRAPH

When a rhetorical analysis works well, it explains *how* a written or visual text means what it does—how unnoticed rhetorical elements are used and how these elements work together in a specific context to persuade or fail to persuade.

For example, consider Stephanie Matamoros's analysis of a famous image, composed and captured by photographer Jonathan Bachman in July 2016. Stephanie was asked to write a four-page rhetorical analysis, and the assignment required her to select an image with a political message.

Stephanie Matamoros
RHET 298

The Power of Silence

Acts of social injustice have occurred throughout U.S. history, and often such acts have sparked protests, both violent and non-violent. Within the last few years, the activist movement known as Black Lives Matter has become an important voice of protest. The movement started as a hashtag on social media in response to incidents where African Americans have been killed in encounters with the police. With the increasing importance of social media, this movement has gained international attention. Traditional news media have reported the violence that has occurred during these protests, but images and videos shared via social media and activists' websites paint a more nuanced picture. **During a protest in Baton Rouge, Louisiana, following the death of Alton Sterling in July 2015, Reuters photographer Jonathan Bachman composed a photograph (fig. 1) to exemplify the peaceful nature of many of these protests.**

Rhetorical Situation setting and relevant events.

Thesis of Analysis.

Fig. 1 Ieshia Evans was arrested for obstructing a highway, fingerprinted, and strip searched in jail.

Text.

Ieshia Evans, the subject of the photo, is a 35-year-old mother and nurse from New York City who traveled to Baton Rouge to participate in the protest to "fight for a better future"

As the subject of the photo, Ms. Evans is a rhetorical element of the text's argument.

for her 5-year-old son. As she told CBS News, "I felt like I was just a bystander and I had—you have a choice as a human being to do something or to not do something... Once the opportunity presented itself, it was just like, 'yeah, definitely'" ("Ieshia Evans"). Evans did not expect to come out of the rally as a symbol of peaceful protest, but Bachman understood the powerful message of his photograph.

In an interview that appears in *The Atlantic*, Bachman said he took the photograph with the intention of sending it to Reuters because he felt that this photograph with Evans "spoke more to the movement" and showed what the protesters were attempting to achieve (Mack).

The media and intended message are part of the Rhetorical Situation.

Bachman was not the only one impressed by Evans's calm demeanor; once Reuters posted the photograph, it went viral as Black Lives Matter supporters shared the photograph throughout social media. A *Facebook* user even stated that there are certain photos that define a moment, while grouping this photograph with other iconic images such as the photo of a Chinese protester standing in front of army tanks in Tiananmen Square in 1989 (Miller).

Audiences find message of photo popular and historic.

Evans's stance in the photograph appears both heroic and vulnerable; she seems confident and relaxed. A slight wind blows her sundress a bit, as if it were a cape. *And yet the image is taken just before the seemingly oversized police force arrests her, leaving the audience to fear for her as they imagine what happens next. Her stance and self-assuredness make her message even more powerful, drawing the viewer to ask, what is she standing for?* By quickly reacting and taking this timely photograph, Bachman was able to capture powerful details, such as her demeanor and stance, contrasted with the uncertainty of the officers, that work together as a powerful ethos appeal.

Details composed and captured by the photograph form an ethos appeal.

In addition to the message of the image, Bachman communicates his authority as a news professional in the way the photograph is composed. Because the image is a medium shot capturing a wide angle of the background, viewers are able to see the entire scene, including the line of police in riot gear behind the two officers who are moving towards Evans. The image of a non-violent, vulnerable individual facing an overwhelming, uniformed force recalls photos from the civil rights movements—a powerful emotional appeal—and links a new

Photo composed to include many elements.

generation of activists to earlier social justice protests such as Bloody Sunday of 1965 and photo from Tiananmen square.

Ethos appeal emerges from similarity of this image with other non-violent protests.

The composition and detail of the photo also imply social commentary. The cracks in the pavement seems to symbolize a fracture between the protesters and officials, with Evans representing peace on one side of the gap and the officers representing impersonal force. While Evans appears to radiate calm resistance, with her feet firmly planted on the ground, her posture straight, and her head upright and forward, the officers portray disproportionate aggression. Evans is not looking directly at the officers, but beyond them, as if she is tuning out the chaos surrounding her. However, it is not difficult for the viewers to picture the next few moments.

Individual elements identified: pavement cracks, individuals portrayed, movement captured.

In their approach, the officers seem to be unsure of what their next move should be. Their feet are in mid-stride, as if they are retreating backwards, and their facial expressions, behind the visors they are wearing, appear to be tense. By capturing their tense, powerful, seemingly chaotic body language in contrast to Evans's calm demeanor, the photograph appeals to viewers' emotions by showing that Evans's protest is fundamentally nonviolent and hopeful.

Analysis of contrasts in the image reveals pathos appeal.

With this photograph, Jonathan Bachman and Ieshia Evans worked together—though unintentionally—to make two points. First, Bachman wanted viewers of the photograph to see that Black Lives Matter protesters are using peaceful means to object to police actions. Second, police often confront such protests ready for a fight, with overwhelming force rather than understanding.

Evaluation of two-point argument composed of different appeals.

The image resonates because the argument is composed of a number of appeals. Portraying the peaceful resolve of a single Black Lives Matter protester, an ethos appeal moves viewers to identify more with Ieshia Evans and her cause than with the situation of the officers. The same image also makes a pathos appeal as the viewer imagines what is next and fears for Evans's welfare and safety. Finally, the image recalls past nonviolent movements and links Ieshia Evans's peaceful act of protest to the ethos and authority of others who took a similar stand such as Martin Luther King and the Tiananmen tank man.

Bachman's photograph and Evans's stance are authoritative enough to resonate with supporters and send a different message from the one suggested by images of violence in the mainstream media.

Works Cited

Bachman, Jonathan. "Taking a Stand in Baton Rouge." 10 July 2016, widerimage.reuters.com/story/taking-a-stand-in-baton-rouge.

"Ieshia Evans, Woman in Iconic Baton Rouge Police Protest Photo, Speaks out." *CBSNews*, CBS Interactive, 15 July 2016, www.cbsnews.com/news/ieshia-evans-woman-iconic-baton-rouge-police-protests-photo-speaks-out/.

Mack, David. "This Photo of a Black Lives Matter Protester Is Incredible." *BuzzFeed*. 10 July 2016, www.buzzfeed.com/david-mack/baton-rouge-blm-photo?utm_term=.hudEE33xrO#.eoakk55PEK.

Miller, Michael E. "'Graceful in the Lion's Den': Photo of Young Woman's Arrest in Baton Rouge Becomes Powerful Symbol." *The Washington Post*. 11 July 2016, www.washingtonpost.com/news/morning-mix/wp/2016/07/11/graceful-in-the-lions-den-photo-of-young-womans-arrest-in-baton-rouge-goes-viral/.

Accurate citation of primary source is a logos appeal.

Accurate citation of secondary sources contributes to author's authority—an ethos appeal.

Questions to Consider

Invention

1. How do you think Stephanie Matamoros discovered this image, and what drew her to it as a subject of a rhetorical analysis?
2. How do you think Matamoros began her invention and discovery once she chose the image as her text?
3. What did she discover using secondary sources?
4. What did she discover when she examined the photo, which was her text?

Audience

5. What restrictions or limits do you think Matamoros had to work with, and what expectations do you think she was responding to?
6. Who is Matamoros writing to, and how do you know?
7. If Matamoros wanted to submit this essay to a regional alternative newspaper such as the *Memphis Flyer* or *Vice Magazine*, what would she have to change?

Authority

8. What terms does Matamoros use to describe the elements in the photo and their relationships?
9. Matamoros is not an expert in media, photography, or image analysis. What does she do to establish an authoritative voice?
10. What is Matamoros's evaluation? Do you agree with it? Why or why not? What would you do to make it more persuasive?

MODULE II-15

A RHETORICAL ANALYSIS OF AN OPINION PIECE

The essay below was selected by a student, Oscar King IV, as the subject of his rhetorical analysis. This opinion piece was written by Froma Harrop, a prize-winning editor and syndicated writer. It first appeared on the site realclearpolitics.com in April 2015. Read the text, and then read King's analysis of it.

On the Internet, Nobody Knows You're a Fraud

By Froma Harrop
April 23, 2015

There's been some tense back-and-forth over the Canadian mother who said she had stopped opposing vaccinations after all seven of her kids came down with whooping cough. Some say we should loudly thank Tara Hills for publicly disowning her anti-vax campaign. Others—me, for instance—are feeling less grateful.

Hills went beyond spreading lies about the "dangers" of vaccinations and exposing her Ottawa neighbors to serious disease. She strongly implied that the best medical authorities are "puppets of a Big Pharma-Government-Media conspiracy," according to *The Washington Post*—and on a site demoniacally named TheScientificParent.org.

You've probably seen the famous cartoon showing a dog at a computer saying to another dog, "On the Internet, nobody knows you're a dog." The word "dog" could have been replaced with "fraud."

As more Americans turn to online forums for advice on everything from where to eat to whether they need surgery, concerns mount about the quality of the information. Readers often use the consensus of forum participants to bypass the views of recognized experts. And because these forums are usually little-monitored, the "weight of opinion" is often determined by the most verbose and those with too much time on their hands.

Millennials have become especially reliant on (apparent) group consensus, according to a report by PricewaterhouseCoopers on the "sharing economy." "If trust in individuals and institutions is waning or at best holding steady," the report notes, "faith in the aggregate is growing."

That is, consumers who disbelieve a hotel chain's claims of fine accommodations will show up at the door of a total stranger, renting a room via Airbnb—their trust totally based on reviews submitted by who-knows-who.

As we know, interested parties or crazy people can create a phony consensus. Then you have people like the Ottawa mother, who seemed truly committed to her beliefs but was unable or too lazy to examine expert opinion in reaching them.

In a similar vein, Sarah Watts wrote an interesting essay about her online confab with other millennial new mothers on caring for an infant. At the time, her own mother was on the scene urging her not to worry if baby June cried shortly after a feeding. The crying will stop, the mother's mother said. That advice turned out to be good.

"I had been scouring message boards and Facebook groups during June's nursing sessions," Watts said, "and I had stumbled on discussions of every kind of parenting issue imaginable." Some were issues she had never heard of, such as cord clamping and vitamin K shots.

Most posted questions, Watts observed, resulted in respondents "bandying conflicting research like a weapon, every one of them armed with a battery of qualifiers to describe her personal parenting philosophy." (I might take her skepticism one step further and wonder whether the other "moms" were actually mothers or even women.)

We see the clamor of anonymous and inexpert posts on everything from foreign policy to breast-feeding. Certain forums are purposely designed to buttress one point of view. They attract like-minded commenters, who leave the impression of overwhelming support for a position.

It's crazy out there. Good sites are often so plagued by armies of the uninformed filling their forums with dimwitted comments that smart people stay away. But some well-run forums are hugely interesting.

It's a sign of the times that Californians trying to tighten the vaccination mandate for schoolchildren now worry that the drawn-out legislative process will open the door to anti-vaxxers intent on poisoning public opinion. In many cases, readers won't even know who they are. The scary part is many won't even care.

Oscar King IV was assigned a rhetorical analysis of an opinion piece in his Communications 324 "Editorial and Opinion Writing" course. He was given two weeks to write a five-page paper analyzing a current, written editorial or opinion. He chose to write an analysis of Froma Harrop's opinion piece about questionable information on the Web, which appears above.

Oscar King IV
Rhetorical Analysis
3 Oct. 2016

On the Internet, Everyone but Me Is a Fraud

Froma Harrop, a popular journalist whose column is widely syndicated, speaks against internet ignorance in an opinion piece **from 2015, "On the Internet, Nobody Knows You're a Fraud." The piece itself is a commentary on the methods people on the internet use to come by information.** *While Harrop makes a convincing argument, her reliance on emotional appeals (pathos) and changes in point of view, with few appeals to logic, puts her into the same position as the people she is criticizing, focusing on anecdotes and stories in the news instead of established facts.*

Rhetorical Situation—author and message.

Text.

Thesis of Analysis.

Harrop makes an immediate appeal to the millennials in her audience with the title of her opinion piece: "On the Internet, Nobody Knows You're a Fraud." This title directly appeals to the millennial reader because it refers to the popular "On the Internet, nobody knows you're a dog" meme, as Harrop herself explains. **The article assumes that its audience is at least tangentially aware of the anti-vaccine movement and the stir it has created, even if they are unfamiliar with the specific case of Tara Hills, an anti-vaccine activist and mother of seven who was the subject of some controversy in 2015. To make her point, Harrop outlines Tara Hills's situation.**

Author speaks the same language, knows the same memes, as audience —ethos appeal.

Hills changed her stand on vaccinations after her seven children contracted whooping cough. The issue that Harrop addresses is not about whether vaccinations should be mandated, however. Rather, she criticizes the methods many internet readers use when evaluating online information

Rhetorical Situation —setting, relevant events, and author's purpose.

such as that previously offered by Hills at her site, titled TheScientificParent. Harrop's purpose is twofold: to convince millennials that relying on the judgement of a group is dangerous when evaluating popular sources of information, and to set herself up as a source who can be trusted. This argument is summarized nicely in her fourth paragraph: "Readers often use the consensus of forum participants to bypass the views of recognized experts." Harrop uses shifting points of view—"we" versus "they" or "readers"—and she relies on anecdotes that appeal to readers' emotions to make her points. *The use of "we" helps Harrop include her readers when she makes positive claims, praising them for their good sense. When she makes negative claims, however, she shifts to noninclusive diction—"they," "readers," "Americans"—and draws an emotional distinction between the intelligent people who are reading her column and the foolish people who are not.*

Points of view move reader to identify emotionally with the author, a pathos appeal.

Analysis of pronouns place reader of text on author's side—ethos appeal.

The lines "beyond spreading lies," and "exposing her Ottawa neighbors to serious disease" help to frame Tara Hills as the antagonist. Harrop suggests that Hills did something even worse than lie or allow the spread of disease: she deceived her readers by claiming to have more knowledge on a topic than she actually did. By calling Hills's website "a site demoniacally named TheScientificParent.org," Harrop comments on Hills's implication that the "best medical authorities are 'puppets of a Big Pharma-Government-Media conspiracy.'" Her language condemns what Hills has published about medical authorities, and it is a strong emotional appeal given the frame she has already placed around Hills.

Author continues ethos appeal by casting Hills as deceitful—ethos appeal.

Harrop's shift to a third person commentary, speaking of "Americans" and "readers" who turn to forums instead of experts, again draws a line between the people smart enough to read Harrop's article and the people who are reading forums without consulting experts. She characterizes online commenters negatively and appeals to readers' emotions by noting that "because these forums are usually little-monitored, the 'weight of opinion' is often determined by the most verbose and those with too much time on their hands." Though Harrop supports her point about overreliance on online forums

Author's critique of on-line forums and their participants is short on reasoning and evidence.

by citing a report from PricewaterhouseCoopers, she seems to assume that her characterization of those who participate in them is common knowledge, and she fails to provide support for it. **Instead of relying on logic or evidence, she focuses on her appeals to pathos, and her argument suffers for it. Furthermore, Harrop uses the third person ("their hands") to indicate that these people with too much time on their hands are not the people to whom Harrop is writing. She is thus effective in swaying her audience to her perspective, because if they do not agree with her, they become the aforementioned followers of weighty opinions instead of facts.**

Flattery may appeal to the audience but may also be seen as manipulative.

Harrop's Airbnb example, another instance of majority-favor over expert opinion, is relevant to her millennial readers, yet she again excludes her specific readership from any negative implications by using "their" instead of "you" or "we." This choice is clearly intentional because the following paragraph shifts again into the inclusive "we" and positive diction: "As we know, interested parties or crazy people can create a phony consensus." Offered without context, Harrop's next anecdotal example, Sarah Watts's experience with online parenting advice, works for Harrop as another point of comparison for readers: Watts's mother's commonsense advice versus ridiculous Internet advice. This one example does not encompass all of what the Internet has to offer, however, and *again, Harrop's argument lacks sufficient evidence beyond anecdotes. The anecdote itself, however, is effective in swaying Harrop's audience because it illustrates Harrop's point that group consensus, forum consensus, and the millennial reliance on unsubstantiated information produces a "clamor of anonymous and inexpert posts on everything from foreign policy to breast-feeding."*

Anecdotes used to move reader toward informed choices.

Anecdotes explain and can be persuasive, but do demonstrate fallibility of consensus.

Harrop establishes her opinion piece as a safe space by saying colloquially, "It's crazy out there" with a tacit emphasis on "out there" as opposed to "here with me." At the end of the article, Harrop revisits her primary tool—distinguishing between "we" and "they"—in a final appeal to fear: "In many cases, readers won't even know who they are. The scary part is many won't even care."

Analysis of tone and tenor of essay suggests it may be effective.

Harrop's point is sound, and she is right that readers ought to assess sources of information with a critical eye and a healthy dose of skepticism and not rely solely on group opinions, no matter how popular they are. She does not realize the shortcomings of her own argument, however. Harrop makes effective use of emotional appeals that will resonate with her audience, but most of her claims on the subject lack evidence beyond anecdotes; for example, her evidence for the dangerous consequences of relying on faulty information in Internet forums is limited to the example of Tara Hills and her sick children. Ultimately, while her argument is convincing, she is in danger of becoming the kind of source she decries by relying almost exclusively on emotional appeals and anecdotes instead of offering expert opinion or grounded pieces of evidence.

Evaluation—argument for reason, evidence and expertise is driven by emotional appeals.

Work Cited

Harrop, Froma. "On the Internet, Nobody Knows You're a Fraud." *Real Clear Politics*, 23 Apr. 2015, www.realclearpolitics.com/articles/2015/04/23/on_the_internet_nobody_knows_youre_a_fraud_126360.html.

Accurate citation proves King's scholarly intent.

Questions to Consider

Invention

1. How do you think King discovered Froma Harrop's essay, and what might have drawn him to it as a subject of a rhetorical analysis?
2. How do you think King began his invention and discovery once he chose Harrop's text?
3. What background knowledge did King bring to his analysis of the text?
4. What did King discover when he examined the text?

Audience

5. What restrictions or limits did King have to work with, and what expectations do you think he was responding to?
6. Does King leave out any rhetorical elements that Froma Harrop uses in her opinion piece? If so, why do you think he omitted them from his analysis?
7. If King wanted to submit his ideas and analysis to a popular blog or radio show specializing in journalism, like *On the Media*, what would he need to change and why?

Authority

8. What terms does King use to describe the rhetorical elements and their relationships?
9. As a student, King is not an expert on the media or journalism. What does he do to establish an authoritative voice?
10. What is King's evaluation of Froma Harrop's argument, and what would you do to make it more persuasive?

MODULE II-16

BUILDING AN EFFECTIVE RHETORICAL ANALYSIS

A rhetorical analysis is composed in two steps. First, you take a text apart so you can analyze and evaluate it. Second, you build an argument that walks your audience through your analysis, showing what you discovered so that your audience will come to the same conclusion about the text that you did. The Breaking the Block box titled "Taking Arguments Apart" (p. 142) describes how to analyze an argument.

Invention

Invention and research are the first steps. In this stage you identify the text you will consider, and then study, analyze, and evaluate it.

- Find a written or visual argument to analyze

✓ If your professor has already assigned a written or visual argument for you to analyze, you are in luck. Move to "Begin Your Analysis." If you have to choose your argument, look for a written or visual argument with one or more of the following qualities:

- It provokes strong or emotional responses.
- It is composed of many elements or complex strategies that will yield a great deal in analysis.
- It is famous, distinctly powerful, or remarkably off the mark.
- It addresses important or enduring issues and questions.
- It is undervalued, overvalued, overlooked, or uncritically praised.

Not all arguments will result in an informative or persuasive rhetorical analysis that will suit your purpose, so choose carefully. If you need to find an argument to analyze, ask your professor for suggestions or look in your textbook for examples and possible genres of argument to analyze.

✓ Learn as much as you can about the assigned text or the rhetorical elements you are expected to examine.

Readers will be more likely to agree with your analysis if you demonstrate that you know what you are talking about. If you are analyzing an argument in the form of a poem, for example, you may need to learn about poetic meters. If you are analyzing a literary text such as Brutus's speech in Shakespeare's play *Julius Caesar*, start early and learn as much as you can so you are not grasping for ideas when it comes time to analyze the text and develop your argument.

✓ Let the rhetorical situation guide you, whether you are responding to an assignment in a course or to another situation.

The rhetorical situation is the place where your audience (your professor or others) will hear or read your rhetorical analysis. If you have been reading about classical oratory in your "Rhetorical Arts" course, your professor might not appreciate an analysis of Kanye West's recent music video. However, if you are responding to an assignment for a mass communication course, West's video might be a possible topic.

- Begin your analysis

✓ Your primary goal is to answer one big question:

> How did the writer/speaker/creator persuade, or fail to persuade, the audience to think, believe, or act as intended?

✓ At first you should work like an archaeologist in the field: dig now to discover and identify rhetorical elements, and evaluate later. Stay focused on the rhetorical elements you have been assigned or the elements you have chosen. The Conventions in Context Box entitled "Many Rhetorical Elements = Many Methods of Analysis" (pp. 147–48) discusses different methods of rhetorical analysis.

✓ As you examine the argument you have chosen, answer the analysis questions that follow, which are organized around the primary components of the rhetorical situation. Answers to these questions will become the foundation of your argument and will help you walk your audience through your analysis.

Author or creator

- Who is the author or creator?
- What does the author or creator know about the subject?
- How does the author or creator know what she or he knows?
- In what way does the author or creator rely on other experts or sources?
- How does the author or creator communicate expertise?

Purpose

- What is the author's or creator's purpose, and what reveals or suggests it?
- How does the argument serve the purpose?
- How is the audience made aware of the author's or creator's purpose?
- How could the audience help achieve the purpose?

Audience

- Who is the intended audience: the doubters, the choir, the receptive?
- Is the audience persuadable?
- What are the audience's age, gender, and politics?
- What does the audience think or believe about the issue addressed in the argument?

Setting

- Where, or in what setting, will the reader or listener encounter the argument?
- How is the setting shaped by politics?
- How is the setting shaped by history?
- How is the setting shaped by culture?
- How is the setting shaped by individual interests?

Message

- What is the central thesis or claim, and what are the supporting ideas or points of the message?
- How is *ethos* established?
- Is the *logos* appeal persuasive?
- Are appeals of *pathos* used effectively?
- How is the argument organized?
- How would you describe the style of the argument?

Genre, medium, and design

- What genre(s) is or are used to shape the text?
- How was the argument made public or published?
- How are layout, imagery, colors, and font related to the ideas and points?

When you have identified the rhetorical elements and looked at how they work together, or don't, you are ready to evaluate.

Evaluation

- Was the audience persuaded? Why or why not?
- How would a different audience be more appropriate for the argument's purpose?
- How would the ideas and points in the argument persuade a different audience?

- Where are the appeals effective?
- Is the argument appropriate to the setting? If not, why not?
- How did the elements you are considering work together to persuade?
- What elements are most disturbing or troubling?
- What elements are most memorable or provocative?
- Were you persuaded? Why or why not?

Breaking the Block
Taking Arguments Apart

The trick to writing an effective rhetorical analysis is to take your time examining the elements of a text and avoid worrying about the significance of what you will discover. This exercise should help you focus on the basic steps of analysis. The writing should take 10–15 minutes.

Step One
First, familiarize yourself with the rhetorical appeals (*ethos*, *logos*, and *pathos*) by reading about them on pp. 125–26 in this chapter and in Chapter 17. Next, go to *The History Channel* or *The History Place* website and search their collections of historical speeches for one that interests you. For example, suppose you decide to analyze Michelle Obama's speech at the 2016 Democratic Convention.

Step Two
After reading the speech, use three different colored highlighters (or underlining, circles, and brackets), to highlight examples of each appeal. The speech you chose may not make use of each appeal. For instance, here's an analysis of a portion of Michelle Obama's speech:

> With every word we utter, with every action we take, we know our kids are watching us. We as parents are their most important role models. And let me tell you, Barack and I take that same approach to our jobs as president and first lady because we know that our words and actions matter, not just to our girls, but the children across this country, kids who tell us I saw you on TV, I wrote a report on you for school. — Ethos
>
> Kids like the little black boy who looked up at my husband, his eyes wide with hope and he wondered, is my hair like yours? — Pathos

> And make no mistake about it, this November when we go to the polls that is what we're deciding, not Democrat or Republican, not left or right. No, in this election, and every election, it is about who will have the power to shape our children for the next four or eight years of their lives.

Logos

Step Three
Write for five minutes about the best example of each appeal you find in the speech you have chosen. Imagine you are explaining to someone who has never heard the speech, does not know the context, and is not familiar with the appeals. For example, when Michelle Obama equates her duties as first lady and those of her husband as president to the duties of parents and role models, she describes the qualifications, morality, and foresight needed in a future president in terms every parent can understand and accept as true.

Step Four
The hardest part of a rhetorical analysis is done. All that remains is to decide whether the elements and relationships were effective, whether they persuaded the intended audience, or, if not, why they failed. To determine effectiveness, you may want to research the way a speech or argument was received and what people of the time said about the speech.

- Draft a thesis

✓ Your thesis should be based upon
  - the rhetorical elements that are your focus,
  - the way the author or speaker used the elements as a persuasive strategy,
  - the effect the elements and strategy have on the intended audience, and
  - your evaluation of the success or failure of the writer or speaker in achieving the intended purpose.

✓ Place the argument you are analyzing within the context of similar arguments with similar messages and purposes in similar situations.

For example, one way to evaluate and highlight the strengths and weaknesses of Michelle Obama's speech to the Democratic National Convention in 2016 is to compare it to other first ladies' speeches from previous conventions (see the Breaking the Block box). In the same way, comparing Ryan Lochte's apology for his behavior during the 2016 Olympic Games to the apology of US women's soccer goalie Hope Solo's after being accused of domestic violence may reveal interesting differences in how each made their appeals.

✓ An effective thesis should not only state your findings and evaluation but also reflect the movement of a rhetorical analysis—from examining the elements and their interrelationship, to evaluating how the elements work, to returning to consider the whole with a new understanding. The structure of your argument may also reflect this movement.

Audience

Once you have analyzed how the writer or speaker uses rhetorical elements in an attempt to persuade her or his audience, decided if the author's strategy works, and developed your thesis, you are ready to shape your argument for your audience.

- Understand the rhetorical situation

✓ You can use a rhetorical analysis to inform, persuade, or entertain your audience. Your purpose will determine what you want to emphasize, which will in turn determine the structure of your analysis.

For example, if you are trying to entertain, you will structure your argument to emphasize interesting discoveries and insights. On the other hand, if you are trying to persuade your audience of the persuasive power of the argument, you will structure your argument to emphasize the context of the argument and its lasting effects.

✓ You may have multiple purposes such as to entertain and inform. However, your purpose must be linked to your audience and their expectations.

- Keep your audience in mind

✓ To succeed, your analysis must reflect the needs and concerns of your intended audience.

If you are writing in a non-academic context, your audience may not be familiar with the terms you are using or the argument you are analyzing. Take time to define and contextualize carefully so you do not leave your reader behind.

In an academic context, you will usually be assigned a rhetorical analysis so that you can learn how arguments work and how they fail. Your assignment will be read carefully and graded based on how thoughtfully you have analyzed elements of the argument and how well you articulate the conclusions of your analysis. The Conventions in Context box entitled "Many Rhetorical Elements = Many Methods of Analysis" (p. 147) describes a number of methods that may be required in an academic context.

- Structure your argument to persuade your audience

✓ An authoritative analysis has a clear thesis and an ordered structure. If you move with confidence through your analysis, readers and listeners will follow.

You can organize a rhetorical analysis in many different ways based upon the audience's expectations, your purpose, and what you have discovered during your analysis. For example, if you are emphasizing the rhetorical situation and setting, your analysis may have only one or two points. Or if you are analyzing Michelle Obama's Democratic Convention speech, you might organize your analysis around the use of *pathos* appeals. As you develop the structure of your argument, be sure to discuss it with peers, members of your intended audience, or your professor.

Authority

- The logical links between what you have discovered during analysis and your evaluation must be clear

✓ Describe the rhetorical elements you are using to analyze your subject, providing clear examples of each element, and explaining in detail how it works within the larger argument.

Make sure your evidence is relevant to your main point. For example, during research for an analysis of the Amazon logo, suppose you discover that founder Jeff Bezos describes himself as a legitimately happy person and journalists often mention his constant smile. It is an interesting fact, but it is not related to a rhetorical analysis of the Amazon logo. Be sure to connect the evidence you find to your thesis.

✓ All evidence and sources you use must be documented accurately using the appropriate documentation style. Chapter 22 explains how to use the MLA and APA styles and provides sample citations.

- Make it flow

✓ A successful rhetorical analysis requires attention to the details of the argument you are analyzing as well as the details of your own analysis. See chapter 22 for suggestions that will help you make your analysis flow and make it easier for your readers to follow your argument.

✓ Guide your audience as you move through the different parts of rhetorical analysis.

For example, if you use the Greek philosopher Aristotle's ideas to analyze a work by the British street artist Banksy (see Figure 8.3), you'll probably need to explain what Aristotle said about quoting authorities such as Diogenes.

Figure 8.3
Banksy:
One original
thought.

✓ When the links you are making are as apparent in your reader's mind as they are in yours, not only do you smooth the way for your reader, but you also demonstrate your authority.

- Get peer response

✓ Peer response is market testing for your argument. The more feedback you can gather on your thesis, structure, and mechanics the more confident you will be in your revisions and edits.

✓ Ask your peers to look over your rhetorical analysis and respond to the following:
  - Please circle my thesis, and tell if it is clear.
  - Please identify the rhetorical elements I am using and tell me if they are working for this type of argument.
  - Where do I describe how the elements affect the author's purpose?
  - Are there any statements in my analysis that are not supported by evidence?
  - Are there shifts in subjects or paragraphs that are confusing?
  - Is my evaluation supported by my analysis?

  If the problem cannot be fixed, reconsider its importance. If rewriting or relocating the problematic part does not fix it, delete it.

✓ The documentation within a rhetorical analysis is important because such an analysis relies upon a great many references and quotations. Your peer reviewer can use these questions to make sure your documentation is in order.

- ◉ Is there an in-text citation for every reference, paraphrase, summary, or quotation?
- ◉ Is the source of every reference, paraphrase, summary, or quotation introduced or named?
- ◉ Are there any in-text citations that are not linked to a citation or bibliographic entry at the end of the paper? Are there any citations at the end that are not linked to in-text citations?

- Revise your argument

✓ After a careful analysis of your peer reviewer's comments, you will have a number of ideas and interesting insights. However, as you revise, keep in mind that your thesis must be supported by the evidence and reasoning developed in your analysis. Avoid the temptation to say more than the evidence supports or guess at the writer's or creator's intentions without proof.

✓ The revision stage for rhetorical analysis is very important because, in composing your analysis, you have probably been buried in the details of the text you are analyzing for some time. You know what you mean, but keep in mind that your audience will read your analysis only once. As you revise, make sure to explain clearly how the details from the text you are citing as examples connect to the main points you are making.

Conventions in Context
Many Rhetorical Elements = Many Methods of Analysis

Rhetorical analyses are common assignments in classes ranging from first-year writing classes to graduate marketing courses. In addition to the three appeals, a number of other methods of analysis are used in academic settings.

Two commonly assigned methods for rhetorical analysis focus on the use of genres and on how the rhetorical situation determines how an argument is understood.

Genre Analysis

If you are using this method, you would analyze the genre or genres used to shape the argument. For example, you might investigate how the writer has modified a given genre, how the writer has blended multiple genres, or which genre elements the writer chose to use and which to leave out.

Genre analysis makes it possible to explore the relationship between the content of an argument and the form or genre of the argument. Also, you can use genre to examine how an author responded to audience expectations for the types of texts required in specific situations. For example, you might analyze Ryan Lochte's apology after the incident at the Summer Olympics according to the common elements of an apology, noting in particular the elements that Lochte left out and his use of the apology genre to redirect media attention away from his acts and toward the Olympic athletes (see above). By framing his apology in this way, Lochte attempted to use select elements of the apology genre to recast the narrative of an ugly American and privileged jock that the sports and news media were attaching to him.

Situational Analysis

If you are using this method, you would analyze the elements of the rhetorical situation: audience, message, speaker, purpose, media, setting, culture.

An analysis of the rhetorical situation for a text can reveal much about its success or failure. For example, you might analyze how a speech was received and understood by an audience. Or you might analyze how recent events prior to the speech changed the way the message was understood. An analysis of Michelle Obama's multiple audiences suggests that the way in which the immediate audience in the convention center in July 2016 received and responded to her speech may have affected how the more distant television audience received the speech. During her 25-minute speech, Michelle Obama was interrupted 49 times by uncontained applause. Pundits' comments and informal polls of the television audience suggest that her speech was highly praised, in part because of its positive, exciting tone.

Before selecting and applying any of the methods listed above, be sure to check with your professor to see if the method is appropriate for your class. Also, you will probably need to do some background reading about the method and study how others have developed and applied it.

CHAPTER 9

STATING THE FACTS

In 2013, Megan Thode filed a lawsuit against Lehigh University and the professor who gave her a C+ in a graduate course in psychotherapy, claiming she was owed 1.3 million in lost future wages. The lawsuit went viral in 2013, with stories appearing in national publications such as *Forbes* and *USA Today* as well as news outlets in Australia and Great Britain.

Thode's lawsuit alleged breach of contract and sexual discrimination. The central issue during the trial, however, was a much more mundane question of fact. Thode's lawyer argued that the "0" she received for class participation was in fact an attempt to push her out of the graduate program. The professor, on the other hand, argued that Thode's participation consisted of silence, outbursts, and cursing—unacceptable in a class training professional therapists.

It may seem strange that one party can see a "0" as a breach of contract and sexual discrimination while another party sees the same "0" as unacceptable class behavior. And yet disagreements about facts are what keep courtrooms busy.

MODULE II-17

WHAT AUDIENCES EXPECT OF A STATE-THE-FACTS ARGUMENT

We all recognize a fact when we encounter one, don't we? A **fact** can be defined as

- information that is true,
- a statement based on irrefutable, sound logic,
- a concept that is not doubted or questioned, or
- a thing that is known to exist.

How then, you may ask, is it possible for a reasonable person to doubt a fact or call something a fact when it is clearly not? After all, a fact is a fact, right? Not exactly.

Why Are Arguments of Fact Necessary?

Nearly everyone knows humans have five senses, and many people have heard that George Washington had wooden teeth. The trouble is, neither statement of "fact" is true. In addition to the five senses, you can also sense acceleration and relative temperature. And George Washington's dentures were made of lead, ivory, and animal teeth.

It is possible to attach the word *fact* to any information or statement, but calling something a fact does not mean it is true. Generally, we accept an assertion as a fact only if it can be verified. For example, any statement about the composition of George Washington's teeth can be verified or refuted by examining the actual object or consulting a source.

When a fact or facts are in dispute, a state-the-facts argument is called for. Depending upon your purpose, you can state one fact, such as that Washington's teeth contained ivory, or you can make an argument about a set of related facts, such as the argument made by Megan Thode's lawyers in the example that opens this chapter. When you present a state-the-facts argument, you are trying to persuade your audience to accept the information, statement, concept, or thing that is the subject of your argument as verifiably true.

William Bernbach, a famous advertising executive, once made the following observation:

> Facts are not enough.... Until you wrap all these facts in a talented expression to which people respond, until you cloak those facts in the artistry which makes people *feel*, you are not going to communicate.

If you want to persuade your audience of the facts you know, the facts alone are not enough, for two reasons. First, your audience has been overwhelmed with assertions of fact that turn out not to be true. For example, how often does the fast food you order look like the meal advertised? Second, facts do not speak for themselves, so you have to communicate both the fact and the fact's significance.

Reasonable people, including the doubters in your audience, will generally accept as true a fact that has been established beyond doubt, such as the fact that water boils at 212°F. Sources or reasoning that you can use to verify facts that are not as well established include reference books like *The World Almanac and Book of Facts*, respected news magazines and newspapers like *The Wall Street Journal*, and peer reviewed, academic journals.

Using Invention to Find a Context for Facts

Writers or speakers persuade and assure their audience of the truth of the facts they are presenting by providing an appropriate **context** for them. Facts need context to make them meaningful, and context is discovered and developed during research and invention. Context is not only the situation or setting in which you find facts; it is also the situation *you* create when you combine and communicate facts to your audience. In the absence of context, readers can draw the wrong conclusion from facts. Consider these well-known facts about the attack that happened in New York City on September 11, 2001, when terrorists hijacked two commercial aircraft and intentionally crashed them into the Twin Towers of the World Trade Center:

> The Twin Towers were attacked on 9/11.
> The first plane that hit a tower was Flight AA 11.
> The emergency number in New York is 911.
> New York City has an 11th Avenue and an 11th Street.
> New York state was the 11th state to join the union.
> From a distance, the towers looked like the number 11.

Each separate statement of fact is true, but combining them suggests a relationship among the facts that isn't real. If you found this list on the website *Illuminati Conspiracy Archive*, that context suggests a conspiratorial interpretation of these tragic events. However, a mathematician could explain that this list is actually an example of the "law of truly large numbers": in any large sample, such as the numerous facts about New York City, seemingly meaningful coincidences will appear as an example of synchronicity. The mathematician's explanation provides a very different context and shapes the facts differently. Though the facts remain the same, the two different contexts lead to two very different ways of understanding them.

Making Facts Acceptable to Your Audience

Your audience has no reason to believe what you believe, which is why you need to provide the **source of your facts**. Simply saying that Washington's teeth are not made of wood is not as persuasive as providing a photograph of Washington's lead and ivory dentures, identifying their current location, and including a link so readers can verify the facts themselves. In the same way, your professor is unlikely to take seriously a research paper that lacks sources or has citation errors. Even if your facts are true, your inability to identify their sources can cause your audience to question your facts.

Consider the two news stories shown in Figures 9.1 and 9.2. Both are about the National Security Agency's effort to monitor the playing of fantasy games such as World of Warcraft and Second Life. Which is more persuasive? The facts are the same in both stories. However, the second is more persuasive because the source of the facts and quotations is identified. In addition, the second story is backed by the reputation of the *New York Times*, a major news organization. As the Responsible Sourcing box entitled "The Chain of Custody" shows, when you use a credible source well, its authority transfers to your own argument.

The Times Tattler
By staff reporter
Online games might seem innocuous, but they had the potential to be a "target-rich communication network" allowing intelligence suspects "a way to hide in plain sight." Virtual games "are an opportunity!" an anonymous source declared.

Figure 9.1 In this hypothetical example, the facts are from an anonymous source, and the author is anonymous as well. Without more information about the source, the facts seem questionable.

The New York Times
By Mark Mazzetti and Justin Elliott
Online games might seem innocuous, a top-secret 2008 N.S.A. document warned, but they had the potential to be a "target-rich communication network" allowing intelligence suspects "a way to hide in plain sight." Virtual games "are an opportunity!" another 2008 N.S.A. document declared.
Published: December 9, 2013

Figure 9.2 The news comes from sources that are meticulously identified by the named authors of the article. In this case the readers are more likely to put their trust in the journalists, even though they do not know them.

Making Your Facts Authoritative

Identifying your or your source's **perspective** reinforces the authority of your statement of facts for two reasons. First, honest people can interpret the same set of facts, and the context in which they are presented, very differently. Second, unethical writers and speakers sometimes try to pass off misinterpretations and biased views as objective reality. **Bias** is an inclination, belief, or feeling for or against an idea, person, or group. When you acknowledge your bias, you are providing full disclosure.

Of course, having a particular perspective and bias is not necessarily bad. For most experts and scholars, bias is the result of their training in a specialized discipline. You would hope that the architect you hire to design a house would be biased in favor of following building codes and rules about the weight-bearing capability of building materials.

The degrees or certificates a person holds, or his or her job or title, often indicates the kind of bias that person will have. A specialized journal or academic text has a certain bias born of expertise as well. If you find an article published in the professional journal *Law and Human Behavior*, you can be sure it will be biased toward a legal and psychological perspective on human behavior.

Responsible Sourcing
The Chain of Custody

To protect evidence, detectives at crime scenes use gloves, sealable plastic evidence bags, and cameras to photograph evidence and the larger scene. They also keep a detailed log of where and how evidence was discovered. This approach to handling evidence, known as chain of custody, ensures that evidence presented in court is uncorrupted, that it was discovered and transported carefully, and that its source has been documented.

In the same way, ethical writers, speakers, researchers, and scholars carefully protect their research and sources. To assure your reader that your facts are beyond doubt, think of your sources as evidence that needs to be protected to be persuasive.

1. **Save everything**. Save all the documentation information you will need. Photocopy all hard-copy articles, along with the journal's title page and its table of contents page. Save copies of any electronic texts in a Word or PDF format, and be sure to indicate the name of the web publisher, date of publication, source database (if it came from that type of source), and address. Always save electronic copies in two separate locations, such as on your hard drive, in cloud storage, and on a thumb drive or other external device.

2. **Don't contaminate evidence**. Cautious detectives take care not to leave their fingerprints all over evidence and would never pick up and bag only one bullet casing while leaving the others on the ground. Similarly, researchers should not contaminate their sources by using them out of context or in a way that is contrary to the source's meaning. When quoting only part of a sentence, for instance, make sure that the entire sentence supports the point you are making, not just the part you are using.

3. **Explain what you have found**. When you integrate a source into your writing, you are like a detective explaining evidence in a courtroom. Introduce your source completely, noting what makes the source authoritative and explaining how the source is relevant to your argument. Disclose any possible bias the source may have. Quote, summarize, or paraphrase the source honestly and accurately. Finally, help your reader understand its significance and how the source supports or is related to your argument.

Genres that State the Facts

Readers and listeners look to specific genres, such as news stories or résumés, because they provide a context that gives facts meaning. Genres that state the facts are important to academic writing as well as journalism and business. As the following list shows, different genres are better suited to different purposes.

- **Accident report**: a report used to establish the facts of what led to an accident, happened during the accident, and resulted from the accident.
- **Annotated bibliography**: a list of articles, books, and artifacts about or related to a specific topic and the facts of each, in the form of a description and evaluation.
- **Lab report**: a formal account of an experiment, including the question to be answered, the procedures followed, and the full results.
- **News article**: an account of recent events that provides facts and their sources, along with background information or context.
- **Research paper**: an academic argument that uses evidence drawn from sources to support a claim.

MODULE II-18

A STATE-THE-FACTS GENRE: RESEARCH PAPER

Each academic course you will take has different requirements for research papers. Professors in different disciplines will expect you to establish contexts, use sources, and show your perspective on the facts in a different way. Nevertheless, for most research-paper assignments that call for a state-the-facts argument, you will be expected to provide data and information you have discovered through research that supports your claim—the undisputed knowledge that you have gained from examining, analyzing, and evaluating that data and information.

Lauren Glass wrote the following research paper for a college writing course. It is an example of a state-the-facts argument. In this excerpt, we see Glass using a statement of facts to set up an examination of a larger debate: is it possible, ethical, or clinically beneficial to diagnose children as psychopaths?

Psychopathology and the Ethics of Labeling Youth
By Lauren Glass

The rise in diagnoses of adolescent psychopathology has triggered questions among psychologists and other specialists. One open question is whether it is possible to diagnose a child as a fledgling psychopath and whether such a diagnosis is ethical. *Until this question is resolved, psychologists should avoid diagnoses of childhood psychopathy and must reconsider the diagnostic tools that lead to such assessments.*

Context

Perspective and thesis

The notion of a psychopath was first constructed in France during the 1800s, but the process for classifying an adult psychopath was not perfected until 1991 by **Robert Hare, a Doctor of experimental psychology at University of Western Ontario and professor emeritus of the University of British Columbia.** Dr. Hare developed the Hare Psychopathy Checklist, used to assess cases of psychopathy *(Hare, 2003).* The Hare PCL-R checklist is a diagnostic grading scale that allows specialists to assess the individual in question through an interview and analysis of personal records. Individual characteristics are then compared to that of a prototypical psychopath. The PCL-R measures twenty specific traits that are highly correlated with psychopathy. A few of the measured traits include,

Perspective

Source of Facts

Facts

- glib and superficial charm
- grandiose (exaggeratedly high) estimation of self
- need for stimulation
- pathological lying
- cunning and manipulativeness
- lack of remorse or guilt
- shallow affect (superficial emotional responsiveness)

- callousness and lack of empathy
- parasitic lifestyle *(Hare, 2003).*

Source of Facts

Each of the traits is ranked between 0 and 2, based on how well it applies to the individual being tested. A prototypical psychopath would receive a total of 40, the maximum score. A score of 30 or above qualifies a person for a diagnosis of psychopathy. People with no criminal backgrounds normally score around 5, while non-psychopathic criminal offenders score around 22 *(Hare, 2003).*

The danger of a psychopath lies predominantly in their sadistic, violent nature. Delinquent offenders with pronounced psychopathic traits display these tendencies earlier *(Brandt et al., 1997; Forth & Burke, 1998)*, commit more crimes, and engage in criminal activity more often *(Forth & Burke, 1998; Myers, 1995)* and more violently **(Brandt et al., 1997; Spain et al., 2004)** than young criminals who are not psychopathic. Psychopathy scores have also been found to correlate significantly with the severity of conduct problems, antisocial behavior, and delinquency in adolescents *(Forth & Burke, 1998).*

Facts

Two authors of a single source

Psychopathy has been shown to predict future violence in adults both while in prison and after discharge *(Salekin et al., 1996).* Studies of institutional violence indicate moderately strong correlations between psychopathy score and verbal and physical aggression *(Edens et al., 2001; Spain et al., 2004).* Though no checklist has yet been created for children, a version of Hare's Checklist has been created for adolescents. The checklist for adults was altered to account for the impulsivity that is characteristic of this age. Using the adolescent-adjusted PCL-R, researchers found that higher psychopathy scores in adolescents were associated with the reoccurrence of violent, undesired behaviors *(Forth et al., 1990)* and shorter intervals between episodes of these behaviors *(Brandt et al., 1997).*

Facts

...

Paragraphs cut for brevity

There are, however, **critics of the PCL-R such as** *Dr. Daniel Seagrave,* a **clinical and forensic psychologist** *and Dr. Thomas Grisso,* **Professor of Psychiatry, Director of Psychology, and Director of the Law-Psychiatry Program at**

Two Perspectives

the University of Massachusetts Medical School. *Writing in the journal* Law and Human Behavior, *Seagrave and Grisso (2002),* **question the validity of the PCL-R, especially for adolescents.** They point out **the PCL-R was constructed for adults and has a high false-positive rate in adolescence, as this is a period of considerable developmental change.**

Source of Facts

Facts

Others who oppose the test and diagnosing adolescent psychopathology condemn it because of the possible damage it might inflict upon a child. Psychologists claim that it will subject children to discrimination *(Seagrave & Grisso, 221)* and cause them to identify with other psychopaths. The potential emotional damage would increase dramatically if the child was genuinely not psychopathic.

Critical perspectives

In spite of the risks false positive results present, it is essential to identify fledgling psychopaths. **Many psychologists are concerned with the psychological effects a child will experience if diagnosed.** Labeling affects children with other mental disorders, such as A.D.H.D. or O.C.D., significantly. However, assuming a child is indeed psychopathic, his or her mental stability will probably not be altered by this label. Since psychopaths are characterized by superficial charm, manipulativeness, and a lack of empathy and guilt, it is likely if not definite that such a child will not be upset by this diagnosis. Psychopathic youth will not fall victim to the belief that something is wrong with them. If they are truly psychopathic, they may feign an overdramatized reaction. In reality, however, their perceptions of their self-identity will not be influenced.

Author's perspective

References

Source of Facts

Brandt, J.R., Kennedy, W.A., Patrick, C.J., & Curtin, J.J. (1997). Assessment of psychopathy in a population of incarcerated adolescent offenders. *Psychological Assessment*, *9*(4), 429.

Edens, J.F., Skeem, J.L., Cruise, K.R., & Cauffman, E. (2001). Assessment of "juvenile psychopathy" and its association with violence: A critical review. *Behavioral Sciences & the Law*, *19*(1), 53–80.

Forth, A.E., & Burke, H.C. (1998). Psychopathy in adolescence: Assessment, violence, and developmental precursors. In *Psy-*

chopathy: Theory, research and implications for society (pp. 205–229). Springer Netherlands.

Hare, R.D. (2003). *Manual for the Revised Psychopathy Checklist* (2nd ed.). Retrieved from http://www.mhs.com/product.aspx?gr=saf&id=overview&prod=pcl-r2

Harris, H.E., Burket, R.C., & Myers, W.C. (1995). Adolescent psychopathy in relation to delinquent behaviors, conduct disorder, and personality disorders. *Journal of Forensic Science, 40*(3), 435–440.

Salekin, R.T., Rogers, R., & Sewell, K.W. (1996). A review and meta-analysis of the Psychopathy Checklist and Psychopathy Checklist-Revised: Predictive validity of dangerousness. *Clinical Psychology: Science and Practice, 3*(3), 203–215.

Seagrave, D., & Grisso, T. (2002). Adolescent development and the measurement of juvenile psychopathy. *Law and human behavior,* 26(2), 219.

Spain, S.E., Douglas, K.S., Poythress, N.G., & Epstein, M. (2004). The relationship between psychopathic features, violence and treatment outcome: The comparison of three youth measures of psychopathic features. *Behavioral Sciences & the Law, 22*(1), 85–102.

APA Style

Perspective

Perspective

Questions to Consider

Invention

1. Glass was allowed to choose any topic for this assignment. What may have prompted Glass to write about this subject?
2. Assuming that Glass is not an expert on the subject, how do you think she gathered ideas and evidence?
3. What did Glass discover about diagnosing adolescent psychopathology, and what new insights do the facts she provides give the reader?

Audience

4. To whom is Glass writing, and how do you know?
5. Glass makes assumptions about her audience. What are these assumptions, and how do they affect the facts she presents?
6. Based on how Glass talks about the facts, what does she want her intended readers to think after they have finished reading?

Authority

7. How does Glass let the reader know what she has discovered and that her information can be trusted?
8. Which facts, if any, need further verification? Which facts with supporting sources are there, if any, that may not be accepted by the intended audience? Why not?
9. Do you accept Glass's argument, based on the facts she presents? Why or why not? What could she do to make her argument more persuasive?

MODULE II-19

A STATE-THE-FACTS GENRE: NEWS ARTICLE

A typical news article responds to the questions *who*, *what*, *why*, *when*, *where*, and *how*, with answers the writer has discovered through conducting interviews and research.

Clive Thompson is a technology writer and blogger interested in how people use technology for personal expression, often in surprising, counter-intuitive ways. He wrote the following state-the-facts argument for *Wired* magazine. With the help of data analysis and a well-known concept from cognitive psychology, he corrects a faulty perception—baby photos are taking over Facebook.

Science Says: The Baby Madness on Your Facebook Feed Is an Illusion

Everyone knows what a hassle new parents are on Facebook, right? They overshare. They post endless pictures of their new bundle of joy, flooding your feed with drooling infants. Last summer saw the creation of a browser extension—UnBaby.Me, since renamed Rather—that fought back against the tide, auto-detecting baby images and replacing them with less-annoying material, like cats or bacon. "A brilliant and sanity-preserving idea," a Forbes writer gushed. Except for one thing: The entire premise is wrong. [Context] [**Facts and Thesis**]

Recently, *Meredith Ringel Morris—a computer scientist at Microsoft Research—gathered data on what new moms actually do online. She persuaded more than 200 of them to let her* [*Perspective*] [*Source of Facts*] *scrape their Facebook accounts* and **found the precise opposite of the UnBaby.Me libel.** After a child is born, *Morris discovered,* **new mothers post less than half as often.** When they do post, **fewer than 30 percent of the updates mention the baby by name early on, plummeting to not quite 10 percent by the end of the first year.** Photos grow as a chunk of all postings, sure—but since new moms are so much less active on Facebook, it hardly matters. **New moms aren't oversharers. Indeed, they're probably undersharers. "The total quantity of Facebook posting is lower," Morris says.**

Facts | Context | Facts and thesis restated

And therein lies an interesting lesson about our supposed age of oversharing. If new moms don't actually deluge the Internet with baby talk, why does it seem to so many of us that they do? Morris thinks algorithms explain some of it. **Her research also found that viewers disproportionately "like" postings that mention new babies. This, she says, could result in Facebook ranking those postings more prominently in the News Feed, making mothers look more baby-obsessed.**

Context | Facts

I have another theory: It's a perceptual quirk called a frequency illusion. **Once we notice something that annoys or surprises or pleases us—or something that's just novel—we tend to suddenly notice it more. We overweight its frequency in everyday life.** For instance, if you've decided that fedoras are a ridiculous hipster fashion choice, even if they're comparatively rare in everyday life, you're more likely to notice them. And pretty soon you're wondering, why is everyone wearing fedoras now? Curse you, hipsters!

Perspective | Facts | Context

Frequency illusions are self-perpetuating cycles enhanced by lazy journalism and punditry. One reason people think new mothers post a lot of baby pictures is that trend pieces and op-eds claim they do. (Indeed, trend journalism is essentially a form of intellectual trolling designed to create frequency illusions. "Why is everyone suddenly listening to Wilco again?") Yes, some moms post about their kids every 10 minutes. You may have one in your feed right now. But the behavior is not widespread or incessant.

Facts

The way we observe the world is deeply unstatistical, which is why Morris' work is so useful. It reminds us of the value of observing the world around us like a scientist—to see what's actually going on instead of what just happens to gall (or please) us.

Perspective

Questions to Consider

Invention

1. What might have prompted Thompson to write about this topic? Make your best guess.
2. Assuming that Thompson is not an expert on Facebook postings, algorithms, or frequency illusion, how do you think he gathered his ideas, information, and evidence?
3. What did Thompson discover about the subject of Facebook postings, and what new insights do the facts he provides give the reader?

Audience

4. To whom is Thompson writing, and how do you know?
5. Thompson makes assumptions about his audience. What are these assumptions, and how do they affect the facts he presents?
6. Based on how Thompson talks about the facts, what does he want his readers to think after they have finished reading his article?

Authority

7. How does Thompson let his readers know that what he has discovered and what he says about Facebook baby postings can be trusted?
8. Which facts in this article, if any, need further verification? Point out any facts with supporting sources that may not be accepted by the intended audience, and explain why.
9. Do you accept Thompson's argument, based on the facts he presents? Why or why not? What could he do to make his piece more persuasive?

MODULE II-20

BUILDING A STATE-THE-FACTS ARGUMENT

The following steps and examples will help you build a persuasive state-the-facts argument using the lenses of invention, audience, and authority.

Invention

- Find a subject

✓ Finding a subject is also a matter of finding your scope and focus. If you have been assigned a subject, it is likely that your **scope**, the context or breadth of knowledge that you are to draw upon, has been determined for you, but you may need to refine your **focus** by clarifying the single data point, detail, subject, or image you will explore and discuss. If you are free to choose your own subject, always look for an issue or subject you care about and that will interest your audience.

✓ Finding a subject can be as easy as discovering mistaken beliefs, questionable facts, or misleading or overstated assertions of fact. Read blogs, popular magazines, and editorials, looking for the following:

- information that seems too good to be true;
- statements of fact presented with no supporting evidence;
- arguments based on faulty logic;
- concepts or ideas that go unquestioned, are assumed to be true, or seem to be "common sense";
- conclusions that overstate or make more of the facts than is reasonable.

The Breaking the Block box entitled "Using Stasis Questions to Find Questionable Facts" can help you to find a subject.

✓ Develop a research question. A good research question will guide your research and inform your thesis. A research question is

- worth answering,
- relevant to your audience,
- relevant to the subject,
- yet to be asked, or if it has been asked, existing answers are unsatisfactory, and
- not overly complicated.

- Find factual evidence

✓ If you are questioning assertions of fact made by others, these questions can help you rigorously examine their facts.

- Are the facts disputed or commonly accepted?
- Are the asserted facts generalizations? If so, can you think of exceptions?
- What kind of logic or reasoning are the facts based on?
- What are the sources of the facts?
- How authoritative are the sources?
- How does the author know that the facts asserted are true?
- What kind of proof (data, research studies, observation) would be necessary to validate the facts?
- What proof do the sources quoted provide to validate the facts?

(See the Responsible Sourcing box (p. 166) for more on types of sources.)

✓ Sometimes you will not find facts that either confirm or disprove an assertion. Still, you can use reasoning and logic to challenge questionable assertions of fact.

For example, you will not find definitive research proving that playing football causes Chronic Traumatic Encephalopathy (CTE). Nevertheless, you can make a reasoned argument that repetitive concussions, common among football players, are not good for the developing brain. Therefore, children should not play tackle football.

- Develop a thesis

✓ Your initial thesis is a working thesis, based on the evidence that you have discovered. It should evolve as you do further research and develop your argument.

✓ Your thesis should be an assertion of fact that the rest of your argument proves. A thesis that goes beyond the facts offered to back it up may lead a skeptical audience to distrust your entire argument.

Breaking the Block
Using Stasis Questions to Find Questionable Facts

Stasis questions of fact can help you move past first impressions and common understandings to find facts that may not necessarily be true. The writing component of this exercise should take 10 minutes.

Step One

Use your browser to search for "trending news stories." You are likely to find sites such as "Trending Now—Yahoo News," "Most Popular Stories and Videos on CNN," and "BBC News—Trending." Find a news story about an event or issue that interests you. Read about the event or issue on two different news sites such as *The New York Times* and *Buzzfeed.com*, noting how each site covers it.

Step Two

Using information from the two different news sites, find answers to the following secondary stasis questions of facts

- Did something happen, or is there an issue?
- What are the facts?
- Is there a problem concerning the event, issue, or facts?

- What cause or change brought about the event or issue?
- Can what happened be reversed, changed, or affected?

Step Three
Look for differences in the way two different sites or two different news organizations report the news about the event or occurrence. Write for 10 minutes comparing the similarities and differences in how the two sites report the facts of the same event or issue. Ask yourself the following questions:

- What facts are presented in the same way (with the same context and perspective) on both sites?
- What facts are presented differently? Does one site present facts that the other site does not include?
- What accounts for the different facts and the different presentations of facts?
- Do contrasting facts suggest that one set of facts is wrong, misunderstood, or misrepresented?
- How would you double-check the facts reported?
- What can be or needs to be corrected?

Audience

- Identify your audience

✓ The ideal audience for a state-the-facts argument does not know the facts you are stating, believes a contrary set of facts, thinks your facts are questionable or false, or believes that the facts call for different decisions or a different course of action than what you are advocating. It is also possible your intended audience is a professor who wants to see if you know the facts and can present them in an organized way on paper.

✓ Audiences are more likely to trust reasonable speakers and writers. Therefore, it will be important to acknowledge contrary facts. For example, imagine you are stating the fact that exercise by itself will not lead to weight loss. During your research, however, you find an article in a national magazine that shows high impact training (HIT) can lead to weight loss without changes in diet. If you do not concede or acknowledge this point, you risk appearing uninformed to your audience. Concession does not mean surrender, however. The article's facts may be true, but most people are unwilling to train with the intensity and consistency required of HIT. You can argue that for most people, reducing calorie intake and moderate exercise constitute a more reasonable way to lose weight.

- Organize your argument

✓ Once you have your purpose, audience, and the context of your facts in mind, the conventions of your genre will help you organize your argument. In an academic setting, the most common genre for a state-the-facts argument is a research paper. Other possible academic genres include a lab report or historical account. These genres also state the facts but organize them differently.

✓ To better understand the elements of the genre you have been assigned or the genres that are available to you, do some research.

For example, when writers are given an assignment, they first ask the assigning editor what kind of genre he or she is expecting. If the writer is free to choose the genre, a good next step would be to look at other examples of brief articles based on statements of fact that have been printed in the publication the journalist is writing for. For an academic assignment, look at the genres the professor is assigning and ask the professor what type of argument she is expecting or what genres have been successful in previous classes.

✓ Whether you are writing in an academic setting or in another writing situation, your audience will expect a logical structure. If you are going to persuade people that facts they accept as true are wrong and that the facts you are presenting are correct, you need to begin by respectfully moving your readers away from the facts they currently believe. A simplified outline for a state-the-facts argument could look something like this:

I. State thesis and establish context.
II. Honestly represent misunderstood facts.
III. Explain why and how misunderstandings or faulty interpretations come about.
IV. State the correct facts with evidence and reasoning that validates them.
V. Concede or acknowledge any parts of the audience's understanding that may be true or valid.
VI. Restate the validated facts.

- Draft your argument

✓ State-the-facts arguments are built upon sources that verify the facts at the heart of the argument. Therefore, when writing your first draft, be sure to include in-text citations for all summaries, paraphrases, and quotations and prepare a preliminary list of works cited or references.

✓ As you draft, keep in mind that your audience is likely to read or hear your argument only once. Your reader will not necessarily be able to guess information that you know and take for granted, such as how psychologists view diagnostic tests or how Facebook algorithms work. To help your reader understand and accept your argument, be sure to explain your perspective and the context of the facts you state.

Responsible Sourcing
Primary Research, Secondary Research, and the Rest

In addition to teaching the content of a discipline, professors also teach methods of investigation and a value system that allows researchers to build upon the work of those who have gone before. (Chapter 16 describes the academic situation.) In this value system, your conviction and reasonable opinions count for little in the mind of a skeptical reader. Persuasive arguments are built upon clear and valid reasoning and verifiable evidence and facts.

Primary Research: The gold standard of persuasive power, primary research consists of original investigation, research, and discovery done by a researcher in an attempt to answer a question. High-quality primary research is disseminated by respected sources like peer-reviewed journals, authoritative research institutes, or top-quality publishers.

Secondary Research: Secondary research makes use of information provided by others, including primary research that has been published by reliable sources. Necessarily, secondary research is as persuasive as the sources it draws upon. Secondary research can be found in peer-reviewed journals and scholarly books.

Some statements look factual, and sometimes even scholars include statements in their arguments that are not facts and do not meet the rigorous standard of primary or secondary research.

Assertions: An assertion is a positive statement that does not include supporting evidence or reasoning. Assertions are often generalizations. In the absence of supporting evidence and reasoning, an assertion cannot be called a fact, even if it is provided by an expert.

Opinion: An opinion is merely a statement of personal belief. Opinions vary in persuasive power. For example, astrophysicist Neil DeGrasse Tyson's opinion about Pluto's status as a planet is likely to sound more persuasive than that of someone who is not an expert in Tyson's area of expertise. However, without supporting facts and reasoning, an opinion cannot be understood or presented as a fact.

Authority

- Check your logic and accuracy

✓ Logic is the foundation of a fact, and a logical fallacy such as a hasty generalization is an example of a statement that is not supported by logic or reasoning. Check to ensure that each statement of fact you present is supported by solid evidence and logic. Chapter 24 will help you identify fallacies of presumption, beliefs that are not supported by evidence, which can undermine statements of fact.

✓ Facts that are common knowledge or indisputable do not need supporting evidence. No reasonable person would deny that World War II ended when surrender documents were signed on the USS Missouri on September 2, 1945. If you are stating the causes of the war, on the other hand, your evidence and reasoning must be solid and well cited.

✓ Verify your facts. Even if you believe that a fact you state is beyond doubt, you need to verify that the fact you believe is true. When using sources to prove a statement is factual, make sure the source speaks directly to the fact and provides proof that will persuade your audience.

✓ Experts, editors, and fact checkers have already verified peer-reviewed, academic articles and information published by well-respected sources such as the *New York Times* and the FBI crime statistics database. Even the most reputable publishers are not 100% accurate, however, and a few scholars have fabricated results. With this caution in mind, verify key facts you present by checking more than one reliable source.

- Make it flow

✓ An argument that flows anticipates the reader's questions and moves the reader effectively from one point to the next. Make your state-the-facts argument flow by focusing on and eliminating obstacles that get in the way of reading and understanding.

Facts and quotations that seem to come out of nowhere confuse your reader, so introduce each fact or quotation and place it in context. Abrupt shifts in topic can also stop a reader. To move readers efficiently from one point to the next, use transitions to review the main point of the preceding paragraph and explain its relationship to the main point in the next paragraph.

✓ Clarity is an experience, not a set of words or sentence structures. Slow down when describing complex facts and ideas, and be sure to define unfamiliar terms or concepts.

✓ Some facts are better seen than read or heard. Facts that are easier to convey using graphics include large data sets (statistics, percentages, ratios), images (landscapes, paintings, or photos), processes (assembly instructions, dance moves, chemical interactions), or relationships (family trees, atoms in a molecule, branches of government). Often the best way to help your reader understand the facts you are stating and achieve your purpose is to illustrate your point with a graphic or image. Help readers "read" your graphic by telling them what to look for and, if necessary, walking them through its parts, step by step. For example, the infographic in Figure 9.3 may appear to be a rather simple pie chart. However, it captures nine different data points, and the facts it presents are easy to understand.

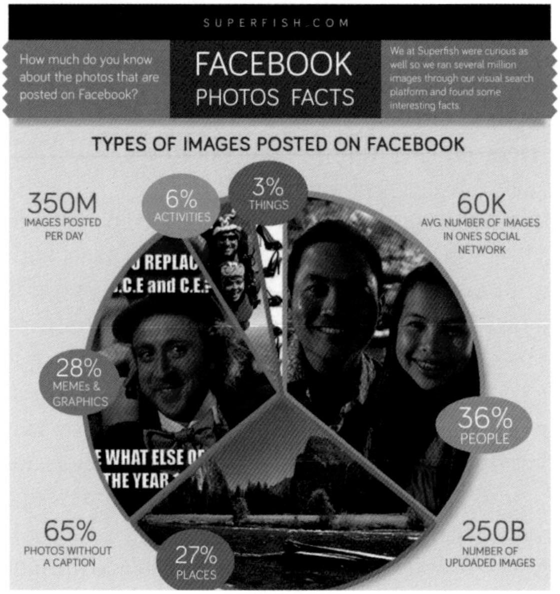

Figure 9.3 The images draw the eye, and the colored bubbles prioritize important facts about content. Facts that are a lower priority are in less vibrant colors and are positioned farther from the center of the image.

- Get peer response

✓Think of peer responses as market testing your argument before you share it with the public. For peer review to work, your readers need to understand your audience and your purpose so they can read as if they are part of your intended audience.

✓When asking peers to respond to your argument, always start with the big things, such as logic and structure, and work towards the small things, like punctuation and spelling. Ask your peers to look over your argument and respond to the following.

- How would you describe the scope and focus of my state-the-facts argument?
- Please circle the sentences of paragraphs that indicate why the audience needs to know the facts, and tell me if my purpose can be clarified.
- Please circle any sentences that appear biased or that may affect my interpretation of the facts.
- Please circle any statements that sound factual but are not supported by logic, evidence, or an authoritative source.
- Are you persuaded by my facts, and if not, what would it take to persuade you my statements are factual?

- Revise your argument

✓ Think of revision as moving your thoughts and ideas from your mind to the mind of the reader. For example, if you've begun your argument by refuting or debunking statements of facts you are arguing against, can the reader tell when you've moved on to present the facts you know to be true?

✓ One of the best ways to revise is to think about what each paragraph adds to your argument. First, make a list of steps you need your audience to make with you before they will accept your facts. For example, given the thesis, what is the first point you must support? What does your audience need to know or believe before they can accept your final point? Then read through your argument and, next to each paragraph, write down how it supports your thesis, not what it means. For example, paragraph two presents a set of facts you will argue are not true. Paragraph three raises the question, what if these facts are not true? Finally, compare your list of the necessary steps with your description of what each paragraph actually does.

When you have described the function of each paragraph, read through your margin notes and consider whether each step makes sense and helps the reader move through your argument. Have you skipped any steps or mistakenly assumed your reader knows or agrees with you? If necessary, revise to ensure that each paragraph moves your reader logically through your argument.

CHAPTER 10
DEFINING

Freestyle, Crunk, Bounce—there are many types of hip-hop music. However, since the mid-1990s, hip-hop culture and rap music have been defined first by the East Coast and then by the West Coast sound. Initially, jazz samples and extraordinary feats of lyrical wordplay were markers of the East Coast sound, while West Coast rappers sampled funk and portrayed the gritty, gangsta life in graphic rhymes.

Multiple sub-genres have emerged, ranging from hypnotic cloud rap to the dexterous mixing of turntablism. Most sub-genres borrow from previous, existing genres such as Reggaetón, with its roots in Puerto Rican dancehalls; early rap themes of violence, drugs, and sex; and pop music beats. Because genres borrow from genres, some commonalities appear again and again. For example, rapping remains, by and large, a masculine, urban art form with recurring themes of aggression and fast money, whether the lyrics are spoken in Mandarin, modern Greek, or a southern drawl.

And then there is Mare Avertencia Lirika, whose Zapotec ancestry and feminist beliefs inform lyrics that decry social injustice for the poor of Oaxaca and the Indigenous peoples of Mexico. Her music is unlike anything you have ever heard, yet it is a redefinition of genres you know well. In fact, the history of hip-hop is a history of redefining. Mare Avertencia Lirika's Zapotec resistance rap is just one in a chain of redefinitions that can be traced back to the Bronx of the 1970s and DJ Kool Herc.

What is true of hip-hop is true more generally: all definitions are built upon other definitions. Why create a new word or redefine a word when the words, the definitions, and the things they refer to, like hip-hop, are commonly understood? Does

Mare Avertencia Lirika really make rap better with her definition? Why redefine when existing definitions seem to work just fine?

In fact, redefinition isn't about a better word—it is about a more persuasive message for a different situation. If it were not for those who redefined the genres they heard to produce their own new message, like TLC and Missy Elliot before her, Mare Avertencia Lirika would not be able to speak from her own experience—for her people—with such resounding power and volubility.

If you think of redefining as just adding more words to an existing definition or combining definitions, then there might seem to be little point in doing it. However, if definition and redefinition can be a form of persuasion, then there are some very powerful reasons to redefine.

MODULE II-21

WHAT AUDIENCES EXPECT OF A DEFINITION ARGUMENT

Open a local or national newspaper, and at the heart of the biggest stories you are likely to find a definition in dispute. For example, the current Israeli–Palestinian conflict rages over a definition: how are the borders of Israel and Palestine to be defined? The debate about gun control and the Second Amendment boils down to how the constitutional phrase "a well regulated militia" is defined. On a university campus, the way "hazing" is defined can mean the difference between long-lived tradition or a student-handbook violation.

Why Would I Need to Define?

In an academic setting, a definition essay is a common assignment. Such assignments may ask you to define an idea or event using existing words and classifications. In history and psychology courses, you may be expected to define terms such as "colonialism" or to explain how observations of behaviors and events fit existing definitions or classifications. In a composition or writing class you may be asked to write a personal definition—what a word, phrase, or idea such as "social justice" means to you.

Because so much depends on definitions, a definitional argument needs to be clear, decisive, and based on evidence. Persuasive definitional arguments redefine an existing word or argue for a new word and new definition. Therefore, you must take a position by explaining why the previous definition should be replaced and why a new definition is necessary, or by persuading the audience that the new word and its definition are accurate, insightful, and better than other possibilities.

Types of Definitions

To **define** is to state the meaning or meanings of a word or phrase, establish the boundaries or extent of a word or phrase, designate the qualities or characteristics that a word or phrase refers to, and resolve misunderstandings about a word's or phrase's meaning. Whenever you are trying to persuade someone to think or act differently, you are probably going to use a definition or make a definitional argument. Because definitions are the building blocks of opinions and persuasive arguments, tradition provides you with different types of definitions. Knowing which type to use based on your purpose and your intended audience will help you build a persuasive argument.

Formal Definition

A **formal definition** describes the range of qualities and characteristics that differentiate the word or phrase from other similar examples. To make a formal definition, the word to be defined is first placed in a larger class or category of things or ideas with similar qualities and characteristics. For example, an oak tree can be placed in the larger category of trees. The formal definition then shows how the word to be defined, like "oak tree," is different from all other things and ideas within the larger group "tree":

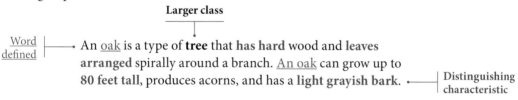

Larger class

Word defined

An oak is a type of **tree** that **has hard** wood and **leaves arranged** spirally around a branch. An oak can grow up to **80 feet tall**, produces acorns, and has a **light grayish bark**.

Distinguishing characteristic

When people look a word up in a dictionary, they expect to find a formal definition. Formal definitions can appear in any type of argument, but they are exceptionally useful in arguments of analysis and evaluation, where you must compare one object or idea with others in a larger class. For example, you could argue that alternative rap (the phrase to be defined) does not get the airplay of other types of hip-hop music (larger class) because it blends and borrows from genres not commonly associated with hip-hop culture such as country, electronica, and folk music (distinguishing qualities). The Conventions in Context box entitled "Common Mistakes in Formal Definitions" will help you build a persuasive definition. For more on arguments of analysis and evaluation, see Chapter 12.

Conventions in Context
Common Mistakes in Formal Definitions

For a formal definition to be effective, it needs to follow the structure readers expect.

The word must belong to a larger class: the word you define cannot be its own larger class. For example, you can't say an oak tree is a type of oak tree. Such a class would be too small, as it would not contain any similar, comparable trees you could use to distinguish an oak.

The class must contain comparable items: your larger class must contain comparable or similar objects or ideas. Therefore, you can't say an oak tree is a type of wood. Trees are composed of wood, but a larger class of trees does not also include types of lumber.

The class cannot be too big: you could say an oak tree is a type of living organism. However, distinguishing an oak from all other organisms, a gigantic class, would take a great deal of energy and time.

The definition must be precise: the word or phrase must be distinct from all other examples in the larger class or category. For example, the following definition describes a meter and other forms of measurement: A meter is a type of metric measurement divisible by numerations of 100. This definition fails because it can also define a liter.

A good definition is built on qualities, characteristics, comparisons, and differences. If the building blocks of a definition are faulty, so too is the definition.

Operational Definition

An **operational definition** describes how a thing or idea affects the environment, is observed or measured, or is the result of a process.

For example, an NBA three-point shot is a shot made from behind a line marking an arc with a radius 23 feet 9 inches from a point directly under the basket. Go to any NBA court or watch any NBA game and you will find the same operational definition.

Operational definitions are well suited to state-the-facts arguments, cause-and-effect arguments, or any argument where you clarify or establish exact qualities or characteristics of a thing or idea. If you were to argue that global warming is due to human activity, you would first have to establish an operational definition of "human climate disruption." You might say that human-based climate disruption is defined as 440 parts per million of CO_2 in the atmosphere measured over a five-year period. For more on state-the-facts arguments and cause-and-effect arguments, see Chapters 9 and 13.

Extensional Definition

In an **extensional definition**, every part of an object or idea is identified. For example, a "s'more" is composed of graham crackers, a chocolate bar, and a toasted marshmallow. Extensional definitions are not appropriate for objects with many parts, such as the universe, or abstract concepts, such as love.

Extensional definitions are helpful in arguments in which you need to break a big idea into smaller parts, such as cause-and-effect arguments and arguments that propose a solution. If you argue that NCAA rules about amateurism are unfair to college athletes, you might describe all the parts of the NCAA's amateurism policy and explain how each part hurts athletes or denies them opportunities. Cause-and-effect arguments are discussed in Chapter 13, and arguments that propose a solution are discussed in Chapter 14.

Definition by Example

A **definition by example** presents similar words, ideas, or examples that have a specific quality or trait in common with the word, phrase, or idea to be defined. If you wanted to define a *Cajon*, for instance, you could point to different examples of the instrument (see Figure 10.1).

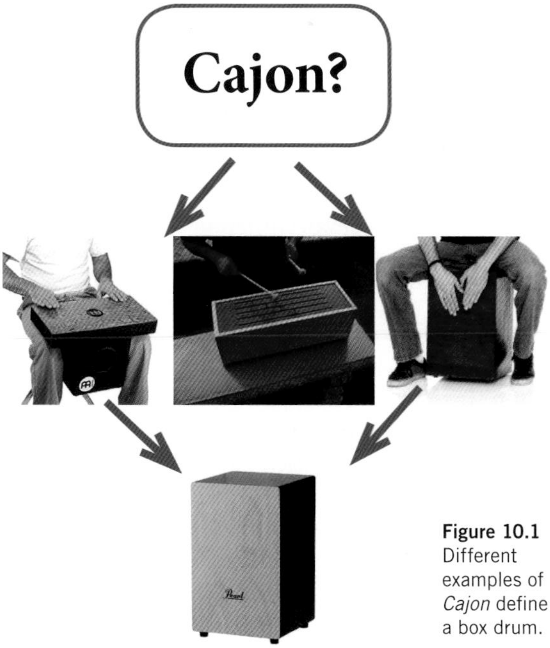

Figure 10.1 Different examples of *Cajon* define it as a box drum.

A definition by example highlights several traits or qualities, making it useful when defining a complex or abstract idea. Example definitions are useful in any persuasive argument and are often found in literary and rhetorical analysis arguments. For instance, if you wanted to argue that Jack London's short story "To Build a Fire" is an example of the naturalist literary movement, you would first define naturalism by identifying common traits or qualities of other naturalist short stories, and then show these same qualities in London's story. Chapter 16 covers textual analysis, and Chapter 8 can help with rhetorical analysis arguments.

Etymological Definition

An **etymological definition** shows the derivation or origin of a word and traces changes in its meaning over time. The contemporary word "cure" has Latin (*cura*) and Old French origins. Over time, it has been used to describe the care of souls (fourteenth century), the act of covering or concealing (fifteenth century), a medical treatment (seventeenth century), and an odd person (nineteenth century). Authoritative etymological definitions can be found in the *Oxford English Dictionary.*

Rhetorical analyses (Chapter 8) and determinations of cause (Chapter 13) are just two of the argument forms that use etymological definitions. For example, if you wanted to persuade people to avoid websites and discussion boards where contributors write extreme, racist, or sexist posts, you might remind your audience of the etymology of the word "troll": "In the early seventeenth century, a troll was a foul-smelling, ugly dwarf or giant with big ears and a menacing disposition who lived in dark caves or under bridges and harassed passersby. Feeding trolls, whether supernatural or electronic, is never a good idea."

Using Invention to Find a Reason to Define

There are many reasons or purposes for defining or redefining a word. During invention, try out different purposes to see how they support different types of arguments. Let's consider five different reasons for defining and the kinds of arguments they can help you build.

1. **Propose a better definition.** In this case, you are arguing that the definition you propose is more appropriate to the current setting and usage, is closer to the original meaning, or is a necessary update of a current word.
   - You can define by establishing the best, most precise word for the thing, idea, person, or event you are describing. For example, the word "amateur" may no longer apply to student-athletes who get scholarships and a paycheck, and "student worker" is too general. A more accurate word may be "athletic worker."

- You can define by returning a word to an older, previous definition. For example, "random" used to mean arbitrary or unplanned. Now it is used to suggest something odd or strange. You might argue that people should go back to using the word "random" to mean unplanned or haphazard.
- You can redefine by pointing out that a word's meaning has shifted in common usage or among a group. For example, for many, a "friend" is someone you like and trust. However, over one billion Facebook users understand "friend" as a verb, and they can "friend" people they do not know.

2. **Challenge an existing definition**. You can challenge a definition of a word by inventing alternative definitions or researching other larger classes or sets in which the word fits. When you challenge an existing definition of a word, you are also often challenging its use in a discussion or debate. The Supreme Court and gun-rights activists interpret the phrase "a well regulated militia" in the Second Amendment of the Constitution to mean private citizens who may be called upon to act as a militia. Gun-control activists challenge this definition and argue that the Constitution's framers intended "militia" to mean professional soldiers only. A change in the accepted definition—for example, by changing the larger class to which militias belong—could change the debate.

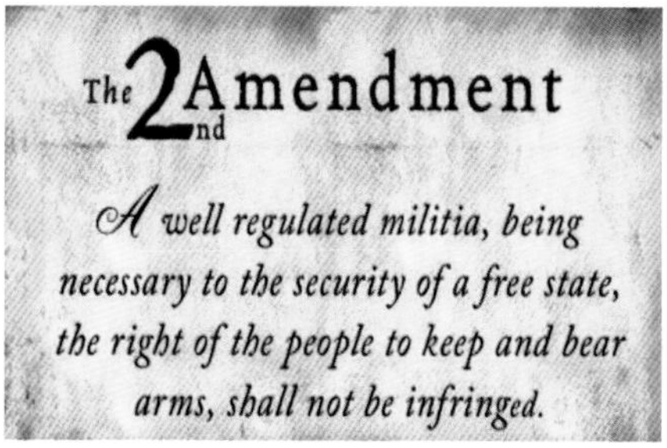

Figure 10.2 The wording of the Second Amendment to the US Constitution.

3. **Create a new word and definition**. Sometimes a new development in society or technology requires a name and a definition for that name. For example, Richard Dawkins first used and defined the word "meme" in his 1976 book *The Selfish Gene*. According to Dawkins, a "meme" is an idea, cultural trait, or behavior whose movement within a population is similar to that of a virus.
4. **Add a new element or idea to an existing definition**. In 2013, the Supreme Court struck down the federal law barring recognition of same-sex marriages. As a result, the legal definition of "marriage" now includes same-sex wedded unions, which were previously excluded.
5. **Help readers better understand words and ideas**. Definitions can inform an audience and, by doing so, establish common ground or agreement. For example, before anyone would buy "wearable tech" or invest in the online currency know as "bitcoin," they must first understand what each is. In other words, these two concepts are a mystery until they are defined.

Making Your Definition Reasonable and Acceptable to Your Audience

Keep in mind that your audience may be inclined to resist your definition. In any debate about diets and food production, some vegetarians may be sympathetic to the redefinition in the phrase "meat is murder." However, if you are trying to persuade those whose diet includes cold cuts, redefining "meat" as "murder" will simply mark you as unreasonable. Modifying or adding to the definition of "meat" as "a source of protein that requires twice as much energy to produce as other proteins" is more likely to strike even a doubtful audience as a reasonable statement.

In order to determine what will be acceptable or reasonable to your audience, you will need to consider their disposition toward and current beliefs about the word or phrase you are defining. You will also need to determine what your audience might find silly or self-serving.

For example, some might be sympathetic to the Dairy Council's argument that people should think of ice cream as a post-workout protein food (Figure 10.3). But it is just as likely that some will see this definition as a clever way to increase ice-cream sales.

Figure 10.3
Is ice cream a healthy choice?

Making Your Definition Complete and Authoritative

Understandably, your audience has beliefs about how a definition works, questions about the need for defining or redefining a word they think they know, and expectations about the insight necessary to justify a redefinition or a new word altogether. In other words, first you need to establish your authority—prove you know how to define—and then you need to persuade your audience of the benefit or insight of your definition or redefinition. Only then will your audience give up their old definition and accept your argument.

Effective definitions provide insight, a new understanding and clearer vision of the subject, and persuasive definitions often illustrate this insight with examples. Defining muscle pain as soreness provides no new understanding or insight, for example. However, if your trainer defines pain as the process of weakness leaving the body, she may have just given you a new way to think about your workout. If she adds a visual example of a muscle with micro-tears that grows bigger and stronger as it heals, her insight may persuade you to work harder. The Responsible Sourcing box entitled "The Dictionary Trap" will help you avoid less than insightful definitions.

Responsible Sourcing
The Dictionary Trap

Obviously, dictionary definitions are useful during research or as the source of a definition you will redefine in your argument. However, building an argument around a dictionary definition or relying heavily upon what a dictionary says about a word can be a trap.

General dictionaries available in print or online, like the *Merriam-Webster's Collegiate Dictionary*, are helpful primarily for settling debates and checking spelling. If your professor has assigned you a definition essay, however, she is probably expecting you to pull together different sources with different perspectives to develop a coherent, insightful definition of your own. Because of these expectations, a dictionary definition will appear to be an uninspired choice. After all, if readers or listeners can look up the definition in a dictionary, what do they need you for?

If you are tempted to begin an essay with or otherwise use a definition drawn from a general dictionary, ask yourself the following:

- What does my reader expect?
- What does the definition provide that is insightful?
- What does the dictionary definition do that I couldn't do?

A professor is likely to view a citation for a dictionary definition as a shortcut that indicates a lack of mental effort.

Genres That Define

Nearly all genres of argument make use of definitions. The following genres focus primarily or typically on persuading an audience to accept a definition of a word, phrase, or idea.

- A **commercial** usually serves to define a new product or service or redefine a product or service.
- **Committee by-laws** define the identity, purpose, duties, and rights of a committee or other type of group.
- A **diagnostic manual** used by physicians defines illnesses and symptoms.
- An **opinion piece** is a short, journalistic argument in which the author tries to persuade the audience of her or his opinion.

- A **research paper** can redefine existing knowledge by describing new discoveries and new knowledge.
- A **review of scholarly literature** defines the subject of articles and books.

MODULE II-22

A DEFINITION GENRE: OPINION PIECE

Stephen L. Carter's curiosity led him to explore the usage and history of the word "blockbuster," which he discusses in the opinion piece that follows, which was first published in September 2016. Carter is the William Nelson Cromwell Professor of Law at Yale. In addition, he is a columnist for *Bloomberg View* and a best-selling author. Carter was also a history major at Stanford University and served as a clerk for US Supreme Court Justice Thurgood Marshall. In his opinion piece, Carter uses a number of methods to redefine and recall earlier definitions of "blockbuster."

Hollywood's Idea of a Blockbuster Is All Wrong

By Stephen L. Carter

The looming Labor Day weekend marks the end of a dismal season at the multiplex. "Hollywood's blockbuster machine frequently stalled and sputtered this summer," writes the Associated Press, "leaving behind a steady trail of misbegotten reboots, ill-conceived sequels and questionable remakes." Even an apparent hit like "Suicide Squad" can be described as a disappointment, because its likely worldwide take in the $700 million range is significantly less than Warner Brothers hoped for. Certainly it will not reach the $1 billion threshold that nowadays is apparently viewed as the definition of a blockbuster.

[Word]

[Purpose—challenge an existing definition]

I don't have a theory on why the audience is shrinking. But the language maven in me is intrigued by the word blockbuster itself. Why do **we define a blockbuster by earnings?** Once upon a time Hollywood had a more qualitative definition; maybe it's time to recover it.

[**Current usage**]

The word served originally as *the nickname for the massive bombs dropped by the Royal Air Force during World War II. A blockbuster literally blew things up.* So it's easy to understand how, **after the war, journalists began to use the word to**

[*Operational definition*]

[**Etymological Definition**]

show that some event had come as a potent and unwelcome surprise. When the U.S. Supreme Court in 1957 ordered du Pont (as it was then known) to divest its holdings in General Motors, Life magazine called the decision a "Judicial Blockbuster."

In 1946, the New York Times described the upset of Wimbledon tennis champ Yvon Petra as "the blockbuster of the season." **When the Washington Post in 1949 derisively referred to the activities of British Foreign Secretary Ernest Bevin in the Middle East as** "Bevin's Blockbuster," **readers understood the implicit argument that his interference could lead to catastrophic results.** Evolution of this sort from the wartime usage is easy to understand. The events in question were (metaphorically) explosive. The effects were disruptive. But when did we start calling hit movies blockbusters?

...

Let's go back to 1947, *when the writer and critic Leon Gutterman referred to the film "Crossfire" as* **"that vivid dramatic blockbuster which deals with anti-Semitism."** *He could not have been talking about money. True, the film earned a small profit—just over $1 million—but by this time any number of films were already earning in the eight figures on minuscule budgets. Similarly, when a 1951 advertisement in the Los Angeles Times for the 1949 Cécile Aubry vehicle "Manon" quoted a critic who called the film* **"a sex blockbuster,"** *the reference could not have been to box office.*

What made **both "Manon" and "Crossfire" important films was their disruptive quality.** *There was anti-Semitism in "Crossfire." There was sex in "Manon." But neither film was a big hit, so they weren't blockbusters because of their earnings.* **They were blockbusters because they were moderately successful while dealing with topics the major studios had largely avoided.**

Consider the original "Ben Hur." In his glowing 1959 review, Bosley Crowther of the New York Times defined "the so-called 'blockbuster' spectacle film" as one "which generally provokes a sublimation of sensibility to action and pageantry." **But in praising the film for its possession of these qualities, he could not have known how successful it would be. When the Times announced a year later** that

Etymological Definition

Example of historical usage

Etymological Definition

Paragraphs omitted for brevity

Usage analyzed

Extensional Definition

Parts of the Blockbuster idea identified

Example of historical usage

Etymological Definition

a "blockbuster" film version of Lawrence Durrell's "Alexandria Quartet" novels was on the way, the article referred not to the expected box office earnings, but to the expected scope in time and place, and to the length of the film, estimated at perhaps four hours.

Example of historical usage

What's useful about thinking of the word blockbuster this way is that we understand that we mean something other than a hit—we mean in some sense an achievement. So although a movie can be both a hit and a blockbuster ("Avatar," for example) it can also be a huge hit without being a blockbuster (the second "Star Wars" trilogy), and vice versa.

New insight

The point is that a blockbuster, whether or not a hit, should always be disruptive. It should show us something different and new. If Hollywood wants audiences back in the theaters, surely that's the way to go.

Questions to Consider

Invention

1. What do you think motivated Carter to analyze and redefine the term "blockbuster"?
2. The author is a historian, an expert in rhetoric, and a professor of law. How would you expect his methods of gathering evidence to be similar to or different from your own?
3. Imagine you were assigned to write a definition essay that takes a position about whether movies should be valued primarily for their box-office profit as opposed to their artistic merit. What would be your first three steps?

Audience

4. Is the author speaking to readers who share his curiosity about the word, or is he addressing readers who have not previously thought about it? How do you know?
5. The author makes some assumptions about his audience. How would you describe his intended audience?
6. What does Carter intend his readers to think, believe, or do after they have finished reading his opinion piece?

Authority

7. This piece first appeared in *Bloomberg View*, the branch of *Bloomberg News*, a financial news service trusted by investors and financiers around the world, that publishes columns, opinions, and editorials. How do you know that the definition is accurate and not biased?

8. How does Carter demonstrate that you can trust his sources?
9. By the end, do you have a good understanding of "blockbuster" and how and why its meaning has changed over time? What more do you need to know to accept Carter's redefinition or to make your understanding complete?

MODULE II-23

A DEFINITION GENRE: YOUTUBE COMMERCIAL

These photos are from the 2015 Super Bowl commercial entitled "Always #LikeAGirl" for *Always*, Procter & Gamble's feminine care product line. The commercial does not directly define the product, but it does define the values the company wants consumers to associate with it. First, the commercial explores the common understanding of the phrase "like a girl" by asking volunteers what it means to run or throw like a girl. They act out uncoordinated or feeble movements. Then, director Lauren Greenfield asks if "like a girl" is an insult. The commercial ends with a boy and girls speaking and acting confidently as they redefine what it means to be "like a girl."

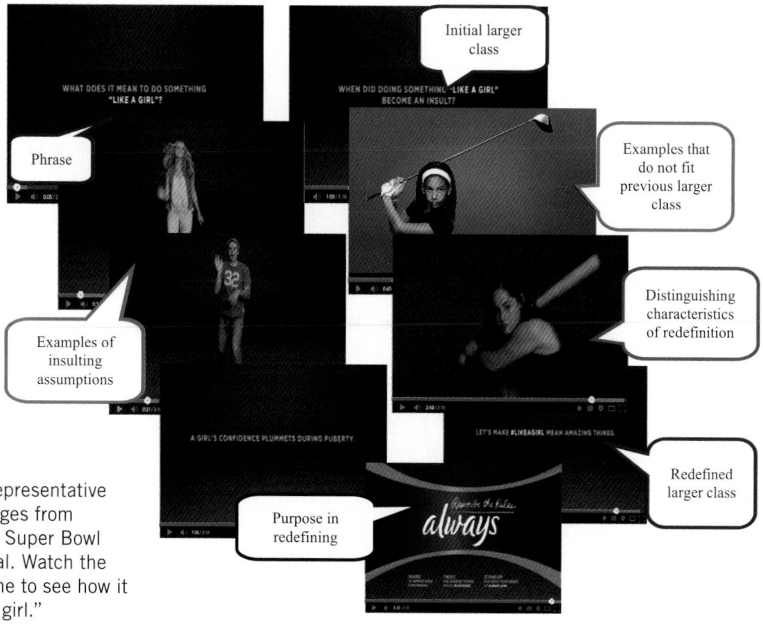

Figure 10.4 A representative sequence of images from the "Like a Girl" Super Bowl 2015 commercial. Watch the commercial online to see how it redefines "like a girl."

Questions to Consider

Invention

1. If you were to make a similar commercial redefining a stereotype, such as the idea that working-class people do not support the fine arts, how would you begin your invention and research process?
2. The audience for the "like a girl" commercial is women. If you were to create a commercial with the same message for college age men, what kinds of images would you use and where would you find them?
3. The commercial is composed of actual interviews. How could you use questions and the responses of friends, peers, and strangers in your invention process?

Audience

4. What does the director's use of live interviews reveal about her audience?
5. What age group do you think the director intends to talk to, and how do you know?
6. What do you think the director wants her audience to do or think?

Authority

7. If you discovered the interviews were scripted and the speakers were actors, how would that change your view of the message?
8. Does the blue background, clothing, and age of the interviewees contribute to or limit their authority?
9. If you were to produce a similar commercial for the same audience, what would you do to establish authority?

MODULE II-24

A DEFINITION GENRE: RESEARCH PAPER

For her final Honors seminar, Cedar Smith explored the science of happiness. She looked to psychologists and experts to better understand why some people are consistently happy while others are not. The excerpt below is her first step—persuade her audience to reconsider their understanding of *moods*, a central term in the current research of happiness, and the relationship of moods to well-being.

An Ever-Changing State: What the Science of Happiness Can Teach Us about Our Moods

If someone asked you to describe your current mood, most likely you would have an instant response. You know exactly how you feel, and you are probably aware that mood influences every second of your life. Few of us think about mood or what a mood is. Yet mood is related to other parts of your life; it shapes your experiences and outlook and can affect your mental health and general well-being.

To explore and understand mood, we must first define it. When we think of moods, we think of *emotions, of feelings, of attitude, of sentiment.* Generally, a mood is **a temporary feeling marked by an overriding emotion or sentiment.** However, a mood is **not simply an emotion like sadness, which is typically provoked by an event and is specific, intense, and focused. A mood is less intense and may not be provoked by anything, and yet** moods are powerful.

As William Morris and Paula Schnurr, the authors of *Mood: The Frame of Mind*, have noted, moods **"are capable of altering our affective, cognitive, and behavioral responses to a wide array of objects and events"** (2). Think back to a time when you were in what would be labeled as a bad mood. **Most likely, you had no desire to interact with people, maybe you wanted to be left alone, or were angry and had no urge to engage in your favorite activities. Moods can change your perspective, your desires, and your thoughts. And moods can wreak havoc on individuals' lives.** From Major Depressive Disorder, Generalized Anxiety Disorder, Seasonal Affective Disorder, and Bipolar Disorder, these disturbances in moods are major psychological problems that impede and affect the lives of many.

Moods can be understood as positive and negative. A **positive** mood **is difficult to define, but in its essence it is a general feeling of well-being.** We can use the terms happy mood and positive mood interchangeably; as Sonja Lyubomirsky explains in her book *The How of Happiness: A Scientific Approach to Getting the Life You Want*, **"the hallmark of happiness, feelings of joy, delight, contentment, vigor, thrill, curiosity, interest, serenity, and pride," are the same aspects of positive** moods (258).

- Word
- Purpose in Defining
- *Larger class*
- **Example, mood is not like an emotion**
- **Distinguishing characteristic**
- **Distinguishing characteristic**
- MLA in-text citation
- **Example, mood is like this**
- **Distinguishing characteristic**
- **Distinguishing characteristic**
- **Distinguishing characteristic**

Lyubomirsky cites a number of studies that show that "**happy** moods, no matter the source, **lead people to be more productive, more likable, more active, more healthy, more friendly, more helpful, more resilient, and more creative**" (258). So how can we experience a positive mood for ourselves? **The science of happiness tells us that expressing gratitude, savoring experiences, and laughter are all things that can put us in a positive** mood.

New Insight

On the other side are negative moods. **A negative mood is a state of tension, nervousness, worry, anger, guilt, sadness, self-dissatisfaction, and/or distress.** People may attribute negative moods to unstable and uncontrollable external events or internal enduring aspects of self (Morris and Schnurr 151). The things that put us in a negative mood are similar to if not the same as the things that bring us out of a happy mood, notably, complaining and ruminating.

Distinguishing characteristic

New Insight

MLA in-text citation

As the research shows, a mood is not a feeling or simply an emotion, but a long term cognitive state that can shape the way we experience events, express ourselves, and can even change the way we think and interact with the world. Now that we understand moods more deeply, let's look at what cognitive psychologists have discovered about our ability to alter or effect our own mood and the moods of others....

New Insight

Works Cited

Lyubomirsky, Sonja. *The How of Happiness: A Scientific Approach to Getting the Life You Want.* Penguin Press, 2008.

Morris, William N., and Paula P. Schnurr. *Mood: The Frame of Mind.* Springer-Verlag, 1989.

MLA style Works Cited

Questions to Consider

Invention

1. In the excerpt above, what is Smith's purpose?
2. Since Smith is not an expert, she needed to rely on invention and research to help her establish an authoritative voice. What do you imagine were her first and second steps when inventing?
3. What types of definitions are used in this excerpt from Smith's research paper about mood? How do they contribute to your understanding of the word or idea being defined?

Audience

4. Often, Smith appears to talk directly to her audience by posing questions. How does such an approach affect her readers and their view of the author?
5. What does Smith assume her readers think about mood before they read her argument, and what does she want readers to think, believe, or do after they have finished?
6. Smith makes assumptions about what her audience knows and thinks. Where do you see Smith using these assumptions to build her definition?

Authority

7. How does Smith let her readers know that her definitions are accurate and can be trusted?
8. Where in the definition did you wish you had more context or background? Why?
9. By the end, do you have a good understanding of the concept of mood? What more do you need to know to accept the definition or to make your understanding complete?

MODULE II-25

BUILDING A DEFINITION ARGUMENT

The following checklist and guidelines will help you to build a persuasive definition argument. It is a guide; it is not the only way to write a persuasive definitional argument.

Invention

- Find a subject

✓ Many academic disciplines and areas of research have their own dictionaries that define specialized terms and concepts such as *Barron's Medical Guides* and *The Sailor's Word Book*. Dictionaries are an excellent place to start, but as the Responsible Sourcing box entitled "The Dictionary Trap" explains, your audience will be looking for more insight than a dictionary provides.

✓ If you have been assigned a subject for a definition argument, your invention should focus on looking around to see what others think, what experts and scholars have said, and what is currently known about the word, phrase, or idea.

✓ If you are free to select your own subject to define, remember that subjects with known specific physical qualities, such as water or a Cajon box drum, may not yield the insight your audience expects. However, definitions of abstract or ever-changing ideas such as "blockbuster" or "free market" can yield a great many insights, in part because they can be placed in many different larger classes or categories.

If you are stuck, see the Breaking the Block box below entitled "Using Stasis Questions to Find a Subject to Define."

- Research to refine your definition and gather evidence

✓ Research can reveal definitions as sources of disagreement between different groups or different perspectives.

For example, the definition of "climate" in the *Glossary of Agricultural and Environmental Sciences Terms* includes variations in soil temperature. *The Facts on File Dictionary of Weather and Climate* includes surface ground and water temperature, but not temperatures below the surface such as in the soil. As you can imagine, studies of climate that do or do not include soil or water temperature at depth could result in very different interpretations of data.

✓ Research will also help you understand the nuances, qualities, and characteristics that the audience might attribute to a concept.

For example, the term "philanthropy" in the United States used to mean indirect giving designed to improve the conditions of the poor in general, such as building better schools or teaching people to grow new crops. Recently, however, researchers have found that giving cash directly to poor persons, known as "direct philanthropy," has the same if not greater long-term, positive effects than indirect support. The definition of philanthropy has, therefore, been expanded.

- Develop a thesis

✓ The thesis of a definitional argument must take an arguable or a debatable position, clearly state the focus (the word or phrase to be defined), indicate the scope (the larger class or category), and suggest a purpose for defining or redefining.

For example, Stephen L. Carter's casual opinion piece frames his thesis about the term "blockbuster" with a question, and in so doing defines the scope: current usage of the term, which is defined by earnings, and past definitions, which were based on quality. His focus also indicates his opinion: the older definition of "blockbuster" is better and should be recovered.

Breaking the Block
Using Stasis Questions to Find a Subject to Define

Stasis questions of fact can help you move past first impressions and common understandings to discover deeper insights. The writing component of this exercise should take 10 minutes.

Step One
Identify the top news story of the past week. Look at versions of the story on respected websites such as the *Chicago Tribune*, *Wall Street Journal*, or *CNN*.

Step Two
Answer the following secondary stasis questions of definition.

- How is the event or issue characterized? Is it a problem, a debate, a tension, an impasse, a misunderstanding?
- What exactly is the event or issue in question?
- Does the event or issue belong to a larger class or category?
- Can the event or issue be broken into smaller parts?
- How is the event or issue related to the larger class or its smaller parts?

Step Three
Look for differences in how different news organizations, commentators, or witnesses define the event or related issue. Then, write for 10 minutes comparing the similarities and differences among the definitions of the event or issue. Ask yourself these questions:

- What types of definitions are used, and why?
- If the event or issue is placed within a larger category, would it be possible to use other categories? If so, how would the definition change?
- What qualities or characteristics are used to define?
- Does the definition offer a new insight or does it confirm an existing understanding?
- Does the definition support a larger argument? If so, how is the definition used?
- Would an alternative definition support a different argument? Briefly, what would that argument be?

Audience

- Understand the rhetorical situation

✓ Definitions can be determined by different situations, the larger culture, and local usage. Since every rhetorical situation is different, different audiences may understand words and phrases in significantly or subtly different ways.

For example, in the "Like a Girl" commercial that played during the 2015 Super Bowl, a young woman named Erin is asked to run like a girl. She is given no further instruction and so she flings her arms and legs about, pantomiming uncoordinated running. She is then asked how the phrase "like a girl" used as an insult affects girls between 10 and 12 years old. In response, she speaks eloquently about how the insult drops their self-esteem. In a matter of minutes, this young woman moves from the rhetorical situation of a commercial set where the phrase "like a girl" is defined as a director's acting instructions, to a different rhetorical situation where the phrase is defined by the experiences of adolescent girls.

✓ Consider culture and setting. When you construct an argument using definitions, you are also arguing about culture and how we know it.

For example, in the culture of stand-up comedy, the terms "killed" and "bombed" mean to make an audience laugh—or to fail to do so. In a different setting, such as an airport security checkpoint, use of the same words may lead to some awkward conversations with TSA agents. Therefore, before you can move your reader or audience to accept your definition, you must clearly understand how they define and use words and phrases.

- Discover your audience's definition

✓ Identify the larger class or category your audience uses to define the word. If you listen to how someone uses a word, you may learn what it means to him or her.

In the "Like a Girl" commercial, the first portrayals of throwing or running like a girl show that the male actors and those past puberty understand the phrase as an insult—the larger class.

✓ Question the larger class or category. Sometimes the class used to define a word is inaccurate or problematic. Offering an alternative, more accurate larger class can lead to a new insight that persuades your audience to accept your definition.

✓ To build your argument, explain why the class or category that is the foundation of your audience's definition is inaccurate or problematic, and then propose a new class or category and corresponding definition. The following questions will help you examine the class or category that is the foundation of your audience's definition:

- ⊙ Is it the best class or category, and what are the alternatives?
- ⊙ Is the current class or category the result of bias?
- ⊙ What are the consequences of using the current class or category?
- ⊙ Who or what benefits from using this class or category to define?

- Organize your definition

✓ As always, look to audience expectations and the conventions of the genre or genres you use for an initial organization of your argument.

✓ Each type of definition has a logical structure (see pp. 173–76). Working with a skeptical audience, your first step in constructing an insightful definitional argument will be to explore your readers' current understanding, and then move them to the definition you will argue for.

A simplified outline for a definitional argument that redefines a word or phrase could look something like this:

I. State thesis and establish context
II. Explain faults of current definition
III. Concede or acknowledge strengths of old definition
IV. Distinguish word or phrase from others in class with examples
V. Describe new class or category
VI. Restate thesis

- Draft your definition

✓ As you draft, remember that defining is precise work; it can take time and several drafts to get your definition argument right.

✓ Other than personal definitions, most genres of definition depend upon invention and researching sources. As you draft, always link the material you find in sources to the citation information you will need for your paper.

Authority

- Check your logic

✓ Unless your professor requires a different type of definition, a definitional argument should follow the logic of a formal definition:

- ⊙ The definition you argue for must be grounded in an acceptable larger class or category.
- ⊙ The larger class or category must account for all the characteristics and qualities of the word or phrase you are defining or redefining.

The Conventions in Context box entitled "Common Mistakes in Formal Definitions" in Module II-21 expands on the logical errors that can happen when defining.

✓ The logic of the definition type you use must be apparent in your argument. For example, an operational definition of "direct philanthropy" would require a description of how it affects impoverished people and their community.

✓ If you use specialized terms, phrases, or acronyms or make a significant change in an existing definition, you will need evidence and sources that support your use of the specialized words or your redefinition. For example, if your professor sees you repeatedly using the acronym SAD (Seasonal Affective Disorder), he or she may wonder how you came across this concept and if you are using it correctly. In this case, providing a clear definition from a solid source—such as, in this case, the latest edition of the *Diagnostic and Statistical Manual of Mental Disorders*—can be a way of demonstrating the depth of your research.

- Make it flow

✓ Transitions such as "for example," "in particular," and "in contrast" are very important in a definitional argument. Replacing a familiar definition that your audience knows with a new and unfamiliar one can be disorienting. Transitions ease your reader from one idea to the next and differentiate a stronger definition from an inferior one.

- Get peer response

✓ Peer response is crucial for a successful definition argument because other readers can tell you not only whether your argument is persuasive but also whether you started with a good understanding of how your audience defines and uses the word, phrase, or idea you are writing about.

✓ Ask your peers to answer the following questions:
  - Please circle my thesis and tell me if it is supported by my definition.
  - What is my purpose, and which sentence tells you why I am defining the word, phrase, or idea?
  - What type of definition am I using? Is it complete? Why or why not?
  - Do I mention any qualities or characteristics of the word or idea that are not supported by my definition?
  - What insights have I missed?

- Revise your argument

✓ After you get comments from your peers, you may find that they missed attempts to redefine or highlight subtle nuances of your word or idea. Revise with the following in mind:
  - Your reader will read or hear your argument once. What is obvious to you is so because of your hours of work and research;
  - Simply defining or redefining a term is not enough, because
  - Skeptical readers have no reason to change their understanding of a word or idea until you give them persuasive reasons.

✓ If a definition does not seem to be working, experiment with different types of definitions and multiple definitions. Formal definitions are the most common, but a formal definition may not suit your purpose or your audience's disposition.

✓ The definitions of most words or familiar phrases are a complex of thoughts, sentiments, and emotions. For example, "taxes" would seem to be a well-defined word. However, some see taxes as a wasteful inhibitor of innovation, while others see them as an expression of civic and patriotic duty. When definitions fail to persuade, typically it is because the author focused on a single part or nuance of the idea or word he or she is writing about and forgot other important, widely recognized meanings. Before you revise, map out all the reasonable meanings your audience may have for a word or idea, and then think about how your redefinition responds to your audience's current thinking.

CHAPTER 11
NARRATING

Discussing his film *The Imitation Game*, actor Benedict Cumberbatch was asked if he had ever witnessed the type of homophobia suffered by the film's protagonist, Alan Turing, the brilliant British mathematician who designed one of the first computers. Cumberbatch replied that "there was incredible homophobia at my school," and then he told a story that takes the reader back to 1994 and the Harrow boarding school in London.

> I was just finishing an essay in the school dining hall at breakfast, and I looked out the window and heard a commotion, a pair of feet scampering by, and then a horde just charging after shouting, "Wankers! Faggots!" and I thought, "What... is going on?" I asked these kids coming back from the house who were breathless from the hunt, "What are you doing, you insane idiots?"... They explained it, and I said, "And you're a Sikh, you're Jewish, and you're from Kenya. Do you want to just sit down and talk about the strife that your people have suffered because of your religion, race, creed, or color? I mean,... You've really got to wake up to the fact that the world is full of disgusting prejudice because we are all different from one another."

Cumberbatch could have stopped after his initial response, but he went on to tell a story. Why? More to the point, why do we continue to read after the answer to the initial question is clear?

You already know the answer. If your eyes have ever glazed over while reading a textbook or you have ever nodded off as you reviewed a spreadsheet, but leaned in to hear better as someone tells a story, you know that narratives are compelling.

Reading Cumberbatch's story, you can almost hear the desperate footsteps through the window even though the danger and hatred of the moment are years and miles from you. If you have heard Cumberbatch speak, you can probably even imagine his voice dripping with disgust. And that was the point of the story in the interview, and the point of Cumberbatch reminding his fellow students of the prejudices toward their own groups. Without an emotional appeal in the form of a narrative that touches the reader, some points cannot be made nor arguments won.

If Cumberbatch had quoted statistics of attacks against gays, recounted the history of hate crimes, or told his classmates that their behavior was contrary to the honor code, no one would have been moved. The narrative creates an emotional connection and appeals to our capacity to empathize with the person hounded by a prejudiced group.

No other rhetorical device can elicit emotions as a narrative can. Narratives are the go-to for *pathos* appeals: using emotions to move the audience to believe the source, be persuaded by the message, and think or act as the message argues.

MODULE II-26

WHAT AUDIENCES EXPECT OF A NARRATIVE ARGUMENT

You tell stories and use narratives every day. Perhaps you told your friends a narrative to explain why your Friday night was the best ever, or you listened to narratives of how others selected their college or university to prepare yourself to make your own decision. Lawyers use narratives in opening and closing statements to organize evidence and testimony that might otherwise overwhelm or confuse the jury. A religious leader may use a simple parable, a brief story or narrative intended to teach or portray a moral lesson.

Narratives are powerful, yet they have limits when used as evidence for an argument. For example, a Yelp review detailing one person's experience with a rude waiter at a restaurant on one particular day is probably not an accurate representation of that waiter or restaurant. Because they usually cannot be generalized, narratives do not have the same persuasive power as verified facts, valid statistics, or the testimony of experts. The Responsible Sourcing box entitled "Narratives Are Not Proof" (pp. 212–13) explains the limits of narratives and sourcing errors that can happen when quoting or referencing research.

Nevertheless, a narrative can be highly persuasive. You can claim new knowledge as a result of the personal experience you narrate. Your detailed narrative can be proof of an event you saw or experienced. Finally, a narrative, even a fictional one, can illustrate and explain what has been proven or will be proven with reasoning and other forms of evidence.

Why Would I Need to Use a Narrative?

A **narrative** is a story or an account of events sequenced and structured in a meaningful way. Traditional narratives have a beginning, a middle where there is some kind of conflict, and an end where the conflict is resolved. A **narrative argument** uses a story—either a true account or a fictional story, or both—to persuade an audience of a position. Typically, the persuasive power of a narrative does not depend upon evidence, reasoning, or the expertise of the author or sources as do other arguments. The persuasive power of narratives is commonly based in their ability to appeal to, provoke, and direct the emotions and sentiments of the audience.

The purpose of a narrative argument may be to persuade the audience to change a previously held position, gain an insight from the narrative message, or be moved to take a stand or act.

In academic settings, brief narratives are often used at the beginning of an argument to help the audience grasp a complex situation or issue. In addition, narratives can make abstract facts and statistics concrete for readers. For example, the fact that there are 1.3 million victims of domestic violence each year is not very compelling. The story of how one victim survived domestic abuse thanks to her friends' intervention appeals to the audience's emotions, making the abstraction moving and persuasive. Sometimes the narrative itself is the point. For example, ethnographers gather and examine narratives systematically to better understand the cultures, customs, and values of different societies. Narratives are often required assignments in the sciences, business, and even engineering, in the form of, say, a field report, case study, or failure analysis.

As a student, you may be asked to describe past events and complex ideas, make dry evidence and reasoning come alive in the mind of your audience, or adopt an alternative perspective so you can anticipate future consequences and choices. In order to do so effectively, you'll need to invent, reach your audience, and establish authority using the elements of a persuasive narrative argument.

Inventing Using the Elements of a Narrative

To serve your persuasive purpose, your narrative should usually have the following elements. You can use these elements as invention tools by shaping and structuring them in different ways to build your narrative.

- **A protagonist—someone or something of interest**. A protagonist is a living (though not necessarily human) actor at the center of the story. The audience should be able to identify with the protagonist, with the protagonist's intentions or a difficulty the protagonist faces, or with the quality or virtue the protagonist represents.
- **A conflict—a reason to care**. The protagonist faces a conflict that usually consists of at least two options or two forces that push and pull. An **internal conflict** happens within the mind or thinking of an individual or a character. An **external conflict** is a struggle or dilemma caused by another person or by the situation an individual or a character finds himself or herself in.

  For example, Lin-Manuel Miranda weaves internal and external conflicts throughout the musical *Hamilton*. The lead character's internal conflict is trying to be more than what society allows a fatherless child to be. It is mirrored by the external conflict of the new nation trying to establish its independence among nations while recognizing that financial interdependence with previous enemies may make the nation stronger.
- **A progression—a reason to keep reading/listening**. A protagonist facing a conflict should move or progress toward some kind of resolution. Stories move or progress as characters talk and move through different settings, situations change, and events happen and are resolved. Different progressions change the message of a story.
- **Resolution—the payoff**. The traditional narrative moves from an introduction of the protagonist and setting, to the conflict, to the resolution of the conflict. The resolution is where the questions, challenges, and dilemmas the protagonist faces are answered, responded to, or simply understood differently than they were before.

In a successful narrative argument, the story cannot just entertain or offer escapism. It must have a point that persuades the audience to think, believe, or act differently. For this reason, a story that persuades must provide a payoff or resolution of the conflict in a way that moves readers or listeners to question their previous perspective and adopt a new one. For example, at the resolution of Benedict Cumberbatch's brief narrative, he makes the boys fresh from the hunt aware that the same kind of prejudice can make them the hunted.

Providing a Context for Your Audience

Imagine that you are riding a bus, and the person sitting next to you breaks into a story about eating a hotdog in the rain. Without some kind of introduction, explanation, or reason for the narrative, you may want to change seats. The following elements contextualize a narrative within an argument so that your reader knows what you are doing and why.

- **An introduction and a thesis** provide context and state your position. A narrative thesis can be **explicit** or clearly stated, or it can be implied or **implicit**—suggested but not directly stated. Some narrative arguments consist of just a thesis, a narrative, and a conclusion. Others are structured more like a traditional argument, with a thesis, evidence, and reasoning, in addition to the central narrative.
- **Perspective** identifies the author's relationship to the narrative and the events in the narrative. Early in your narrative argument, your reader should be able to identify your perspective. Your perspective must also support your argument. Finally, your perspective must remain consistent throughout the argument; otherwise your audience may become distracted. There are three common perspectives:

    1. **First-person perspective** uses the pronouns *I* or *me* and suggests that the narrative is yours and about you. Also, you can use *we* to encourage your audience to share your first-person perspective. In a narrative argument, a first-person perspective can enhance your authority because it is delivered as testimony.
    2. **Third-person perspective** uses pronouns like *she, he*, or *they*. Narrative arguments using the third-person perspective rely upon observation or records of past events and individuals. Your description of how another person feels or thinks will not carry the same weight as your own reactions to an event or a direct quotation or other documentation of the third party's reactions.
    3. **Second-person perspective** relies on pronouns like *you* and *your* and indicate that the narrative is the reader's. Necessarily, narrative arguments using this perspective are speculative or hypothetical.

- **A conclusion** can help you establish authority while reinforcing your argument. The answer to the "so what" question is the significance of the story and why your message or insight is important to the audience. Answering this question before your audience even thinks of it establishes your authority as a person offering an argument and not just telling random tales. If your audience can clearly see the significance of your narrative, they can project the lesson or insight of your narrative argument onto their own lives, experiences, or decision making.

Genres That Use Narration

Narratives are used in many types of arguments, and there are many genres of narrative argument. Below is a brief list of genres that use narrative arguments either frequently or primarily. They are found in academic settings and beyond.

- An **advertisement** may use a narrative to connect a quality or sentiment to the item or service advertised.
- A **how-to essay** can use a narrative with the second-person perspective to describe a procedure or practice.
- **Case studies** are narratives of events or situations that the writer analyzes to understand real-world problems and opportunities and develop effective responses.
- An **opinion piece** is a brief, journalistic argument in which the author tries to persuade the audience of his or her opinion.
- An **ethnographic essay** narrates the activities, situation, and cultural context of individuals and provides an anthropological analysis of the significance of the details that make up the narrative.
- A **personal narrative** is a self-told, true story of experiences and events that led to a new understanding or insight.

MODULE II-27

A NARRATIVE GENRE: OPINION PIECE

In the following opinion piece, *New York Times* columnist Nicholas Kristof looks at the issue of animal and livestock rights through the lens of his own experience growing up on a farm. Kristof wrote this in July 2008 in response to California proposition 2, the "Prevention of Farm Animal Cruelty Act." The proposition passed in November 2008, making it illegal in California to pen chickens or calves in a way that does not allow them to sit, stand, and move around.

A Farm Boy Reflects

In a world in which animal rights are gaining ground, barbecue season should make me feel guilty. My hunch is that in a century or two, our descendants will look back on our factory farms with uncomprehending revulsion. But in the meantime, I love a good burger.

Thesis

This comes up because the most important election this November that you've never heard of is a referendum on animal rights in California, the vanguard state for social movements. Proposition 2 would ban factory farms from raising chickens, calves or hogs in small pens or cages. — Significance

And it's part of a broader trend. Burger King announced last year that it would give preference to suppliers that treat animals better, and when a hamburger empire expostulates tenderly about the living conditions of cattle, you know public attitudes are changing. — Significance

Harvard Law School now offers a course on animal rights. Spain's Parliament has taken a first step in granting rights to apes, and Austrian activists are campaigning to have a chimpanzee declared a person. Among philosophers, a sophisticated literature of animals rights has emerged. — Significance

I'm a farm boy who grew up here in the hills outside Yamhill, Ore., raising sheep for my F.F.A. and 4-H projects. At various times, my family also raised modest numbers of pigs, cattle, goats, chickens and geese, although they were never tightly confined. — *Perspective: I (1st person)*

Our cattle, sheep, chickens and goats certainly had individual personalities, but not such interesting ones that it bothered me that they might end up in a stew. Pigs were more troubling because of their unforgettable characters and obvious intelligence. To this day, when tucking into a pork chop, I always feel as if it is my intellectual equal. — **Progression**

Then there were *the geese, the most admirable creatures I've ever met.* We raised Chinese white geese, a common breed, and they have distinctive personalities. *They mate for life and adhere to family values that would shame most of those who dine on them.* — *Conflict*

While one of our geese was sitting on her eggs, her gander would go out foraging for food—and if he found some delicacy, he would rush back to give it to his mate. Sometimes I would offer males a dish of corn to fatten them up—but it was impossible, for they would take it all home to their true loves. — **Progression**

Once a month or so, we would slaughter the geese. When I was 10 years old, my job was to lock the geese in the barn — **Progression**

and then rush and grab one. Then I would take it out and hold it by its wings on the chopping block while my Dad or someone else swung the ax.

The 150 geese knew that something dreadful was happening and would cower in a far corner of the barn, and run away in terror as I approached. Then I would grab one and carry it away as it screeched and struggled in my arms.

Progression

Very often, one goose would bravely step away from the panicked flock and walk tremulously toward me. It would be the mate of the one I had caught, male or female, and it would step right up to me, protesting pitifully. It would be frightened out of its wits, but still determined to stand with and comfort its lover.

Conflict

We eventually grew so impressed with our geese—they had virtually become family friends—that we gave the remaining ones to a local park. (Unfortunately, some entrepreneurial thief took advantage of their friendliness by kidnapping them all—just before the next Thanksgiving.)

Resolution

So, yes, I eat meat (even, hesitantly, goose). But I draw the line at animals being raised in cruel conditions. The law punishes teenage boys who tie up and abuse a stray cat. So why allow industrialists to run factory farms that keep pigs almost all their lives in tiny pens that are barely bigger than they are?

Thesis expanded

Defining what is cruel is, of course, extraordinarily difficult. But penning pigs or veal calves so tightly that they cannot turn around seems to cross that line.

Significance

More broadly, the tide of history is moving toward the protection of animal rights, and the brutal conditions in which they are sometimes now raised will eventually be banned. Someday, vegetarianism may even be the norm.

Thesis restated

Perhaps it seems like soggy sentimentality as well as hypocrisy to stand up for animal rights, particularly when I enjoy dining on these same animals. But my view was shaped by those days in the barn as a kid, scrambling after geese I gradually came to admire.

Relevance

So I'll enjoy the barbecues this summer, but I'll also know that every hamburger patty has a back story, and that every tin of goose liver pâté could tell its own rich tale of love and loyalty.

Conclusion

Questions to Consider

Invention

1. What prompted Kristof to use a narrative to persuade?
2. What invention process did Kristof probably use for his narrative argument?
3. What information and what events did Kristof leave out purposefully, and why do you think he made such decisions?

Audience

4. Being as specific as you can be, how would you describe the intended audience of this narrative argument?
5. Based on Kristof's argument, what specific opinions held by the intended audience is Kristof attempting to change?
6. If you were to cast the Kristof editorial as a 60-second film, how would the narrative begin and what would be the image that delivers the thesis?

Authority

7. What makes this narrative believable and relevant to the intended audience?
8. The title suggests that Kristof is a farm boy. Does his experience add to his authority and contribute to the persuasive power of his opinions? If not, why not?
9. Why does Kristof mention Yamhill, the F.F.A., and the 4-H, and what is the likelihood that readers of the *New York Times* fully understand the significance of these references?

MODULE II-28

A NARRATIVE GENRE: ADVERTISEMENT

The Guinness & Co. advertisement entitled "Empty Chair" begins as a woman opens a pub for the day. Setting up, she places a pint of Guinness on an empty table.

The beer remains untouched and the table vacant even when the bar is crowded. The scene is repeated, indicating that placing the beer is part of the routine of the bar.

Finally, a military man carrying a duffle steps in, looks at the table, the beer, and bartender. As he picks up the beer, the other patrons lift their pints to toast his return.

During the commercial (which is available at youtube.com), the only words spoken are those of a narrator at the end. "The choices we make reveal the true nature of our character." The images, however, expand on this explicit thesis with an implied thesis—Guinness is such a fine beer that one can use it to remember, honor, and welcome home a friend.

Questions to Consider

Invention

1. Working backwards from the finished commercial, try to imagine the invention process that led to the Guinness narrative.
2. Advertisements are always brief, yet some detail is included while some is left out. What information is missing and why?
3. Try a different narrative using a different protagonist than a soldier. What message are you left with?

Audience

4. Being as specific as you can be, how would you describe the intended audience of this narrative?
5. If you had to write out the Guinness advertisement in words, what kind of narrative and perspective would you use to persuade the same intended audience of the same thesis?
6. If you were to cast the Guinness advertisement as a 60-second radio commercial, how would the narrative begin? What sounds and whose voice(s) would be heard, and what words would deliver the message?

Authority

7. What makes this narrative believable? What makes it easy to relate to?
8. Watch the Guinness advertisement online. How do the use of color, background music, and the placement of the narrator's words build trust?
9. The thesis is not directly stated. How do the producers of the ad make sure you get the right message?

MODULE II-29

A NARRATIVE GENRE: PERSONAL NARRATIVE

In her composition course, Kelly Hu was asked to write a personal narrative paper about an unexpected lesson she learned. Drawing on her own experience, she wrote the following narrative argument.

Kelly Hu
College Writing
December 9, 2011

Game, Set, Match

The 2009 Roxy tournament was the most important tennis tournament I had played that year. If I did well, my ranking would move high enough for me to be considered for tennis scholarships. Things did not go as planned—planned for me by my father and my coach. However, during the match that was to be the last I have played, I learned that sometimes your impulses speak for you when you can't and make decisions for you when you must.

Perspective: I (1st person)

Thesis

Years earlier, sixth grade was the best year of my life in terms of my tennis career. **I represented Jack Kramer Club's junior tennis team in the South Bay League. Through the course of two years, I became the number one singles player and played an undefeated season. On Fridays, Anna, my best friend since second grade, and I would play practice matches after school. We went to different middle schools, but Fridays were our days to play tennis with each other, and it had been that way since the first time we played against each other in second grade. I was always really proud of myself for beating Anna because her dad was a professional tennis player and hit with her every day. But I didn't care whether or not I beat her every time because she was my best friend, and I just wanted to play as much as possible.**

Protagonist's background

Things changed in seventh grade, when my undefeated career came to an end and I experienced a quick and drastic change in my life. I lost my first match. It was the worst loss I ever experienced because of the sheer embarrassment of losing to an arrogant girl three years younger than I. I told myself I was just having a bad day, but regardless, the match seriously damaged my ego. Since that moment, my confidence was never the same and I eventually lost almost all of my sense of self-belief.

Conflict

Though my life never solely revolved around tennis, **I used my success in the sport as a way to measure and define my**

Relevance

value in the world. *After my loss, I couldn't have felt any more hurt. But then Anna told me that she couldn't hit with me on Fridays. I was even more devastated when I later saw her hitting with another girl on Fridays. From then on, I started associating my ability to win with my ability to be loved.* — *Conflict*

Part of me pictured how different my life would be if I didn't have to stress about playing in competitions and winning my matches, but I forced myself to snap out of it and think about how angry Mom and Dad would be and how disappointed my Coach would be if I admitted that I'm not sure if I still want to play competitive tennis. I just kept playing. — **Progression**

I finally acknowledged that I didn't want to be a competitive tennis player when I was a freshman. It was difficult, but I could no longer avoid admitting that I just don't have the competitive drive, natural confidence, and strong sense of self-belief to be a successful player. *There were countless times when I wanted to tell my parents that I needed a break from tennis and that I didn't want to play so competitively anymore. But I could never find the courage to say it to their faces. I kept wondering, "Would they think of me as a quitter if I told them that I wanted to stop playing tournaments? What if they get mad at me, or worse: disappointed?" It was a prolonged and continuous struggle to come up with how I should break the news to my parents and my Coach. I would have never guessed that my actions would speak for me.* — *Conflict*

During the most important match of my life, I knew I couldn't torture myself anymore. For two years I had contemplated how I would tell my parents that I'm not a born tennis competitor, but I always chickened out of telling them the truth. I had to think fast. My opponent tossed up the tennis ball and served it to my side. As an act of impulse, I hit the ball out of the boundaries. The umpire called, "Game, set, and match." — **Resolution** *My game had always spoken for me.* **How I played had been the foundation of who I was and who I would be—and it did so again.** — **Significance** *I didn't look at Dad or Coach this time. I just walked to the net, shook my opponent's hand, and smiled.* — *Conclusion*

Questions to Consider

Invention

1. Hu was required to write a personal narrative, but how do you think she discovered the deeper meaning and the resolution of this story? Did she know it at the time or did she recover it? What invention strategy is best for recovering memories? Which invention strategies help you see things differently?
2. What information and what events did Hu leave out purposefully, and why do you think she made such decisions?
3. Hu tells us her position—the message of the narrative—at the end. If she had not done so, what message or position might a reader infer from the narrative alone?

Audience

4. If the intended audience were parents or readers of parenting magazines, how would Hu have to change the essay?
5. Personal narratives written in academic settings can be tricky. What type of narratives, messages, and positions are appropriate for this situation, and what kinds would be inappropriate?
6. How could the introduction be rewritten to make the message more explicit or more directly stated? Would that be a good choice given the intended audience? Why or why not?

Authority

7. What makes this narrative believable?
8. Which parts of the narrative support Hu's conclusions, and are there any parts that do not support her conclusions?
9. How would the persuasive power of this narrative argument be different if Hu had told us that the events happened to a friend?

MODULE II-30

BUILDING A NARRATIVE ARGUMENT

Narratives are versatile, and an interesting one can be very entertaining. For this reason, many people assume that narratives are easier to write than formal arguments. In fact, persuasive narrative arguments require all the careful development that any other type of argument requires.

The following checklist and guidelines will help you to build a narrative argument. As always, your writing process is unique and can change with every argument you write. The checklist is a guide; it is not the only way to draft a narrative argument that is relevant, authoritative, and persuasive.

Invention

- Define your narrative subject

✓ If you have been assigned a narrative argument, it is unlikely you have been given a specific narrative that you must use. Instead, you have likely been assigned a general issue that you must personalize, such as "a dispute in your community" or "a moment that shaped your identity." Such assignments ask you to draw from your own experience and memory—the raw materials of your narrative argument.

In addition to your own experiences, you can also build persuasive narrative arguments by narrating the activities, successes, and failures of others that you have witnessed or know well. For this reason, looking around, recalling events with family and friends, and interviewing people you know can be a great source of narratives that persuade. See the Breaking the Block box entitled "Recall Your Narrative Map."

✓ Research will give you ideas, subjects, and structures.

If Lin-Manuel Miranda had not picked up a biography of Alexander Hamilton, he would not have researched Hamilton's personal letters. If he had not read Hamilton's letters, he would not have visited Weehawken, New Jersey, where Aaron Burr shot Hamilton in 1804. And if Miranda had not visited the site where the two old friends, both orphans, turned guns on each other, he would not have been able to write the song, "Aaron Burr, Sir," that introduces the Hamilton–Burr relationship that was so central to the evolution of the United States. Each bit of research provided details necessary to build a persuasive narrative.

✓ It is easy to mistake an anecdote for a persuasive narrative. However, anecdotes are not insightful. An anecdote is a brief retelling of an event that happened to the teller. It may describe a conflict, but it simply ends without resolution. A narrative argument, on the other hand, uses a narrative to illustrate a specific insight.

- Draft a working thesis

✓ Use a draft thesis to explain the relevance and significance of your narrative.

A draft thesis can also provide material for an introduction or a conclusion. For example, in an earlier draft of her personal narrative about an unexpected lesson, Kelly Hu's draft thesis looked like this:

> I couldn't make the decision to stop playing competitive tennis, but during the tournament, my desire to quit came out in my play. I learned I needed to define my own value and success and not let others or fear determine who I am.

Her final thesis is different, but the draft thesis helped her develop a conclusion.

Breaking the Block
Recall Your Narrative Map

Often, a narrative argument begins with a memory. This exercise will help you recover significant events that can serve as the raw material for a narrative argument. The listing and writing part of this exercise should take 15 minutes.

Step One
Recall a location where you have spent a large amount of time. It could be your high school, a workplace, a community center, a relative's or friend's home, or the family business. Draw a detailed, bird's-eye view of the location. Draw it not as it is now, but as you remember it.

Step Two
Annotate your map. The following sample questions can help:

- Where was the safe place you ran to when you were in trouble?
- Where did you go to meet friends or be seen?
- Where did you do something you still regret?
- What place smelled the best and what did it smell like?
- What place smelled bad and why?
- Where did the hero of the community live?
- Where did your enemy live?
- Where did you get your first kiss?
- Where was there always music?
- Where was your worst fight?
- Where was your greatest achievement?

Step Three
Select one place on your map. Close your eyes and put yourself there in your mind. Try to remember what you usually thought and felt in that place. Imagine what you would do if you could go back. Open your eyes and write for 10 minutes as fast as you can. Do not worry about errors or slow down to make corrections. Then set your writing aside for at least a day.

Step Four
Look at what you have written and identify thoughts that surprise you, ideas that are unusually meaningful, or changes in perspective you did not expect. You may not find deep insights, and don't be disappointed if nothing jumps out at you right away. What you have is a map of memories and the building blocks of a narrative argument. Pick a story or idea from your writing, or one from the map, and continue to explore and flesh it out.

Audience

- Understand the rhetorical situation

✓ If you are writing in an academic setting, you will need to explore the rhetorical situation of the assignment. Necessarily, many disciplines use the term "narrative" differently.

For example, a historical narrative often relates events that occurred in a region or nation, and a case study explores the experiences of an individual or a business. Be sure you understand the type of narrative you are being asked to write and how your professor expects you to build and use narrative in your argument.

✓ The context of any academic assignment is usually the readings and lectures of the course. The readings for the course will usually provide a great many clues to the types of narrative argument your professor expects of you.

For example, an anthropology professor will have you read ethnographic narratives about the experiences of ethnic groups. If you are assigned to write such a narrative, the readings will show you how to gather information and how to shape it to meet the professor's expectations.

✓ Your narrative and your thesis should be proportional to each other and reflect audience expectations. For an opinion piece about animal rights, New York Times columnist Nicholas Kristof could have provided a detailed account of horrors in the meatpacking industry. However, such a lengthy discussion would have overwhelmed his thesis.

- Discover your audience's interests

✓ With your purpose in mind, research the interests, likes, and dislikes of your intended audience, as well as their disposition not only toward your argument but also toward the subject of your narrative.

The purpose of the beer ad was to sell more beer. To achieve such purposes, advertising companies do extensive audience research and test their ads with focus groups. The makers of the beer ad determined that their audience is moved by patriotic stories.

✓ The persuasive power of your argument will depend upon the significance your audience finds in your narrative. If your readers can imagine themselves in the protagonist's position or if they can imagine confronting the same conflict, they are more likely to agree with the thesis of your narrative argument. If you research your audience, you can make an educated guess about the audience's ability to identify with the subject of your narrative.

✓ Insights that contradict conventional wisdom are often memorable. Readers might expect Kelly Hu's personal narrative to be about winning her tournament or at least soldiering on and rediscovering her love of tennis. Another typical ending would have her discussing her decision with her father and coach. Readers probably don't expect the insight that an instinctive swing of a racket and an intentional loss can be a statement of independence and self-discovery that speaks louder than words. Then again, if you are talking to tennis players, they may not find such a narrative as insightful. Research your audience just as you research your subject.

- Organize your argument

✓ There are a number of ways of organizing a narrative, each with different benefits.

  - **Chronological narratives**, arranged as the events happened in time, allow you to develop a story from beginning to end. This is a traditional form of storytelling, easily recognized and understood.
  - **Fractured narratives**, such as those with flashbacks, bounce around in time to focus on a specific event or idea from many different angles or perspectives. These narratives can be confusing if the reader does not understand why jumps in time are necessary.
  - **Thematic narratives** draw together experiences and memories of different times that are related to the theme. In his opinion piece about animal rights, Nicholas Kristof structures his reflections around the theme of the dignity and sacrifice of the geese raised on his family farm.
  - **Multiple narratives** about different subjects, all of them supporting your main argument or thesis, can also provide multiple perspectives and be persuasive.

✓ The structure of your argument should be shaped by your purpose and message. If your purpose is to share a personal insight, you can focus on the narrative itself and imply your thesis. If you are trying to persuade your audience to accept an idea, belief, or behavior that is new to them, your thesis may have to be more explicit.

- Draft your argument

✓ A great story is not necessarily a persuasive narrative. Remember that the narrative must serve the argument, not just entertain. As you write your first draft, keep your working thesis in mind. Doing so will help you construct a narrative that supports or demonstrates your argument.
✓ Make sure your evidence and narrative are related and support your thesis.
✓ If you are arguing for a new perspective on a historical event, historical accounts and eyewitness testimony will be most persuasive. If you are trying to persuade an audience that an outcome will happen or should happen, or that a specific course of action should be followed, statistics and facts about similar scenarios or narrated events can be persuasive.

Responsible Sourcing
How to Use a Narrative in an Argument

Narrative arguments are most effective if you already have the audience's trust. This is why the bar is much higher for persuasive narratives than for entertaining ones. Remember, narratives are not anecdotes. If you are not sure which you are writing, check the note below.

When using a narrative, you have choices:

1. Use a true narrative or make one up.
2. Use your experience or another's experience.
3. Make the position or message of the narrative explicit or implicit.
4. Use a narrative to introduce a position or message or use a narrative to demonstrate or explain a position or message already introduced.

A made-up narrative can explain an idea or a concept as a parable does. However, be sure that your reader does not misunderstand a made-up narrative as true, especially if it contains some true or historical elements.

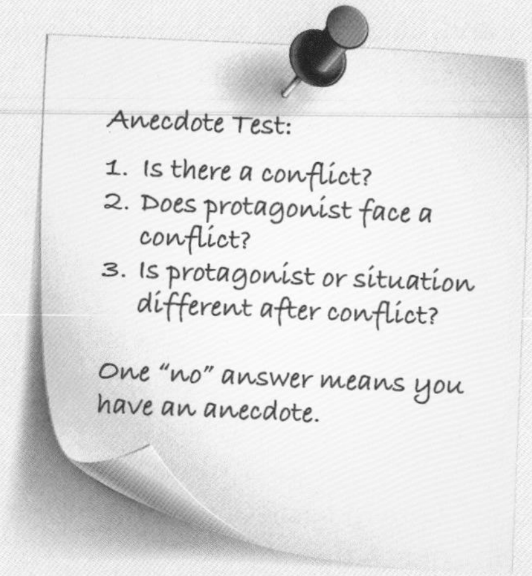

Anecdote Test:
1. Is there a conflict?
2. Does protagonist face a conflict?
3. Is protagonist or situation different after conflict?
One "no" answer means you have an anecdote.

A true narrative based upon real experiences and events can be used like testimony or an eyewitness account. If you are providing a narrative told by someone else or narrating another person's experience, you must treat the narrative as a source. This means

- introduce the source of the narrative clearly,
- quote, summarize, or paraphrase the narrative accurately,
- cite the source of the information correctly.

Remember, narratives alone are not proof, and you should not ask your audience to generalize from a single narrated event or experience. However, narratives can be the perfect tool for making complex ideas or concepts easier to grasp.

Authority

- Check believability and logic

✓ A narrative argument can be based on a fictional narrative or an age-old parable, but it must be believable and logical. If you are drafting a real or realistic narrative, avoid speculative details, distracting descriptions, and illogical leaps.

✓ In fiction, the reader's or listener's freedom to interpret can make a story richer. However, if an argument is to be persuasive, there can be no confusion about the significance of your narrative.

For example, have you ever watched a commercial and afterwards wondered what the advertiser is selling? Such ambiguity is not only a relevance problem; it makes it impossible for the viewer or reader to connect any insight they may derive from the narrative with the argument. Authority arises from the significance of the insight your reader finds in the narrative. Make sure they find what you want them to find.

- Make it flow

✓ In an academic setting, "flow" commonly refers to how an argument or essay hangs together and moves the reader or listener from one point to the next. One way to think about flow is to use a concept common to television and movie production—the through line. A through line holds a script together and drives the action forward. In terms of writing, a through line holds all the paragraphs in an argument together in a specific way. For example, Kelly Hu's through line is also her thesis:

> sometimes your impulses speak for you when you can't and make decisions for you when you must.

As she pulled the parts of her narrative argument together, she needed to make sure her audience would understand the line that connects Fridays with Anna, the 2009 Roxy tournament, and her fear of angering her father. She linked these parts together, as well as the sentences and paragraphs that made up the story, using transitions ("years earlier," "from then on"), references to previous parts of the narrative ("after my loss"), and direct statements ("It was the worst loss I ever experienced..."). Hu guided her readers to follow the through line even though they did not know specifically what it was. When you direct your audience in this way, they will experience flow, and when you don't, they will go their own way.

✓ Transitions, like road signs, help the reader or listener link ideas that may be separated by many paragraphs or pages.

For example, just after Kelly Hu describes the conflict of not knowing how to tell her parents and coach that she wanted to quit tennis, she has the following transition sentence:

> I would have never guessed that my actions would speak for me.

Hu's next paragraph then dramatically describes how she expressed her decision to quit by intentionally hitting the ball out of bounds. Transitions in narrative arguments are very important because the narrative can take up a large portion of the paper, and you may need to remind your reader of the through line connecting a point you made early in the argument to a point made near the end.

- Get peer response

✓ Ask your peers to look over your argument and identify the following:
  - If the thesis is directly stated, please identify it. If the thesis is implied, please summarize it.
  - What do you think is the point of the narrative and the insight that can be drawn from it?
  - Is the narrative too big for the thesis, or does the thesis make claims not supported or explained by the narrative? Please explain.
  - How is the narrative used? To explain a complex idea? Dramatize a point? Describe an event or experience?
  - If the narrative is true, what makes it believable?
  - How would you describe the through line that holds the elements and details of the narrative together?
  - Is the insight of the narrative too vague, obvious, or confusing? What makes you think so?

- Revise your argument

✓ Revision is re-seeing. Rely on the responses of your peers or professor to help you see your narrative argument through the eyes of your audience.

✓ Revision also continues the process of invention. You may have started with a true narrative but later find that it does not help the reader achieve the insight you had hoped for. Perhaps another person's experiences, a myth or story from literature, or an invented narrative would work better. Always cite narratives you find elsewhere or take from previous readings.

✓ Stories take many forms. A chronological ordering may be how you remember something, but perhaps a thematic ordering of events, or starting with the ending, would suit your argument better. Revision is a chance to re-see, re-invent, and re-shape to make the most persuasive argument possible.

CHAPTER 12

ANALYZING AND EVALUATING

You may think that professional snowboarders have a great life—that they don't have to sit in class and write papers, and the only thing they have to analyze and evaluate is the brand of beer to choose and the best hot-tub temperature to set at the end of the day. However, snowboarders who plan to have substantial pro careers do need to use analysis and evaluation. From the top of the slope, a jump may look small, but before successful snowboarders head down the ramp, they need to analyze it carefully. They need to analyze the ramp trajectory speed (RTS) and evaluate the equivalent fall height (EFH) and landing angle.

Otherwise, the three-foot deck drop, combined with a modest RTS of 50 feet per second, can send a snowboarder way out over the landing to a painful spill on the hard, flat run-out.

Analysis and evaluation are common forms of argument that shape many different genres. In addition to scientific and technical tasks, such as determining the safety of a snowboarding ramp, analysis and evaluation are common in many academic fields.

For instance, your professor may ask you to analyze and evaluate different marketing strategies, the camera angles in a scene from a movie, or the psychological motivations of Iago and Othello. Analysis and evaluation should be nothing new to you, though, because you do these tasks every day when

- Amazon asks you to review the DSL camera you just purchased,
- your professor requires a literature review,
- your boss asks you to develop a report that explains last year's sales, or
- you assess players to add to your fantasy league team.

MODULE II-31

WHAT AUDIENCES EXPECT OF AN ANALYSIS AND EVALUATION

Although analysis and evaluation are two separate activities, and can be separate forms of writing, evaluation depends upon analysis, and analyses usually conclude with an assessment or evaluation of their subject.

- When you write an **analysis**, you examine a complex item, idea, or event by looking at its parts and considering how the parts work together. A rhetorical analysis, a common assignment in college and university courses, is the focus of Chapter 8.
- When you write an **evaluation**, you provide an assessment or judgment about the subject of your analysis. To make an assessment, you use standards of judgment, or **criteria**, to evaluate how the parts work together and comprise the larger item, idea, or event.

Genres such as movie reviews and customer reviews found on sites like Amazon and Yelp are all shaped by analysis and evaluation. As a student, you may be asked to analyze a work of literature and write a literary analysis. Or you may be asked to analyze a company's financial data and then evaluate its business plan. Professors of every discipline analyze and evaluate, and they will ask you to do the same. An analysis is sometimes all that is necessary for the assignment or writing situation, but in this chapter it is treated as an essential part of evaluation.

Why Would I Need to Analyze and Evaluate?

Three types of assignments or situations typically call for an analysis and evaluation: an assignment that asks you to explore an item, idea, or event; an assignment that requires you to demonstrate authority and competency; and an assignment that asks you to educate or inform an audience.

Exploring items, ideas, and events is what people who work at universities, research centers, intelligence agencies, and even some corporations do. Students are often asked to practice analysis and evaluation so that they can explore a subject on their own as opposed to simply being told what to think about it.

In a meteorology class, for example, you might be given a map that looks like a hairy United States and asked to do an analysis and evaluation to determine the best location for a wind turbine farm. The map in Figure 12.1 is an analysis of the speed and direction of prevailing winds on a given day. Using this analysis and a criterion, such as the wind speed necessary to generate 10 kilowatts of power, you could evaluate different possible locations and decide on the best place to locate a wind turbine.

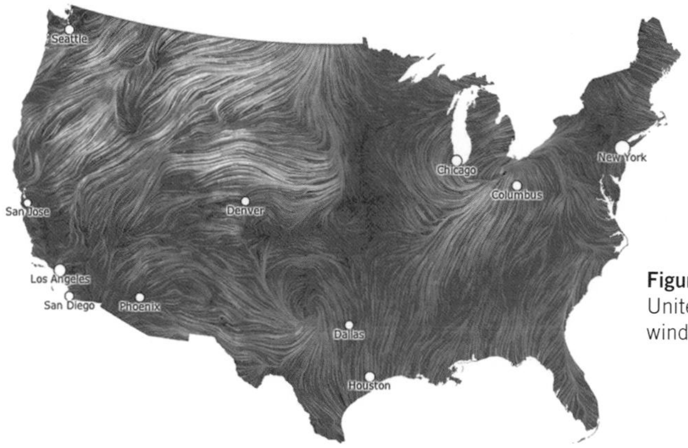

Figure 12.1 United States wind map.

Demonstrating authority and competency can be important for persuading your instructor that you have mastered your subject, which will in turn help you achieve a good grade. For example, in an engineering lab, you could be asked to explain why manhole covers are round and to prove your reasoning. To answer the question, you would need to conduct an analysis and evaluation by: 1) analyzing round manhole covers, their purpose, and the purpose of the holes they cover; 2) developing criteria that you can use to see if other shapes might better meet these purposes; and 3) evaluating the other shapes to see if they meet your criteria. The question isn't really about your knowledge of manhole covers, though, but about your ability to analyze and evaluate solutions to problems as an engineer would.

Educating or informing an audience is another reason people analyze and evaluate subjects. Because this type of argument breaks complex subjects into parts and then examines the parts and how they work together, analysis and evaluation is also an excellent teaching tool. In an economics class, for example, a group assignment might call for your team to analyze the fuel burned per mile for a person traveling by plane and again by train. With this information, your team could then evaluate the carbon footprint, dollar cost, and other effects of both types of travel. For your class presentation, you would present your criteria, analysis, and evaluation so your audience can understand how you came to your findings. In this way, you would show your audience how an everyday decision can lead to costs of all kinds, both obvious and not-so-obvious.

A writer can shape an analysis and evaluation argument in many ways. However, an effective analysis and evaluation emerges from thoughtful invention and research, is attentive to the audience and their disposition, and has the authority not only to sound reasonable but also to have persuasive force.

Beginning Your Analysis with Invention and Research

Focus, scope, and discovery are the elements of an analysis and evaluation that set the direction of your analysis and keep you on track.

- Focus: The subject of your analysis is its focus. For example, a consumer review of the iPad mini focuses on the smaller version of Apple's popular iPad. A thoughtful invention process will help you identify and refine your focus.
- Scope: During the invention process, looking at other items, ideas, or events similar to your focus will help you analyze your subject. To analyze the iPad mini, for example, you would look at similar 7-inch electronic tablets. These tablets are your scope. If the members of your audience are thinking about buying a tablet, you would not include desktop computers in your analysis, but you might include regular tablets. If you decide to talk about an iPad in terms of a desktop, however, you'll need to make it clear to your audience why you chose such a large scope—with seemingly unrelated items—for your analysis.
- Discovery: In an analysis, the writer locates and names significant elements, traits, patterns, and strategies that make up the thing, idea, or event that is the focus. An analysis of the iPad mini's processor speed, battery life, and display quality will lead to specific data and findings you can use to compare it with the other tablets within your scope.

Shaping Your Analysis and Evaluation to Meet Audience Expectations

A chef looking at reviews of knives may be looking for durability and sharpness and may not care if a meat cleaver was forged at a foundry that uses renewable energy, just as someone reading a Yelp review of a farmer's market may be looking for one committed to the use of renewables and sustainable farming methods rather than a particular kind of vegetable or fruit. In other words, to write an effective, interesting analysis, you need a specific audience, and you need to know their disposition and expectations.

- Criteria: The criteria consist of the values, standards, or metrics you use to judge the evidence for your evaluation. The criteria you use to analyze and evaluate a subject should be shaped by
  - similar items, ideas, or events within your scope,
  - your purpose and your audience's expectations, and
  - the time and resources you have to analyze and evaluate.

Any item, idea, or event can be valued or measured in an astounding number of ways. For example, if the focus of your analysis and evaluation is Girl Scout Cookies, you could look at the energy used to produce a box of cookies. Or you could analyze and evaluate how the human body metabolizes a Thin Mint. As you can see, you have a great deal of creative freedom when deciding upon the criteria of your analysis and evaluation. Once you have determined your criteria, the evidence you will discover as you apply it will shape your argument.

In fact, your criteria will determine the evidence you use—and the evidence you exclude—in your argument. For example, if your criteria include measures such as tastiness, crispness, and sweetness, you will be arguing about the flavor and mouth feel of the cookies. If, however, your criteria are based on industrial baking practices, packaging technology, and shipping logistics, you will not be talking about the yummy goodness of Thin Mints. The argument you will be making with the latter criteria is based on the quality and efficiency of the industrial food-processing bakeries that hold the Girl Scout Cookie license.

When you are trying to narrow down the large number of possible values, standards, or metrics you could use to evaluate your subject, you must think of your purpose and the members of your audience, their expectations, needs, and disposition. Your audience may not care about the marketing of Girl Scout Cookies, only their flavor. An audience of marketing professionals, though, might feel differently. An evaluation of the iPad mini without a price comparison may not be of much use to a consumer. An app developer, on the other hand, may not care about price but needs an analysis and evaluation of the processor speed and memory capacity. If your purpose is to help parents select the best tablet for a seven-year-old, other metrics such as durability may be more important.

Module II-35 provides a brief checklist that will help you identify and narrow down your criteria.

- Evidence: Your review of the criteria you used to analyze your subject will generate evidence for an evaluation. The analysis of the iPad mini, for example, provides evidence about its processor speed, display resolution, and battery life.

Making Your Assessment Persuasive by Establishing Authority

Your criteria may be composed of relevant metrics and your focus may be clear and relevant to your audience. However, for your readers to accept your analysis and evaluation, they must recognize your authority. And authority is determined by the reasoning and logic of your assessment. An assessment often describes the relationship between the subject analyzed and the broader scope into which it fits, and may look like this: "The iPad mini is best in its class of sub 8 inch tablets, and is a standout in terms of battery life. Its higher price, however, sets it apart from similar tablets." Or if you are writing an analysis of gourmet cookies for readers of a cooking and food magazine, and your criteria do not include flavor, your readers may question your reasoning. In addition, if the scope of your criteria is flavor and mouth feel, but your assessment focuses on packaging, a reader will have good reason to question how you came to your conclusions.

Genres That Analyze and Evaluate

The basic elements of an analysis and evaluation are always the same. However, each genre that analyzes and evaluates presents these elements differently. For example, a person's life history would be treated differently in a biography than it would be in a eulogy written for the family and friends attending a memorial service. The audience for a biography expects a detailed account of the subject's life and a dispassionate analysis and evaluation of their achievements, setbacks, and relationships. A eulogy may also analyze and evaluate, but it will commonly focus on positive personal qualities and achievements as recalled by those that loved and admired the deceased. Among the many genres that call for analysis and evaluation are the following:

- A **review of a cultural product such as a film, a television series, or a popular song** examines a specific work using qualities and traits found in similar, successful works of that genre. The reviewer then comments on the achievement of the work based on the criteria.
- **Image reviews** are used to identify common, innovative, and effective traits or qualities of images, as well as abnormalities and errors. A medical technician can evaluate an image to diagnose illnesses, for example.
- A **cost-benefit analysis** analyzes a plan or potential opportunity like a contract. The criteria are typically limited to financial or market-share metrics. Business and government groups use this genre of analysis to compare the impact of different business or policy options.
- A **literary analysis** considers the literary techniques that are evident within a poem or novel, for example, and evaluates how the techniques work to make a distinct, meaningful expression of the genre. Unlike a review, which indicates whether a book is worth reading, a literary analysis starts from the premise that the work is worthy of careful attention.

- A **product review** in a consumer publication is an application of criteria composed of practical metrics that are of concern to a consumer. A product review typically analyzes and evaluates a specific make or model of an item and then compares it to other makes and models, which are analyzed using the same criteria.

MODULE II-32

AN ANALYSIS AND EVALUATION GENRE: BLOG ENTRY: THRILL-RIDE REVIEW

The attached is one of many articles by Joel Bullock found on *The Coaster Critic*, a website that specializes in theme park and thrill-ride reviews, news, and tips. Bullock started the site in 2006 because he was frustrated with the poor quality of the reviews he found on other sites, and he wanted to blend his passion for rollercoasters and writing.

World-Class Woodie Puts Dollywood on the Map

By Joel Bullock

By some random chain of events my family decided to take a summer vacation in Tennessee. This gave me the opportunity to stop at Dollywood on our way back home. I had heard a lot about **Thunderhead, the 2004 GCI wooden coaster** that topped many enthusiast's Top 10 lists. Also, Thunderhead had been awarded the Golden Ticket Award for the best **Wooden Coaster in the World**. Needless to say, I was expecting an amazing ride and for the most part I wasn't disappointed. Thunderhead's location *in the mountainous park was very scenic. The Timber Tower had just opened next to the ride and the area had several "back-country" themed buildings in the newest section in Dollywood known as Thunderhead Gap.* As my wife and I approached the queue I noticed the Golden Ticket signage under the main sign. It was good to see that Dolly and her park management weren't clueless about the success of the ride.

Focus—Thunderhead at Dollywood

Scope—Wooden coasters in the world

Criteria—location

Evidence concerning location

As we entered the station I noticed that the trains *were millennium flyers. They were padded with leather and the lead car was themed. The* ride op *had personality, which is always a big plus in my book. She sent every train out of the station with "Let the thunder rollllllll!!!!!"* **An excited station is high on my list of what makes a world-class coaster and so far Thunderhead was doing great.** If the ride op wasn't enough to get people in the queue excited, *then the unique station fly through did. At about midway through the coaster's twisted course, the trains curve back around the queue and fly through the station. The roaring train every few minutes kept the waiting riders anticipating their ride.* Nice touch GCI!

Finally, we board the comfortable trains and were lifted up the modest 100 foot lift hill. The swooping drop led to a banked twisting turn and then another and so on. Thunderhead's twister layout offered some great lateral G-forces *and a seemingly fast, but pretty smooth, ride. There were a few nice pops of* airtime *and the station fly through had a great head chopper effect. After returning to the station, the train was packed with smiles and laughs. Thanks to its unabusive* ride, my wife and I decided to immediately ride it again.

Why only an 8.5? **I just don't think it did anything all that amazing. It was a great ride and the overall experience was fast, fun, and smooth. I didn't walk away with any big 'wow moments' or legendary launches of airtime. Also, it was just more fun than thrilling.** The majority of my highest rated coasters are thrilling and really get the adrenaline pumping. Not to take anything away from Thunderhead, it's definitely a crowd pleaser. It's great that a smaller park like Dollywood can boast one of the top **wooden coasters in the world,** probably for years to come. The park may have quite a one-two punch if Mystery Mine turns out to be a winner. **Final Rating 8.5—(Great Approaching Excellent).**

Evidence of ride comfort

Criteria—station environment

Assessment

Evidence of station environment

Evidence of ride G-forces and comfort

Criteria—G-forces and airtime

Criteria—ride comfort

Assessment

Scope—Wooden coasters in the world

Assessment summary

Questions to Consider

Invention

1. What prompted Bullock to start a blog called *The Coaster Critic* and to write about this rollercoaster in particular?
2. It must be difficult taking notes on a coaster. How do you think Bullock gathered ideas, information, and evidence for his analysis and evaluation?
3. What did he discover about his subject?
4. What do you think is the source of the evidence Bullock uses to build his analysis and evaluation? Time at the park? Other sources of information? Explain.

Audience

5. What restrictions or limits did Bullock have to work with, and what expectations do you think he was responding to?
6. How does Bullock's writing differ from academic writing?
7. Which aspects of Bullock's writing are appropriate for an academic analysis and evaluation and which are not?
8. Who is Bullock writing to, and how do you know?

Authority

9. How does Bullock let the reader know that what he has discovered about the ride and what he says about it can be trusted?
10. What has Bullock left out of his review, and why do you think he left it out?
11. What is your overall opinion of Bullock's review? How would you make his review stronger and more persuasive?

MODULE II-33

AN ANALYSIS AND EVALUATION GENRE: ONLINE RESTAURANT REVIEW

Online reviews are not only popular but also prevalent. You can find reviews of nearly any item you might purchase online, whether it be from Amazon, Home Depot, or another Web-based retailer. And after you make a purchase or use a service, you are often asked to write a review.

The crowd-sourced reviews found on the website Yelp are intended to provide helpful tips to other consumers. Yelp contributors offer reviews of many types of business and activities, including restaurants, hotels, bars, auto-repair shops, and so on. As you will see in the following review posted by Anthony Sasso, Yelp reviewers often use the elements of an analysis and evaluation.

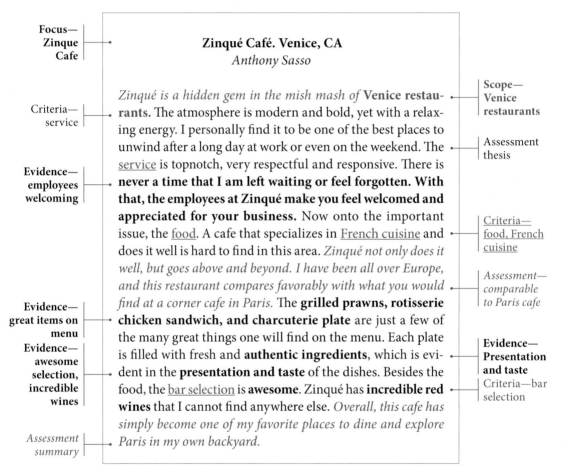

Zinqué Café. Venice, CA

Anthony Sasso

Zinqué is a hidden gem in the mish mash of **Venice restaurants.** The atmosphere is modern and bold, yet with a relaxing energy. I personally find it to be one of the best places to unwind after a long day at work or even on the weekend. The service is topnotch, very respectful and responsive. There is **never a time that I am left waiting or feel forgotten. With that, the employees at Zinqué make you feel welcomed and appreciated for your business.** Now onto the important issue, the food. A cafe that specializes in French cuisine and does it well is hard to find in this area. *Zinqué not only does it well, but goes above and beyond. I have been all over Europe, and this restaurant compares favorably with what you would find at a corner cafe in Paris.* The **grilled prawns, rotisserie chicken sandwich, and charcuterie plate** are just a few of the many great things one will find on the menu. Each plate is filled with fresh and **authentic ingredients**, which is evident in the **presentation and taste** of the dishes. Besides the food, the bar selection is **awesome**. Zinqué has **incredible red wines** that I cannot find anywhere else. *Overall, this cafe has simply become one of my favorite places to dine and explore Paris in my own backyard.*

Focus—Zinque Cafe

Criteria—service

Evidence—employees welcoming

Evidence—great items on menu

Evidence—awesome selection, incredible wines

Assessment summary

Scope—Venice restaurants

Assessment thesis

Criteria—food, French cuisine

Assessment—comparable to Paris cafe

Evidence—Presentation and taste

Criteria—bar selection

Questions to Consider

Invention

1. What do you think prompted Sasso to write about this subject?
2. How do you think Sasso gathered ideas, information, and evidence?
3. What did Sasso discover about his subject?
4. What evidence tells you that this piece of writing is an analysis and evaluation?

Audience

5. What restrictions or limits did Sasso place on himself, and what expectations do you think he was responding to?
6. Who is Sasso writing to, and how do you know?
7. If Sasso reviewed this restaurant for a group of friends, how would it be different? What elements might be the same?

Authority

8. How does Anthony Sasso let the reader know that what he has discovered about the café and what he says about it can be trusted?
9. What has been left out, and why?
10. How successful is Sasso's Yelp review? Would you eat at this restaurant, based on his review? How would you make this review stronger and more persuasive?

MODULE II-34

AN ANALYSIS AND EVALUATION GENRE: REVIEW OF A CULTURAL EVENT

Evaluations are common assignments in various college courses because they require you to think critically and evaluate a subject dispassionately, often using criteria or a method developed in a specific discipline such as analyzing the brush strokes of a Monet painting or the oxygen intake of an engine.

Alvaro Gonzalez wrote the following essay for an assignment in a college writing course. He had visited traditional museums on school field trips and was curious to see and write about an example of the "new museum movement" with an open design allowing for multiple interpretations of artifacts from different cultures. Also, he had never seen an exhibit focused solely on pre-Columbian people and cultures of the American continent prior to Christopher Columbus's arrival. As you read his essay, notice how his analysis informs his evaluation. Gonzalez also uses comparison and contrast in his evaluation of the success of the museum exhibit.

Jorge Pardo brings the New Museum to LACMA

Alvaro Gonzalez

Surprisingly, the world of museums is a contentious battleground of ideas and visions. The struggle between the "New Museum" and the "Modern Museum" is one example of the war of ideas. *The new exhibit of the Los Angeles County Museum of Arts (LACMA) Pre-Columbian art collection* is an example of **a new, young curator attempting to advance New Museum ideals against dated Modern Museum expectations**.

The split between the New Museum movement and the more traditional Modern Museum plays out in many ways. In the new LACMA exhibit, the conflict between new and modern is most apparent in the *information provided, the architecture, and the museum/audience relationship.*

The Modern Museum rarely discloses the name of its curators or the ideals that inform their work. Because *Jorge Pardo, the curator of "Latin American Art: Ancient to Contemporary," and his vision for the exhibit were promoted with the opening of the collection*, the connection between the Art of the Americas exhibit and New Museum's ideologies are easily discoverable. *The architecture of the exhibit, which is very non-linear and immerses the audience, is the most obvious New Museum trait of the exhibit (Pardo).*

The typical modern museum separates the audience and the gallery. The museum/audience relationship in the Modern museum model is cold and distant, as Eilean Hooper-Greenhill explains in *Museums and the Interpretation of Visual Culture* (7). It can be likened to the relationship between a boss behind a desk and an employee standing attentively, respectfully, and quietly in front of it. Pardo's

Fig. 1 One of the Latin American galleries at the Los Angeles County Museum of Art.

Scope—world of museums

Focus—LACMA Pre-Columbian Art exhibit

Assessment thesis —curator of exhibit trying something new

Criteria—information, architecture, museum/audience relationship

Evidence—curator identified, architecture flowing

Discovery—museum ideal curator is working against

Evidence—non-traditional exhibition of artwork

exhibit calls for the same degree of attention and consideration, but it does so by breaking certain relational norms. *Pardo refuses to give into the structured norm of the modern boxed gallery museum. The pillars and the walls upon which the artworks are mounted are made of multi-layered, warm wood (fig. 1). In addition, the walls of the exhibit aren't white and straight but made of flowing curves, immersing the audience in a sense of motion. By giving the gallery motion, Pardo removes the idea that exhibits have a start and a finish line; he encourages free-range observing.*

Evidence of break with tradition—exhibit uses flowing wood

Jorge Pardo's exhibit attempts to build a closer bond between artifact and audience. Pardo draws his audience into the viewing experience without compromising or redefining everyday artifacts. An example of re-contextualization of the typical Modern Museum is seen in the Lando Hall of California History where **baskets and tools are placed next to a recreated hut behind glass.** This approach separates the audience from the artifacts, often losing the genuine artifact in the larger and possibly inaccurate recreation.

Discovery—attempt to build closer bond

Discovery—artifacts traditionally exhibited

The majority of the pieces of the Pre-Columbian art exhibit are items for everyday use such as vessels for grain or for drinking, spoons and forks, items used for sport, and even dolls.

Discovery—artifacts of new exhibit

Pardo's exhibit encourages the appreciation of the intrinsic qualities and details of the artifacts by placing them in the traffic flow. He varies the sight lines and uses juxtaposition. At one point Pardo asks us to reconsider contemporary art by placing modern lounge furnishings within a Pre-Columbian cave.

Evidence—new exhibit highlights intrinsic qualities

One element of the Pardo exhibit grates against the New Museum approach. The anthropological wallpaper identifying artifacts with the times of their creation, created by Pardo, encourages passive observation instead of an active learner experience. This effect detracts greatly from the overall exhibit.

Assessment—wallpaper does not fit New Museum ideals

The museum and Pardo as curator have attempted to distinguish this most recent LACMA exhibit by breaking many established Modernist ideals. Pardo does a good job of breaking away from the established traditions of the Modern Museum and creates a more captivating exhibit that aligns itself with new ways of imagining the museum.

Assessment—exhibit an immersive break from tradition

Though there are shortcomings, such as the anthropological wallpaper, **Pardo demonstrates what is possible when we break away from the Modern museum. Not only can the presentation of the artifacts change, the entire exhibit can be transformed.**

Works Cited

Hooper-Greenhill, Eilean. "Culture and Meaning in the Museum." *Museums and the Interpretation of Visual Culture*, Routledge, 2000, pp. 127–30.

Pardo, Jorge. "Latin American Art: Ancient to Contemporary." Los Angeles County Museum of Art, 27 July 2008.

MLA Citations

Questions to Consider

Invention

1. Gonzalez could have written about any museum exhibit in his city. What do you think prompted him to write about this subject?
2. How do you think Gonzalez gathered ideas, information, and evidence for his argument?
3. What did he discover about his subject?
4. What evidence tells you that the Gonzalez's essay is an analysis and evaluation?

Audience

5. What restrictions or limits did Gonzalez place on himself, and what expectations do you think he was responding to?
6. How does Gonzalez's essay differ from other types of academic writing like a research paper?
7. Who is Gonzalez writing to, and how do you know?

Authority

8. How does Gonzalez let the reader know that what he has discovered and what he says about his subjects can be trusted?
9. What has Gonzalez left out, and why do you think he did so?
10. How successful is Gonzalez's review? What could he do to make his essay stronger and more persuasive?

MODULE II-35

BUILDING AN ANALYSIS AND EVALUATION ARGUMENT

The following steps will help you build a persuasive analysis and evaluation. As with every writing task, use the lenses of invention, audience, and authority to help you build a persuasive analysis and evaluation argument. It is a guide; it is not the only way to write a persuasive definitional argument. You might return to invention and discovery, for example, if you find that your criteria are not right for your audience.

Invention

- Find your subject for analysis and evaluation

✓ If you have been assigned a subject, you still may need to refine your focus. Alvaro Gonzalez was assigned a 500-word analysis and evaluation of a museum exhibition in Los Angeles. Clearly, he could not analyze and evaluate every artifact on display. Also, it would be difficult to write 500 words about a single artifact, such as the one shown in his paper, Figure 1. Instead, he decided to focus on the architecture of the exhibit.

✓ If you are free to select a subject, consider the time you have available, and the energy you can commit. Suppose you have two weeks to complete an analysis and evaluation of a marketing campaign targeting 18–27-year-old consumers. Analyzing and evaluating Coca-Cola's global marketing campaign could take weeks. On the other hand, focusing on the label of the Coke Zero can may not give you enough material to fulfill your professor's expectations.

✓ Once you have a subject to focus on, identify the scope of your project: the category that contains similar items, ideas, or events. For example, if your focus is on Coke Zero marketing, you might notice that all the drinking cups at a basketball game are printed with the logo for Coke Zero. You decide that marketing tie-ins between soft-drink companies and college sports might be an interesting scope for your marketing project. This scope would allow you to focus on the Coke Zero marketing strategy linked to the NCAA final four.

- Begin discovery

✓ Look for unexpected traits, patterns you did not see before, elements that deserve further examination, and strategies that are unusually effective.

The use of contrasting color and lighting in an ad for Coke Zero that appeared during the NCAA "March madness" season (Figure 12.2) seems significant, for example. The light focuses on the two men shouting with excitement and surprise. Their eyes appear to be focused on the contrasting bright red Coke trademark located in the black field. Coke, then, appears to be the source of the light, the excitement, and the "madness." Also, the heavy use of black and contrasting red colors, the absence of the word *diet*, and the tie to NCAA basketball, which attracts a largely young male audience, all suggest that the Coke Zero ad campaign is aimed at men.

Figure 12.2 A Coke Zero advertisement tied to the NCAA Basketball tournament.

✓ Look for other sources of information about the patterns, trends, statements, and unstated assumptions that you have noticed. With your hunch about Coke Zero in mind, for instance, you might conduct some research in a business database such as *ABI/INFORM Complete* using the terms "Coke ads" and "color in ads" as search terms.

- Draft a working thesis

✓ If you have sharpened your focus on your subject and started to discover more about it, you will probably reach a tentative evaluation about how your subject relates to the broader scope in which it fits. For an evaluation of the Coke Zero campaign, for example, you might come up with the following tentative assessment:

> The Coke Zero / NCAA final four advertising campaign targets 18- to 27-year-old men in an attempt to increase sales.

At this point, you will need to look to your audience to help you determine your criteria for analysis and shape your argument.

Audience

- Understand the rhetorical situation

✓ Knowing what your audience is looking for in an analysis and evaluation will help you to shape your argument. Readers of a film review, for example, usually expect an assessment of the story, characters, and acting. However, if a reviewer spoils the end of the movie, readers are unlikely to return to that reviewer ever again.

- Define your criteria

✓ Determining the values, standards, or metrics that make up your criteria is not difficult if you follow the following four steps:

1. **Select what you will measure**. Place the focus of your analysis in a larger class of similar items, ideas, or events. Gonzalez placed the pre-Columbian exhibit within the class of all museum exhibits. Then, list all possible qualities, characteristics, and traits most have in common. Gonzalez's list could have included a huge number of items, ideas, and events, such as museum tours, exhibit arrangement, ticket prices, staff professionalism, and parking.
2. **Audience expectations and your purpose will reduce the options**. Only the qualities, characteristics, and traits expected by the audience and those you believe the audience needs to know about should be analyzed and evaluated. Given Gonzalez's purpose, to share his assessment of a new type of museum exhibit, he decided that his audience did not need to be informed of parking availability. He knew, however, that his professor expected a detailed analysis and evaluation of the quality of the new exhibits.
3. **Choose how you will measure**. There are many ways to measure. Select the methods that your audience expects and will help you achieve your purpose. How you measure will also determine the type of discoverable evidence you can use to persuade your audience. For example, if you are measuring the success of a Coke Zero–NCAA Basketball ad campaign, your audience would expect evidence concerning sales numbers during the tournament. If, instead, you are measuring the value of the NCAA tournament tie-in as a business strategy, your audience will expect evidence showing the investor value of Coca-Cola North America during the campaign (Figure 12.3).

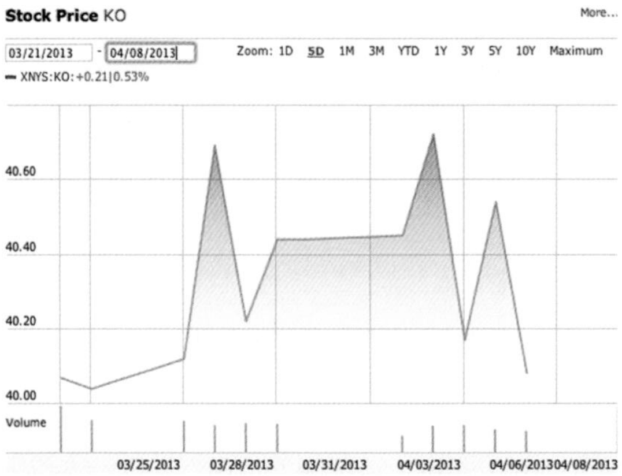

Figure 12.3
The chart shows Coca-Cola stock rising during the 2013 NCAA basketball tournament and falling after the final game.

4. **Make your final selection** of what and how you will analyze and evaluate based on time, page limits, and resources. A Yelp review of a restaurant may allow you to mention only three criteria and analyze each one briefly. However, a researched, 25-page analysis and evaluation of a new Transportation Security Administration (TSA)–enhanced screening procedure may require 8–10 criteria, each described and justified in detail.

✓ Once you know what you want to analyze and how you will measure it, you must analyze your subject fully using each of the criteria, and your assessment cannot say more than is supported by the evidence you have discovered.

- Organize your argument

✓ The processes of discovery, invention, and research will continue as you draft and revise. For example, you may find compelling evidence that does not fit your criteria but is relevant and will be persuasive to your audience. As you apply your criteria to the evidence, then, you may need to revise or refine it, or even reconsider your tentative thesis.

✓ The organization of your analysis and evaluation will depend upon the expectations of your audience. Because Alvaro Gonzalez was working on an assignment for a writing course, for example, he was able to consult the assignment sheet the professor handed out, and he also asked the professor directly how best to organize his thoughts.

Suppose, though, that the professor who assigned the analysis and evaluation of the Coca-Cola marketing campaign did not describe her expectations in detail. An analysis and evaluation of this type is a common genre used in business and in business schools and colleges. Therefore, the course textbook and some simple research will tell you what this genre looks like and how to organize your argument.

If the professor and textbook offer little guidance, ask yourself, "How has this subject been analyzed and evaluated before?" If you are assigned a business case study and asked to analyze and evaluate the decisions of a manager, the structure and organization of other business ethics case studies will be your guide.

✓ You can use or adjust one of three basic outline types to fit your purpose and your audience's expectations.

1. A **criteria structure** helps you highlight the traits, qualities, and practices of the category to which your subject belongs (for example, advertising campaigns, museum exhibits) and demonstrate how your subject meets, or does not meet, the criteria.
2. A **point-by-point structure** allows you to emphasize the argument that emerges from or makes use of an analysis and evaluation. For example, Gonzalez uses the result of his analysis to make a case for "New Museum" exhibits.
3. A **scope/subject structure** allows you to emphasize the relationship between the larger category and your subject as well as any differences between them.

Criteria Structure

I. Introduction
   1. Focus & Scope
   2. Evaluation & brief assessment

II. Body of Argument
   1. First criterion
      a. Ideal trait, quality, or practice
      b. Subject's trait, quality, or practice
   2. Second criterion
      a. Ideal trait, quality, or practice
      b. Subject's trait, quality, or practice
   3. Third criterion ...

III. Conclusion
   1. Review evidence
   2. Restate assessment

Point-by-Point Structure

I. Introduction
   1. Focus & Scope
   2. Evaluation & brief assessment

II. Body of Argument
   1. Explain the criteria.
   2. First point of argument
      a. Criterion assessed
      b. Evidence assessed
   3. Second point of argument
      a. Criterion assessed
      b. Evidence assessed
   4. Third point of argument ...

III. Conclusion
   1. Review evidence
   2. Restate assessment

Scope/Subject Structure

I. Introduction
   1. Focus & Scope
   2. Evaluation & brief assessment

II. Body of Argument
   1. Explain the criteria
   2. Subject's larger category
      a. Relevant traits, qualities, or practices
      b. Assessment of the larger category
   3. Describe your subjec
      a. Subject's traits, qualities, or practices.
      b. Assessment of the subject

III. Conclusion
   1. Review evidence
   2. Restate assessment

- Write your final assessment and refine your assessment

✓ Your judgment must be based on the criteria, the evidence, and how your subject fits into the larger scope of similar items, ideas, or events.

✓ Keep in mind that you are not simply sharing your opinion; you are applying your criteria. You may love your iPad mini, but if you have discovered that the iPad mini does not fit the criteria you have established as well as other small tablets on the market, you must say so.

Returning to the analysis and evaluation of the Coke Zero marketing campaign, it is possible that the campaign was a success if you apply one criterion but a failure if you apply different criteria. In other words, the campaign could have matched the objectives of the Coca-Cola Company perfectly and yet failed to make people more aware of Coke Zero, resulting in no overall increase in sales.

✓ The best way to write a final assessment or thesis for an analysis and evaluation is to see how others have done the same and how they use the thesis to shape their argument.

For example, Alvaro Gonzalez's thesis sets up the rest of his essay, where he provides background information on his subject, defines the criteria he uses to analyze and evaluate, and then walks through each discovery and the evidence that informs his final assessment.

- Draft your analysis and evaluation

✓ As you draft, remember that your reader will be encountering your analysis and evaluation for the first and probably only time. Often, clarity and simplicity will serve your purpose more effectively than other options. State your criteria, explain the meaning of the evidence you found carefully, and make sure others can see how you moved from what you saw or experienced to your evaluation.

✓ Different audiences expect different elements in an analysis and evaluation, depending on the genre. A music review may not state all of the criteria, and in a lab report the scope may be assumed and unstated. Though you can organize the elements of an analysis and evaluation to enhance your persuasive power (see p. 235), some elements, such as your purpose, your criteria, and your evidence, are essential.

Authority

- Check the logic of your assessment

✓ To persuade your audience of your analysis and evaluation, you need to establish your authority to evaluate your subject and avoid making mistakes that could give a reader or listener reasons to doubt your judgment. The questions that follow will help you to check your logic.

Does your scope—the larger category of similar items, ideas, or events to which your subject belongs—allow you to make a reasonable assessment? For example, if your scope includes all types of computers including desktops, praising the iPad mini for its portability may seem unfair. Your audience may have reason to question the relevance and wonder if you are loading the deck by comparing the iPad to computers that were never meant to be portable.

Does the evidence support your final assessment? If you state in your final assessment that the stock price for Coca-Cola increased following the Coke Zero advertising campaign, your reader or listener may wonder if there were other causes for the increase. You need to provide evidence for the cause–effect relationship.

✓ Remember, sources are persuasive only if they are authoritative, and authority, in part, is established with excellent documentation. The Responsible Sourcing box entitled "How to Handle Web Sources" can help.

- Make it flow

✓ State your focus and scope early to give your audience context.

✓ No matter what genre you adopt, your analysis and evaluation should have a clear structure. Readers will expect an analysis and evaluation to have some very specific qualities. See Chapter 24 for advice that will help you make your argument flow.

Move your readers or listeners through your argument by giving them a roadmap at the beginning and transitions between paragraphs. For example, in the introduction to an evaluation of the iPad mini, you could say, "Most small tablets offer portability and vivid displays. How, then, does the new iPad mini compare with the other entries in this market? To find out, I recently visited my local computer store and conducted a comparison. Here is what I discovered."

✓ Use transitions to remind readers of the significance of what you just said and forecast what is coming next, as in this example, from the Coca-Cola analysis: "As the evidence suggests, the Coke Zero campaign is clearly aimed at 18- to 27-year-old men. Did it reach that audience? An analysis of the sales numbers for the months following the campaign provides the answer to that question."

Responsible Sourcing
How to Handle Web Sources

The Internet makes it possible for information to live in many places and to be constantly updated. The tradeoff is that the multiple places and constant updates make it much more difficult than it used to be to direct others to the specific place where you found your sources. For example, all three of the following URLs will lead you to a version of the wind map image shown in Figure 12.1 on page 219.

1. https://www.pinterest.com/pin/127367495681719483/
2. http://hint.fm/wind/gallery/
3. https://flowingdata.com/2012/03/28/live-wind-map-shows-flow-patterns/

In order to document the wind map correctly and make it easy for your reader to find it, you need to cite the most direct link to the author or originator of the data. Both the MLA and APA documentation styles require you to include a DOI (digital object identifier) or the URL for the site in your works-cited or references entry.

The exact image used in Figure 12.1, for example, is not available at any link because the image is a screen shot of a moving wind map, produced by the creators of hint.fm—the source of the map and image. To provide the most accurate citation to the source, you would need to provide the URL for the hint.fm site.

- Get peer response

✓ Peer response is not saved for the end. Discuss your ideas, such as what you want to focus on and how you might measure with classmates, friends, and your professor. Keep track of their ideas so you do not have to ask twice.

✓ Ask your peers to look over your analysis and evaluation and, using a highlighter and a pen for notes, respond to the following:
  - Please circle my thesis, and tell me what you predict the rest of the essay will say.
  - Where do you see a statement of my scope and focus?
  - Please highlight the items, ideas, or event I analyze and evaluate.
  - What measures am I using to analyze and evaluate? How do you know?

  - ◎ What did I forget to analyze or evaluate?
  - ◎ Is my final assessment supported by the evidence that results from my analysis?

- Revise and edit your argument

✓ Check to make sure that the words or phrases you use to describe the items, ideas, and events you analyze, and the words used to refer to the values, standards, or metrics you use are consistent throughout your argument.

✓ Review all of the quotes, summaries, paraphrases, and images you use as evidence, and the accuracy of your citations and the contextualization provided by your captions.

CHAPTER 13

DETERMINING CAUSE

Why did we go to the moon and why haven't we been back?

How did the Ohio State University campus police obtain a Mine Resistant Ambush Protected (MRAP) military personnel carrier? What effect will it have if it is ever used?

We want answers and always have. We want to know if humans can exist in outer space and what would happen if a campus police officer rolled up to a tailgate party in a wheeled tank. In fact, people have asked "why, how, and what?" so often that we have developed methods of answering questions and, in the process, advanced a great many human endeavors.

Each of the questions above is an attempt to discover a cause or an effect. For example, if you know the political, financial, and social conditions that made it possible and, for a little while, reasonable, for surplus military equipment to be sold at a discount to police departments, you know the cause. In turn, if you have an idea of how tailgaters four beers into a party typically respond to authority figures, you can anticipate the effect of a campus cop in a tank stopping by to ask them to turn it down.

This chapter will show you how to build a strong, persuasive argument that identifies causes and effects.

MODULE II-36

WHAT AUDIENCES EXPECT OF A CAUSAL ARGUMENT

An argument that defines and explains the cause of an effect or traces the effects of a cause is called a **causal argument**. In addition, arguments that disprove and dispute causes or effects are also causal. Often, knowledge cannot advance until a faulty belief in a cause or an effect is disproven.

Academic disciplines and many professions have specialized means of looking for causes and effects. In fact, causal arguments are the foundation of most academic discussions and everyday debates.

Figure 13.1
Doctors did not stop bloodletting until it was proven that an imbalance of the humors (blood, bile, and phlegm) was not the cause of illness.

Why Would I Need to Write about Cause and Effect?

Making an argument that identifies cause and effect is not as simple as declaring that one thing caused another. As a student, if you are asked why a poet chose a specific rhyme scheme, why in 1890 the US frontier was said to be closed, or what chemical effect Mentos candy has on diet soda, you should be prepared to respond with an argument that persuasively describes causes and effects based on evidence. An effective causal argument persuades the audience by helping readers understand the relationship between a cause and an effect.

As you learn how a discipline generates and discovers knowledge, you will also see how it deals with cause and effect. The Conventions in Context box provides some examples.

Conventions in Context
Cause and Effect in Academic Disciplines

Different academic disciplines use cause and effect arguments in different ways.

Sciences: The scientific method, in which we make observations, form a hypothesis about what we see, experiment to test the hypothesis, and then revise it, is a system that distinguishes between correlations (simple links between events or data points, without evidence of a causal connection) and situations where one data point or event is altered or caused by another. For example, a scientist who measures higher global temperatures also observes increases of atmospheric CO_2 over the same time period. However, this correlation does not mean the increase in CO_2 actually causes higher global temperatures. Scientists must do experiments to prove or disprove the hypothesis that higher levels of CO_2 cause higher global temperatures.

Theology: One causal argument is the first-cause argument for the existence of God, who in this argument is the prime mover and first cause of all actions and changes in the universe. In this argument, take away God and you take away all subsequent effects and events.

Engineering: Engineers consider closed systems, like electronic circuits, and examine the effects caused by various inputs. For example, an engineer may input static electricity to a circuit to see how the materials and function of the circuit change.

Law: To establish guilt, a lawyer must prove to the jury that there is a causal link between the accused person's actions and the crime. For a lawyer to link you to a hit-and-run accident involving a UPS truck, she would have to prove that the smudge of brown paint on your car was caused by a collision with the truck. However, if you can prove an alternative causal link, such as that your brown garage door scraped your fender and left a smudge, you can create doubt about the lawyer's causal argument.

Types of Cause-and-Effect Relationships

A cause can be categorized in three different ways, and the evidence required to prove each type of cause differs.

1. A **sufficient cause** is all that is required for an effect to occur. For example, an enormous increase in static charges in a cloud is sufficient—it is enough—to cause lightning.

   The sufficient cause of lightning is a large static charged cloud. A sufficient cause is the strongest link between cause and effect, so it requires undeniable evidence to be persuasive.

2. A **necessary cause** is one of many causes of an effect. For example, heat, often in the form of lightning, is a necessary cause of fire, but heat by itself is not enough to cause a fire, just as lightning does not always cause a fire. To cause a fire, heat, oxygen, and fuel (like wood) must be present.

   Fire has three necessary causes—heat, oxygen, and fuel.

   A single necessary cause is not enough to establish a cause-and-effect relationship. To form a strong link to an effect, all necessary causes must be explained. Because necessary causes merely contribute to an effect, their relationship to the effect is not as strong as that of a sufficient cause.

3. A **contributory cause** is one of many causes that can be linked to an effect, but it is neither necessary nor sufficient. Underground mining can contribute to minor earthquakes; however, it is not a necessary cause because there are many reasons for earthquakes, and it is not a sufficient cause because many mines operate for years without earthquake activity. Because it is only contributory, the persuasive force of this type of cause is modest compared to proven sufficient or necessary causes.

If you have found a cause-and-effect relationship, it is one of these three, which means you do not need to invent a new way of characterizing the cause-and-effect relationship you are exploring.

Now that you understand how causes are related to effects, you are ready to explore how causal arguments are structured.

Using Invention to Structure a Causal Argument

Causal arguments can be structured in three basic ways:

- an argument that starts with a cause and links to an effect,
- a casual chain argument, and
- an argument that starts with an effect and links to a cause.

A strong thesis often mirrors the structure of the argument that follows. Below, you will find three ways to structure a thesis and its supporting arguments.

1. Argument That Starts with a Cause and Links to an Effect

    [X cause(s)] → [Y effect(s)]

    The increase in the minimum wage has caused entry-level jobs to disappear in our area.

The simplest versions of this structure allow you to argue that a cause or a number of causes are linked to one or more effects.

You can also use this simple structure to invent an argument that disagrees with a causal claim made by someone else, and then argue for a different effect. The ¬ symbol is used by logicians to indicate negation or "not."

    [X cause(s)] ¬ [Y effect(s)]
    [X cause(s)] → [Z effect(s)]

    The increase in the minimum wage did not eliminate entry-level jobs in our area. Instead, the wage hike reduced turnover in entry level-jobs.

An argument that moves from a cause to an effect always looks forward, since causes always come before effects.

2. Causal Chain Argument

    [X cause(s)] → [Y effect(s)] → [Y cause(s)] → [Z effect(s)]

    The first car skidded, which caused the second car to hit the first car, which caused the third car to hit the second car.

A causal chain argument claims that two or more effects are linked and that the sequence was set in motion by a first cause or causes.

A strong casual-chain argument requires careful research and solid reasoning. Different people will have different perceptions of the same events, which is why the person making this argument must prove the first causal link, eliminating other possibilities, before moving on to the next effect in the sequence.

3. Argument That Starts With an Effect and Links to a Cause

    [Y effect(s)] ← [X cause(s)]

    The militarization of police tactics is an effect of the military equipment in their inventory.

This structure starts with an effect or effects and describes its cause or multiple causes. Arguments from effect to cause can include multiple effects brought about by multiple causes.

In addition, you can use this structure to dispute the cause or causes proposed by someone else. For example,

> **[Y effect(s)] ← [W cause(s)] ¬ [X cause(s)]**
>
> The militarization of police tactics are an effect of military methods and practices used to train police officers, and not an effect of the military equipment in their inventory.

Until you do the research to discover all possible effects, you can't be sure you know what happened. In addition, if you do not consider all possible explanations for the effects you see, you will not find the evidence to persuade your audience of the cause you argue for.

Making Your Causal Argument Acceptable to Your Audience

The most basic expectation of a causal argument is that the writer will answer the *why*, *how*, and *what* questions. Why did the event or change happen? How is the cause related to the effects? What are the effects?

Answers to the *why* question often begin with the word *because*—the conjunction indicating causality. When arguing for a cause, keep in mind that your audience may think that a different cause is more likely. After all, there is no point in building a causal argument for an audience that already thinks as you do. Therefore, you cannot simply identify a cause and move on to its effects. You need to consider other possible causes and then eliminate them with evidence. Finally, you must use evidence and reasoning to prove the cause you are arguing for is the most likely.

When your audience asks *how*, one of the three types of cause-and-effect relationship is the answer. Each type of cause-and-effect relationship has a different level of persuasive force, and not every type will support every argument. For example, if you are arguing that fracking in Oklahoma must be shut down to prevent further earthquakes, those who benefit from the 100-million-barrel Oklahoma oilfields will require evidence proving that fracking is a sufficient or one of a few necessary causes of recent earthquakes. A contributory cause argument simply will not persuade oil producers. Obviously, the type of cause-and-effect relationship you argue for must come from the data and events you analyze, and without evidence and solid reasoning you can't establish a cause-and-effect relationship.

When you focus on the effects and their consequences, you answer the "what happened or what resulted" question. Because a cause always precedes an effect, you must persuade your audience of the cause and its relationship to the effect or effects before they will accept your thesis that the effect or effects you are arguing for result from a specific cause. Audiences will expect answers to the *why*, *how*, and *what* questions. If you have the answers, you are ready to make your argument more authoritative than competing arguments.

Breaking the Block
Using Stasis Questions to Find Causes and Effects

Stasis questions of cause and consequence can help you look deeper. The goal of this exercise is to find a subject for a causal argument in the form of a research paper. The writing component of this exercise should take 10 minutes.

Step One

Search the news for events whose cause or effect is debated, for example, the effect of a candidate's economic platform or the cause of an accident. If nothing jumps out at you, the following prompts can help you find a causal issue.

- Name three events that are well known or common, like an injury at a music festival, the election of an unlikely candidate, or the sinking of a ship.
- Think of a plan, scheme, or trip in your experience that ended badly or had unexpected consequences.
- List all the machines, devices, or appliances you've owned that stopped working or malfunctioned for no obvious reason.
- Look at things you handle or see every day, like your smartphone. What effect does the shape or functions have on you?
- Think about purposes or final outcomes. For example, what is the purpose of body armor and helmets worn by police? Are they only to protect, or do they send a message? What are the effects of mega-amusement parks on the surrounding environment?

Step Two

Choose the most interesting or confusing events, changes, or final outcomes and write for 10 minutes developing answers to the following secondary stasis questions.

- Why did an event or change happen?
- How are the possible causes and possible effects of an event or changes related?

- What are the possible effects?
- What possible causes or effects do not make sense or can be eliminated?
- What was the immediate or most obvious effect?
- What other consequences will become apparent later or in other locations or situations?

Step Three

Reflect upon what you have written. Could reasonable people point to other causes or effects? What would they base their contrary conclusions on? How could you prove your observations or theory?

Making Your Causal Argument Authoritative

Building authority is a matter of using logical reasoning to help your reader understand the evidence that supports your argument. Like showing your work in a math class, if your audience can follow your reasoning, checking accuracy if need be, and then come up with the same conclusion you do, you have also demonstrated your authority.

Your audience will recognize your authority, or not, in the way in which you answer the *why*, *how*, and *what* questions. For example, if someone argued that last week's earthquake in Logan County was caused by the fracking rig that started operation in the county two weeks ago, that person could be making a ***post hoc ergo propter hoc*** fallacy. The *post hoc* fallacy is an overestimation of the significance of a sequence of events. Just because fracking preceded an earthquake does not prove it caused the earthquake.

If someone had undeniable evidence that a fracking rig drilling and pumping high-pressure liquid into a fault did in fact cause an earthquake, however, he or she would be making a hasty generalization by then arguing that all Oklahoma earthquake swarms are an effect of fracking. A **hasty generalization** fallacy is an overestimation of the significance of the sample size or number of observations made. One observation (sample size of 1) of a single fracking-caused earthquake does not prove the cause of all earthquakes in Oklahoma. Many more observations (a greater sample size) are required to support such a conclusion.

Solid reasoning is a product of careful, logical thinking. Inductive and deductive reasoning, the two primary types of reasoning used in a causal argument, are explained in detail in Chapters 17 and 24.

Reasoning is persuasive but evidence is convincing, and direct evidence is stronger than circumstantial or indirect evidence. To understand the difference, imagine that as you wake up in the morning you hear the pitter patter of falling water and smell cool, fresh air drifting through your bedroom window. If you conclude, as you leave for work, that a rain shower is the cause of your wet bike seat, your argument is based on circumstantial or indirect evidence. **Circumstantial or indirect evidence** is evidence that requires an inference or interpretation to connect a cause to an effect.

You have no direct evidence of rain, but you are inferring that the rain happened because you experienced the sound of falling water and a wet seat. **Direct evidence**, on the other hand, is undeniable evidence that directly supports your conclusion, such as actually seeing raindrops fall from the overcast sky onto your bike.

Audiences judge your authority by the reasoning and evidence you use. Chapter 20 will help you evaluate the persuasive power of evidence.

Genres that Determine Cause

A cause-and-effect argument can be one part of a larger argument or paper. Below is a brief list of genres that make use of causal arguments and often consist primarily of causal arguments.

- A **lab report** is the record of a completed experiment, including the original hypothesis that predicts causes and effects.
- A **closing argument** is a restatement of arguments in a courtroom, with a lawyer describing the guilt or innocence, or liability or lack of responsibility, of a defendant in a court case.
- A **historical analysis** is an examination of historical events and artifacts to determine cause-and-effect relationships between individuals, acts, ideas, and events.
- A **political cartoon** expresses a political view for the purpose of persuading the audience.
- An **editorial** is a short journalistic argument in which the author tries to persuade the audience to think, believe, or act differently.
- A **research paper** can argue for a new understanding by offering a thesis about a possible cause-and-effect relationship, backed by credible evidence.

MODULE II-37

A CAUSAL ARGUMENT GENRE: EDITORIAL

The following editorial is from *Nature: International Weekly Journal of Science.* Though the argument is subtle, the journal's editorial board felt the need to restate in clear terms the innocence of a man falsely accused of spreading HIV/AIDS in North America.

26 October 2016

How researchers cleared the name of HIV Patient Zero
Genetic analysis of historical virus samples proves the epidemic arrived by another route.

In 1982, the Canadian air steward Gaétan Dugas wrote of his worsening illness in a letter to Ray Redford, his former lover. Believing he had what was being called "gay cancer," Dugas had shaved his hair ahead of expected chemotherapy. He felt nude without it, he said. Like an alien.

Hook and introduction of subject

Dugas told friends he was ready to fight and beat the cancer, but he died in 1984. By then, scientists and public-health officials had a new, more formal, name for the illness that claimed his life—HIV/AIDS. *Dugas was given a different label, too. As the attention of politicians and journalists was drawn to the unfolding crisis, he was identified as 'Patient Zero' of the US epidemic. He was demonized as a knowing and callous reservoir of infection and as a deliberate transmitter of disease. He was regularly compared with Mary Mallon, better known as Typhoid Mary—the cook who, several decades earlier, ignored instructions not to prepare food, and infected dozens in New York City with that bacterial disease.*

Effect of "Patient Zero" label

Thirty years on, samples of the virus that closed down Dugas's immune system still exist. And in a research paper this week, disease scientists report how they have analysed its genetic sequence (M. Worobey et al. Nature http://dx.doi.org/10.1038/nature19827; 2016). The results are important for two reasons. In clinical terms, they show that Dugas's virus was, in many ways, unexceptional. And in human terms, they clear his name.

Source of primary research exonerating

Dugas was identified as Patient Zero in a 1987 book about the AIDS epidemic, *And the Band Played On* (St. Martin's), by journalist Randy Shilts, who died in 1994. Shilts painted Dugas as a villain, and turned a typographical curiosity into a badge of dishonour. US scientists had spoken to Dugas as they investigated a cluster of cases of the new syndrome in Los Angeles in 1982. Because he didn't live in the state, his case notes were marked as Patient O

Causal chain resulting in "Patient Zero" label

Hasty generalization that led to faulty cause argument and "Patient Zero" label

for "Outside of California." When vocalized, the designation became muddled with the number zero. As Shilts said when he first heard the description: "Ooh, that's catchy."

The author introduced the air steward to the world as the original sinner. A man whose reckless behaviour and disregard for the health of his (many) sexual partners helped the AIDS epidemic to take hold. He became known as a lover driven by hate, and a foreigner who brought death and disease to US shores. The myth helped to drive the political response to the disease. It was used to demand laws to stop the deliberate transmission of the virus, and fuelled hostility towards a community that many believed had brought the disease on themselves as a perverse condemnation of their lifestyle.

Effect of "Patient Zero" label for Dugas and gay community

Medical historians have chipped away at the pernicious story of Dugas as Patient Zero for years. *They have pointed out, for example, how he helped epidemiologists to trace a significant number of his sexual partners.* And how the scientific advice at the time was contradictory and distrusted by people whose sexuality medics had considered a psychiatric problem until just a decade earlier.

Evidence for his exoneration

The latest genetic analysis completes the exoneration. *The virus arrived in New York City from the Caribbean around 1970.* There is nothing in the samples from Dugas that implicate him and his behaviour as key to its subsequent rapid spread. In his 1982 letter, Dugas wrote that "my mind is finding peace again." RIP.

True cause predates Dugas

Thesis and conclusion: Dugas' memory and reputation exonerated

Questions to Consider

Invention

1. What do you think prompted the editorial board of *Nature* to select this subject?
2. The editorial was likely a group project. How do you imagine two or more writers would have researched and invented as they drafted this editorial?
3. Given the brief format of an editorial, a great deal of relevant history and information from the primary source must have been left out. How do you think the writers decided what to keep in and leave out?

Audience

4. The source of the research used above is from an article in the journal *Nature* entitled "1970s and 'Patient 0' HIV-1 genomes illuminate early HIV/AIDS history in North America," with ten authors specializing in and writing for an audience that understands the technicalities of viral epidemiology and phylogenetics. This article was published in the same edition of the journal *Nature* as this editorial. Based on this information, how do you think the primary source differs from the editorial?
5. Why do you think the editorial's writers repeated the findings of the longer article in an editorial?
6. Who is the intended audience of the editorial?
7. Why do you think the editorial begins with a brief narrative, and why does the thesis appear in the conclusion?

Authority

8. Without a named author, is the argument persuasive? What makes you think so?
9. The editorial disputes an earlier casual chain argument with findings that prove a different casual chain. How do we know the exonerating argument can be trusted?
10. What would you do to strengthen this argument?

MODULE II-38

A CAUSAL ARGUMENT GENRE: POLITICAL CARTOON

Causal arguments can be complex, and they can also be very brief and visual. In this political cartoon (Figure 13.2), notice how cartoonist Adam Zyglis makes a causal link between US drone strikes and growing anti-American sentiments in countries such as Yemen, Afghanistan, and Pakistan, where drones are used to attack targets.

Effect

Cause

Figure 13.2 A cause-effect argument in the form of a political cartoon.

Questions to Consider

Invention

1. All ideas have a specific inspiration. What do you think prompted the cartoonist Adam Zyglis to select his subject?
2. How do you think the invention strategy of a political cartoonist would be different from the invention strategies used by an essay writer? A reporter? A student writing a research paper? How might they be similar?
3. If you were asked to develop an idea for a political cartoon, and you wanted to show a relationship between one change or event and another, what would be your first step?

Audience

4. The cartoon argues a conclusion based on a causal link. What kind of evidence and what kind of reasoning are necessary to arrive at the cartoon's conclusion?
5. How would you describe the audiences for this cartoon?
6. What background knowledge does cartoonist Adam Zyglis assume his audience already has?

Authority

7. What are the markers of authority in the cartoon? Are the expectations of authority different for a political cartoon than they are for an editorial?
8. Why doesn't the cartoon examine other possible causes and additional effects?
9. List any other causes of anti-American sentiments you can think of that may be more probable than drone strikes.

MODULE II-39

A CAUSAL ARGUMENT GENRE: RESEARCH PAPER

In the following essay for a psychology course, entitled "Resilience and Development," student Elicia Flemming examines the causes of identity development and then argues that educational institutions must understand and respond to the stressors that can inhibit the academic success.

Assessing the Desire for Success: How Bi-Cultural Identity Development Strains Academic Motivation in Immigrant Youth

Elicia Flemming

Immigration shapes America. The population of immigrants is increasing at a rapid rate, and by 2040, one-third of all children will be growing up in immigrant households (Suárez-Orozco, Gaytán, Bang, Pakes O'Connor, & Rhodes, 2010). Unfortunately, two-thirds of the immigrant population experience steady declines in academic performance during their education while another fourteen percent of immigrants are labeled as low achievers from the start of their academic careers (Suárez-Orozco, Gaytán, Bang, Pakes, O'Connor, & Rhodes 2010).

Introduction of scope and focus.

To assist immigrants on their paths towards academic success, schools and colleges must be aware of and respond to the psychological stresses that challenge identity development and academic achievement. In this paper, I argue that the challenges of successfully developing a bi-cultural identity negatively affect immigrant academic achievement and personal development.

Thesis

During the process of assimilating into American culture, immigrant adolescents are faced with the challenge of maintaining the values of their home culture while simultaneously attempting to assimilate into their new culture (Rodriguez, Morrobel & Villarruel 2003). This dual-sided development of identity provides a consistent source of pressure for **new immigrants who are essentially undergoing the process of assuming new identities in America.** Understanding the process and pressures working against positive identity formation can help educators and society ease immigrant academic success and assimilation.

General cause challenging identity development

Identity development—the general effect

Jacquelynne Eccles' theory of Expectancy Value Perspective explains that **positive identity formation is an effect** of *three linked causes, positive personal motivation, participation in socially appropriate behaviors, and realistic personal assessment.* Motivation is, perhaps, the most important of the three, because without it the other two causes are unlikely.

General cause composed of a three part casual chain

Positive motivation is tied to positive acts. An individual must first be motivated to identify new and different activities

First linked cause

and actions they are willing and able to complete and then they must behave, over time, in a way that corresponds with these motivations (Eccles 2000). In the context of academic performance, students who are motivated to excel must first identify new behaviors that will contribute to their social success. **For example, in the original culture, an immigrant may have been labeled a good student if he or she sat silently and did not disrupt the class with talking. Such behaviors, which the immigrant mastered and grew comfortable with, may be inappropriate in an American academic context. Motivation in academic setting often means a willingness to put oneself in new, uncomfortable situations and try activities that the student has not yet mastered.**

Example of link between motivation and positive acts

Effect of motivation

Motivation is necessary, but not sufficient to positive identity formation, especially in academic situations. *A student must also engage in socially appropriate behaviors. If students are motivated to behave in a way that corresponds to socially appropriate behaviors,* **they are essentially forming an identity as a good student. A willingness to try new activities and practice new behaviors is also tied to the third cause, which is the ability to assess one's own skills and abilities.**

Second linked cause

Effect of participation is socially appropriate acts

Link between first, second, third necessary cause

Eccles explains that *self-perceptions of personal skills and competencies shape how successful an individual perceives he or she will be. This awareness, in combination with perceptions related to goals that are shaped by a larger social context, allow an individual to assess the value of the behavior in relation to the social context.* **For example, motivated immigrant students who have learned how to behave in class and take part in appropriate behaviors learn over time how to judge their own work and compare their efforts to those of their classmates. As a result, when a student receives praise for hard work, he or she is likely to repeat the same study habits on the next assignment. If a student sees that his or her in-class work habits and participation are less than the work and participation of praised students, that student is likely to study more or ask for help—another form of positive participation in appropriate behaviors.**

Third cause of positive identity formation

Example of causal link

Expectancy Value Perspective theory demonstrates that motivation, an understanding of appropriate behaviors, and

Summary of Eccles research.

having positive ideas about being successful in combination with the values of the larger social context are essential to identity formation for immigrant students (Eccles 2000). **Unfortunately, the chain of causes that result in positive identity development can be strained or disrupted by particular challenges associated with immigrant status.** Because the majority of America's immigrants have *low-socioeconomic status and often reside in urban, poverty stricken areas, these particular contexts may not promote educational success.* **Latino immigrants, for example, place more significance on their interpersonal relationships with family, extended family, and members of the community (Rodriguez, Morrobel & Villarruel 2003). If the family values finding a job as more important than getting good grades in school, motivation for academic achievement will be unsupported and is likely to disappear. In this way, the student's emphasis on family may override conflicting notions of what is valued in the dominant school-group setting.**

Causal chain easily broken

Cause leading to lower academic achievement

Example of causal link breakdown

Negative effect of break in causal chain

Immigrants also face stressors and impediments that may keep them from participating in socially appropriate behaviors that contribute to positive identity development. *Immigrants experience stress related to exclusion, which are "the institutional barriers of acceptance and inclusion in the culture and economy of our nation" (Roffman, Suárez-Orozco & Rhodes 2003). This institutional barrier sends implicit messages about who belongs in the context of American culture and who doesn't.*

Institutions may limit or inhibit participation

Institutions are not the only source of exclusionary behaviors that stress immigrant students. When studying the academic performance of blacks and Latinos in school settings, Reynolds and Beehler found that *the psychological distress caused by being a victim of individual racism, or being exposed to racism, positively correlated with intrinsic motivation and participation (Reynolds & Beehler 2010). In this way, the psychological distress that is caused by being negatively targeted or judged on the basis of race or immigrant status causes a lack of achievement in school.*

Individual racism also a cause

Conflict between cultures makes the process of assessing strengths and weakness more difficult. For immigrants, identi-

fying in what ways they are successful may be more challenging when they are in a new, unfamiliar environment. Unfortunately, the social setting immigrant children are surrounded by may also assist in setting up personal expectations for failure among youth. Peers, school administrators, teachers, community members, and the media often stereotypes them as lazy, irresponsible, unintelligent, and dangerous. Such stereotypes negatively shift immigrant perspectives on their ability to achieve success within this social context (Roffman, Suárez-Orozco & Rhodes 2003). **The critical process of identity development involved with assessing personal strengths is disrupted because of the individual's difficulty in accurately viewing his or her strengths and weaknesses in a different, sometimes harsh country.**

Stereotypes and low societal expectations a cause

Effect stereotypes and low expectations

Despite the stressors and the difficulties, the development of a bicultural identity results in substantial benefits. **Students who successfully overcome the challenges of this identity communicate more easily with friends, make friends with students from other academic backgrounds, and achieve a higher amount of academic success** (Suárez-Orozco, Gaytán, Bang, Pakes, O'Connor, & Rhodes 2010).

Positive effects of casual chain

In conclusion, immigrant adolescents face a far more difficult time than their nonimmigrant peers. Due to the amount of academic decline that is observed within the immigrant culture, it is critical that our educational institutions pay attention to and accommodate the psychological distress and challenges that lead to low academic performance. If immigrant youth are provided with resources that ease the formation of a bi-cultural identity and help undo the increased psychological distress that they experience, we will begin to witness positive feelings of belonging within the context of American culture and positive perceptions for the future. When positive outlooks are achieved, immigrant youth will be more motivated to excel in school and will break past the barriers that limit their success in America.

Summary and final appeal

References

Eccles, J. (2000). Who am I and what am I going to do with my life? Personal and collective identities as motivators of action. *Educational Psychologist*, 44 (2), 78–89.

APA Citations

Reynolds, A.L., Sneva, J.N., & Beehler, G.P. (2010). The influence of racism-related stress on the academic motivation of Black and Latino/a students. *Journal of College Student Development*, 51(2), 135–149.

Roffman, J.G., Suárez-Orozco, C., & Rhodes, J.E. (2003). Facilitating positive youth development in immigrant youth: The role of mentors and community organizations. In F. Villarruel, D. Perkins, L. Borden & J. Keith (Eds.), *Community Youth Development Programs, Policies, and Practices* (pp. 90–117). London, United Kingdom: Sage Publications.

Rodriguez, M.C., Morrobel, D., & Villarruel, F.A. (2003). Research realities and a vision of success for Latino youth development. In F. Villarruel, D. Perkins, L. Borden & J. Keith (Eds.), *Community Youth Development* (pp. 47–78). Thousand Oaks, CA: Sage Publications.

Suárez-Orozco, C., Gaytán, F.X., Bang, H.J., Pakes, J., O'Connor, E., & Rhodes, J. (2010). Academic Trajectories of Newcomer Immigrant Youth. *Developmental Psychology*, 46(3), 602–618.

Questions to Consider

Invention

1. Assuming that Flemming was free to select her topic, how would you imagine she discovered her issue?
2. Imagine you were inspired by Flemming's causal analysis to examine the effects of motivation, participation, and assessment on a different group, such as new recruits in their first week of military boot camp. What would you do, and where would you look for information as you invent?
3. What information does Flemming appear to have discovered during research, and what did she develop or create herself?

Audience

4. The research Flemming found establishes a causal chain. How does she describe the relationships in this chain?
5. Why would a professor in an education psychology course ask students to write a cause-and-effect paper? What skills and competencies could such a paper demonstrate?
6. Flemming's voice is formal and direct. How do you think her voice would be different if she were to write an editorial arguing that public schools do not have the resources to support immigrant students?

Authority

7. Flemming is not a psychologist or educational expert. What does she do to make her findings and argument authoritative?
8. What types of evidence does she provide, and is the evidence sufficient to establish a cause-and-effect relationship?
9. What would you say is the major strength of Flemming's argument? How would you change her argument to make it more persuasive?

MODULE II-40

BUILDING A CAUSAL ARGUMENT

Use the checklist below to apply the lenses of invention, audience, and authority to your causal argument. Remember, your writing process will be unique and can change with every paper you write. The checklist can guide you as you develop your ideas and revise your writing; however, the editorial decisions are up to you.

Invention

A persuasive causal argument starts with invention, research, and synthesis.

- Find a causal question that you can use to build an argument

✓ If you have been assigned a subject, such as the causes and effects of advertising, be sure to look beyond the first thing that comes to mind. In such a situation, many students begin look to the obvious, such as advertising's effect on how teenagers see themselves. However, other options are available, such as what causes advertising agencies and photographers to select slender models rather than those with more normal body proportions.

✓ If you are free to find your own subject, the Breaking the Block box entitled "Use the Fishbone Diagram" will help you find an event, change, or end state that makes you curious about how it came to be. For example, what are the effects and potential dangers of marijuana use for automobile drivers?

✓ Often, the best path is to question causal relationships that are claimed by others, taken for granted, or go unquestioned by exploring the logic behind the assumed link.

For example, many people assume that children shouldn't watch too much TV because it is bad for their intellectual development. However, Steven Levitt and Stephen Dubner, the authors of *Freakonomics*, question the assumed causal link because research they uncovered found that watching a great deal of TV had no educational or intellectual effect, positive or negative.

Breaking the Block
Use the Fishbone Diagram

Manufacturing and service industries spend a great deal of time tracking down the causes of mistakes and errors so they can correct them. One trick they use to discover causal links is the fishbone diagram.

The backbone of the fish is like a timeline that leads to the effect—in this case a manufacturing defect. Each bone is a category of common or possible contributing causes of defects.

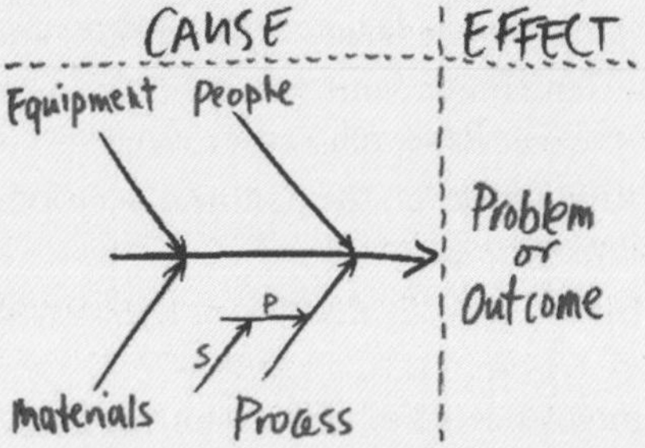

To use a fishbone diagram to discover possible causal relations, follow these steps.

Step One: Draw the Diagram

1. To find a cause, write the effect (event, change, or end state) you want to explore on the right side of a page, forming the fish head.
2. Draw the backbone line with fish bones branching from it, a few up and a few down.

Step Two: Flesh out the Diagram

1. Observe, recall, and research all possible causes.
2. Write down one cause on each fishbone.
3. Review each possible cause to discover whether evidence or reasoning proves there really is a causal link. Cross out the causes that do not hold up.

Step Three: Build an Argument
You are now ready to write a draft thesis, outline your argument, and continue to research evidence that will convince your audience of the causal links you have discovered.

Audience

- Understand the rhetorical situation

✓ Research and discover as much evidence of a causal link as you can, but when deciding which research to use, try to anticipate your audience's objections and reservations. To do that, you will also need to research your audience.

If you argue against fracking by presenting evidence of a link between fracking and a recent earthquake cluster, and your audience has worked in the oil exploration industry, they are likely to believe the opinion of a geologist, but not just any geologist. Research some industry publications to find out which experts are being quoted, what their specialization is, where they work, and what makes them widely respected.

✓ In an academic situation, your audience—your professor—may know the causes and effects but wants to see if you do. Or your audience may want to see if you can use the methods taught in the course to identify causes and effects. In this case, you will be expected to describe your method in as much detail as the discoveries you make. In addition, you must carefully document your evidence and be sure not to make statements the evidence and reasoning cannot support.

- Organize your argument

✓ The three basic structures of a causal argument—starting with a cause or causes and determining an effect or effects, a causal chain, or starting with an effect or effects and determining a cause or causes—do not limit the ways in which you can compose your argument. However, the nature of the causal relationship you are arguing for should be reflected in the structure of your argument.

✓ If you are arguing for multiple causes or multiple effects, it is best to present them chronologically. If they occurred very close together or at the same time, the one that best supports your argument and explains the link between cause and effect should be last, since the last point made is often the one best remembered.

- Draft your argument

✓ As you draft, remember that you are describing a causal relationship your audience did not see or understand before, or you are critiquing a causal relationship that they believe is correct and accurate. Take enough time to develop each relationship fully and explain in detail the evidence you have that proves the relationship you are arguing for. Remember, your readers or listeners would not hold their current view of the event or change you are talking about unless they were convinced that their view is correct.

✓ Just as architects and designers make models first to identify difficult connections and test assumptions, drafting is a form of modeling. Be sensitive to the difficulties you experience as you draft. If a paragraph describing a cause or an effect just does not come together, that difficulty may indicate a link that just is not there or be a sign of strained logic.

Authority

- Check your logic

✓ To be logical, evidence of the causal relationship needs to be presented using either inductive or deductive reasoning. Chapter 17 will help you clarify your inductive or deductive argument.

✓ Check to see whether reasoning and evidence prove a causal link. Conducting research and using solid reasoning and evidence will not only help you prove a causal link but also eliminate alternative causes and effects.

✓ The Responsible Sourcing box entitled "Introducing Evidence and Support" will help you present your evidence authoritatively.

✓ Do not bury evidence that argues against your position. If you found it, others will. Exploring and eliminating alternative causes or effects not only makes a causal argument more persuasive; it is also a way of anticipating the counterarguments that may occur to your audience.

Responsible Sourcing
Introducing Evidence and Support

In a causal argument, you will generally use evidence from sources in two ways, either as direct evidence that a causal link does or does not exist or as expert opinion to back up your causal argument.

Direct Evidence

When introducing direct evidence of a causal link, you need to give your reader assurances that the evidence provided by the source is accurate, properly developed, confirmed by other experts, and relevant to the subject. In the following example, notice the language the writer uses to introduce and contextualize the sources. Words and phrases that help to establish the sources' authority are in bold.

> Many smokers have turned to E-cigarettes as a healthy alternative to traditional cigarettes. However, **a recent study** entitled "Hidden Formaldehyde in E-Cigarette Aerosols," **published by the *New England Journal of Medicine***, indicated that even in E-cigarette cartridges that did not contain formaldehyde, formaldehyde-releasing agents formed when the cartridge was heated **(Pankow). The American Cancer Society has studied the effect** of exposure to formaldehyde in traditional cigarettes for years, **and it has been shown to cause cancer** in laboratory animals and is linked to cancers in humans. Though traditional cigarettes have many more toxins, there is a clear link between the formaldehyde found in E-cigarettes and cancer.

Expert Opinion

When using an authoritative source to support your argument, you need to show clearly that the source is an expert in the subject of your argument. In the following example, notice how the source providing support for the writer's conclusion is introduced and contextualized.

> Therefore, E-cigarettes are not the healthy alternative that manufacturers advertise them to be and many ex-smokers wished them to be. In fact, Dr. James Pankow, professor of chemistry and engineering at Portland State University who has studied commercially available tank system E-cigarettes that use a variable-voltage battery, argues, "It's way too early now from an epidemiological point of view to say how bad they are." However, in his expert opinion, "the bottom line is, there are toxins and some are more than in regular cigarettes" (Pankow).

- Make it flow

✓ A strong causal argument makes connections that are acceptable to a skeptical audience that did not know or understand them before. In short, you are trying to link things your audience does not think are linked. To avoid a break in flow, map out your argument. Ask yourself, what must my audience believe before they accept my next point?

✓ Be sure to define important terms, phrases, and ideas. Your audience may not be familiar with terms or phrases such as "fracking" or "sufficient cause," and even if they are, they may not be familiar with the relationships you are describing.

✓ Use transitions between paragraphs and ideas to help your reader understand why you are shifting to a new point and what they can expect from the next paragraph or idea.

- Get peer response

✓ Peer response should not be limited to your classmates. Try to find responders who are close to or have the same viewpoints as those of your intended audience. No matter who provides a response to your argument, be sure your responders understand your intended audience and your purpose.

✓ The following questions and requests can help your peers provide responses you can use.
  - Please circle my thesis and tell me if it clearly identifies a cause or causes, the effects of a cause, or casual chain?
  - In the body of my argument, have I identified and described all relevant causes and effects? If not, which ones are missing?
  - How would you describe the causal relationship I am arguing?
  - What causes or effects have I discussed, and are any beyond the scope of my argument?
  - Do I prove enough evidence to prove a causal relationship?
  - Please underline every sentence that provides persuasive evidence of a causal link.
  - What is the significance of the cause and effect I describe?

- Revise your argument

✓ Make sure all your reasoning is supported by evidence, your evidence is introduced, contextualized, and linked to your argument, and all sources are correctly documented.

✓ Causal arguments are sequenced arguments. Check to make sure your sequence is logical. Also check to make sure your transitions take account of what you have just proved and direct your audience to your next point.

✓ It is too easy to get lost in the mechanics and logic of a causal analysis and forget your purpose. In an academic setting, make one last check of the assignment requirements. Are you required to make a causal argument or simply inform your audience of a causal relationship? Did you use the types of sources and documentation style that are expected?

CHAPTER 14

PROPOSING A SOLUTION

Crowdfunding sites raised $2.7 billion in 2012 and $16.2 billion in 2014. At the current rate of growth, the crowdfunding industry is expected to generate $500 billion by 2020. To give you an idea of how much money that is, a stack of 500 billion one-dollar bills would be six and a half miles high. You may be thinking that crowdfunding is an amazing example of the Internet's capacity to make it rain money. Crowdfunding sites, however, are also a vehicle for something even more powerful: proposal arguments.

Without a persuasive proposal on a crowdfunding site, those without money would not be able to solve problems or create new opportunities. In fact, the Internet we know today would not exist if J.C.R. Licklider of MIT had not written memos proposing that the Advanced Research Projects Agency (ARPA and later DARPA) research networking concepts with the goal of building a "Galactic Network."

Proposals are not reserved for major policies or projects like a galactic network, however, and usually they are very practical. If you've asked a friend whether she would trade her pudding for half a sandwich or asked someone to marry you, you've made a proposal. Some proposals are successful and some are not. The persuasive force of a proposal is not due to what is being proposed; after all, how often have you heard a proposal and thought "seriously?" or "sounds too good to be true." Proposals are persuasive due to careful invention and research, an understanding of the needs and desires of your audience, and an air of authority that makes you and your argument credible.

MODULE II-41

WHAT AUDIENCES EXPECT OF A PROPOSAL

A **proposal argument** is intended to persuade an audience to accept a solution to a problem or undertake a specific response to an opportunity. To do that, it identifies and informs the audience of a problem or opportunity, proposes a solution or response, shows with evidence and reasoning that the solution or response is superior to or more beneficial than other solutions or responses, and assures the audience that the solution will solve the problem or the response will achieve the stated goal.

Why Would I Need to Write a Proposal?

If you want to start a dance crew, change a zoning law, sell your bike on Craig's list, negotiate a labor contract, or propose marriage, you need to explain how things will be better in the future if your audience accepts your proposal today. In fact, if you want to bring about any change that you cannot do alone, a well-crafted proposal is the way to move others to help you achieve your ambition, campaign, agreement, or vision.

In academic settings, professors often assign proposals to develop specific competencies and writing skills such as "create a marketing strategy," "apply for a research grant," or "offer an alternative reading of a novel or data set." Professors also use proposal assignments to assess the ability of students to apply what they have learned. For example, in a political science class, your professor may ask you to study a number of Senate election campaigns and then propose a campaign strategy for an imaginary candidate. In a course with a service learning or applied learning project, you may be asked to develop a proposal that identifies a local problem and proposes a solution.

Types of Proposals: Practical and Policy Proposals

One way to think about proposal arguments is to examine their focus and scope. If a proposal deals with an immediate, practical problem, such as the need for a new labor contract or to replace your old bike, then it is a **practical proposal**. The scope of a practical proposal is limited to whatever is needed to respond to the problem or opportunity. The focus is on the specifics of the problem or opportunity, the specifics of the fix or response, and details such as when the solution should be in place and how the opportunity will work.

On the other hand, a **policy proposal** is focused on larger, more general issues and has a larger scope. Most of the people who joined the fight for net neutrality—the idea that Internet service providers should treat all content equally and not favor or block particular content or websites—probably stated their position but did not suggest detailed regulations for the Federal Communications Commission to enforce. Rather, they focused on preserving the general policy of net neutrality.

The reasoning and evidence supporting practical proposals are different from those supporting policy proposals. The memos proposing a Galactic Network drafted by J.C.R. Licklider described general benefits and not the specifics of how such a network would work. But once ARPA was on board, practical proposals followed, including solutions to real networking challenges, detailed schematics, and designs of switches and routers.

No matter what type of proposal you are writing, you might think of it as a way of helping your audience overcome a series of obstacles. Overcoming obstacles requires preparation, an understanding of the obstacles ahead, and an understanding of your team's capacities. When it comes to building an effective proposal, invention is your preparation.

Using Invention to Develop a Proposal

When using invention to develop a proposal, always consider the following two elements:

1. **A problem or opportunity**: Before your audience can decide to adopt your proposal, they must be aware of the problem or opportunity. Next, they must understand that it is a serious problem they can help to solve or a significant opportunity they can seize.

   For example, if you try to persuade your readers to support Title II reclassification of ISPs under the Communications Act of 1934, you are unlikely to inspire much excitement in your audience. However, with some thoughtful invention and careful research, you can recast your proposal in terms your audience will grasp: the Internet will slow down if you do not add your voice to the campaign for net neutrality.
2. **A solution**: Once your audience members recognize that the problem or opportunity you describe is important and urgent, they will expect a solution or a way to respond. Research will help you discover how others have responded to similar problems or opportunities as well as how previous proposals have failed or been ignored.

   In 2008, a young man surprised his girlfriend with a marriage proposal during a Houston Rockets basketball game. He was rejected at center court and left holding the ring box. Clearly, the proposal made perfect sense in his head, but it is just as clear that he did not do his research or fully think through all the possibilities. Research your audience so your proposal has a chance.

Making Your Proposal Acceptable to Your Audience

Thinking about the following aspects of a proposal will help you tailor it to your audience:

- **A Focus on the Right Audience**: It may seem obvious to say that proposals should be made only to those who might adopt your solution, but proposals are often made to the wrong audience.

  For example, you may be able to persuade US college students to accept your proposal for new laws ending government censorship of the Internet in China. However, they have no power to bring about such a change. The only individuals who could act on such a proposal are members of the Chinese Communist Party. In fact, the US government, as well as companies like Google and Facebook, have repeatedly proposed to the Chinese Foreign Ministry that they should tear down the "Great Firewall," arguing that such censorship harms trade relations.
- **A Rational, Doable, and Effective Call to Action**: Part of the challenge of building a persuasive proposal is rising above the noise of the countless proposals, opportunities, advertisements, and solutions we hear every day. To stand out, you must show that your solution or response is superior to earlier or competing proposals. A rational, doable, and effective call to action is more likely to be heard.

  The Battle for the Net consortium, a group of technology companies and nonprofit advocacy organizations, had only five days to pressure the FCC to adopt net-neutrality regulations (see http://blog.cloudflare.com/battleforthenet/). To rise above the noise, participating websites had to show that their proposal was more widely supported than those opposed to the regulations. The consortium also had to overcome apathy and motivate as many comments as possible. With three easy clicks of a mouse, anyone on the Internet could overcome seemingly large obstacles, a large government bureaucracy influenced by powerful lobbyists, and act. The campaign demonstrates that the persuasive power of a proposal is based not only on the reasoning and evidence but also on the audience's understanding of why and how to take action.
- **Incentives**: "Change is hard" may be one of the only clichés that is as overused as it is true. You want your readers to believe, think, or behave differently, but it is usually so much easier for them to continue as they have done in the past. And how they have thought about and done things in the past has worked out pretty well. When developing your proposal, keep in mind that you must offer real incentives that motivate your audience in three ways:
  - the future benefits of adopting the proposal overwhelm the audience's natural instinct to resist change;

- change is easier than simply ignoring the proposal and worth the effort given the proposed benefits; and
- urgent action is necessary to ensure the proposed benefits.

Making Your Proposal Authoritative

To convince an audience to adopt it, a successful proposal has the following elements:

- **Reasons and evidence**: Before your audience will act upon a solution or response, they must believe that a problem or opportunity is real and that the solution or response is rational and doable. By offering compelling reasons and solid evidence to back them up, you can convince your audience to believe you and adopt your proposal. In other words, reasons and evidence establish your authority.

  Your reasoning does not have to be sophisticated, but it must resonate with your intended audience. When Emma Watson addressed the United Nations to promote the "HeForShe" Campaign, her intended audience was men and boys who were put off by the word "feminist." Watson proposed that the word itself was not important, but rather that gender inequality and gender stereotypes are serious problems that also affect men. She argued that too many young men silently suffer mental illness for fear of being considered less of a man if they ask for help. To prove her point, she cited statistics from a report entitled "Suicides in the United Kingdom, 2013 Registrations," proving that young British men are more likely to die by suicide than from auto accidents, cancer, and heart disease. She concluded that more young men are likely to die of suicide if the current trend is not reversed. In this way, she recast what some men and boys see as a feminist issue into a shared experience that inhibits and injures all generations.
- **Alternative solutions and conviction about the best solution**: You must convince your reader or listener that your proposed solution is the best possible one. Therefore, you must present alternatives, analyze each fairly, and then explain why they will not provide the desired result. Once you have eliminated alternative solutions and responses, your audience will look to you for a better option that will solve the problem or a better response that will result in the opportunity described. Conviction happens in the minds of your audience members, so you must build it for them.

  For example, if your history-major roommate proposed to build and host your website for a dollar a month, it is unlikely that you would (or should) simply accept the offer. However, if your roommate has provided an impressive portfolio of websites she built and maintains, along with a stack of thank-you letters from happy customers, you might do well to hire her.

- **Integrity**: How your audience responds to your proposal may depend upon whether you are presenting a **transparent argument** so the audience can understand your purpose. If your audience can see that your proposal is not motivated simply by self-interest, that their future and yours will both be better if your proposal is adopted, they are more likely to be persuaded. On the other hand, if your purpose remains obscure, your audience will be suspicious. And as you know, suspicion does not lead to persuasion. But integrity is persuasive.

  For example, imagine you see what would normally be a $500 bike for sale on Craig's list for $300, and the seller will meet only at a Best Buy parking lot. You would be right to be suspicious. However, if the seller also has stated that she is leaving for the Peace Corps in a week and she wants to meet where she works for security reasons, you understand that her purpose is reasonable. Transparent arguments are persuasive because they contribute to your authority.

Genres That Propose a Solution

Proposals are a part of everyday life, and people have been composing proposals for as long as they have found reasons to work together. Tradition provides several genres of proposals that have proven effective in very different situations:

- **Position paper**: a written statement of an individual's or organization's views, disposition, or response toward an issue, policy, or question. It often includes counter-positions or counter-proposals.
- **Pop-up advertisement**: an online advertisement designed to entice or draw viewers to another website providing goods and services.
- **Advocacy speech**: a speech made on behalf of, and for the benefit of, an individual or a group, or a speech in support of a position or proposal.
- **Op-ed piece**: a brief persuasive argument typically found in a magazine or newspaper ("opposite the editorial") in which the author proposes a way of thinking, believing, or acting.
- **Proposed budget**: a financial estimate of future costs, obligations, and expenses.
- **Business proposal**: a text written to describe a business transaction to a potential client or customer. The proposal includes the goods and services offered, anticipated outcomes, and the price of the goods or services.

MODULE II-42

A PROPOSAL GENRE: ADVOCACY SPEECH

In September 2014, actress Emma Watson of the *Harry Potter* movies delivered an advocacy speech to the United Nations General Assembly. Her proposal was intended for an audience that may not have identified with the problem she describes. In the six months after she delivered her speech, it received nearly seven million YouTube views.

Notice how she urges her audience to move past obstacles as she redefines the problem.

Gender Equality Is Your Issue, Too

Today we are launching a campaign called "HeForShe."

I am reaching out to you because I need your help. We want to end gender inequality—and to do that we need everyone to be involved.

Purpose and Incentive: involve everyone to end gender inequality

This is the first campaign of its kind at the UN: we want to try and galvanize as many men and boys as possible to be advocates for gender equality. And we don't just want to talk about it, but make sure it is tangible.

I was appointed six months ago and the more I have spoken about feminism the more I have realized that fighting for women's rights has **too often become synonymous with man-hating. If there is one thing I know for certain, it is that this has to stop.**

Problem: feminism perceived as anti-man

For the record, feminism by definition is: "The belief that **men and women should have equal rights and opportunities. It is the theory of the political, economic and social equality of the sexes."**

Reason: definition of feminism requires equal rights for men and women

...

A few paragraphs have been left out for brevity

Apparently I am among the ranks of women whose expressions are seen as too strong, too aggressive, isolating, anti-men, and unattractive.

Why is the word such an uncomfortable one?

I am from Britain and think it is right that as a woman I am paid the same as my male counterparts. I think it is right that I should be able to make decisions about my own body. I think it is right that women be involved on my behalf in the

Conviction: women of Britain hold these rights, so can other countries policies and decision-making of my country. I think it is right that socially I am afforded the same respect as men. But sadly I can say that **there is no one country in the world where all women can expect to receive these rights.**

Problem: gender inequality persists

No country in the world can yet say they have achieved gender equality.

These rights I consider to be human rights but I am one of the lucky ones. My life is a sheer privilege because my parents didn't love me less because I was born a daughter. My school did not limit me because I was a girl. My mentors didn't assume I would go less far because I might give birth to a child one day. These influencers were the gender equality ambassadors that made me who I am today. They may not know it, but they are the inadvertent feminists who are changing the world today. And we need more of those.

Conviction: her life is evidence that change in countries, cultures, and schools is possible

And if you still hate the word—**it is not the word that is important but the idea and the ambition behind it.** Because not all women have been afforded the same rights that I have. In fact, statistically, very few have been.

Reason: the word is not important, but the ambition for equality is

...

<u>Men—I would like to take this opportunity to extend your formal invitation. Gender equality is your issue too.</u>

<u>Audience: men</u>

Because to date, **I've seen my father's role as a parent being valued less by society despite my needing his presence as a child as much as my mother's.**

Problem: gender inequality affects men

I've seen young men suffering from mental illness unable to ask for help for fear it would make them look less "macho"—in fact in the UK suicide is the biggest killer of men between 20–49 years of age, eclipsing road accidents, cancer and coronary heart disease. I've seen men made fragile and insecure by a distorted sense of what constitutes male success. Men don't have the benefits of equality either.

We don't often talk about men being imprisoned by gender stereotypes but I can see that they are and that when they are free, things will change for women as a natural consequence.

If men don't have to be aggressive in order to be accepted women won't feel compelled to be submissive. If men don't have to control, women won't have to be controlled.

Reason: stereotypes compel men to continue stereotypes

Both men and women should feel free to be sensitive. Both men and women should feel free to be strong.... It is time that we all perceive gender on a spectrum not as two opposing sets of ideals.

If we stop defining each other by what we are not and start defining ourselves by what we are—we can all be freer and this is what HeForShe is about. It's about freedom.

I want men to take up this mantle. So their daughters, sisters and mothers can be free from prejudice but also so that their sons have permission to be vulnerable and human too—reclaim those parts of themselves they abandoned and in doing so be a more true and complete version of themselves.

...

And having seen what I've seen—and given the chance—I feel it is my duty to say something. English Statesman Edmund Burke said: "All that is needed for the forces of evil to triumph is for enough good men and women to do nothing."

In my nervousness for this speech and in my moments of doubt I've told myself firmly—if not me, who? If not now, when? If you have similar doubts when opportunities are presented to you I hope those words might be helpful.

Because the reality is that if we do nothing it will take 75 years, or for me to be nearly a hundred, before women can expect to be paid the same as men for the same work. Fifteen point five million girls will be married in the next 16 years as children. And at current rates it won't be until 2086 before all rural African girls will be able to receive a secondary education.

If you believe in equality, you might be one of those inadvertent feminists I spoke of earlier.

And for this I applaud you.

We are struggling for a uniting word but the good news is we have a uniting movement. It is called HeForShe. I am inviting you to step forward, to be seen to speak up, to be the "he" for "she." And to ask yourself, if not me, who? If not now, when?

Thank you very, very much.

Solution: when women are free of gender inequality and stereotypes men will be free as well

Incentive: ensure daughters and sons are free from prejudice

Reason: stopping gender inequality requires good men and women to act

Problem: inaction will result in continued inequality and suffering

Conviction: inadvertent feminists have and will continue to make change

Solution: men unite with women in HeForShe movement

Questions to Consider

Invention

1. Proposals try to bring about change, but often resistance prevents change. What resistance may have inspired Watson to develop her proposal?
2. Watson supports her proposal with evidence from sources. Where would she have looked to find this evidence?
3. If you wanted to make a similar proposal to boys and men in the United States or in another country, how would you go about researching your subject and audience?

Audience

4. Watson addressed the United Nations, but who was her intended audience, and how do you know?
5. What resistance does Watson's proposal have to overcome in the minds of its intended listeners?

Authority

6. Watson is not an expert on gender issues, and in fact her fame as an actress may get in the way of her argument. How does she establish authority?
7. Sometimes, creating conviction in the minds of your readers or listeners is the most difficult part of writing an effective proposal. How does Watson convince her audience that her proposal is rational, doable, and potentially effective?
8. Is Watson's proposal transparent? Is her purpose aligned with the incentive she gives the audience?

MODULE II-43

A PROPOSAL GENRE: POP-UP ADVERTISEMENT

On September 10, 2014, a consortium of more than 80 websites called the Battle for the Net initiated a campaign called "Internet Slowdown Day." The campaign proposed that net-neutrality regulations be adopted—in other words, that all Internet traffic is to be treated equally and no internet service provider (ISP) is allowed to charge different prices for different types of data or traffic.

The proposal was in the form of a pop-up ad (Figure 14.1) linked to the *Battle for the Net* website (Figure 14.2).

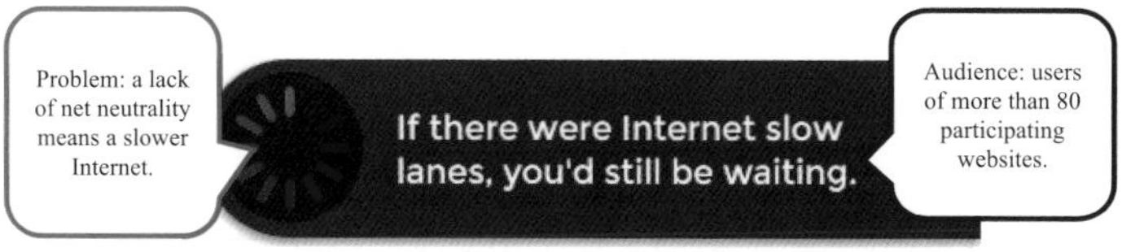

Figure 14.1 The spinning wheel of death. When users clicked the pop-up, they saw this:

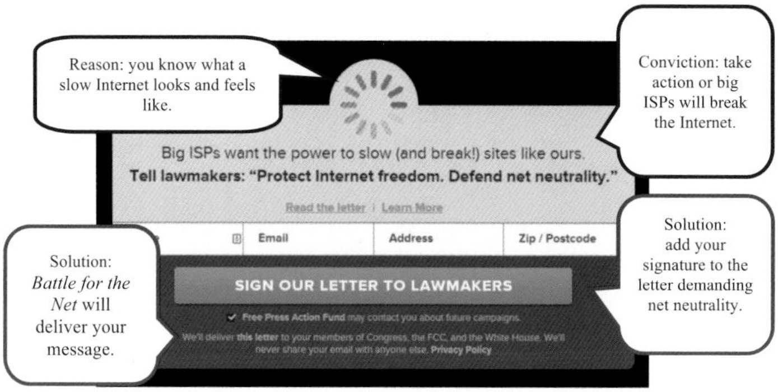

Figure 14.2 Users sent more than 4.7 million comments to the FCC.

Questions to Consider

Invention

1. Imagine that you need to develop an alternative ad opposing net neutrality. How would you begin your invention process?
2. Proposals like this one are an attempt to make an audience aware of a potential problem. If in conducting your initial research you discovered that cable providers would invest in technology enabling incredibly fast download speeds if they were free to charge higher rates for specific types of data downloads, where would you look for additional information and data about your subject and audience?
3. Sometimes the best way to start a proposal argument is to start where your audience is. Visualize why people your age, for example, might prefer their Internet provider to charge different rates for different types of Internet content. Now visualize the reasons and evidence that would give your audience an incentive to oppose net neutrality.

Audience

4. Based on the imagery alone, what do the creators of the pop-up ad believe is a primary concern of the audience?
5. What obstacle stands in the way of participating websites achieving their purpose?
6. Is this a transparent argument? Why did the websites participate in this campaign?

Authority

7. Creating authority visually can be a challenge because a visual argument needs to convey authority in a different way than by a written or spoken argument. Describe the authority portrayed in the pop-up ad that would lead the audience to believe the proposed response is a good idea.
8. How will the audience benefit if they respond as the ad suggests? Who will the Battle for the Net consortium benefit?
9. You can create authority if you can demonstrate that you understand your audience's situation, needs, and interests. Has Battle for the Net established authority with the intended audience? Why or why not?

MODULE II-44

A PROPOSAL GENRE: POSITION PAPER

Veronica Pacheco wrote the following position paper as part of her "College Composition" portfolio. This context implies that the professor is the audience. However, the way in which Pacheco describes the problem of endangered sharks suggests that she has another intended audience in mind as well, namely those who care about animals or the environment but are unaware of the practice and impact of shark finning.

Consider the Shark

Veronica Pacheco

Although sharks in movies like *Sharknado* and *Jaws* are portrayed as cold, vicious killers, sharks are like other animals; they can feel pain. *Shark finning, on the other hand is cold and vicious. It is the practice of slicing off a shark's fins while the shark is still alive and throwing it back into the ocean* ("Shark

Education"). *Shark fins are harvested for the sake of a single kind of soup. The Chinese are the largest consumers of shark fin soup, a delicacy at banquets and important dinners. For the sake of this soup, 99% of shark protein is wasted, these animals are put through unnecessary suffering, and shark finning threatens the balance of the oceans' ecosystems.*

Problem: shark finning

Sharks should no longer be hunted solely for their fins because the methods are inhumane, finning threatens the ecosystem, and there are alternatives that will protect the wild population.

Thesis: stop animal cruelty and protect the ecosystem

Shark finning is cruel and inhumane and must end. After a shark is caught and the fins sliced off, the live shark is tossed back into the water. Unable to swim, the shark slowly sinks toward the bottom where it is defenseless and can take days to die an agonizing death as it is eaten alive by other fish ("Shark Education"). Finning is inhumane. In addition, some of the methods used to catch sharks are harmful to the environment. Longline fishing practices are the most significant cause of losses in shark populations worldwide. Longlining involves floating a main line, around 100 feet, on the surface of the water while smaller secondary lines are baited and hang beneath the main line. Longline fishing is indiscriminate; all kinds of sharks are attracted to the bait. Experts estimate that within a decade most species of sharks will be lost because of longlining ("Longline Fishing").

Reason: finning causes unreasonable and unnecessary suffering

Reason: longline fishing kills many species indiscriminately

Currently, twenty species of sharks are listed as endangered by the International Union for Conservation of Nature (IUCN). Since 1972, populations of many shark species have fallen by over 90% ("Shark Education"). As the graph below shows (fig. 1), shark populations have collapsed in the Northwest Atlantic where the US longline fishing fleet is based. Through careful

Reason: many species of sharks are endangered

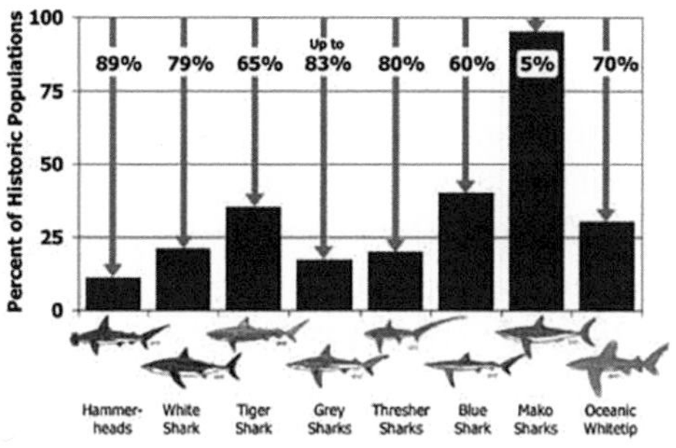

Fig. 1
The research team led by Julia Baum collected data from 15 years of longline fishing trawler logbooks. Graph provided by Tobey Curtis and the Fisheries Blog.

management, though, a few species are making a comeback.

Loss and devastation of shark populations around the world affects the oceans and those who depend on shark meat as a main food source in third world countries. If longlining and shark finning continue to increase, these practices will inevitably lead to the extinction of shark species. Hence, the oceanic ecosystems of the world will forever be altered.

Why bother saving the sharks? Sharks and humans alike are both part of the food web. Every organism depends on other species and the ecosystem as a whole to survive. The extinction of sharks impacts not only the sharks but also all the other organisms such as small fish. A reduction in sharks can lead to a reduction in seafood that serves as a source of nutrition for a large segment of the world's population. For example, tiger sharks are key to the quality of seagrass beds and ecosystem balance. If that shark population is greatly reduced, then the ray population will explode, causing a significant drop in medium sized fish and green sea turtles, which live and feed in seagrass beds ("Shark Education"). Without tiger sharks to control their prey's foraging, this important habitat will be lost. **The balance of biodiversity is vital to life.**

Reason: reduced shark population affects ocean and people

Incentive: protect biodiversity, which protects seafood stock

How do we start to fix this problem? **Breeding sharks specifically for culinary purposes in shark farms would enable humane harvesting methods and leave the wild shark population untouched.** Finning is illegal in federal waters; however, enforcement on the ocean is nearly impossible ("Shark Education"). Because shark farms could be regulated, raising sharks for food could be made as humane as possible.

Solution: shark farms

Another solution would be to change the appetites of those who buy and consume shark fins. **A number of organizations have held contests asking renowned chefs to develop soup recipes without fins, and the results are encouraging.**

Solution: change appetites

Further, a change in the overall attitudes about sharks can make a difference. Let's face it, sharks are unappealing, unlike cute polar bear cubs and other endangered species. However, **Shark Week on the Discovery Channel has already done a great deal to help people understand and respect these complex creatures.** Clearly, television programs alone won't save sharks from suffering painful, wasteful deaths. However, as Shark Week shows, the negative connotation that surrounds

Solution: change attitudes

Conviction: attitudes are changing

sharks can be changed, and further efforts will continue to make people more inclined to contribute to the cause.

Clearly, shark finning is an inhumane fishing method and the ways the fins are harvested are wasteful and cruel. **You may not eat shark fin soup, but you can protect sharks by boycotting and protesting restaurants that serve such soup. Share the story of sharks and the inhumane act of finning, and join and support international organizations that are dedicated to protecting the shark and marine ecosystems, such as Sea Shepherd, the Humane Society International, and Wild Aid.** *These organizations are having an impact,* **and by joining them you can ensure that they continue to work to protect sharks.** The next time you hear the daunting theme music from the movie *Jaws*, instead of screaming in fear, just consider the shark.

Conviction: increased awareness is already happening and will continue

Solution: support the protection of sharks

Incentive: protect sharks

Works Cited

Baum, Julia K. et al. "Collapse and Conservation of Shark Populations in the Northwest Atlantic." *Science*, vol. 299, no. 5605, 2003, pp. 389–92. www.jstor.org/stable/3833388.

Curtis, Tobey. "Jaws Returns: Signs of Recovery in Well-Managed Shark Populations." *The Fisheries Blog*, 4 June 2012, https://thefisheriesblog.com/2012/06/04/jaws-returns-signs-of-recovery-in-well-managed-shark-populations/. Accessed 3 Oct. 2015.

"Longline Fishing Threatens Seabirds and Other Marine Life." *The Humane Society of the United States*, 25 Sept. 2009, http://www.humanesociety.org/issues/fisheries/facts/longline_fishing_marine_life.html. Accessed 6 Oct. 2015.

"Shark Education—Shark Finning Facts." *Sharkwater*, Sharkwater Productions, 2016, www.sharkwater.com/index.php/shark-education/. Accessed 12 Oct. 2015.

MLA format

Questions to Consider

Invention

1. A proposal is often an answer to a question. What question do you imagine Pacheco was trying to answer with her proposal?
2. Where do you think Pacheco looked for her initial research about her subject and audience?
3. What information and data appear to be discoveries Pacheco made during research?

Audience

4. Based on her language and examples, what can you infer about the audience that Pacheco had in mind for her proposal?
5. What resistance would Pacheco's proposal have to overcome in the minds of its intended readers?

Authority

6. How does Pacheco build conviction that her proposal is possible and doable and will have the desired effects?
7. Pacheco is not an expert on the subject she writes or speaks about here. What does she do to establish authority?
8. Pacheco wrote this proposal in response to a class assignment. How would her attempt to establish authority be different if she were writing an op-ed for a local newspaper?

MODULE II-45

BUILDING A PROPOSAL

Finding a solution to a problem or identifying the best way to respond to an opportunity is the first step in developing your position paper—a step that involves invention. The second step is to shape your proposal so that your audience sees the problem and solution as you do. Ensuring that your audience recognizes the overwhelming rightness of your proposal and the authority of your argument is the final step. Your process may not look like others. Feel free to follow the checklist item by item or adapt it to your way of writing.

Invention

- Find a problem or an opportunity

✓ If you are free to select a problem or an opportunity, first look within. You probably face challenges both large and small every day. For example, how do you protect yourself from identity theft, or how do you keep track of the different interest rates on your student loans? You have probably found ways to solve problems such as these that others would like to hear about.

✓ Look around and research the problems that concern others. Often people voice problems as complaints, grievances, or criticisms.

Editorials and opinion pages are an excellent source of problems to address in proposal arguments. Editorial writers air grievances and criticize a wide variety of acts, events, and policies. Within an academic setting, every discipline has its own internal problems—for instance, how can a social scientist research different cultural behaviors without imposing his or her own beliefs and values?

Websites like Livehacker.com, AddictiveTips.com, and even Pinterest.com don't solve problems but show how others have responded to problems and issues that many people experience. Others, like OpenIDEO.com, encourage participants to find practical and policy solutions for large social issues.

- Invent and research solutions

✓ If you have looked around, researched, and found no solutions, reconsider the problem. Most problems that look new are actually reformulations of old problems.

For example, email spam is a contemporary version of an old problem. In fact, communication systems—from the telegraph to the CB radio—have always had the problem of noise. In this case, widening your scope and looking into communication history could be useful. Perhaps the solutions that early users of the telegraph developed to reduce line noise could be reformulated to reduce spam.

✓ Some problems seem unsolvable. In such a case, it may be helpful to change your scope. Remember that solutions can range from practical acts and decisions by individuals to major policy shifts.

For example, Veronica Pacheco realized that she couldn't ask her American audience to ban shark fin soup in Asia in order to protect sharks. She then proposed the very doable solution of joining organizations that protect sharks and marine life in general.

✓ Do not hesitate to propose a solution that has already been tried or has been written off.

For example, the average age of a farmer today is 55, and the number of small and family farms is diminishing. If the trend continues, we may run out of people who know how to farm or want to learn. One idea for addressing this problem is not new: you could propose starting chapters of Future Farmers of America (founded in 1928) in cities, colleges, and universities that do not have them.

Once you start exploring a problem or opportunity, you are likely to find a number of options. The Breaking the Block box entitled "Using Stasis Questions to Develop a Proposal" will help you develop the best proposal.

Breaking the Block
Using Stasis Questions to Develop a Proposal

The stasis questions of procedure and proposal can help you find a subject for a proposal argument and a solution. The writing component of this exercise should take 15 minutes.

Step One
Find a news story about an event, development, or problem that interests you. For example, you may have read that Jerry Jones, owner of the Dallas Cowboys, bought a helicopter to avoid long commutes to his office, and this news may lead you to wonder how others in Dallas can deal with traffic congestion.

Step Two
Read about the event, development, or problem on reputable news sites such as *Time* magazine or scientificamerican.com, and then write for 15 minutes and develop answers to the following secondary stasis questions:

- Is a response necessary?
- Who should respond?
- What kind of response is possible?
- What kind of response is necessary?
- What must be done to respond?

Step Three
Reflect upon what you have written and try to develop alternative answers, different proposals, and other purposes. For example, if at first you argued that a response to congested Dallas traffic is necessary, but it is not possible for everyone to buy a chopper, imagine an alternative. Instead of an individual response, perhaps you could propose a high-speed commuter train built on top of Dallas's busiest highways and paid for by a city gas tax.

- Draft a working thesis

✓ In a proposal argument, the thesis is in two parts: the problem or opportunity that must be resolved and the proposed solution or response.
✓ Your thesis should also indicate the reasons and evidence you will use to argue for your proposal. Four common ways to structure reasons and evidence are:

1. Bad consequences—doing nothing or adopting other proposals will result in these bad consequences...
2. Good consequences—adopting your proposal will result in good consequences or desired outcomes...
3. Best practice—the solution you are proposing has succeeded in solving the same kind of problem in other locations at other times...
4. Principled action—your proposal is the only one that reflects the best values or ideals...

Audience

- Understand the rhetorical situation

✓ The context of a proposal is often defined by an audience that does not see the need to act, is hesitant, or is resistant to act as you propose. Build your argument around your audience's position. If they don't see a problem, begin with a discussion of the problem. If they favor a different response, start with a critique of the alternative.

✓ The rhetorical situation should guide your research and the evidence you use. You may have evidence proving that a proposed commuter rail network will ease traffic congestion, but your audience may be more worried about the higher taxes needed to pay for it. Without evidence and reasoning addressing their concern, persuasion will be unlikely. Always keep in mind the obstacles you are inviting your skeptical audience to overcome.

- Identify the appropriate audience

✓ Each problem will affect, or each opportunity will be available to, a limited number of people. In other words, your intended audience should be those who can directly or indirectly bring about the change you propose.

✓ When you define the problem or opportunity, you will define the audience best situated to respond to your proposal.

For example, if the problem is slow Wi-Fi in the classrooms and dorms, the people best situated to respond are in the campus Information Technology office. You do not need to make a proposal to your student government to address slow Wi-Fi speed.

- Organize your argument

✓ Proposal arguments are about creating expectations. If your audience accepts the problem or is intrigued by the opportunity, they will then ask what should be done. Having created the expectation, you then provide your solution or response. The Conventions in Context box entitled "Outlining Is High Speed Prototyping" will help you organize your proposal.

Conventions in Context
Outlining Is High Speed Prototyping

Designers and fabricators use 3-D printers to try out different shapes and structures quickly at a low cost.

Effective writers do the same with outlines. Outlining your argument, even after you have a draft in hand, can help you see the structure of your proposal and try out different organizations quickly. Below is one outline for a proposal argument, but like any prototype or model, you must adapt the outline to suit your purpose and audience.

I. Introduction
- A. Introduce the problem with a brief narrative
- B. Briefly describe consequences and your solution
- C. State your thesis
- D. Outline your argument

II. Narrative of situation
- A. Define the problem
- B. Describe the history of the problem
- C. List factors contributing to the problem
- D. Explain consequences if the problem is not addressed

III. Body of argument
- A. Describe the solution
- B. Give the first reason to adopt your solution with supporting evidence
- C. Give the second reason and evidence
- D. Give the third reason and evidence

IV. Alternative solutions
- A. Summarize one or more alternative solutions
- B. Concede good points of alternative solutions

C. Refute—explain why alternative solutions will fail
D. Summary

V. Conclusion
A. Summarize your argument
B. Summarize failing alternative solutions
C. Make your final appeal for adoption of your proposal

- Draft your argument

✓ The persuasive force of your solution or response depends wholly on your audience's acceptance of the problem or opportunity you describe. Therefore, it may be best to start with a clear description of the problem or opportunity, as it will set the stage for the rest of your argument. In addition, if you are working with a solid outline, you can work on different parts and sections of your argument at different times without fear of losing track of your argument's structure.
✓ If you get stuck, sometimes a redraft with a different audience in mind will help. Ask yourself what other group may help achieve your purpose. Who else is best situated to fix the problem or see the opportunity you see?

Authority

- Check your ethos and logic

✓ Your ethics—the principles that guide your behavior—are not self-evident to your audience. It is possible for a good and honest person to be perceived as a sketchy fraud if his or her argument does not establish a sense that the author is trustworthy.
✓ *Ethos* is the way in which an author or speaker moves an audience to believe that the source of the message is trustworthy and authoritative. To make sure your *ethos* is apparent to your audience, you should first strive for a transparent proposal argument, one in which your purpose is obvious to your audience and consistent with the action you are proposing that your audience adopt. Second, your audience will gain confidence in your proposal if you can show that your method of arriving at it was rational and exhaustive.
✓ Your logic also contributes to your trustworthiness. Check to make sure the following logical links are clear and rational:

1. Your analysis of the problem or opportunity is clear and reasonable.
2. The outcome, consequence, or result you anticipate if a change is not made is based on solid logic and evidence.
3. Your solution or response directly addresses the problem or opportunity.
4. You provide a fair summary and serious examination of alternative solutions, and evidence guides your analysis of alternative solutions or responses.
5. The outcome, consequence, or result of your proposed change is also based on solid reasoning and evidence.

✓ When using images as evidence, transparency and solid logic are especially important because images can be very persuasive and because your audience knows how easily images can be manipulated. The Responsible Sourcing box will help you use images ethically and logically.

Responsible Sourcing
Images Can Define—and Deceive

Responsible sourcing is not simply a matter of accurate documentation, but also of integrating and using information from your sources ethically. Photographs, in particular, are an excellent way both to document and dramatize problems and to describe opportunities. However, images can deceive. Skeptical audiences are aware that images can be manipulated to misrepresent or obscure.

Figure 14.3 The three different versions of this image were posted on reddit by redditor Antonskarp. The first appears to show the capture of an enemy, next compassion for an enemy, and finally aid given to a comrade.

The three images of the soldiers tell three different stories, yet they are simply differently cropped versions of the same image. Whether you are including images to portray a problem or a solution, responsible use will add persuasive power to your argument, and you will avoid raising suspicion in a skeptical audience.

- Make it flow

✓ In three areas of your proposal, logical flow requires your special attention. First, your readers or listeners must accept that the problem or opportunity is urgent and relevant to them. Second, the audience must see a relationship between the problem or opportunity as described and your proposed solution or response. Third, audience members must see the proposal as rational and doable.

- Get peer response

✓ Peer response is most useful when your respondents understand the audience for your proposal and can imagine themselves as members. Therefore, clearly describe for them the thinking and disposition of your intended audience.

✓ To help your peer reviewers focus on your purpose, your audience, and the genre you are using, ask them to read the following requests and questions before they read your draft.
  - Please summarize the problem or opportunity.
  - Will the audience believe there is a problem or an opportunity? If not, why not?
  - Does the problem or opportunity require urgent attention? If not, why not?
  - How would you summarize the solution or response?
  - Is the solution rational, or does it seem unrealistic? Is the solution or response doable, or is it unlikely to achieve the results described?
  - Have alternate solutions or proposals been considered and dealt with fairly?
  - Can you identify the incentives for acting on the problem or opportunity?
  - If sources are used, do you understand why their opinions should be trusted?
  - What can be done to make the proposal argument more persuasive?

- Revise your argument

✓ Once you have a solid draft, revision is your chance to rearrange the major parts of your proposal to see if you can squeeze even more persuasive power from your ideas.

✓ Argue against your proposal. Take ten minutes and try to imagine all the possible ways in which someone could argue against your proposal. Where are the weak links in your reasoning that an opponent may exploit? Do you promise greater incentives than your solution can truly provide?

✓ Your reader will need to know quickly why you are directing your proposal their way and what specifically you are proposing. Try rewriting your thesis or restructuring your argument to answer these questions as soon as possible.

✓ As you revise, pay attention to your tone and tenor. When making proposals, a common pitfall is to adopt the tenor of a know-it-all. Also, a tone that suggests your proposal is the only reasonable option may lead your audience to question your reasonability. Clearly, you need to express confidence that your proposal or response is best, but avoid denigrating or badmouthing other proposals. Your audience is more likely to listen to someone who shares their interests in making things better, so don't talk down. Remember, you are trying to build a partnership.

PART III

APPEALING TO YOUR AUDIENCE

CHAPTER 15

UNDERSTANDING YOUR AUDIENCE

If you are a hot new chef and want to win *Top Chef*, what do you need to know? In this cooking competition, the best chefs in the nation compete in cooking challenges and try to impress the judges.

Would it help to know that one judge was raised in an Italian American home but learned to cook by reading French cookbooks? Do you need to know that when asked what food they would need on a desert island, one judge said Champagne, dark chocolate, *spaghetti alla carbonara*, mangoes, and beef jerky?

Rhetoric is not cooking, but like a great chef, the persuasive writer or speaker understands that it's the members of the audience who declare the effort a success or failure.

You may have a great deal of talent, ideas, and resources you can use to make an argument. But if you want to persuade others, you need to know the situation that will shape how your words and ideas will be heard or read.

MODULE III-1

RHETORICAL SITUATION DEFINED

A **rhetorical situation** is a context in which someone tries to persuade someone else or members of an audience. It consists of a writer or speaker, a message, an audience, and the limits or conditions that shape and give meaning to the moment in which the audience hears the message. Limits and conditions can be as varied as having only 500 words to describe an important issue, or the willingness of an audience to sit in the hot sun as they listen to your valedictorian speech. Practically speaking, writers and speakers use the idea of a rhetorical situation to make their ideas appealing and persuasive in the mind of their intended audience.

Therefore, before responding to or making any public statement or argument, you need to gather information about the situation.

The rhetorical situation (see Figure 15.1) consists of all the elements that affect how an audience understands an argument. The audience, writer/speaker, and message form a triangle at the heart of the rhetorical situation.

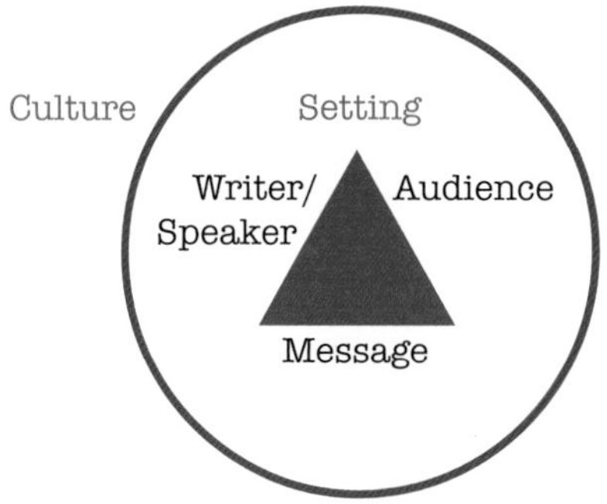

Figure 15.1 The rhetorical situation.

- **Audience**: the individual or group who will read, hear, or observe your argument. Your audience could be your professor, the readers of your blog, or a stadium full of people.
- **Writer/Speaker**: the one who creates and delivers the argument—in this case, you.
- **Message**: the language, imagery, sound, media, and technology that make up the argument intended to persuade the audience. A research paper, text message, and the State of the Union address all qualify as messages.

The rhetorical triangle always happens within a specific situation that is shaped by the immediate setting and surrounding culture.

- **Setting**: The setting is the time, place, and context in which your audience encounters your argument. Your audience might find your argument on the op-ed page of the local newspaper, for instance. The setting is also defined by the exigency that brings the writer or speaker and audience together. **Exigency** is the issue, urgent need, or recent event that motivates the speaker's message and so gives meaning to the setting. Your town's proposal to start charging a toll for crossing a nearby bridge might inspire your op-ed piece.

- **Culture**: All rhetorical situations exist within some larger cultural environment. Culture is composed of beliefs, values, and practices that make it possible for the individual to express ideas and experiences, and for an audience to understand these expressions. Your town may have its own culture, and different academic disciplines have very distinct cultures.

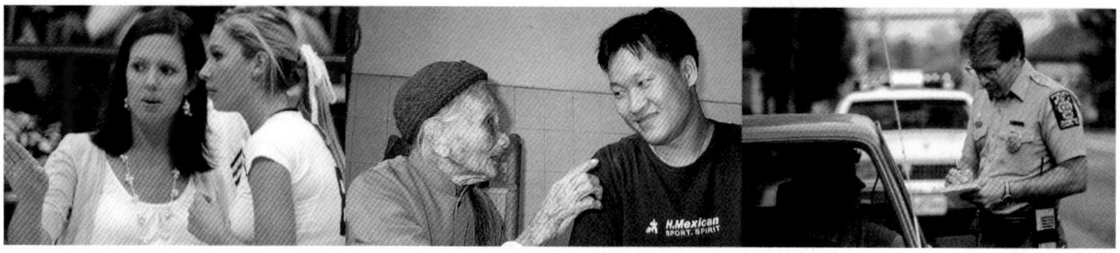

Every time you talk or write to someone, you are in a complex rhetorical situation.

If the rhetorical situation seems complicated, consider that you respond appropriately to complex rhetorical situations all the time without thinking about it.

Most of the information you need to examine and understand a rhetorical situation comes from you or your experience. The rest is easily discoverable.

MODULE III-2

AUDIENCE DEFINED

An **audience** is the individual or group who will read, hear, or observe your argument. If rhetoric is having the right word at the right time for the right audience, then everything depends upon addressing an audience you understand.

Intended and Secondary Audiences

Many people may hear or read your words and ideas; however, not everyone in your audience needs to hear you and not everyone is essential to your purpose. As you develop your argument, you will identify the **intended audience** you hope to persuade. These are the people who will help you achieve your purpose once persuaded. For example, if you intend to persuade your new boss of your skill and dedication, your new boss is your intended audience.

A **secondary audience** consists of others who read, hear, or observe your arguments. There are two kinds of secondary audience.

1. **Someone who can influence your intended audience**. If your intended audience is your boss, for instance, a secondary audience may be the boss's administrative assistant who also reads your document. If she hands it to your boss with positive comments, she could help persuade your intended audience.
2. **Your professor, who creates a fictional intended audience**. For example, a marketing professor may require your group to develop an advertising campaign for an imaginary company. You will write to persuade this imaginary company's CEO, but your professor, your secondary audience, will grade your work.

Simple and Complex Audiences

An audience can also be simple or complex. A **simple audience** is composed of one individual, or people with similar characteristics—such as age and education—and dispositions. **Disposition** is an individual's tendency of thought, preferred view, or initial understanding of an issue or your argument.

A **complex audience** may have a wide range of characteristics and dispositions and include individuals who will not be persuaded and those who already agree with you. In general, as introduced in Chapter 1, there are three kinds of audience members:

1. **The Doubters**: those who strongly disagree with you and are unlikely to change their minds despite your reasons and evidence.
2. **The Choir**: those who already agree with you and need no further persuasion.
3. **The Receptive**: those who have not considered your position, are undecided, or are leaning in a different direction but will give you a chance to make your argument.

The people most likely to be persuaded are the receptive. However, not everyone who can be persuaded can also help you achieve your goal. For example, you may convince your mother you would be an excellent class president, but if she cannot vote in the class election, she cannot help you get elected.

MODULE III-3

ANALYZING AN AUDIENCE

Persuasive writers and speakers analyze, define, and target those who can and need to be persuaded. When you do an **audience analysis** as you build an argument, you are trying to find answers to these questions.

- Who needs to be persuaded so you can achieve your goal?
- Among those who need to be persuaded, who *can* be persuaded?
- If they can be persuaded, what do they think and believe now?
- What do they expect and require of a writer or speaker?

There are a number of ways of discovering the characteristics and dispositions of audience members:

1. **Address your assigned audience**. If you have been assigned an audience, the characteristics and disposition of its members are close at hand. If your advertising agency has been hired to sell high-end headphones to 18- to 35-year-old musicians, vocalists, DJs, and producers, you need only examine this group. If you are writing for a professor, your audience was assigned when you picked the course, and his or her disposition will probably be on display during class.
2. **Invent your audience**. Imagine you are the first human to talk to an alien. You do not know the alien's language, culture, or purpose. All you can do is to try to observe and then guess what actions and sounds will be meaningful. Students face a similar problem. Until they have observed and understand how professors talk, what they value, how they behave, and what they expect, students can only guess what a professor expects. Over time, if students are attentive and research their audience, wrong guesses are corrected and solid information begins to flesh out the nature of the audience. Direct and effective communication is then possible.
3. **Discover your audience**. If you have not been assigned an audience, your audience may become clear as you build your argument. For example, suppose you want to propose that Election Day each year should be a holiday. Initially, you may not have an audience in mind. However, as you research the subject, you may discover that your congressional representative is a member of the House Committee on Administration that can propose changes to federal election laws. Once you have discovered and defined your audience, you can target it with reasons and evidence. (Chapter 1 can help you research an audience.)

Audience Analysis Checklist

Analyzing your audience is not like reading a Match.com profile. Just because someone shares your background, interests, and ethnicity does not mean the two of you will see an issue in a similar way. Each member of an audience is distinct, and an audience of distinct individuals does not share identical characteristics and dispositions.

However, if you are writing or speaking to more than one person, it is difficult to shape your argument without making some generalizations about your audience and the setting. The more informed your generalizations, the more persuasive your argument will be. The checklist in Figure 15.2 will help you analyze your intended audience so you can clarify your purpose and shape your argument. If you can answer all the checklist questions, you will have a good profile of your audience. Your argument will be more effective if it is based on a real audience as opposed to an invented one.

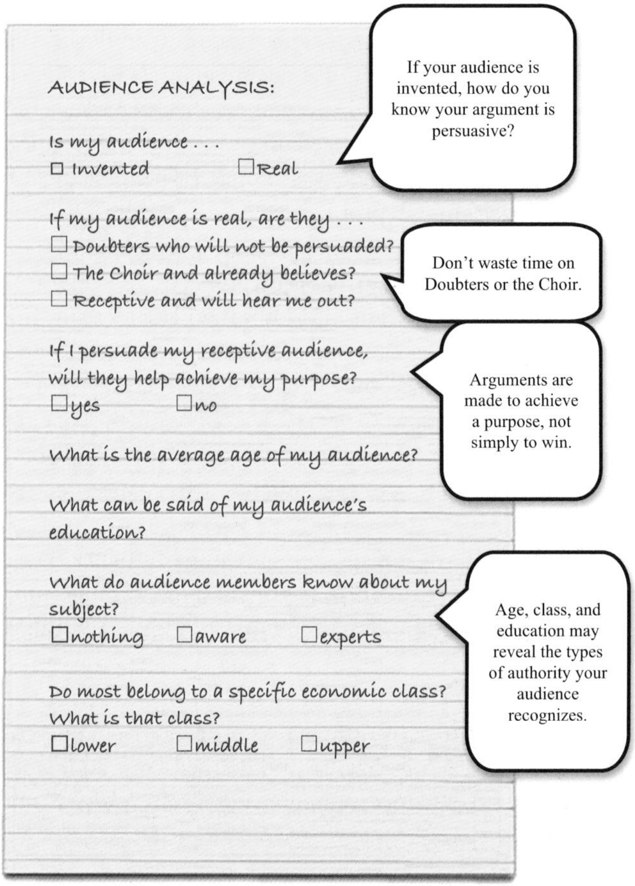

Figure 15.2
This checklist will help you begin to clarify your audience with some basic generalizations.

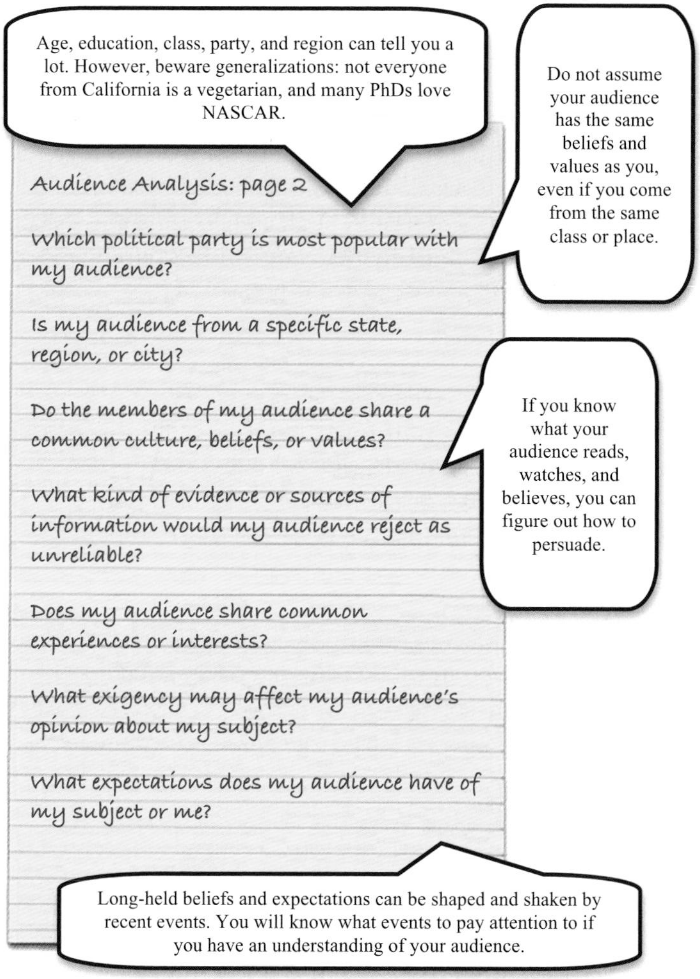

Age, education, class, party, and region can tell you a lot. However, beware generalizations: not everyone from California is a vegetarian, and many PhDs love NASCAR.
Do not assume your audience has the same beliefs and values as you, even if you come from the same class or place.
Audience Analysis: page 2
Which political party is most popular with my audience?
Is my audience from a specific state, region, or city?
Do the members of my audience share a common culture, beliefs, or values?
If you know what your audience reads, watches, and believes, you can figure out how to persuade.
What kind of evidence or sources of information would my audience reject as unreliable?
Does my audience share common experiences or interests?
What exigency may affect my audience's opinion about my subject?
What expectations does my audience have of my subject or me?
Long-held beliefs and expectations can be shaped and shaken by recent events. You will know what events to pay attention to if you have an understanding of your audience.

Targeting Your Audience: Mistakes to Avoid

Many arguments fail to persuade because the speaker has misunderstood or oversimplified the intended audience. Avoid these common mistakes when thinking about your audience.

1. "I am writing to everybody."
   If you really want to talk to everyone, you would need to translate your argument into an estimated 7,000 world languages. Writing to a general audience is like trying to send a meaningful email to everyone, everywhere.

2. "I am talking to those who have had similar experiences."
   Why? Sharing experiences is wonderful, but if your audience already agrees with you, what are you going to achieve?

3. "My audience is made up of people who can relate to me."
   Students who choose their own audience and purpose often would prefer to talk to people of their own age, background, values, and dispositions. Such conversations are important and comfortable, but if audience members share your dispositions and values, it is unlikely that you will have strong differences of opinion where you can demonstrate your rhetorical skills.

4. "They know what I mean."
   Your readers or listeners do not know what you mean. A receptive audience will recognize your topic, but they do not know why you believe as you do, why you think your proposal is the best move, or why the evidence you have found is so important to you.

Experiences and interests are often linked to values and dispositions

5. "They don't like me or care what I say."
   Disagreement is not hostility. A person who thinks differently from you may simply have no evidence or reason to think, believe, or act as you do. If you think your readers or listeners are hostile, you are unlikely to explore why they think as they do, or to shape your message to provide the evidence and reasons they need to change their mind.

6. "I think this joke is funny, so my audience will too."
   Comedy is hard. A joke can break the ice or develop a point, but think of your audience's needs. In many formal settings like a university or a business, a joke may undercut the authority and trust you are trying to establish.

7. "If they just read to the end, it will all make sense."
   Most of us will read only the first paragraph of an article or story if it is not interesting. Your professors will read every page, but at what point will he or she make a decision about your grade? Each sentence, point, and paragraph should contribute to your persuasive power. If, on the other hand, a professor losses track of an argument somewhere in the middle, how likely is it that the remaining pages will be so impressive that she forgets the confusing part?

Effective writers and speakers target receptive members of an audience. You probably do not know them, they may come from very different backgrounds, and their way of thinking may be confounding to you. Still, you can persuade your audience if you work to understand their characteristics and dispositions as well as the setting and culture that shape meaning and understanding. The Breaking the Block feature entitled "Inventing the Audience" will help you refine your understanding of your intended audience.

Breaking the Block
Inventing the Audience

Moving from an invented audience to a real, intended audience is an important process of writing and revision.

This exercise can help you discover a subject that is of interest to a specific audience, or help you develop educated guesses that will lead to a richer understanding of your audience. It combines observing and note-taking with analysis and writing. For this exercise, observe or think for 10 minutes and write for 10 minutes.

Step One: Analyze a small group

Think of a small group of 5 to 15 people. It could be the people at a lunch table, the foursome on the golf course in front of you, the small group talking in the back of a bus, or a choir you heard recently.

- Observe or try to recall some qualities of the group members, such as their dress, mood, tone, and habits.
- List three subjects in the news or of current interest that they are probably aware of.
- List three events that have likely caused most of them distress.
- List three causes or charities a majority of them could probably support.
- Now think of a single topic that could cause a huge argument among the members of this group.

Step Two: Reflect

What was the most difficult part of inventing this audience, and what was easy? If you had to address this group on the single topic that would cause an argument, how would you begin and what kind of language would you use?

MODULE III-4

USING APPEALS, MEDIA, AND CONVENTIONS TO INFLUENCE YOUR AUDIENCE

An analysis and understanding of your audience prepares you to shape the meaning of your argument by using appeals, media, and conventions that will help persuade them.

Appeals

Tradition provides three types of appeals to the audience's disposition and values and also provides a way of determining the best time to use each appeal. You make an **appeal** whenever you structure an idea or select specific types of information so that both are attractive and persuasive to a specific audience. There are many ways of appealing to someone. If you use a chocolate cake to express your affection to a friend, you are appealing to his or her sweet tooth. In Western cultures, three types of appeal have become cultural practices: *pathos*, *ethos*, and *logos*.

- ***Pathos*** is the way in which an author or speaker arouses or uses emotions to move the audience to believe the source, be persuaded by the message, and think or act as the message argues. At the end of an editorial, when the writer ends with a call for action based on pride, a sense of duty, or sympathy, for example, they are using emotions to motivate the readers to act. *Pathos* can use any emotion, including anger, delight, or outrage, as well as empathy. However, only audiences that share, or have been persuaded to share, your view, disposition, or argument are likely to be moved by *pathos*. Academic audiences, those expecting evidence-based arguments, and the highly skeptical are unlikely to be moved by *pathos* and may see such an appeal as manipulation.
- ***Ethos*** is the way in which an author or speaker moves the audience to believe that the source of the message is trustworthy and authoritative. A student who describes in detail an expert's credentials and uses proper documentation is making an *ethos* appeal. Think of *ethos* as a way for the audience to evaluate the honesty, accuracy, and passion the speaker has for his or her subject. It is difficult to imagine an audience that does not acknowledge some type of authority, whether it be based on experience or expertise. However, not every audience will be persuaded by every type of *ethos* appeal. If the basis of your or your sources' authority meets your audience's expectations and you deal with your subject seriously and opposing opinions fairly, then you will appear credible.
- ***Logos*** is the way in which an author or speaker moves the audience to believe that the message is true, valid, and beyond doubt. When someone says your

argument is well reasoned and logical, that person has been moved by a *logos* appeal. Because *logos* appeals are based upon solid reasoning and evidence, they are often more complex arguments than those heard in casual conversation. For example, if you are delivering a toast at your office holiday party, an *ethos* appeal will fall flat. However, if you are making a presentation that may change the direction and business model of the entire office, facts, figures, and data will be expected and necessary for persuasion.

Appeals shape meaning, but audiences will also consider the timing or appropriateness when evaluating your appeals.

Kairos

Kairos is an ancient Greek word that does not have an exact translation in English. However, if you have ever been sad and had someone say just the right thing at just the right time to turn your mood around, you have experienced *kairos*. A *kairotic* moment has been lost if, after a conflict or an argument, you think of the perfect comeback—but it is too late.

Kairos was used by the Greeks to describe moments that seem to call for a certain kind of response, speech, or argument. In short, *kairos* can be translated as the right time or opportunity, which is why *kairos* is often linked to appeals. For example, Dilios's speech prior to the final battle with Xerxes' Persian army is a *pathos* appeal to the 300 Spartans' courage, sense of duty, honor, love of country, and loyalty to their king.

Had Dilios instead used a *logos* appeal by analyzing the strengths and weaknesses of the 150,000 Persian soldiers, his speech would not have been timely and would not have spurred the 300 to fight bravely to the last. In other words, it would not have taken advantage of the *kairotic* moment.

The *kairos* of an academic setting is shaped by the assignments, due dates, professor's expectations, and subject of a course as well as more personal exigencies such as your desire to succeed and the pressure you feel to do well. In an upper-level sociology course on race relations and public policy, the exigencies that bring you and other students to the class are graduation requirements, an interest in the subject, and an interest in readings concerning race relations in the United States. However, if an unarmed person of color were shot and killed during a traffic stop near your campus, the exigencies would change the *kairotic* moment of the next class, as many students would look to the course and professor for a way to understand and respond to the tragedy.

If you keep *kairos* in mind, you will realize that issues, events, and the audience's needs are always changing within the rhetorical situation, and they in turn change how individuals think, making them receptive to different types of appeals and arguments. Knowing about exigency enables you to explore what is most on the mind of your audience—like a happy occasion or recent tragedy—and use this knowledge to build your argument.

The Message in the Medium

A **medium** is what you use to extend your thoughts to others, such as a printed page, a PowerPoint presentation, or a webpage. The medium sits between you and the audience. "The medium is the message" is a famous phrase, but it is often misunderstood. What the twentieth-century communication philosopher Marshall McLuhan meant by it is that each medium can create subtle but long-term social effects that we may not notice but that shape the meanings we derive from the messages we receive. For example, in the 1950s, television created a new kind of home entertainment that discouraged family conversation. A message of the medium of TV can thus be that family time is quiet time.

Figure 15.3
TV brought the family together—quietly.

Practically speaking, every medium and even every form or genre has social effects that condition how your audience will understand what you write or say before you begin. For instance, older people are more likely to trust what they see on the Internet if web pages resemble traditional sources of trusted information like magazines and newspapers.

In an academic setting, consider the difference between a traditional research paper printed on paper and a Prezi presentation. The medium of paper forces the argument to unfold in a linear, point-by-point, way. A Prezi, on the other hand, allows the presenter to move through and bounce between any number of points without concern for an order or hierarchy. Media are patterns you can play with, but keep in mind that every medium—paper or Prezi, for example—will communicate different meanings to an audience.

Conventions

Conventions are expected or required ways of doing things, from the width of the margins to punctuation to documentation format. The proper use of conventions communicates your care for your audience and your subject. For example, if you see a misspelling in a newspaper article, you may begin to doubt the reporter's skills and the newspaper's professionalism.

Audience Expectations

When someone buys a ticket for Disney on Ice or Coldplay, they arrive at the venue with specific expectations. If Coldplay does not play "Paradise" or Elsa does not glide around an ice-crystal palace while singing "Let It Go," there will be some very angry audience members. However, if Chris Martin ends the final set with a rendition of "Let It Go," his fans may find a new reason to love him. Audience expectations are an opportunity, not a limitation. However, you cannot fulfill, confound, or play with an audience's expectations unless you know them, and know them well.

Your professor may expect a research paper, but he may be delighted with a research paper cast as a brief documentary film shot with an iPhone. Then again, your chemical biology professor's detailed written description of what a lab report should look like accompanied by perfect examples written by previous students should be an indication that her expectations are not to be played with. If you know what you must do, what you can do, and what freedoms you have—in other words, the expectations of your audience—you have all you need to build a persuasive argument that achieves your purpose.

Gaps in Your Audience's Understanding

You must assume your audience knows something about your subject; otherwise, they would be unlikely to read or hear you. However, what we do not know also shapes how we understand others. I think I know how my car works, but when my mechanic said my serpentine needed tightening, I wondered if there might be a snake under the hood, while he assumed I knew he meant the serpentine belt.

Unanticipated gaps in your audience's understanding can lead to confusion. However, gaps also provide the writer or speaker with an opportunity to educate, as well as to demonstrate a deep understanding of the subject.

MODULE III-5

COMMON ACADEMIC ASSIGNMENTS: WHAT DOES YOUR AUDIENCE EXPECT?

In academic settings, your audience—the professor—has many expectations for the purpose, features, and documentation style of each course assignment.

Types of Academic Assignments

It is impossible to list every type of academic assignment, but some types are more frequently assigned than others. Each responds to a different set of audience expectations, and each represents a different purpose you may be required to adopt. Let's look at some common assignments.

- **Blog or Journal**: Your purpose is to document your initial thinking so it can be evaluated as part of a larger portfolio or series of assignments. Your audience—your professor, and possibly your classmates—will expect a draft of your thoughts-in-progress about a subject of study, assignment, or reading.
- **Prospectus**: A prospectus is a formal research proposal with the purpose of persuading a professor that your research question is appropriate and the proposed research is focused, reasonable, and doable. Professors who assign a prospectus want you to compose a brief description or portrayal of an area of research, a draft research question and plan, and a working list of sources you plan to use.
- **Annotated Bibliography**: An annotated bibliography is a list of sources such as articles, chapters, or books about a specific subject, with a brief summary of each. Some professors also want to know how each source fits within your research plan or argument. The list is typically organized and formatted using a documentation style such as that of the Modern Language Association (MLA) or the American Psychological Association (APA). Its purpose is to demonstrate that your research is on track and your sources are relevant to your subject and research question.
- **Review of the Literature**: A review of literature, or lit review, is a survey, an analysis, and an evaluation of the commentary and scholarship about a specific subject found in academic articles and books. Your purpose is to demonstrate familiarity with a subject and the current state of scholarship about it.
- **Report**: Each discipline and each professor may expect different things from a report. For example, a book report is very different from a technical report. In general, the purpose of a report is to describe the status of work done or describe the results of a specific task so the professor can evaluate your progress or the depth of your understanding. Your professor may expect a brief

description of a subject, a process, observations, or progress on an assignment or task. He or she will rarely require original research other than a description of your research process and initial thinking and findings.

- **Essay**: An essay is a short argument whose purpose is to persuade. It is one of the most common university assignments and as a result can take many forms. Your professor will expect you to demonstrate that you know the material or subject and that you can apply or think beyond what you have read and researched to make an argument.
- **Research Paper**: A medium-length assignment that requires the use of researched sources to support an argument. A successful research paper demonstrates that you can gather relevant information beyond the assigned reading and pull it together to support your argument. The assigned topic will likely reflect the professor's expectations and way of thinking about the discipline.
- **Thesis**: A thesis is a clear argument concerning a limited subject or issue that the writer has exhaustively researched. (A thesis in this sense is not the same as a thesis statement.) Master's students write a thesis as the last requirement for obtaining their degree, and some undergraduate seniors also must write a thesis in their major. Its purpose is to demonstrate a depth of understanding about the subject.
- **Article**: An article is a short scholarly work that can be drawn from a research paper or a thesis and be refined and formatted for publication. The purpose of an article is to contribute to the discussion about or knowledge of a specific discipline. It must be of the same quality as other works published in the discipline.
- **Dissertation**: A dissertation is a book-length, multi-chapter argument about a subject or issue written as the last requirement of a Ph.D. degree. The purpose of a dissertation is to prove that a doctoral student is ready to become a professional scholar or professor. The student's committee of professors will expect a well-written and documented work that the student can also defend orally.

Chapter 16 explains specific types of assignments found in different disciplines.

Documentation and Purpose

Documentation has one primary purpose: to make it possible for your professor and other readers to find and review the original sources of your research. You provide bibliographic information about your sources because your audience may want to read more on the subject, and skeptics need to be able to check your research and your interpretations.

All documentation styles are structured by the disciplines that have developed or adopted them. When you use a style such as MLA, you have adopted the purpose of that style. The Conventions in Context box entitled "Influencing the Audience by Using Proper Documentation" will help you understand that documentation says as much as the words describing a source. A more detailed explanation of how to document sources is found in Chapter 22.

Conventions in Context
Influencing the Audience by Using Proper Documentation

Some professors may read documentation errors as more than just errors. If you think of documentation as a way of demonstrating your authority and persuasive power, you will understand why.

The list of references from a student paper that follows (Figure 15.4) shows a writer unwittingly sabotaging his or her own authority and persuasive power. At first glance, it looks good. But a professor with expertise in the subject will see other things.

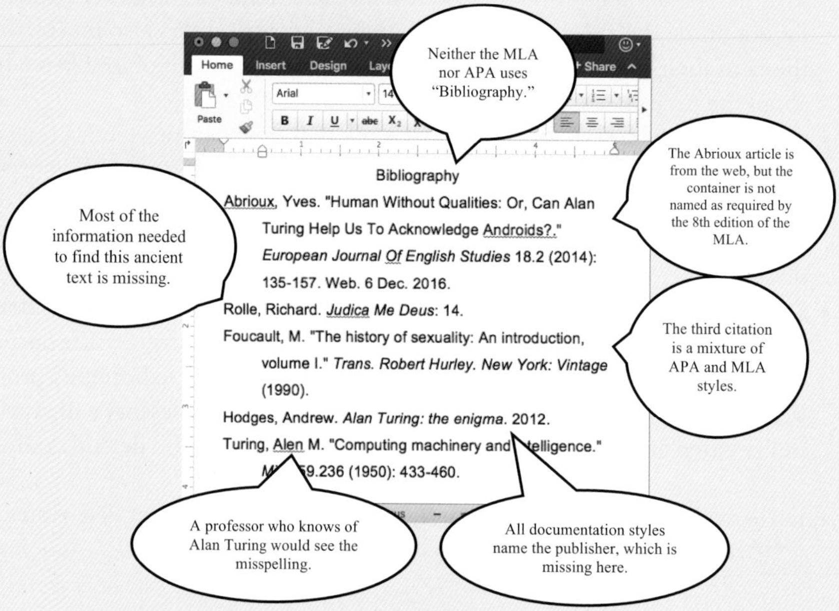

Figure 15.4 At first glance, the citations look good and appear to be in the proper style. However, a few small errors shape the message on the page as much as the words do.

It would be difficult to persuade a professor that you are serious about your purpose, and that the research supporting your argument and message is trustworthy, with these errors.

CHAPTER 16

UNDERSTANDING THE ACADEMIC SITUATION

How does a high-school nerd become the popular kid on campus with friends everywhere and party invitations every weekend? How do students who have never changed a tire learn aircraft engineering and maintenance? Maybe you've wondered how the same five people always seem to score front-row seats at games. Closer to home, was your brother or sister the type who never cracked a book, squeaked into college, and is now a member of the honors society? What is the secret sauce?

When it comes to popularity and scoring great tickets, answers are hard to come by. However, the academic secret sauce is much easier to discover, for a very simple reason: All American colleges and universities are built around a similar academic culture. If you know what this culture involves, you can learn to read the rhetorical situation in each classroom, even though specific professors will have different expectations.

MODULE III-6

WHAT YOU NEED TO KNOW ABOUT WRITING IN UNIVERSITIES AND COLLEGES

The rhetorical situation of a classroom or lab is a bit different from other rhetorical situations, as illustrated in Figure 16.1.

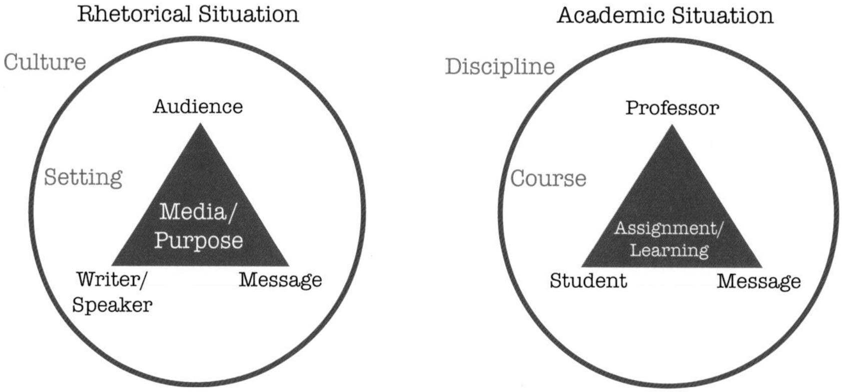

Figure 16.1 The complex rhetorical situations in an academic setting will reflect the discipline of your course and professor.

If you understand the rhetorical situation on the left as described in Chapter 15, then the academic situation on the right should look familiar. But to break it down in detail, see the side-by-side comparison of a general rhetorical situation and an academic rhetorical situation in Figure 16.2.

As Chapter 15 describes, all rhetorical situations exist within some larger cultural environment. As a student you work within the academic tradition; however, in a single course you need to focus on the cultural principles, values, and practices of the specific discipline that course represents.

There are many ways to define a **discipline**. As a student, the best way to think of a discipline is as the practices used by a group of scholars who

- are motivated to increase understanding and contribute to what is known;
- study a common subject or focus on a related set of questions;
- apply the same or similar habits of critical thinking, methods of discovery, and innovative practices; and
- communicate in and are organized by formal, specialized ways of exchanging and evaluating information.

General Rhetorical Situation / Academic Situation

General Rhetorical Situation	Academic Situation
Audience The individual or group who will read, hear, or observe an argument.	**Professor** The individual who teaches the course and evaluates you as a student.
Writer or Speaker The one who creates and delivers the argument.	**Student** You, the one studying a subject and doing assignments to be evaluated by the professor.
Purpose The goal the writer or speaker hopes to achieve by persuading the audience to change opinions, principles, or behavior.	**Learning** Demonstrating your understanding, skills, competencies, and knowledge in your work and contributions.
Setting The time, place, and context where an audience encounters an argument.	**Course** The specific academic setting where you study an aspect of a subject discipline and are then evaluated on your understanding by a professor.
Culture Principles, values, and practices that make it possible for the individual to express ideas and experiences, and for an audience to understand these expressions.	**Discipline** Similar or common methods of examining a subject, common habits of critical thinking, and formal ways of communicating that allow scholars to exchange and evaluate information and contribute to what is known.

Figure 16.2 Comparing a general rhetorical situation and an academic rhetorical situation reveals important differences.

You may have noticed that a physics professor and a creative writing professor do not teach in the same way. This is partly because they are different people, but mostly because they have years of study, training, and practice in different disciplines that lead them to think, do research, and teach differently.

No text can predict your professor's assignments or expectations. Therefore, relying on any sample paper, template, or outline (except those provided by your professor) is the same as ignoring your audience. For this reason, students who plagiarize papers are likely to be disappointed by their grade, even if their fraud is not discovered, because the author of a purchased paper has no idea what your professor expects in a specific course or assignment.

To understand your audience within the academic situation, you need to study your professor, learn his or her expectations, and understand the markers of authority in their discipline. The checklist in Figure 16.3 will help you examine the rhetorical situation of any class.

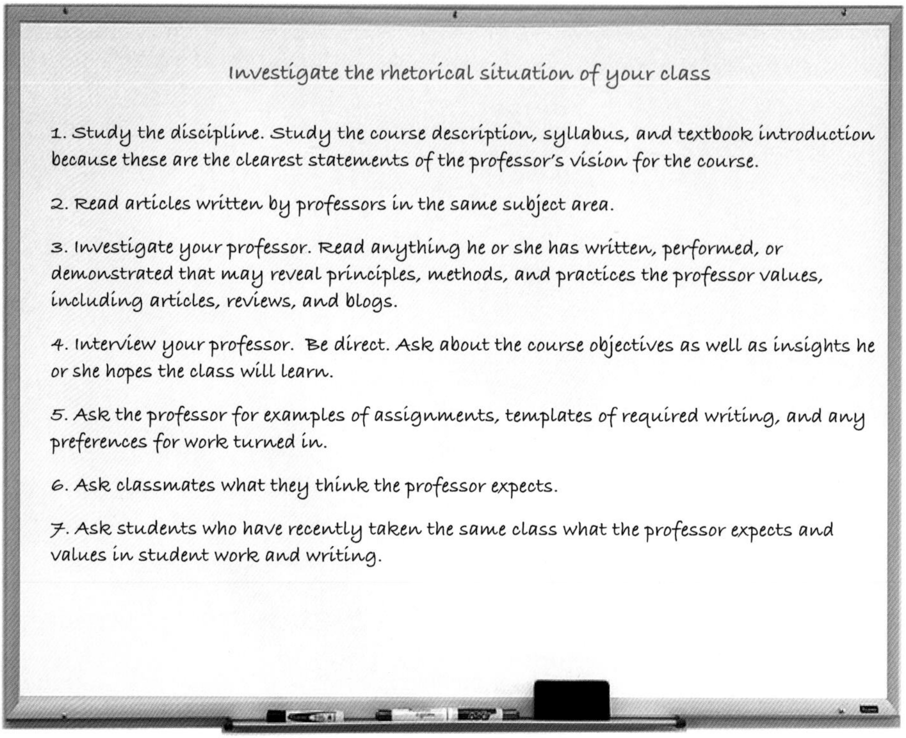

Investigate the rhetorical situation of your class
1. Study the discipline. Study the course description, syllabus, and textbook introduction because these are the clearest statements of the professor's vision for the course.
2. Read articles written by professors in the same subject area.
3. Investigate your professor. Read anything he or she has written, performed, or demonstrated that may reveal principles, methods, and practices the professor values, including articles, reviews, and blogs.
4. Interview your professor. Be direct. Ask about the course objectives as well as insights he or she hopes the class will learn.
5. Ask the professor for examples of assignments, templates of required writing, and any preferences for work turned in.
6. Ask classmates what they think the professor expects.
7. Ask students who have recently taken the same class what the professor expects and values in student work and writing.

Figure 16.3 Though each discipline is different, the expectations of professors and markers of authority are not secret, and they are easily investigated and understood.

The modules that follow provide guidance as you consider your audience and work to establish authority within the most common disciplines.

Responsible Sourcing
Prioritizing Audience Saves Time and Grades

All students have to prioritize to save time and energy. Often, it's worth taking time to discover what your academic audience is looking for before spending time on an assignment.

Imagine it is late at night. You have homework in all your classes, a midterm essay to write, and little time. As you think about your next steps, you realize you have many options for the essay, but the results of those options may not be so clear. As the decision tree in Figure 16.4 shows, some decisions can take you where you want to go, while others can lead to less happy results.

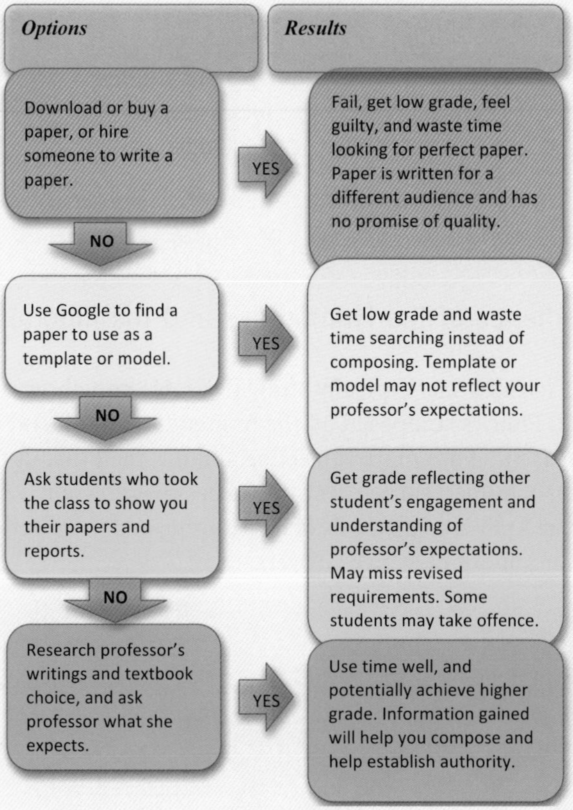

Figure 16.4 Decisions that take a second to make often have long lasting consequences.

MODULE III-7

THE HUMANITIES AND THE LIBERAL ARTS AND SCIENCES

The humanities and the liberal arts and sciences are among the many different ways to study humanity, human culture, human relationships, and human existence. The humanities (for short) typically include arts such as English and history and social sciences such as economics and political science.

These are a few of the subjects and departments often organized within the humanities:

cultural studies
economics
English
geography
history
languages
linguistics
literature
philosophy
political science
psychology
religious studies
social science
sociology
urban studies

Reading the Audience of the Humanities and the Liberal Arts and Sciences

Unlike the natural sciences that typically study definable and observable subjects, such as the material Pluto is composed of, the humanities and liberal arts and sciences concern subjects that are more subjective and may be difficult to pin down, such as the meaning of human existence or the causes of aggression. As a result, the humanities are better known as methods of questioning and interpretation than as sources of facts, solutions, or objective answers.

Scholars of the humanities spend their time studying texts (novels and survey results, for example), images (political posters and maps), and practices and events (rituals and performances). In addition, they study the relationships *among* texts, images, practices, and events. For example, American literature professor Robin Miskolcze spent years studying seafaring novels, poetic descriptions of sailing, and eighteenth-century newspaper accounts of shipwrecks in an attempt to understand the source of the maritime phrase "women and children first." She discovered a relationship between the phrase, chivalrous British Naval officers, and the expansion of the American Navy.

In another discipline, anthropologist Clifford Geertz went into the field to study the significance of a ritual—outlaw cockfighting in Balinese culture. Years of interviews and analysis revealed the relationship between social status, wealth, and battles between chickens.

As a student of the humanities, you will be asked to understand and analyze the meanings others have found and then make your own meaningful statements. To add your voice to the discussion, you will use the ways of knowing and communicating developed by scholars of English, anthropology, political science, and religious studies, to name just a few.

But keep in mind that professors of the humanities do not just want to know what something means. They also want to know the mechanics of meaning and how knowledge has evolved over time. At first glance, an assignment in the humanities may appear to ask you to explain what something means. But you may also need to explain how it has come to mean what it does. For example, what does it mean when Deadmau5 wears his big mouse head on stage? Does his mask function in the same way and mean the same thing as the masks worn by actors of Chinese Opera? How have such modern performance masks become so important? How are these masks related to other masks worn by other performers in other times and places? Asking what and how masks mean can lead to discoveries of unrecognized relationships. Questions such as these are an important part of invention in the humanities.

A formal paper for the liberal arts should clearly state a thesis based upon an interpretation or analysis, describe the approach or criteria used to interpret or analyze, and then provide evidence in support of the thesis statement. A formal paper written for one of the social sciences, such as psychology or sociology, should clearly and objectively report the findings of an observation or study.

Building Authority in the Humanities and Liberal Arts and Sciences

The humanities and the liberal arts and sciences use refined methods of questioning and interpretation. You can communicate authority in these disciplines by carefully and critically reading primary sources (text, image, practice, or event) and secondary sources (comments and critiques about primary sources). In addition, citing primary and secondary sources accurately will demonstrate that you value what scholars and professors in these disciplines value and know how to investigate and talk about the questions and issues they care about.

Of course, different disciplines have different expectations, so different professors will look for different markers, or signs, of authority. For example, political science arguments commonly strive for objectivity and rely upon verifiable data and formal logic. The social sciences rely upon the scientific method to discover general truths that may in turn explain other questions or events, as Module III-10 on the natural sciences explains below.

Theology and literature, on the other hand, do not assume an objective truth. In these disciplines, authority is founded upon interpretations or judgments built upon relevant evidence.

As always, the best way to understand any rhetorical situation and the audience that will read or hear your argument is to do research. Fortunately, courses are built to deliver information that will help you understand the rhetorical situation of the course, and professors are available to answer questions. All you need to do is look around, read, and ask.

MODULE III-8

THE FINE, VISUAL, AND PERFORMING ARTS

The fine, visual, and performing arts consist of the study, practice, and performance of artistic expression. Artistic expression can make use of materials and instruments, to create works of art.

The fine, visual, and performing arts can be organized in many different ways within a university. Here are some typical subjects and departments:

- animation
- art
- art history
- conceptual art
- dance
- digital arts
- ethnomusicology
- film & TV
- history of dance
- kinesiology
- music
- music studies
- photography
- sculpture
- stagecraft
- theater arts

Reading the Audience in Fine, Visual, and Performing Arts Courses

The arts (for short) such as dance and theater are not practical in the same way that cooking or piloting skills are practical; they do not complete a task or solve a problem. However, they are a crucial expression of what it is to be human, and they are essential for understanding how people experience their lives and their relationships with others.

Scholars of the arts, such as art historians and musicologists, work very much like scholars of literature in their consideration and interpretation of a work of art. On the other hand, a professor of sculpture and 3-D design may spend time in a studio covered in marble dust to express emotions with form, materials, and an air hammer.

Too often, students underestimate the intellectual demands of fine arts courses and misread audience expectations. The arts student's audience is composed of individuals who have committed a great deal of time and energy to the creation of art and to an understanding of art and the creative process. You can begin to understand this audience in terms of four areas of creative thought and scholarship.

1. **Aesthetics** is the theoretical or historical study of ideas about beauty, the sublime, the profound, art, and the ways in which art is received. For example, cinematic arts professor Akira Mizuta Lippit looked at the aesthetics of the avant-garde and experimental films and discovered that these films are apart from the traditional form. According to Lippit, the external space of the avant-garde makes the concept of cinema thinkable.
2. The **history of art** and ideas looks at art and creativity in terms of history. How ideas of the beautiful have changed over time, how creative techniques have developed, and how specific artists and their work have influenced those who follow are some of the concerns of art history professors. For example, in his article "The Ambiguity of Caravaggio's *Medus*," art and literature professor Paul Barolsky tries to understand how the Italian Renaissance painter Caravaggio used an expression of shock to portray a sudden awareness of mortality.
3. **Art production** involves the technical skills necessary to put on a modern stage play, animate a cartoon, or cast and fire a plate or vase. For example, Professor Vita Berezina-Blackburn teaches courses such as "3D Animation: Form, Light and Motion," and "Motion Capture Production and Experimentation." Her work helps students learn how to give personality to animated figures and animals.
4. **Performance** is the focus for departments such as music, dance, and theater. Like any mature discipline, music, dance, and theater have formalized ways of describing, recording, and critiquing movement and placement, tone, and tenor. Mastering how such qualities are talked about is as important as mastering their expression. For example, Nathan Haymer, director of bands at Southern University, not only is responsible for the musical direction and choreography of the Southern University marching band but also teaches and trains elementary and secondary music educators.

Building Authority in the Fine, Visual, and Performing Arts

Creative artists and scholars of the fine, visual, and performing arts often use the word "connoisseur" to describe an authority in one of their fields. A **connoisseur** is someone able to make judgments of a work of art based on his or her knowledge of the history of the artistic genre (such as sculpture or dance), the principles that govern a type of art (such as formal composition in photography and music), and the techniques and components that create the work of art (such as a type of brush stroke in painting).

Your professor, as a connoisseur, will likely teach each course and studio session with high expectations in mind. In fact, it would be an unusual arts professor who did not wish for his or her students to acquire the knowledge necessary to be known as an expert or connoisseur in the discipline.

MODULE III-9

THE PRE-PROFESSIONAL AND APPLIED SCIENCES

Pre-professional and applied sciences (applied sciences for short) provide the highly advanced, professional training required by specialized careers and professional certification agencies. For example, the National Council of Examiners for Engineering and Surveying (NCEES) administers the exams required for an engineering and surveying license in the United States. As a result, a college or university department that teaches engineering students will create courses that prepare students for the NCEES exam and the job demands to follow.

Below are a few pre-professional and applied science subjects and departments.

agriculture
architecture
business
civil engineering
computer science
design
education
engineering
environmental studies
forestry
health science
human performance and recreation
journalism
law
library sciences and museum studies
media studies and communication

Reading the Audience of the Pre-Professional and Applied Sciences

The pre-professional and applied sciences use the principles, values, and practices developed by other, more theoretical fields like physics, art, or the life sciences. But practitioners in these applied fields are not about creative expression, advanced research, or alternative perspectives. Rather, professors in these fields often seek to find the best solutions to real-life problems. They appreciate practicality in others and look for logical principles and practices. For example, you will not find many hydraulic engineers debating the philosophical meaning of a drop of water in the ocean or the existence of water on Pluto. You will, however, find them arguing over the most efficient way to move rainwater out of a city center.

Authority in the Pre-Professional and Applied Sciences

Because the applied sciences offer training for advanced and specialized technical careers, much of the writing required of students mirrors the kinds of writing done in these jobs. Project journals, project reports, lab reports, posters, proposals, and business plans are just some of the types of writing common to applied sciences courses. Again, since professors in the applied sciences focus on solving problems and finding answers quickly, they value many of the same qualities of clarity and precision that professors in the sciences value: efficient, objective, and clear writing and speech that rely on hard data and corroborated observations. The arguments expected in such courses are precise, never flowery or rambling, and the conclusions must be supported by evidence. Necessarily, invention and research in these courses is focused on discovering principles and practices that have effectively solved similar problems or refined similar processes and then discovering ways of adapting them to a new problem or process.

If you are training for a profession in business or engineering, you need to be able to think, write, and speak like a businessperson or engineer. Of course, a software engineer working at Apple will not talk like a software engineer at Halliburton Oilfield Services or one working for a NASCAR team. The language, methods, and practices of the professors and professionals working in the careers you are training for are the best source of information about your audience. Fortunately, many professors of the applied sciences also have on-the-job or consulting experience in businesses in their specialized field.

MODULE III-10

THE NATURAL SCIENCES

The word *science* covers a lot of territory. The empirical or natural sciences are often separated from the disciplines of the social sciences. They examine the natural phenomena of the earth, the stars and other planets, the oceans, plant and animal life, and math and physics. Sometimes called the hard sciences, they may include the following subjects and departments:

biology
botany
chemistry
earth sciences
ecology
geology
life sciences
logic
mathematics
oceanography
physical sciences
physics
space sciences
statistics
systems science
zoology

Unlike the arts and social sciences, the disciplines and departments of the sciences are organized in similar ways within different universities and colleges of sciences (though some mathematicians cannot agree on whether they study an art or a science). New disciplines and departments may split off, such as genomics emerging from the more established discipline of microbiology. In addition, you will find an amazing diversity of scientists in higher education. Neuroscientists are trying to map the quadrillion connections that compose brain circuitry, computational biologists are tracing the family trees of animals, and physicists are trying to imagine how black holes can propel spacecraft.

Reading Audiences in the Sciences

One thing scientists have in common is their reliance on the scientific method. This method is also a clue to the principles, values, and practices of the audience you will write and speak to in the hard sciences and the social sciences.

Briefly stated, the **scientific method** begins with observations of real things, some huge and obvious but some invisible and observed only by traces or symptoms left behind. A scientist then makes a hypothesis about these observations in order to make a prediction. Next, the scientist tests the hypothesis with experiments or additional observations. If necessary, the hypothesis is revised and tested again. All the while, the scientist carefully follows defined rules of his or her discipline so that some other scientist—whether in the lab next door, on the other side of the world, or yet to be born—can understand the hypothesis and repeat the testing, experiments, and observations. Because scientific investigation and reasoning are shaped by the scientific method, that method also determines the invention process of the student and professor.

If the members of your audience spend their days engaged in the scientific method, you already know something about them:

- **Scientists think inductively** (see Chapter 17), meaning that they start with a small or limited observation and use the scientific method to develop a hypothesis and test it with an experiment that becomes a conclusion if the hypothesis is proven true.

- **Scientists think deductively** (again see Chapter 17), because they apply a conclusion developed through the scientific method and test it to see if it also describes other phenomena they observe and new questions that arise. For example, Dr. Tim Coleman proved that gravity waves can cause tornados. If another meteorologist were to use his conclusion to develop a hypothesis that gravity waves may also cause hurricanes, she would be thinking deductively.
- **Scientists are detail oriented.** They build complex models and experiments in which they must try to control many factors in order to study the workings of one factor of interest. For example, imagine all the data and information a meteorologist has to account for when building a computer model of a tornado.
- **Scientists are driven to develop hypotheses** that can be proven with a high degree of certainty and therefore accepted by others. A conclusion will be accepted and used by other scientists only if the experiment was designed, completed, described, and shared in such a way that others can repeat the experiment over and over again with the same result.
- **Scientists are good critical thinkers.** Because scientists and social scientists see the search for truth as their purpose, they are trained to spot sloppy thinking, bad logic, and false statements.

Building Authority in the Sciences

The quick answer to building authority in the sciences is to avoid sloppy thinking, bad logic, and false statements. If only it were that simple.

The language of the sciences is unlike that of the humanities or fine arts. For example, the sciences use many symbols, terms, equations, and tables of data, all of which are specialized for each of the many avenues of scientific investigation.

Fortunately, your authority in the sciences is founded upon the principles, values, and practices of the specific discipline you are studying, and the methods and practices that are the focus of your course. An organic chemistry lab report for a professor at the University of Florida will be similar to one assigned at the University of Washington, because the lab report is a genre based upon the methods and practices of laboratory sciences.

On the other hand, a lab report in a mechanics of materials course taught in a mechanical engineering department will differ from the organic chemistry lab report. The scientific method is the foundation of both, but the two specialties have different expectations because they study very different phenomena in very different ways.

Students of the sciences establish authority by mastering the ways in which a specific course, specialty, department, and discipline talks and writes about the subject of study. In practical terms, on the first day in a science course, be prepared to take notes. But also be prepared to notice how the professor and assigned sources talk and write about the subject of the course.

CHAPTER 17

USING CLASSICAL RHETORIC

Why would anyone use classical Greek rhetoric or any strategy that is more than 2,500 years old? How can ancient terms and ideas be relevant in a world of multimedia, instant messaging, and wearable technology?

If rhetoric were just a bunch of old rules, it wouldn't be relevant. However, rhetoric provides solutions to modern, everyday problems. Specifically, rhetoric shows you how to change someone's mind in person, at a distance, or in the future. Rhetorical strategies can help you figure out how someone changed your mind, countered your argument, or moved a crowd to do their will. Rather than thinking of rhetoric as archaic rules older than the dust of Athens, think of rhetoric as a discussion board that has been solving real-world problems for more than 2,500 years.

In fact, classical rhetoric still shapes our everyday conversations and arguments, and it structures Western thinking and our expectations of what is persuasive. For example, we think movies, arguments, and research papers should have a beginning, a middle, and an end because early rhetoricians found that this structure keeps an audience's attention. We analyze websites and Snapchat images in terms of *ethos*, *pathos*, and *logos* because these are effective ways of describing appeals.

Fortunately, you don't need to know ancient Greek to be persuasive. However, if you are composing in an academic setting or beyond, you should know how others have solved the same problems you will discover. Rhetoric is the key, not just to being persuasive, but also to saving time and energy. After all, why bother reinventing and recreating what others have already figured out? This chapter explains the major concepts of classical rhetoric, and then discusses specific devices and solutions.

MODULE III-11

CLASSICAL RHETORIC AND THE WRITING PROCESS

Early **rhetors**, or teachers of rhetoric, organized what they discovered about effective speeches into five categories, often called the five canons (see Figure 17.1). As a result, these categories of devices and strategies became the first systematic process for composing and delivering a persuasive speech.

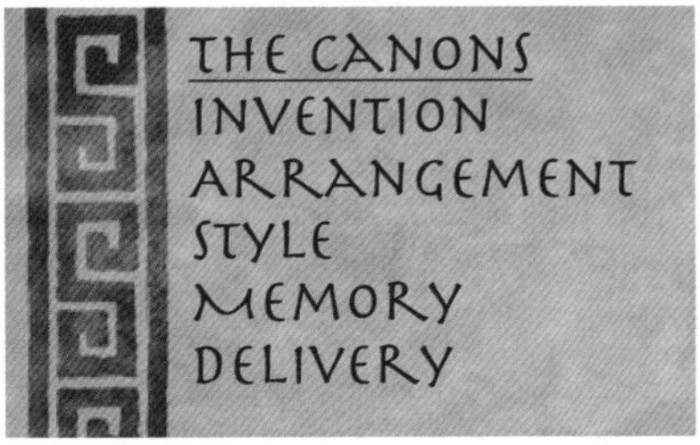

Figure 17.1
The first rhetors studied persuasive speeches, the major genre in their society, which explains the emphasis on memory and delivery.

Five Canons of Classical Rhetoric

1. **Invention** originally meant the discovery of persuasive devices and strategies that a speaker could use during a speech. It was believed that all the strategies and devices a speaker would ever need already existed. All that was needed was to find them.
2. **Arrangement** initially meant the selection of a rhetorical strategy that suited the situation, audience, and speaker's purpose and the selection and ordering of rhetorical devices appropriate to the strategy.
3. **Style**, or how something is said, became a concern once speakers discovered and arranged what they wanted to say. Rhetors often taught three levels of style: grand or highly ornamented expressions, middle style, and plain or everyday language.
4. **Memory** was an essential skill for speakers trying to persuade a live audience in ancient times. Early rhetors taught students to quickly recall alternative devices and strategies so they could adjust their speech on the fly depending upon the changing mood of an audience.
5. **Delivery** included inflections of voice, directive gestures (see Figure 17.2), and even manipulating posture to convey a message. Rhetors took delivery and gesture very seriously, even as late as the nineteenth century.

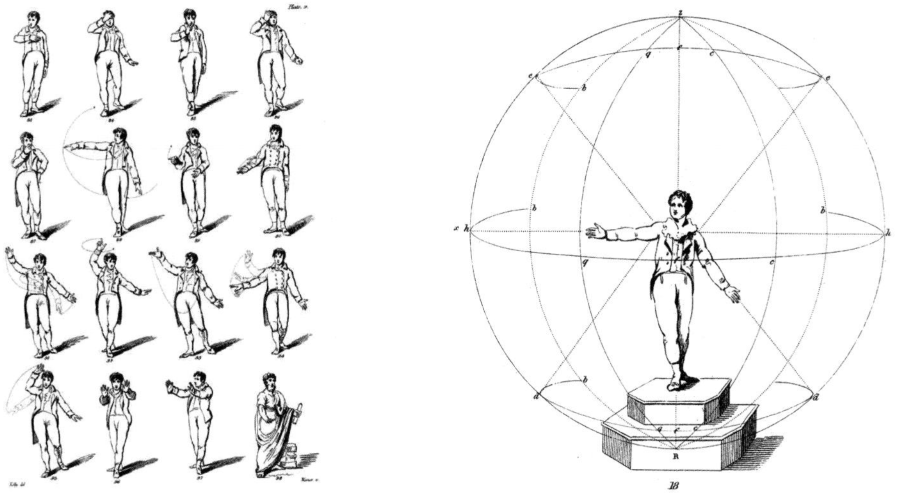

Figure 17.2 These images of gesture instruction come from a nineteenth-century book entitled *Chironomia; or a Treatise on Rhetorical Delivery.*

Obviously, our widespread ability to read and write, contemporary habits of communication, and technology have made speech less important and changed how we use the lessons of classical rhetoric. Though you may not use a grand style, the way in which your voice conveys your attitude, the images and graphs you use to explain your points, and word choice and sentence length are as much a part of delivery as are dramatic gestures. The Conventions in Context box entitled "Gestures of Hand and Word" shows the persuasive power of simple gestures.

Conventions in Context
Gestures of Hand and Word

We typically think of gestures as movements of the body, but writers also make effective gestures that move and persuade an audience, or alternatively they make clichéd gestures that turn an audience off. For example, the phrase "in this day and age" is not only a cliché but also wordy and archaic. Starting an essay with a dictionary definition is another clichéd gesture. After reading such an opening move, your readers may wonder why they need you if they can just Google the word.

A fresh, effective, meaningful gesture is often unexpected. For example, a one-sentence paragraph that crystallizes an important point in your argument can be powerful, as in this famous example:

I have a dream.

In an academic argument, a shift to a personal narrative can bring what would otherwise be a dry subject to life.

Think of gestures you make as a writer in the same way you think of gestures that speakers make. Effective speakers may pound their fists at just the right moment, but if they do it too often it loses its impact. Use gestures—both the ones that readers expect and creative gestures that will surprise them—sparingly, but do experiment with gestures as you draft, and seek feedback about their effectiveness. By using gestures effectively, your distinct voice will arise from the page as if you are speaking, and your argument will stand out.

Relevance of the Five Canons Today

Ancient rhetors taught students the canons. Today, cognitive psychology has taught us that when effective writers tackle writing tasks, they use a process composed of four functions that often repeat and overlap, as shown in Figure 17.3. Different people arrange and repeat the functions in different ways when working on different writing tasks.

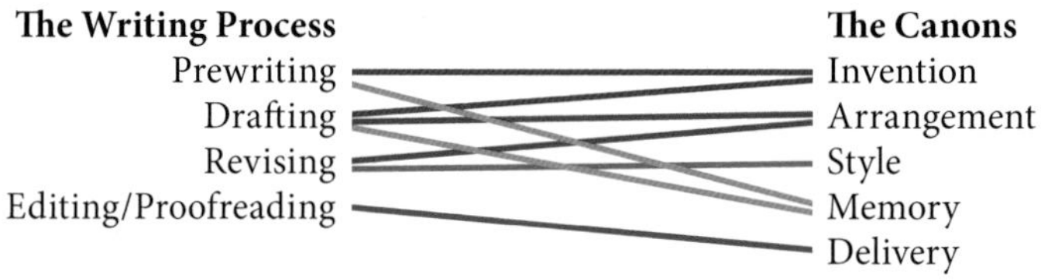

Figure 17.3 The steps of the writing process are related to the canons of classical rhetoric.

- **Prewriting**, another term for **invention**, is still the discovery of what can be said by looking within our own minds and around to the thoughts of others, as well as by researching the ideas of experts and scholars. (For more on invention, see Chapters 3 and 4.) Though we no longer need to commit everything we discover during invention to **memory**, a well-organized bibliography, a research notebook, or a cloud storage account is essential for recording the ideas and opinions you discover and keeping track of sources and documents.
- **Drafting** is the act of recording ideas and arguments on paper or a screen. As you draft, you continue the process of **invention** until the final version of your argument is handed in or published, just as ancient students of rhetoric constantly re-drafted, revised, and practiced their speeches. You will also begin the work of **arrangement** as you move parts, elements, and points around. **Memory**, in the form of careful file saving procedures, is crucial during drafting.

- **Revising** is when you begin working toward your audience, trying out different **arrangements** or organizations to see which suits their expectations and necessities of the situation. Your **style**, such as your tone and formality, emerges as you revise. Decisions you make about the best arrangement or style during revision should be based upon your purpose and audience. It is possible to revise your thoughts even before you have written out your ideas. If you have ever had an ah-ha moment in the shower or a breakthrough that occurred to you after a nap, you were revising in your head.
- **Editing/proofreading** is the fine-tuning of an argument to conform to the conventions of the genre and meet the expectations of your audience. Just as speakers do, writers can use concerns about **delivery** to refine their argument by checking their work for small details that shape meaning, such as consistent margins, precise documentation, and word choice.

Because they are based on the rhetorical situation, the canons of classical rhetoric remain relevant today. They can help you persuade an audience with a message within a setting shaped by a larger culture.

MODULE III-12

ARRANGEMENT OF ARGUMENT

Though we no longer walk around in togas, the following classical elements are still part of contemporary arguments because they continue to solve real, practical problems. More important, these elements are still expected by readers of arguments and non-fiction essays.

Elements of the Classical Argument

- **Introduction, or *exordium***—Because audience members are easily distracted, early orators had to grab their attention at the beginning of a speech and redirect it to the stage or podium. At the same time, the speaker had to give the audience a reason to continue listening. As a writer, you also need to grab your readers' attention, make them care about your thesis, and give them a reason, with each sentence, to continue reading. Effective speakers and writers often used *ethos* and *pathos* appeals to hook and hold attention while introducing the subject in a compelling and relevant way.

- **Thesis or claim**—The thesis is a theory, premise, or claim you will demonstrate using reasoning and evidence. The thesis can be located anywhere in the introduction, but it is often located after the hook and before the narrative.
- **Narrative of what happened, or *narratio***—If a subject is not relevant to the concerns and interests of audience members, they will not hang around long. Early rhetors knew that after grabbing their attention in the introduction, they needed to give audience members a narrative of what happened, providing background information and context to connect them to the subject or issue. In addition, clever orators would describe the background events or conditions in a way that favored their position. Often, speakers or writers share their sense of passion or urgency at this point, which can be a very effective *pathos* appeal.
- **Outline, or *divisio***—First you hook, and then you hold. If you can't persuade your audience members to listen or read to the end, you will not persuade them to change their minds. By promising benefits if readers continue to read, you are more likely to hold their attention. For example, an orator might say "first I will talk about what it means to embezzle public money and why it is a betrayal, and then I will show that Verres used your tax dollars to build his summer home." In addition to holding attention, the appearance of organized thinking, an outline of your points, contributes to your authority. And finally, an outline, reinforced by clear transitions between points, will help the audience remember your argument long after.

- **Proof, or *confirmatio***—Ancient rhetoricians called the main part of the argument, following the introduction, the proof because it was composed of artistic and inartistic proofs. In this section—the most information-rich part of an argument—you need to slow down a bit and convey an authoritative presence to reinforce each piece of evidence you present. As mentioned earlier, data and information are not persuasive unless you explain what they mean, what they prove, and why they are authoritative. In the body of an argument, readers usually expect *logos* appeals: information from authoritative sources, connected to your thesis with solid inductive or deductive reasoning or both. If you don't explain the significance of your information, or how your reasoning supports your thesis, your audience is likely to ask the question that kills an argument: "so what?"
- **Refutation, or *confutatio***—It was not enough to make a strong argument; rhetors also had to show that they understood the alternative perspectives held by their audience and the counter-arguments an opponent might offer. During this part of the argument, the speaker or writer acknowledges alternative

perspectives and refutes counterarguments by critiquing their reasoning. If an arguer does not consider alternative views in this way, the audience can easily conclude that those positions are as valid as the one proposed in the argument. Most issues have more than just two sides. Reviewing alternative perspectives and positions allows you to critique and disprove counter-arguments and demonstrates that you have thought long and hard about the subject. However, if a reasonable argument cannot be refuted, you can't simply ignore it. In such a case, conceding a point or acknowledging a counterpoint is valid and not only will demonstrate your reasonableness but also may strengthen your argument in the mind of a skeptical audience.

- **Conclusion, or *peroration***—Even if the appeals and proofs are persuasive, audience members may become lost in or confused by all the information and reasoning presented. This can be a problem for speakers and for writers whose arguments have more than two points. Therefore, early rhetors emphasized the importance of the conclusion as a boiling down or summary of the argument and an explanation of what to do next: how to think, believe, or act. In addition, early rhetors recognized that logical appeals alone do not lead to conviction or action. The same remains true today. *Pathos* or emotional appeals, such as praise for courage and good behavior, hope and optimism for the future, and justice for those wronged, will still compel people to think, believe, or act immediately.

Outline of the Classical Argument

In addition to the elements of a persuasive argument, ancient rhetoricians found that the most persuasive and memorable speeches followed a common sequence, whether they were spoken in the senate or in the street.

Effective contemporary arguments continue to mirror the outline of a classical argument, and not simply because Aristotle recommended it. Drill sergeants, parents, professors, corporate trainers, ministers, and politicians use the classical structure because it works. And it works because it is based upon what an audience needs to understand and retain in a complex, multi-part argument.

Aristotle's classical outline serves as a great template or starting point as you draft, develop, and arrange your argument. The Breaking the Block box entitled "Fill-in-the-Blank Inventing" can help you try out the classic argument structure.

I. Introduction
- A. Hook and thesis
- B. Narrative
- C. Outline argument

> *Pathos* and *ethos* appeals are often used in the introduction to hook the audience.

II. Body of Argument
- A. Refutation

> *Logos* is essential when refuting opposing arguments.

  - 1. Summary of opposing argument
  - 2. Reasons opposing argument is faulty
  - 3. Evidence
  - 4. Conclusion

> *Logos* is essential when refuting opposing arguments.

- B. Concede opposing argument
  - 1. Summary of opposing argument
  - 2. Reasons opposing argument is strong
  - 3. Evidence
  - 4. Conclusion

> Concessions build authority and can work as an *ethos* appeal.

- C. First Point
  - 1. Reasons
  - 2. Evidence
  - 3. Conclusion
- D. Second and Subsequent Points
  - 1. Reasons
  - 2. Evidence
  - 3. Conclusion

> Each point can be seen as a mini-essay: you may find a *pathos* appeal at the beginning, *ethos* and *logos* appeals as sources are introduced and evidence referenced, and *pathos* again in the conclusion.

III. Conclusion
- A. Summary of points
- B. Summary of opposing arguments' failings
- C. Final appeal for acceptance of thesis

> The final call to action often makes use of a *pathos* appeal.

Remember, the classical outline is just a place to start. Many genres—such as a lab report, a narrative essay, and a eulogy—use different structures, and their outlines are very different from the one above. Researching your topic and your audience will help you determine if you need a concession, for example. Chapter 15 will help you develop the skills to examine the rhetorical situation and determine audience expectations.

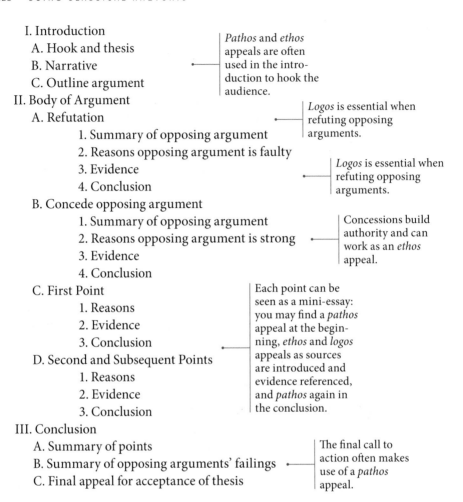

Breaking the Block
Fill-in-the-Blank Inventing

Wouldn't it be great if you could plug your ideas and the research you found persuasive into an app that would then organize your essay for you? Aristotle certainly thought so, which is why he created the classical argument structure. Think of the classical outline as a fill-in-the-blank application.

Step One
At the top of a blank page, write your thesis or the subject you would like to explore at the top. For example, let's try the following thesis:

I. Introduction

A. Thesis—People are fraudulently misusing the service-animal designation that allows people to bring animals such as seeing-eye dogs into areas that do not otherwise allow pets. The result is that individuals who depend upon certified assistance animals are perceived as self-indulgent.

Step Two
Now, think about the background information your audience will need to know. For example, maybe you read about fraudulent service badges being sold over the Internet. Write anything the audience will need to know as your narrative.

B. Narrative—The Americans with Disabilities Act of 1990...

Step Three
Time to fill in the points that will make up the body of your argument. What is the first point or assertion you need to prove to convince someone to accept your thesis? For the thesis above, the first point you have to prove is suggested by the first part of the thesis:

II. Body of Argument

A. First Point: define and explain the service-animal designation

Then move on to fill in the blank for the second point.

B. Second Point: evidence that the designation is being misused or misrepresented

Continue filling in your points until you have exhausted your subject. Also under Body of Argument, write down what someone who disagrees with your thesis would say about your points.

C. Refutation: service animals come in many shapes and sizes

You just outlined the most important part of a classical argument and now have its basic outline. It is possible to write a complex argument without using the structure of a classical argument as outlined here. However, as early rhetors, students, and orators discovered, you will probably find that this structure can help you build persuasive arguments and save time in the process.

MODULE III-13

TYPES OF APPEALS

Another way to think of rhetoric is as the presentation of persuasive **proof**: evidence, appeals, and reasoning that support a thesis and an argument. Tradition provides two types of proof: inartistic and artistic.

- **Inartistic proof** consists of evidence or reasoning that should not require art, or rhetorical devices and strategies, to be believed by an audience. Evidence that was considered true in ancient times included laws, the testimony of witnesses, contracts, oaths, and confessions obtained from torture. Today, we may consider a video of an event, data, or material items like DNA or a moon rock as inartistic proof. For example, it is difficult to deny that US astronauts landed on the moon when confronted with inartistic proof such as moon rocks in museums, photographs of the lunar lander on the moon, and Apollo astronauts who live among us.
- **Artistic proof** consists of evidence and reasoning that the speaker or writer must invent or develop. Ancient rhetors presumed that an audience would accept inartistic proofs, but artistic proofs must respond to the diverse beliefs, expectations, and dispositions of different audiences to be effective. Traditionally, there are three types of artistic proofs, or appeals: *ethos*, *logos*, and *pathos*.

Appeals

You make an **appeal** whenever you structure an idea or select specific types of reasons or evidence that are attractive, provocative, or persuasive to a specific audience. We often say that someone makes or composes an appeal, and yet students are told to appeal to someone's sense of justice, for example. Is an appeal something you make or is it something you hope to inspire in the audience, like sympathy? Oddly, both are true. You compose an appeal to inspire a specific type of thinking or sentiment in your readers or listeners that will make them more likely to accept your argument. As with all elements of argument, an appeal works, or does not work, in the mind of the audience.

Building an appeal is a bit like engineering a roller-coaster ride (see Figure 17.4). The engineer thinks about the emotions and sensations she wants the riders to feel at each point in the ride, and then she draws upon her knowledge of physics and the tricks of the trade to inspire or arouse those emotions or sensations in the riders.

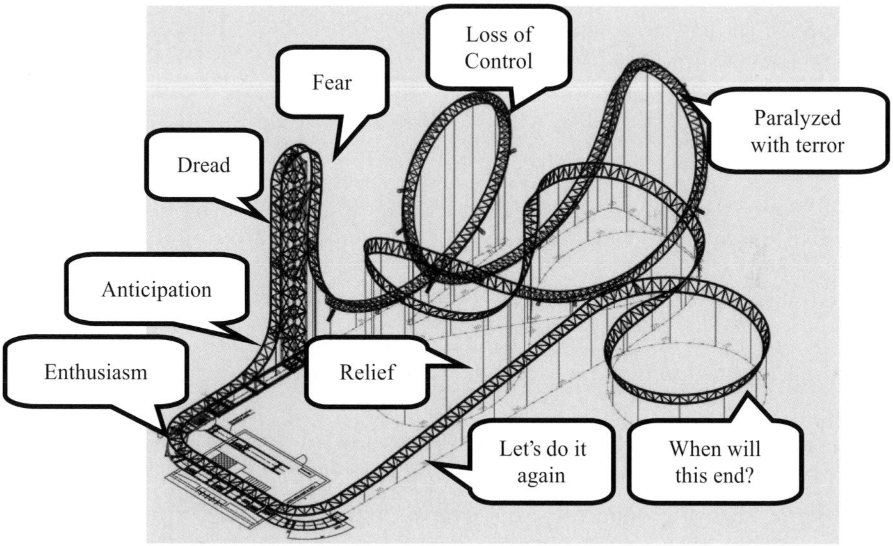

Figure 17.4 Sensations are felt by a person, and appeals work only if your audience responds to your appeal as you intended.

Not all roller coasters live up to expectations—just as not all appeals work. If you know the devices that others have used to make similar appeals and learn about your readers or listeners and how they are likely to respond, you can build an effective appeal. Tradition defines three types of persuasive appeals:

- ***Ethos***, an ethical appeal, is the way in which an author or a speaker moves the audience to believe that the source of the message is trustworthy and authoritative. Citing recognized experts and including their academic degrees and information about their published work are ways of making an ethical appeal.
  Your tone—your attitude toward your subject—is also an effective way of expressing *ethos*. If you deal with your subject seriously and engage opposing opinions fairly, and your writing or speech is appropriate to the audience's expectations and the setting, you will appear credible: the appeal of *ethos*.
- ***Pathos*** or emotional appeals are uncommon in academic contexts, and yet such appeals are the subject of study for a number of disciplines such as communication studies, political science, and theology. In both traditional argument structures and contemporary genres such as the editorial, *pathos* appeals are often found in the conclusion in order to inspire action or change.
- ***Logos***, logical appeals, or better still solid reasoning from reliable evidence provides the persuasive power of academic arguments. Some subjects, such as biology, engineering, and economics, use logic and data as their primary appeal. In fact, most academic audiences expect logical appeals built upon logical reasoning and evidence.

Inductive and Deductive Reasoning

In many situations, your audience will not accept your thesis until you provide the evidence that led to your conclusion or the steps in reasoning that caused you to believe what you assert. In a similar way, it is not enough for a recipe to list the ingredients and show a glossy picture of a beautiful cake. The recipe must also detail the steps that cooks must follow to bake the cake. For this reason, *logos* appeals are commonly built using inductive or deductive reasoning.

Inductive reasoning starts with a desire to explain a specific phenomenon like skyrocketing concert ticket prices or the decreasing use of open office plans.

Inductive reasoning, as illustrated in Figure 17.5, begins with an **observation**. The observer then tries to recall or discover similar observations or **patterns**. Next, the observer develops and tests a tentative explanation, also called a **hypothesis**, that describes the observation in terms of a possible pattern. If the hypothesis proves true or is widely accepted, it becomes a **theory** or general conclusion that can explain the original observation and predict future events.

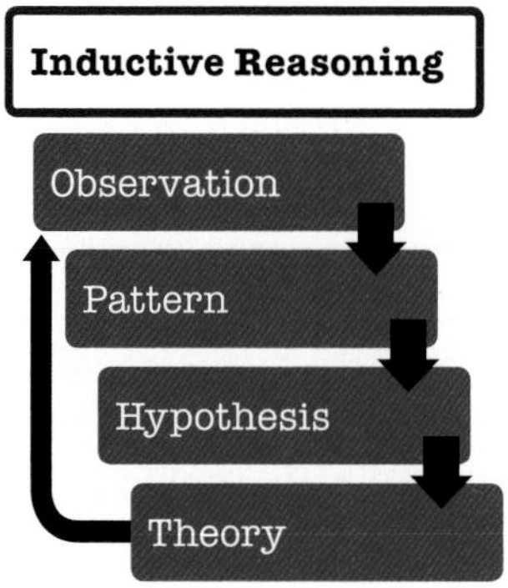

Figure 17.5 Steps in inductive reasoning.

Inductive reasoning results in explanations that are general (not specific) and probably true (not certainly true). The theory that results from inductive reasoning can always be refined by additional observations and observed patterns, and the persuasive power of an inductive argument grows with each observation that tests the perceived pattern and the explanatory hypothesis and then confirms or modifies the resulting theory.

For example, let's say you have noticed that when you go fishing for channel catfish, you get bites only in the spring or early summer when the water temperature is rising. Therefore, you formulate the following hypothesis:

Catfish hypothesis: Channel catfish are easier to catch when the water gets warmer.

The following fall and winter you get almost no bites. However, in spring, the same pattern continues and provides more evidence to support your hypothesis. You then formulate the following theory:

> **Catfish theory**: The best time to fish for channel catfish is in the spring or early summer when waters are warming.

In November, your aunt invites you to go on a camping trip below the Thomas Hill Reservoir in Missouri. You take your fishing gear and are surprised to spend the day pulling in fish after fish. You know the water should be cold and getting colder, but your aunt points out that the power plant discharges warm water half a mile upstream. Additional observations yield a new pattern. Your hypothesis has not lost its descriptive power, but your theory needs to be refined.

> **Revised catfish theory**: The best time to fish for channel catfish is any time you find warming waters.

The revised theory has more persuasive power because the sample size is larger. **Sample size** is the number of observations you make, such as the total number of times you went fishing, that lead to your hypothesis or theory. All of your observations, such as all of the times you went fishing in the last two years—including that one time you caught a catfish in freezing water—must be part of your sample.

If you developed your hypothesis and theory after fishing only once in your life, your sample would be too small and your conclusion too quickly reached. It would be an example of a logical fallacy called a **hasty generalization**. If you exclude from your sample events or observations that seem to go against your hypothesis, your hypothesis would be based on an **unrepresentative sample**, which is also a logical fallacy.

Deductive reasoning starts where inductive reasoning ends, with a general theory. In deductive reasoning, you apply a general theory to a specific observation which leads to a specific conclusion (Figure 17.6).

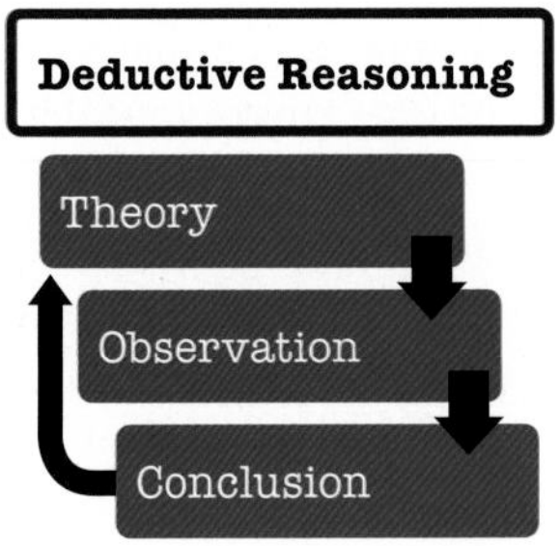

Figure 17.6 Steps in deductive reasoning.

A classic example of the three steps of deductive reasoning involves the ancient Greek philosopher Socrates:

All people are mortal. — Theory
Socrates is a person. — Observation
∴ Socrates is mortal. — Conclusion

(Logicians use ∴ for therefore)

When the theory and observation result in a conclusion that is described by the general theory, the theory is reaffirmed.

If you were to test your catfish theory with deductive reasoning, you would begin with a more specific hypothesis that may explain your fishing experience:

> **Catfish theory**: Channel catfish metabolism increases when waters warm above 40 degrees, stimulating hunger and increased feeding.

To test this theory, you might create an experiment that allows you to observe a control group of channel catfish in a tank of water 35 degrees or colder (test group) and a group of similar catfish in a tank 45 degrees or warmer. If you observe the activity in each tank and measure the amount of food each group of catfish eats, your observations may confirm, contradict, or refine your hypothesis and the more general theory.

If confirmed by scientific observations, you could state your confirmation as a simple argument, or a syllogism, similar to the Socrates deduction.

Increased channel catfish metabolism results in increased hunger and feeding.	Theory
Catfish metabolism increases when in water 40 degrees or warmer.	Observation
∴ Channel catfish are hungrier and feed more in waters above 40 degrees.	Conclusion

Inductive or deductive reasoning is appropriate in different writing tasks for different audiences. A scientist may use induction to develop a theory, and deduction to test the theory. If you are developing a proposal for some future action, induction may be the way to go. If you are trying to figure out how an auto accident happened, you may use what you know about how cars generally skid and spin to deduce what happened and who was at fault in a specific collision. An understanding of your audience and the available evidence will guide you in deciding what form of reasoning to use.

Induction:
specific → general
observation → theory

Deduction:
general → specific
theory → observation
confirmation

MODULE III-14

BUILDING AUTHORITY USING CLASSICAL VIRTUES

Early orators taught that only after being persuaded of the speaker's virtues, or good character, can the audience be persuaded to accept the speaker's message or thesis. Plato and most Greeks of his time valued four virtues: temperance, courage, wisdom, and justice.

Contemporary Virtues

Today virtues, if not Greek virtues, are still relevant to any argument you make, from an argument with a store manager that Ikea should refund the cost of an uncomfortable chair to an editorial maintaining that student athletes should be compensated.

Whom do you trust and whom do you believe? Odds are that people you trust have specific qualities that you look for in order to determine whether someone is worth listening to. When you speak or write, your audience is looking for qualities or virtues that reflect contemporary values such as the following:

- **Honesty** is a virtue we all hope to find in those we engage and work with. People who demonstrate truthfulness, fairness, and integrity are generally considered to be honest.
- **Transparency** includes the understanding that being open and forthcoming about biases and dispositions and being accountable for your own decisions and actions leads to fair treatment and mutual respect.
- **Authority** is the virtue of having valuable experience and knowledge and sharing it when appropriate. Possessing the markers of authority such as a judge's robe or an elective office like a governor is one way in which authority is demonstrated and recognized. Authority is also apparent when writers make true statements that can be proven with evidence or reasoning acceptable to an audience.
- **Civility** is not just a matter of being polite. It is in fact more like the classical virtue of justice because it is apparent in the relationships between individuals. Someone who is civil recognizes the rights and independence of others and respects these rights even when an opponent is disagreeable, annoying, or hostile.
- **Stewardship** may be recognized as beliefs and actions that demonstrate concern for the welfare and needs of others who share our environment and the continued welfare of future generations.

Classical orators would rarely have to demonstrate their virtues, because most members of their audience knew the speakers and their qualities. You, however, will need to demonstrate the qualities or virtues that your readers—such as your professor—will expect.

When writing a research paper, you transfer the authority of your sources to your argument by conducting thorough research and carefully documenting the evidence you cite. In addition, when you represent alternative positions and opposing arguments fairly and evaluate their points in an evenhanded manner, you demonstrate the virtues of honesty and transparency. Every rhetorical situation and each audience has virtues that they value and look for in others. By researching your audience, you can discover the virtues they value.

CHAPTER 18

USING CONTEMPORARY RHETORIC

In 2015, Texas governor Greg Abbott signed SB11, a bill allowing concealed handguns on campuses and in university buildings. The Gun-Free University of Texas movement and University Chancellor William McRaven, a former US navy admiral who opposes the law, see no justification for bringing weapons to otherwise peaceful campuses. Groups such as Texas Students for Concealed Carry on Campus cannot imagine why anyone would restrict a law-abiding citizen's right to protect himself or herself.

The views of those for and against the new Texas gun law couldn't be farther apart, and although the initial debate was somewhat civil, it is hard to imagine that any arguments have changed the minds of those on either side. In short, the debate seems stuck.

You may be thinking that the issue is resolved, since SB11 was signed. In fact, this issue and many others that occupy the news media are simply the most recent arguments in debates begun long ago. If you have ever heard conservative radio personality Rush Limbaugh argue against big government or liberal journalist Robert Scheer make the case for a strong federal government, you are hearing echoes of an argument that dates back to the writing of the Constitution more than 230 years ago.

Contemporary public debates rage on because for issues such as gun rights, tax policy, and protected speech there is no widely accepted consensus and few attempts to truly understand why one side or the other holds a particular view.

Don't give up hope, however; even on big contentious issues, persuasion still happens. For example, though it is hard for us to imagine, eight-hour workdays and 40-hour workweeks are the result of a rowdy public debate that raged for more than 100 years, beginning in 1836.

In fact, groups that seem to be so polarized that they can't even speak to people on the other side can move to understand, if not agree with, their opponents' way of thinking and work toward a resolution. How? Sometimes persuading a resistant audience or moving a debate forward is a matter of offering a new way of seeing the issue, and sometimes progress is a matter of using a new way of arguing.

Stephen Toulmin and Carl Rogers were two influential theorists who developed practical solutions to the problem of persuading extremely resistant audiences, including those who resist an argument without even knowing why.

Toulmin will help you examine and understand the hidden foundation of an opponent's argument or position so you can effectively argue against your opponent and persuade your audience to hold a different position. To do that, Toulmin developed a model and set of terms you could use to analyze and develop practical arguments in any field or discipline. Think of Toulmin's rhetoric as a rhetorical x-ray (see Figure 18.1). Like an x-ray, Toulmin's analysis can reveal the unseen structure of an argument, exposing both faults and strengths. Toulmin's method of analyzing and understanding how individuals justify their thinking, beliefs, and actions helps you find a way past their resistance and skepticism.

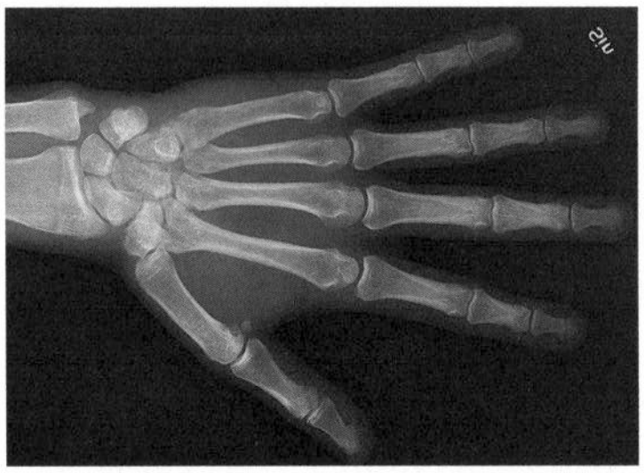

Figure 18.1
An x-ray can't fix a broken bone in your hand, but it can tell you what a strong hand looks like and where the problem is.

Whereas Toulmin looks deeply, Rogers looks at the space between. Rogers's way of thinking about the audience and shaping arguments will help you examine the points that you and your opponent have in common and understand the perspectives and ideas that separate. Beginning with what you share, Rogers shows you how to build an argument that moves you and your opponent closer so you can become partners working toward a shared purpose.

Both Toulmin and Rogers will force you to examine your thinking, the assumptions behind your reasoning, and why you believe what you argue. Both will make you think like your audience and see an argument from your reader's or listener's point of view. If you can anticipate challenges and counter arguments and find common ground with your audience, your argument will be stronger. Toulmin's model and terms of analysis will help you build a strong foundation and structure your argument. Rogers will help you speak with an authority built on empathy and understanding.

MODULE III-15

USING TOULMIN'S MODEL TO ANALYZE AN ARGUMENT

Sometimes people take positions or propose solutions for reasons they can't explain or don't fully understand. And sometimes people take positions for solid reasons that they may not be eager to share. Because persuasion happens only in the mind of the audience, it is necessary to delve deeply into the justifications and reasoning that people rely on to support their thinking, beliefs, and actions. Stephen Toulmin's approach to argument can help with this process.

Stephen Toulmin's (1922–2009) first job was as a science officer with the Supreme Headquarters of the Allied Expeditionary Force during World War II. Later, as a scholar, Toulmin studied everyday arguments in part because he thought that logical reasoning and classical argument rarely appear in ordinary conversations or academic debates. Instead of studying logical reasoning and syllogisms, he looked at how people make **practical arguments**, or arguments in everyday life, and developed what is now called the Toulmin model. Necessarily, Toulmin had to develop a number of new terms to describe practical arguments.

Data/Evidence and Claim

The two most basic elements of Toulmin's model are a claim and data or evidence:

Claim—The statement you will try to convince your audience to accept, using reasoning and evidence.
Data or Evidence—The evidence or reasoning that supports or makes your claim true or believable.

To see how these terms help analyze everyday arguments, let's take a look at an argument related to the issue of guns on campus. The image "Signs can't stop acts of violence" was posted on the Facebook page of the group Texas Students for Concealed Carry on Campus (Figure 18.2). Below the image was a request for the reader to send email to Texas senators asking them to support an amendment that would allow people with concealed handgun licenses to carry guns on Texas college campuses.

Figure 18.2 An image posted on Texas Students for Concealed Carry on Campus Facebook page, May 8, 2015.

If we cast the message of the image as a simple argument, or enthymeme, we can see that the data or evidence functions as an observation and the claim as the conclusion.

> Signs can't stop violence, ⟵ Data or Evidence
> therefore,
> armed citizens can stop violence and should be allowed on campus. ⟵ Claim

If you switch the two, with claim first and data or evidence second, you have a thesis.

> Armed citizens can stop violence and should be allowed on campus,
> because
> signs can't stop violence.

Warrant

What is unstated in the simple argument is the connection between the data or evidence and the claim. In other words, it is unclear how the author got from the evidence of signs to the claim that licensed, concealed handguns should be allowed on campus. The answer to that question is what Toulmin calls a warrant.

> **Warrant**—The assumptions that led you from the data or evidence to a reasonable claim or conclusion.

A warrant is typically thought to be so reasonable or obvious that it does not need to be said aloud. In the diagram (Figure 18.3), the warrant appears between the data and claim but not in the same line, which indicates that it is often unstated.

The warrant of the WhyCampusCarry.com argument was unstated, but we can infer it given the audience and the context of the amendment that was pending before the Texas legislature when the image first appeared (Figure 18.3). You do not need to state a warrant in a practical argument when the reasoning that lets you make the leap from data to claim is assumed to be obvious or based upon an observation, common sense, or a set of values shared by the writer or speaker and the audience. However, if your warrant isn't obvious or accepted by your audience, you may need to persuade your audience of your warrant.

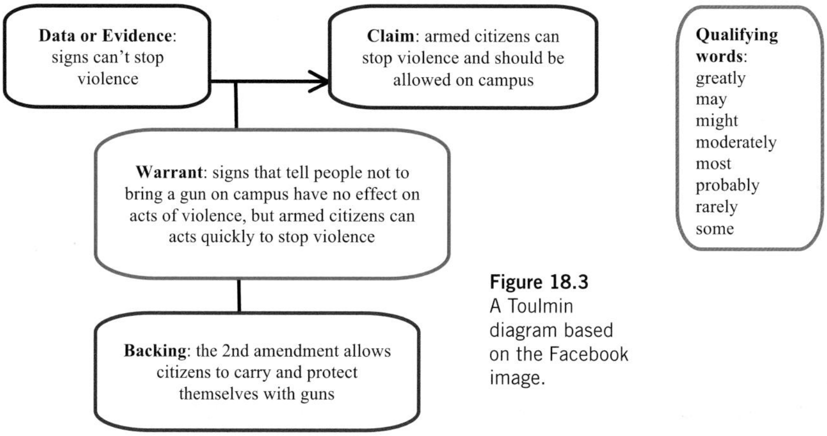

Figure 18.3 A Toulmin diagram based on the Facebook image.

Backing

Whether they are stated or unstated, all warrants must have something that backs them up, which is why Toulmin calls the warrant's support its *backing*.

Backing—Evidence or explanations that support the warrant.

Unlike a warrant, which always leads to or is oriented toward the claim, backing can be a general statement of fact that supports the warrant. In the argument of Figure 18.3, the backing supports the warrant but does not directly support the claim or explain the reasoning that links the data or evidence to the claim.

In an informal, spoken argument, among friends who share your reasoning for example, backing is usually unsaid, which is why the model (Figure 18.3) shows it hanging below the argument and linked only to the warrant. Backing does not need to directly support the argument's claim, but it gives the warrant authority and makes it believable.

Qualifier

In most practical arguments, the truth of a claim cannot be established with absolute certainty. Many claims acknowledge this by including a *qualifier.*

Qualifier—To qualify your claim is to limit it or reduce its force.

Qualifying words such as "possibly," "often," or "a majority" indicate that the data or evidence, warrant, and backing do not prove the claim to be absolutely true (see Figure 18.4). Qualifying words reduce the persuasive force of the warrant and backing; however, because qualifications also demonstrate that the arguer is reasonable, a qualification can enhance a writer's or speaker's authority.

Figure 18.4 If the WhyCampusCarry.Com argument was qualified, a word like perhaps or probably would appear between the data or evidence and the claim.

Rebuttal

Another way to enhance a writer's authority involves dealing with opposing ideas.

Rebuttal—A rebuttal can be contrary evidence, other ways of reasoning, alternative explanations, or counter claims that offer an alternative explanation or prove the warrant and backing are wrong.

For example, it is true that guns can be and are used to stop violent acts by others. However, as the Harvard School for Public Health and the Violence Policy Center research shows, guns are more frequently used in suicide. If the goal is a reduction of violence, more guns may not be the solution (Figure 18.5).

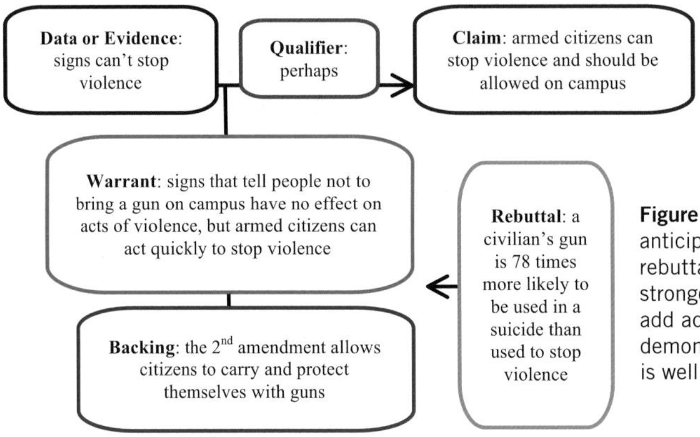

Figure 18.5 If you can anticipate an audience's rebuttals you can build stronger warrants and add additional backing demonstrating your claim is well reasoned.

The WhyCampusCarry.com (Figure 18.2) image is a brief, practical argument. For the sake of brevity, a great deal of the warrants, backing, qualifying terms, and possible rebuttals are not included. However, just as it is assumed that warrants need not be stated because they are obvious, rebuttals may be just as obvious to the intended audience.

You may be wondering, however, why you should weaken your own argument. Qualifiers and rebuttals work in the mind of your audience where persuasion happens. In fact, ignoring alternative explanations or evidence will not prevent rebuttals from occurring to your audience. They will, and if it seems you are unaware or you do not have a response to them, your argument will not persuade your readers or listeners. Adding appropriate qualifications and thoughtfully considering alternative explanations enhances your authority and increases the persuasive power of your argument.

Toulmin analysis can reveal both the strength and weakness of the arguments others make and the arguments you build. For example, a strength of the WhyCam pusCarry.com argument is that its backing is a constitutionaly guaranteed freedom. A weakness is that it does not acknowledge that guns can both prevent and cause violence. The Breaking the Block box entitled "Inventing and Revising with Toulmin" will help you use the Toulmin model and terms to analyze other people's arguments and invent your own.

Breaking the Block
Inventing and Revising with Toulmin

Toulmin's model can help you analyze the arguments of others to develop responses or counter arguments. In addition, Toulmin can help you refine your own argument as you draft and revise. Answering these questions can take between 10 and 20 minutes.

Step One: Read and Analyze
If you are doing research, read the questions below before you read the arguments you have discovered. Take notes as you read.

If you are revising your own argument, ask a friend or peer to read these questions and then read your argument and answer the questions below.

- ✓ Where did the idea come from? Or what are the data and evidence that lead to the claim?
- ✓ What makes you think that this claim is true or reasonable? Or how did the author get from the data and evidence to the claim?
- ✓ Why should I believe this? Or what warrants and backing must I have and agree with to accept this claim?

✓What is left unstated but assumed to be obvious or shared?
✓Is this claim always true? Or are there valid alternatives or limits to this claim?
✓How confident are you in this argument? Or should this claim be qualified?

Step Two: Reflect

A skeptical audience will ask the questions above as they read. If the arguments you discovered during research offer no answers, you have the beginnings of a counter argument. Where would you begin to build a counter argument?

If you can anticipate the same questions and provide answers in your own argument before the questions occur to your audience, your argument will have more persuasive power.

Ask yourself the following:

✓Does your claim rest on a warrant that will be accepted by your audience?
✓Do your warrants have backing?
✓Have you supplied and stated backing for any warrants your audience might question?
✓Have you responded to any conditions or rebuttals?

MODULE III-16

USING TOULMIN'S MODEL TO BUILD COUNTER-ARGUMENTS

Toulmin's model and his terms can help you analyze and understand all kinds of arguments, from simple, practical arguments you encounter every day to more complex arguments about controversial issues. Once you get beyond guesswork and start to understand why someone would make a particular argument, you are ready to build a targeted counter argument.

As Toulmin notes, people sometimes leave warrants unstated because, given the context, the warrant is obvious, or they assume the audience shares a set of beliefs and values or shares a way of reasoning sometimes called common sense.

As with any structure, if the hidden foundation is weak, what is built above may crumble. Therefore, the best place to begin to look for weaknesses or faulty reasoning is in the unstated warrants or backing. And the best way to understand unstated warrants and backing is by examining the context of an argument and noting the writer's or speaker's intended audience.

Using the Model

Let's consider an argument built to oppose the argument that licensed concealed weapon owners should be allowed to carry guns on campus because they can stop violence and because the Constitution guarantees the right to own and carry firearms.

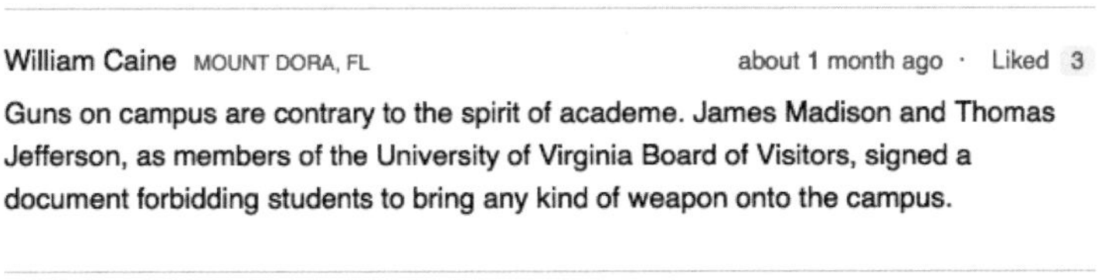

William Caine MOUNT DORA, FL about 1 month ago · Liked 3

Guns on campus are contrary to the spirit of academe. James Madison and Thomas Jefferson, as members of the University of Virginia Board of Visitors, signed a document forbidding students to bring any kind of weapon onto the campus.

Figure 18.6 A comment on a website for the group Gun Free University of Texas.

William Caine's brief comment was posted on a petition website of the group Gun Free University of Texas (see Figure 18.6). The website asks viewers to sign a petition and add their comments supporting the repeal of the new Texas law signed by Governor Abbott called the "Campus Carry" law. Mr. Caine's argument is in the form of a thesis, with the claim in the first sentence and the data or evidence as the second sentence. Cast in Toulmin's model it would look like the diagram shown in Figure 18.7.

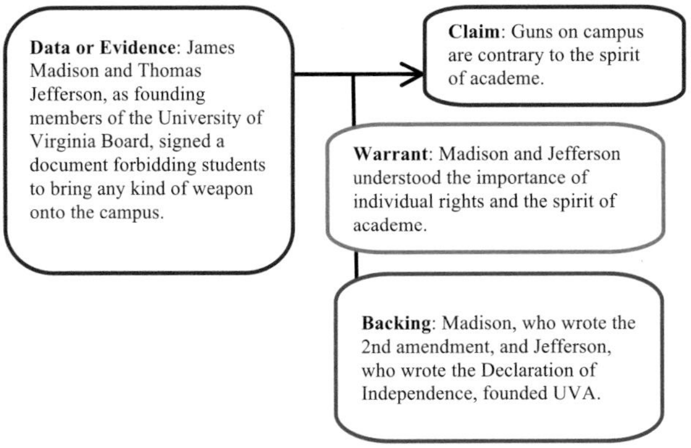

Figure 18.7 The argument against campus-carry laws, within the Toulmin model.

This argument has two strengths. First, Mr. Caine's comment is the result of research on the foundation of nearly all gun rights arguments, including those of WhyCampusCarry.com. It is true that the Second Amendment guarantees the right of citizens to carry and protect themselves with guns. However, Mr. Caine's research shows that authors of the Second Amendment recognized and enforced limits upon this freedom. And this leads to the second strength of this argument.

Even those opposed to Mr. Caine's stated claim are likely to accept the authority of Madison and Jefferson on individual rights and the spirit of educational inquiry that makes up the backing. After all, it would be difficult to argue that Madison and Jefferson intended the Second Amendment to be an unlimited right and then disregard their stated intention of the Virginia campus to be a weapon-free place. Thus, skeptical readers may be inclined to consider the warrant, even if they do not accept the claim.

Both the WhyCampusCarry.com image and Mr. Caine's anti–campus-carry comment are surprisingly complex arguments, but you can use Toulmin's model and terms of analysis not only to analyze them but also to build a persuasive counter argument.

Building Counter-Arguments

All arguments are subject to counter-arguments or rebuttals, but you cannot rebut or argue against what you cannot see. Once you have used Toulmin's model to reveal the underlying structure of an argument, you can look for weakness or missing points to build an effective counter-argument. Let's start with the image in favor of the campus-carry law.

The first warrant of the sign argument is causal; it asserts that signs that tell people not to bring a gun on campus have no effect on acts of violence, but all types of firearms—not just rifles—can prevent or limit acts of violence. An effective rebuttal would question this assumption. Research questions such as the following may yield evidence for a rebuttal.

- Is an increase in the number firearms carried by civilians in a community linked to an increase or a decrease in acts of violence, or do more firearms have no effect?
- How likely is it that a person carrying a weapon who is confronted with a violent act can safely intervene to stop or limit that act?
- When citizens intervene in acts of violence, how often are they able to stop the violence without injuring innocent bystanders?
- How often are weapons intended for personal protection involved in accidental shootings, suicides, or crimes?

If you can find authoritative evidence proving that guns carried by citizens, concealed or in the open, do not stop violence, you have a persuasive rebuttal to the warrant that backs the campus-carry argument.

The warrant of the argument against campus-carry laws is based on the authority of Thomas Jefferson and James Madison, but it also tries to link their authority to the attempt to forbid guns on campuses. Although the authority of these two former presidents cannot easily be challenged, the link can be. In the first place, you might do research to determine whether Madison and Jefferson really did sign a document that banned guns from the University of Virginia. The following research questions may help build a persuasive rebuttal.

- Did the document that Madison and Jefferson signed ban guns in all situations or simply limit the use or presence of guns to certain situations?
- Did the document have any authority in the actual banning of guns on the UVA campus, was it a voted policy of the University of Virginia Board of Visitors, or was it simply a suggestion?
- If the forbidding of guns was the result of a vote by the University of Virginia Board of Visitors, how did Madison or Jefferson vote?
- Did Madison and Jefferson really sign the document?

Obviously, it is impossible to argue against the backing. Madison and Jefferson founded the University and were also key figures in the founding of the United States. Likewise, it may be difficult to argue against the backing of the signed argument. Keep in mind, however, that the backing supports only the warrant (not the claim), and it is the warrant that is the leap from the data or evidence to the claim. Often a counter-argument simply shows your audience that the leap could have gone in a different direction, or simply shows that no one can logically make the leap from the data or evidence to the stated claim.

MODULE III-17

ROGERIAN RHETORIC DEFINED

Rogerian rhetoric is a method of persuasion that attempts to convince the audience to help solve a problem that concerns both the writer and the audience. Unlike an **adversarial argument**, also known as a classical argument, which tries to move or persuade an audience to take one side of a dispute, a **Rogerian argument** attempts to achieve consensus among different parties in a dispute by identifying common ground and unstated areas or points of agreement.

Carl Rogers's goal was to help people of many different, and even opposing, perspectives work together to solve significant problems. Rogers was a psychologist, and in his time he was concerned about the escalation of the Cold War and the potential of nuclear war between the Soviet Union and the United States. Elements of Rogerian rhetoric remain relevant today, and they can be used to build collaborative relationships with extremely resistant individuals to face problems ranging from climate change to who should get a contested parking spot.

Carl Rogers (1902–87) went to college to be a farmer, but he changed his major to history and then theology. He eventually studied psychology, and he developed the idea of the **evaluative tendency** to explain why communication breaks down or is blocked. He noted that we all have a tendency to evaluate and judge what we read or hear from our own frame of reference. We accept ideas that fit within our frame and evaluate negatively and reject those that don't. For example, imagine I say to you,

> For the good of the country, you really must change the way you think about immigration.

The sentence above doesn't explain *how* you should think about immigration, but it is likely your first thought after reading it was similar to one of the following reactions:

> No I don't, you're wrong.
> My thinking on immigration is better than yours.

These responses are examples of the evaluative tendency in action. Friends or colleagues who always seem to disagree or do the opposite of what they are told are also displaying this tendency. In fact, Rogers saw this common tendency as the greatest obstacle to creating long-lasting relationships built on mutual communication. **Mutual communication** is an exchange where both individuals come to a new, deeper understanding of the other's perspectives and can accept why and how the other person thinks, believes, or behaves as they do. You can still disagree with your counterparts within mutual communication, but you see the others' beliefs as justifiable from their position and perspective. For example, moving from the view that "you are just stubborn and in love with your own ideas" to a more empathetic statement such as "now that I understand the future problems you anticipate, I see your point" is a step toward mutual communication.

Significantly, mutual communication requires **empathetic understanding**. As Rogers explained, empathetic understanding does not simply mean understanding a person's background or what someone might say in opposition to your argument. To develop empathetic understanding, you need to dwell so deeply in another person's perspective that his or her thinking, beliefs, and actions make sense to you.

This level of understanding can be scary because you may change your ideas and, be forced to rewrite your argument as you learn more about the views and opinions of your audience.

For example, during your research about climate change and the emission of carbon dioxide (CO_2), you may have discovered all the typical arguments made by those who oppose limiting our dependence upon fuels like coal. However, until you sit down and talk with a coal miner whose family is dependent upon the mining industry or speak with workers in towns like Somerset, Colorado, where mining has shut down, leaving the entire region destitute, you can't really empathize or understand one important opposing argument.

This kind of understanding and empathy is crucial because press releases and position statements are often just summaries of, and sometimes inaccurate representations of, the real reasons that people think and believe as they do. And evaluating and judging a brief statement is not a way of engaging others in a productive debate or solving problems.

This kind of understanding and audience research has the potential to change how you and your audience think. And that type of change was Rogers's objective.

MODULE III-18

A ROGERIAN ARGUMENT: A PERSUASIVE PAPER

The structure of a Rogerian argument is shaped by its objectives and the attitude toward the subject (**tone**) and audience (**tenor**) of the Rogerian approach.

In most arguments based on the classical model, such as an academic argument, your tone is authoritative. You know your subject, you are confident your thesis statement is true, and your evidence proves your position. In a Rogerian argument, however, your tone reflects the attitude you may have had at the beginning of your research—you are interested and hope to learn more about your subject from all who can provide insight, including those with a very different perspective from yours.

Although the tenor of a traditional argument should be respectful, you are trying to persuade the members of your audience to change how they currently think, believe, or act. Necessarily, an adversarial argument presents a subtle, and sometimes not-so-subtle, critique of how your readers or listeners currently think, what they believe, and how they act. A Rogerian argument has a different attitude toward the audience. Rather than assuming the audience is in need of correction or new information, the writer or speaker using the Rogerian structure assumes that the audience's perspective provides valuable insight, and their justification for their current thinking, beliefs, and behavior can contribute to solving the problem at hand.

Alyssa Smith wanted to respond to the many skeptical questions that people had asked her about her home schooling. In her First Year Seminar course, she decided that the most persuasive argument would be one that began where her audience was and moved to middle ground.

Alyssa Smith
Dr. Miskolcze
First Year Seminar
11/12/2015

Homeschooling

Oftentimes, when classmates would find out that I was previously homeschooled, they would ask if it was awesome not having to get up early to do homework or being able to watch TV whenever I wanted. Students would also ask if I ever got to meet people or if I had any friends. Initially, even my grandparents did not approve of my homeschooling. They did not think our parents should instruct us, and that we probably would not succeed later in life because we wouldn't be able to perform at the same level we would if we had attended a public or private school. My grandparents wanted us to have the same schooling they did; the same as 96% percent of school aged children in the United States (Institute).

Hook

Subject introduced

People argue that homeschooling is not an efficient way to educate children. They maintain that parents who have not been trained to be teachers cannot properly educate their children. And, even if a parent has experience or expertise in one area such as math, he or she is unlikely to have the same expertise in a different field like social studies.

Opposing position

A recurring question is whether or not homeschooled children will grow up to be socially awkward, without knowing how to behave in social situations. In fact, a common criticism of homeschooling is that it is used by religious parents to force their beliefs on their children. These parents are viewed as controlling, unwilling to let their kids out into the "real world," and eager to shelter their children from all outside influences.

Opposing perspective

According to the National Home School Association, "Over 2.04 million students are now learning at home, a 75%

Context of opposing perspective

increase from 1999." The potential for abuse or simple neglect is there, especially with the growth in the number of families who are home schooling and the lack of consistent regulation.

As a recent *Slate* magazine article entitled "The Frightening Power of the Home-Schooling Lobby" shows, oversight and regulation of homeschooling is inconsistent, and some states have no required subjects. As a result, there are cases where homeschooled students, suffering abuse and neglect, "fall off the face of the earth so that no one knows they exist," as Loretta Weinberg, majority leader of the New Jersey Senate, is quoted as saying in the article (qtd. in Huseman).

Justification of opposing perspective

My parents never forced me to be homeschooled and always told me that I could enter a public school at any time that I desired. I am so grateful for my parents' decision to homeschool me for nine years, and I would not change a thing about my past education. There were many reasons why my parents decided to homeschool me; some reasons were that they wanted me to develop my own way of thinking without being persuaded by classmates or a closed-minded teacher. It was also a great way for my parents to see how fast or slow a learner I was. I started school a year early and was able to learn at my own pace without being held back by the restraints of a typical public school year.

Perspective of writer

Being homeschooled was actually very challenging because I was being taught with an accelerated curriculum, which fit the way I learn. Many of my friends had other reasons for choosing to be homeschooled. For example, I had a friend at my public high school who was being bullied so much that it was taking a negative toll on his life, so he resorted to homeschooling. Another friend was constantly missing school because she was so badly allergic to peanut butter and many other foods; there was no way to protect her at the public school. Her only alternative was to be homeschooled or to drop out of school. Thankfully, because school is possible at home, she could continue her educational endeavors in the safety of her house without worrying if a classmate would eat peanut butter near her. Without homeschooling, students like these would have no means of education and would most likely become dropouts.

Context justifies position

It is true, that some parents may not have the expertise to meet all their children's educational needs, which is why, "The most significant factor behind growing public acceptance of home schools is the establishment of a vast array of support systems and networking organizations" according to Maralee Mayberry, a professor of the sociology of education (Mayberry 10). Parents do not have to be the sole teachers of their children because homeschooled children can draw upon organizational support groups that provide parents curricular guidance and materials. Qualified teachers are also available who can meet with children on a regular basis to check the quality of their work to make sure they stay on track.

Justification and common ground with opposition

I have also heard stories on the news involving parents who don't let their children outside or do not require them to do any of their work. Because these are people who abuse the system and are not properly homeschooling their kids, they should not represent the vast majority of parents who competently teach their students. Some public schools do not properly teach students, but those individual schools should not represent the work ethic and results of all public schools.

Similarities between perspectives

We all agree, the most important thing is for a child to get a good education, whether in a public school or in a homeschool situation. The article "Exploring Academic Outcomes of Homeschooled Students," by Michael F. Cogan, reports on a study done at a medium sized college located in the upper Midwest to find if there is a significant difference between homeschooled students and students from other forms of traditional education. The study found that homeschooled students achieve higher standardized test scores than traditionally schooled students. The issue of whether or not homeschoolers can perform at the same level as students of traditional schools arises often, but is continually answered with a yes. According to Cogan, "Descriptive analysis reveals [that] homeschool students possess higher ACT scores, GPAs, and graduation rates when compared to traditionally-educated students" (24).

Position addresses concerns of opposition

My grandparents did not approve of my siblings and me being homeschooled until they saw our high grades and other accomplishments later in high school and beyond. Despite

Benefits of combined schooling options

the many arguments people raise when confronted with the question of whether or not homeschooling is a sufficient form of education, there is adequate evidence to show that it is. In fact, I think the combination of the homeschooling option and my later public high school experience was exactly what I needed to succeed in college. And research shows it may be just what many students need.

Similarities summarized

Those who disagree with homeschooling and those who prefer public schools all want a good education for children. Yes, many parents who homeschool need support from professional organizations, and abuses must stop. Regulation and more cooperation with school districts may be the answer. However, rather than critiquing another way of teaching and learning that has proven successful, perhaps critics should consider what is best for each student and family. It seems that if the goal is education, then we should all work to encourage many different ways of educating different students.

Alternatives considered

Appeal for consensus and collaboration

Works Cited

Cogan, Michael F. "Exploring Academic Outcomes of Homeschooled Students." *Journal of College Admission*, no. 208, Summer 2010, pp. 18–25, files.eric.ed.gov/fulltext/EJ893891.pdf.

Huseman, Jessica. "The Frightening Power of the Home-Schooling Lobby." *Slate*, 27 Aug. 2015, www.slate.com/articles/life/education/2015/08/home_school_legal_defense_association_how_a_home_schooling_group_fights.html.

Institute of Education Sciences, National Center for Education Statistics. *Homeschooling in the United States: 2012.* US Department of Education, 2016, http://nces.ed.gov/pubs2016/2016096.pdf.

Mayberry, Maralee. *Home Schooling: Parents as Educators.* Corwin, 1995.

National Home School Association. *Homeschool Fact Sheet.* 2016, nationalhomeschoolassociation.com/fact-sheet.php.

Smith built her Rogerian argument on the questions and responses she received from skeptical family and friends. She also researched the views of others who doubted the effectiveness of homeschooling. As she did, she found research that supported her position, and she was able to identify areas where compromise is possible. As you build your argument, you will need to develop invention and research strategies that focus on your audience and on new perspectives and ideas.

MODULE III-19

REACHING YOUR AUDIENCE WITH ROGERIAN RHETORIC

Throughout your argument, your objective is to demonstrate empathetic understanding and move your readers to believe that you not only understand their position or solution but also understand their perspective and how they came to their solution or position. Empathy cannot be faked. Therefore, to achieve such understanding you must practice empathetic listening during your invention and research. You engage in empathetic listening by placing your evaluative tendency on hold as you come to understand how others are positioned, how they see the world, and how they make sense of what they see. The following checklist can help you use empathetic listening to build an effective Rogerian argument.

Listen to opponents and their ideas.

✓ Listen carefully to people who see the situation or problem differently from the way you do.
- Give your opponents your undivided attention.
- Do not interrupt, disagree, or criticize anything they say.
- Take careful notes or record what they say if they grant permission to do so.
- Pay special attention to their understanding of the context of the situation or problem, their perspective or how they see the situation or problem, and the reasoning they have used to come to their position or solution.
- When they are done talking, count to ten, and then ask if you can ask questions.
- When asking questions, learn not to challenge, and as they answer do not interrupt.
- Paraphrase their position or solution and ask if your understanding is correct. Do not challenge them if they correct you. Instead, take notes, and then try to paraphrase again.

✓ *Read* or *listen to* scholars, experts, and other writers who have addressed the situation or problem in terms much different from your own.
- Take notes on the context, perspective, and reasoning of the writer or speaker.
- Recast what you have read or heard in your own words. If you are doing so in a draft, be sure to highlight the paraphrase of your source or mark it with a different font and add the appropriate documentation.
- Think of additional reasons or evidence that would support the opponent's argument.

Find common ground—the points that are not in dispute. Chapter 6 will help you find common ground and identify the differences you have with your audience.

- ✓ Focus on context. How is the opponent's understanding of the context similar to your understanding? There will be differences, but take note of what you have in common.
  - For example, if your opponents have a different view of gun rights or gun control than you do, what context informs their thinking? Do they understand the issue in terms of self-protection, as a matter of civil rights, or as a matter of public safety? Work to understand how the context makes sense to your opponents.
- ✓ Consider the opponent's perspective. Try to understand what informs and motivates your opponents' thinking, beliefs, or actions.
  - If your opponent understands guns in terms of a family hunting tradition, any suggestion that access to guns should be limited or controlled may be seen through the perspective of family heritage and traditions. You may have never gone hunting, but to build a Rogerian argument, you will need to see and appreciate the issue of guns from their perspective.

Identify differences and conflicts of opinion, and acknowledge strong points in opposing positions or solutions.

- ✓ It is equally important to identify real differences between you and your opponent. If it appears that you do not recognize real differences, your audience members may not believe that you understand the issue or understand their position.
  - For example, if you are talking to someone who collects historic guns about inner-city gun violence, she might agree with you that access to guns should be restricted. However, if you are unaware of why someone would find an antique or historic gun interesting, your audience is unlikely to consider any proposal, as they see no common ground in your position.
- ✓ Concession proves you have listened and learned.
  - When you concede, or acknowledge that an opponent has a good point or is right about something, your readers or listeners will see you as flexible and attentive to their concerns and interests. In this way, you build ethos in the eyes of your audience.

A Rogerian argument isn't about winning. Instead, the Rogerian approach to argument involves learning from those who hold an opposing view in order to solve real problems. As a result, you can find the raw material for a Rogerian argument by paying close attention to your audience or opponents or, really, anyone who thinks about a subject or problem differently from the way you do. The Conventions in Context box entitled "Think before You Speak" provides a way of doing this in the context of social media.

Conventions in Context
Think before You Speak

Have you ever hit send and a second later desperately looked for the cancel or recall button? Most people who have used instant messaging or social media have written a text, an email, or posted a Snapchat they wanted to take back. You don't get do-overs, unfortunately. But if you think about it, you are in charge of what happens *before* you hit the send button.

The poster in Figure 18.8 is a simple meme found in classrooms, in offices, and on sites like Pinterest, but it is also a sentiment that is easy to ignore until you send or post something you wish you had not. Significantly, the poster's advice is consistent with Rogerian rhetoric, and it can help you build cooperative relationships that not only help you solve problems but also help you meet challenges that will pop up next week.

Figure 18.8 THINK before you speak.

Let's break down the poster's message:

- **Is it true?** Not just to you, but also to the person you are writing to? Because if the recipient does not think it is, your message will not be heard.
- **Is it helpful to your reader?** If not, why would he or she bother reading it?

- **Is it inspiring?** For example, you may be thinking that you are just asking your collaborators on a project when they will finish their part. Think about it this way, though: if you want to slow down the project, a nasty attitude or guilt trip laid on your partners will certainly do that. On the other hand, encouragement and optimism may inspire them to work with more confidence and work more quickly.
- **Is it necessary for all who read it?** How many unnecessary messages do you delete every day? On the other hand, whose messages do you always read and tend to keep? You should aim to write messages like those in the second group.
- **Is it kind?** Think about how you respond to kindness and what impels you to cooperate with others. Odds are that you not only value kindness when others show it to you but you also recognize how kindness contributes to your outlook and your working relationships.

Finally, here's a bit of advice: the "reply all" button can get you in trouble as it sends your message to an audience that someone else selected. Take control of your audience by not using the "reply all" button. You can answer the Think questions for one or two people, but it gets more complicated when the list of people you are talking to is large or unknown.

PART IV

CONDUCTING RESEARCH TO BUILD AUTHORITATIVE ARGUMENTS

CHAPTER 19

USING DATABASES AND SEARCH ENGINES

Could you use the image in Figure 19.1 to find your home or something larger like the city of Paris? The answer is no. First, the image presents too much information (it is a map of the entire world) to locate your house. And second, it has too little information—no continents, countries, or cities are named—to locate the city of Paris.

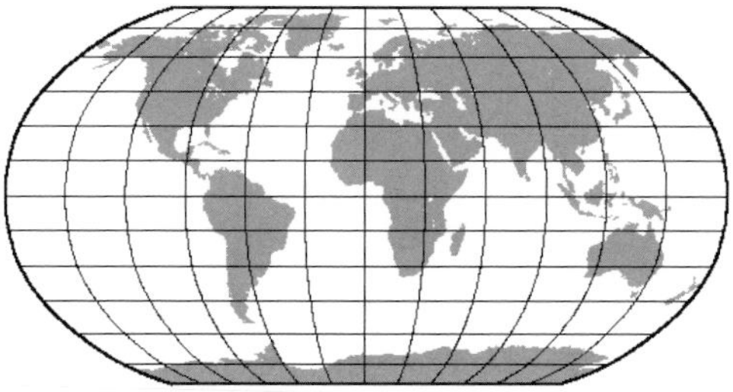

Figure 19.1 A Robinson Projection of the globe.

Different images—and maps—answer different questions and are suited to different uses because each one has a specific orientation, scope, and focus. The same is true of search engines and databases. In fact, to use search engines and databases effectively, you should think of them as types of maps.

It may seem odd, but the article you can download on your smartphone has an actual location. A search engine can find that article because the article is linked to a person (author), an origin (place of publication and publisher), a location (the container of the source such as a website), and even a time (the date of publication).

This chapter will show you how databases and search engines, in effect, create and then search vast maps of documents. It will also show you how to find articles, books, and other works that you need—and even those you don't yet know you need—quickly and with as little energy as possible.

MODULE IV-1

BUILDING AUTHORITY WITH SEARCH ENGINES AND DATABASES

To begin, let's explore the functions of the available resources and tools.

Tools and Resources

A **database** is a collection of indexed information or data. Databases can be large or small, digital or composed of physical records. A box of recipes, your contacts list, the World Wide Web, and your hard-drive directory are all databases.

Examples of research databases are

- The National Digital Data Forecast Database
- The Modern Language Association International Bibliography
- *The New York Times* article archive
- Federal Reserve Bank of Chicago Economic Research Publications

Some databases are open and some are closed. Databases intended to serve the public, such as the "JPL Small-Body Database Browser," which indexes near-earth asteroids, are open and free to the public. Some, such as the Modern Language Association Bibliography or the WGSN database, which indexes future trends, require a subscription or fee to access. In an academic setting, students benefit from institutional subscriptions and can search a great number of specialized databases with appropriate log-on credentials provided by the university or college.

The purpose of a database is to allow scholars to search for and retrieve desired data, information, and documents. Therefore, almost all databases provide a search function, and some databases, such as the World Wide Web; can be searched with any one of the many search engines available.

To search a database, you can use a **search function** or a **search engine**. A search function is typically a simple word-search computer program linked to a database used to identify desired data, information, or documents. A free-standing search engine, like Google or looksmart, is a computer program that indexes and searches open-access websites and databases.

A search engine does not necessarily tell you where a document or information is or provide access to it. However, many databases with linked search functions used in academic contexts do so. Here are some examples of subscription databases with search functions:

Business Source Complete
EBSCOhost
LexisNexis
Westlaw
Jstor
ProQuest

A **library catalogue** is a searchable index of a **library collection**: physical holdings (books, journals, and newspapers), electronic subscriptions (databases and electronic texts), and other resources held and made available by a library. Some libraries now provide a central search engine to make it easier to search their entire catalogue.

Limitations of Resources and Tools

All search engines, like all maps, are constructed with a specific perspective—a limited scope, a defined focus, and an orientation. **Scope** is the area, range, or breadth of subject matter that the search engine covers. **Focus** is the search engine's ability to concentrate on a single data point, detail, subject, or image. **Orientation** determines scope and allows you to focus because it is the direction of your vision or search.

Google may appear to have an unlimited scope because it seems to be looking in every direction at once. But Google has limitations: It cannot search databases that require subscriptions, catalogues that have not been made available to the public, or documents that have not been digitized or indexed electronically. In a similar way, every search function linked to a database has its own limits. These limitations, however, also make it possible for you to select the tools best suited to your search and search only those databases that are likely to hold what you need.

World Wide Web Orientation

Search engines look in different ways. **Google**, for example, attempts to take the perspective of the individual looking out at the world. It assumes the individual wants to search with the largest scope possible and look at the entire World Wide Web.

Google is constantly searching the web; indexing linked sites on countless subjects. Using the words you type in the search box, Google then narrows its search to identify a set of sites in which your search words frequently appear. After selecting those that are most often linked by other sites, it then reduces that set of sites to the most relevant, using your search terms but also other data such as the location of the computer you are using and its past search history. This final winnowing produces the list of results you see.

Google is a powerful search engine, but because its orientation is the World Wide Web and its scope is so expansive, it also has a problem with focus (see Figure 19.2). The speed with which Google can provide 1.8 million hits is amazing, but how long would it take you to find useful, reliable, and relevant information among so many results? A more focused search within a tighter scope may take more of Google's time, but it is a more efficient way to research.

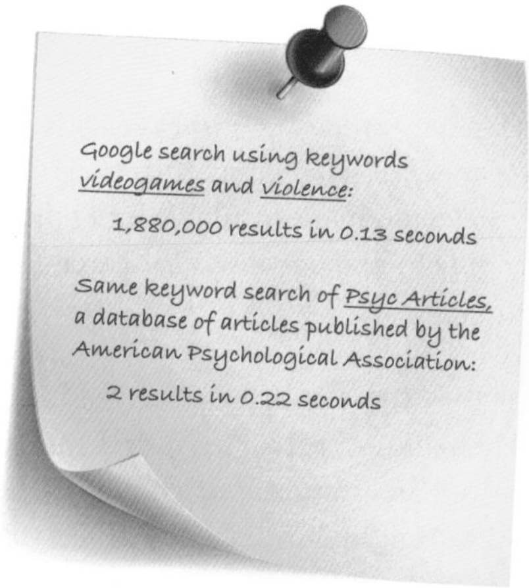

Google search using keywords videogames and violence:
1,880,000 results in 0.13 seconds
Same keyword search of Psyc Articles, a database of articles published by the American Psychological Association:
2 results in 0.22 seconds

Figure 19.2 Different databases yield different results.

Academic Research Orientation

Search engines linked to multiple academic databases, such as **Proquest** and **EBSCO**, take the orientation of a researcher looking into specific disciplines or specialties. These search engines identify and return entries (articles, books, journals) in which the words typed into the search box appear most frequently.

Search engines that take a researcher's orientation, like **Google Scholar**, Google's search engine for academic sources, and **JSTOR**, give you the freedom to shape your search. You can search databases for specific categories such as author, subject, and date, and you can also create searches that *exclude* specific words and types of texts (see Figure 19.3).

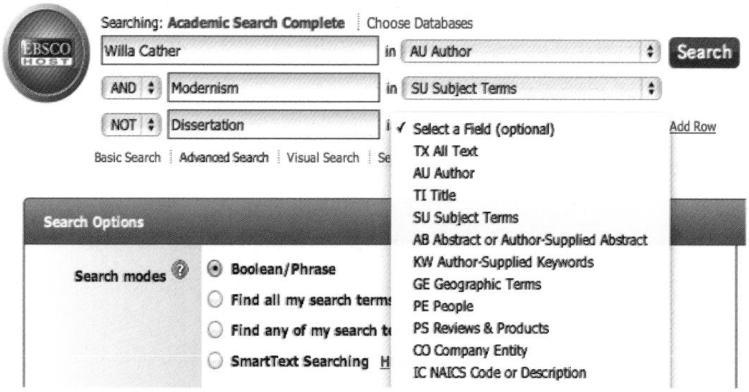

Figure 19.3 Example EBSCO search for publications about author Willa Cather and "modernism." A drop-down menu allows you to exclude dissertations as a type of text. Libraries subscribe to academic databases and linked search engines, and as a result Proquest, EBSCO, and other subscription services will look nearly the same no matter where you are or what library you use to do your research.

A digital library catalogue or **online public access catalogue (OPAC)** search engine is oriented toward the resources and holdings of a specific library. As a result, the OPAC of each library and library system is likely to look different (Figure 19.4). Because many libraries are linked to other libraries, the OPAC of your library may allow you to search a limited number of others as well. For example, the University of Wisconsin Library OPAC links all 13 UW campus libraries as well as a few more.

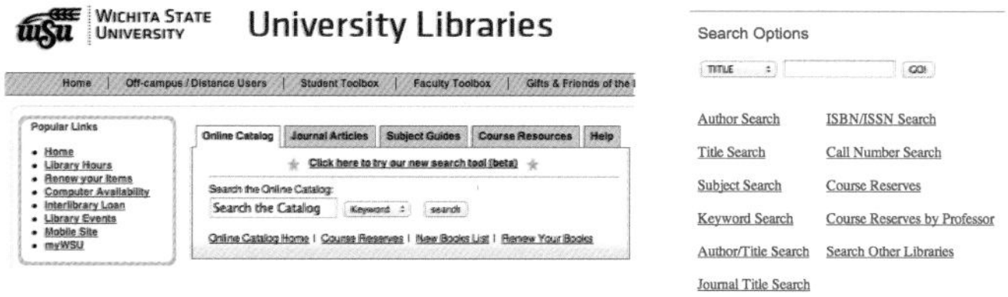

Figure 19.4 Two different OPAC search engines; one from a university and one from a college in Kansas.

Sometimes the greatest discoveries happen when you are simply wandering among the shelves, scrolling through search engine results, moving from source to source, taking nibbles here and there to see what is good. The Breaking the Block box entitled "Grazing" will show you how it is done.

Breaking the Block
Grazing

The most basic form of research invention is grazing, wandering from source to source and taking nibbles here and there. The benefit of grazing is that you are motivated by curiosity and you keep only what interests you. This exercise will take you to five different types of information to graze, and you will write for 10–15 minutes.

Step One: Prepare Your Work Space
Visit each of the following specialized sites.

- *Blog Search Engine*—http://www.blogsearchengine.org
- *Zanran*, a data and statistics search engine—http://www.zanran.com/q/
- *Quora*, a searchable question-and-answer discussion board—https://www.quora.com
- The website of the best newspaper in your area
- A general library database such as *Reader's Guide to Periodical Literature*

In the search box of each site, type in three words that describe your subject, or type in three words that represent an interest of yours.

Step Two: Write

- Identify the three search engines with the most interesting results.
- Graze the sites your search turns up, reading or reviewing the results of your three searches.
- When you find a result, a site, or a document that interests you, cut and paste the URL address onto a blank page. Beneath the URL, write a paragraph about why you found it interesting.
- When you have at least two URL addresses for each search engine search, set aside your work for at least two hours.
- The paragraphs you have are an excellent source for paper or speech topics. Review each paragraph and look for links among the paragraphs and the results they describe.
- Write a couple of sentences describing who would benefit from, or who needs to hear, the data and information you found. You have created an annotated bibliography on a possible topic for further research.

MODULE IV-2

USING DATABASES AND SEARCH ENGINES

Just as when you consult a map, when you use a search engine you must first have a destination or subject in mind. Even a vague one will do at first. When you have an idea, it is time to ask yourself this very basic question: Where does the knowledge I need live?

Deciding Where the Knowledge You Need Lives

Most of us would have little trouble finding departure times for May 4 flights from Boston to Austin; we would visit a travel website. Similarly, most of us would have no difficulty at all finding a gallon of milk in our hometown. In both cases, we know what we need and where it lives. Asking "where do political science data, information, and knowledge live?" may seem odd, but it is the first step of focused research.

Focus on the location. If you have an assignment to compare the ideas of the political scientists Aaron Wildavsky and Alan Wolfe, Google's scope may be far too large and may not provide the focus you need. So narrow your scope. Just as milk is in a dairy case in the back of the store and Kansas City lives on the Kansas–Missouri border, political science scholarship lives in a few specific databases and collections.

To focus within your scope, find out where scholars of your subject keep their ideas, writing, and documents. There are a number of ways to do this, but here are three easy methods:

1. Ask your professor.
2. Ask a reference librarian.
3. Consult the Library of Congress (LOC) subject-heading list.

The Library of Congress Classification (LOC) system assigns a unique call number to each item in the collection. Each call number starts with a letter or sequence of letters. Each letter stands for a general subject area. For example, the LOC assigns the subject of political science the call letter "J." If you look within "J," you will find Aaron Wildavsky's books in the subsection JK which holds documents about US political institutions and public administration (Figure 19.5). You will also find academic journals in the field of political science. To see the entire LOC subject heading list, including subsections such as JK, follow this link to the Library of Congress Classification Outline: http://www.loc.gov/catdir/cpso/lcco/.

replace later

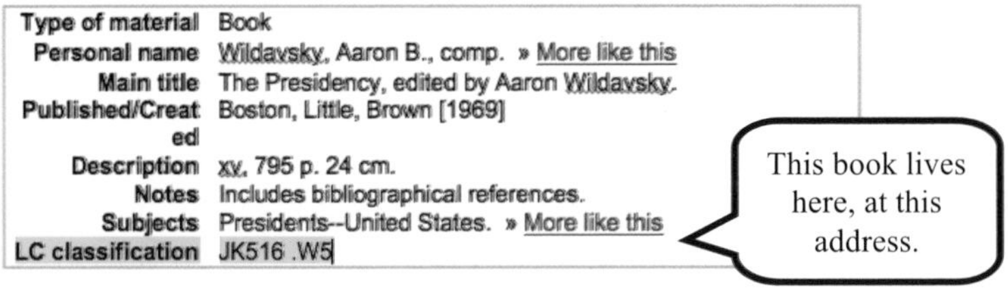

Type of material	Book
Personal name	Wildavsky, Aaron B., comp. » More like this
Main title	The Presidency, edited by Aaron Wildavsky.
Published/Created	Boston, Little, Brown [1969]
Description	xv, 795 p. 24 cm.
Notes	Includes bibliographical references.
Subjects	Presidents--United States. » More like this
LC classification	JK516 .W5

Figure 19.5 The Library of Congress classification number for this book will be the same in every library that uses the LOC.

Breaking the Block
Parachute in to Discover a Topic

Developing your own subject for a paper or presentation may seem daunting, especially if you are in a course that is already disorienting or overwhelming. Do not worry. You probably discovered many of your interests by chance, and you can become interested in unfamiliar subjects as well. Sometimes researchers can force such happy accidents simply by jumping in and seeing where they land. This exercise is a useful way to discover writing topics within specific subject areas. You will need to spend some time in the library.

Step One: Prepare Your Work Space

- Grab a laptop or iPad or two pens or pencils and a legal pad.
- In the library, find the Library of Congress classification outline: the subject list used to organize books and journals.
- If you can't locate it easily, ask a librarian or look it up online: http://www.loc.gov/catdir/cpso/lcco/.
- Choose a subject that interests you (for example, forestry, English, sports, music). Look for the shelves that hold books on this subject and wander from the beginning to the end. Then locate the periodicals on this subject, which may be shelved in a different location.
- Pull three books, journals, or magazines from the shelves, find a desk, and sit down.
- Turn to the table of contents and choose a place to start reading, or flip open the publication at random. Read each one for ten minutes.

Step Two: Write

- After reading and reviewing, make a list of ideas that caught your eye, that interested you, or that you disagree with.

- Choose one of the ideas from your list and write down your thoughts about the ideas as fast as you can for 10 minutes.
- Keep in mind that the best reading notes are usually questions. For example, if you read that Aaron Wildavsky argued that once in office presidents are always drawn to foreign policy over domestic policy, you might ask, "Is that a bad thing?" "What makes Wildavsky think so?" "Is this also true of presidents who had little experience with foreign policy before being elected?"
- Set aside your work for at least two hours. Before you pick it up again, review your assignment and what is expected of you.
- When you review your 10-minute writing, look to see how close your thoughts are to the expectations for the assignment.
- If you see connections, discuss your initial thoughts with your professor or with classmates who can help you evaluate and develop your ideas for the assignment.

There are many paths to the knowledge you need. If you have an assigned topic, zero in on your subject area. But keep in mind that Google and a library catalogue or an OPAC are not the only paths to tracking down the knowledge you need. Academic databases, and their associated search engines, are a fast, efficient path into disciplines and the information that lives there.

Search your library's homepage for databases. You will likely find a link to an alphabetical list or a subject index of available databases. Using the subject index, you will commonly find a number of databases specializing in various disciplines. For example, you can find political science scholarship such as *Worldwide Political Science Abstracts* or the *CQ Press Voting and Elections Collection*. You can also use the "advanced search" function of database search engines such as JSTOR and ProQuest to focus your search on the subject of political science.

Use subject headings to search databases. It is not possible for database managers to anticipate every word a researcher might use to describe a subject. However, most search engines linked to specialized databases and collections use a limited subject-heading list. Sometimes a search engine will offer suggested subject headings as you type in the search box. Sometimes databases will list their subject headings as a drop-down menu. The American Economic Association database has the drop-down menu shown in Figure 19.6.

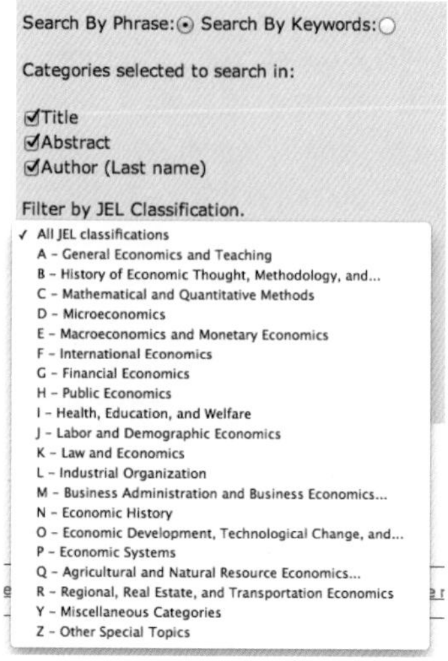

Figure 19.6 An example of a drop down menu of specialized search terms.

Google Scholar allows you to search for articles in journals with specific subjects. Click on the three bars in the upper left corner of Google Scholar. This will open up an advanced search box (Figure 19.7). There you will find a box with the phrase "Return articles **published** in." In this box, you can use the LOC subject headings (see above) to find articles and books within a specific subject or specialty.

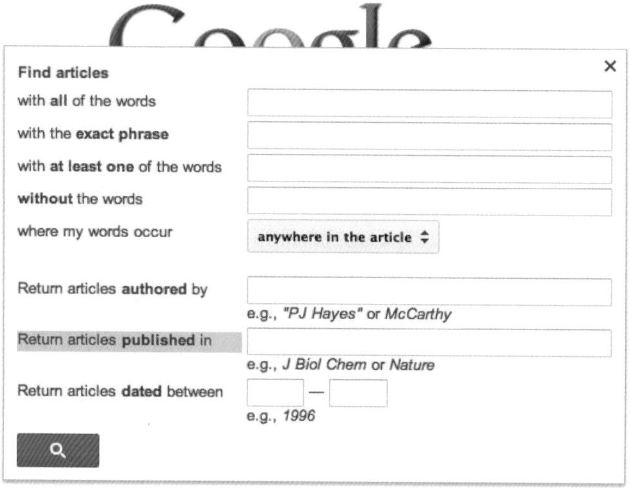

Figure 19.7 The advanced search function in Google Scholar.

Using Tricks of the Trade to Find the Knowledge You Need

As you can imagine, there are tricks of the research trade that yield the most relevant results, or hits, in the least amount of time with the least effort. A **hit** is the information about a source such as an article or a book that a search engine returns on a results page. Here are a few strategies to find what you need efficiently.

Ask an expert for help. In research there are two kinds of experts, librarians and those who have already researched and written about your subject. You can tap the expertise of both.

Major libraries will have reference librarians who specialize in various disciplines, and small libraries are staffed by librarians who are thoroughly familiar with the tools and resources available. If you have a subject, a librarian will point you to the databases and catalogue subject headings that will be most productive.

If a scholar has done the research necessary to write a book and a reputable publisher has published it, odds are that the sources that author used are authoritative. Bibliographies and "works cited" pages in these books are an excellent way to focus and enhance your research. In addition, the sources you read can lead you to additional sources as they are likely to have relied on sources as well.

Learn search-engine tricks. Most search engines use set theory to translate the words and phrase you type into commands the computer can understand. You do not need to learn set theory, but you should learn the tricks that allow you to search precisely and efficiently.

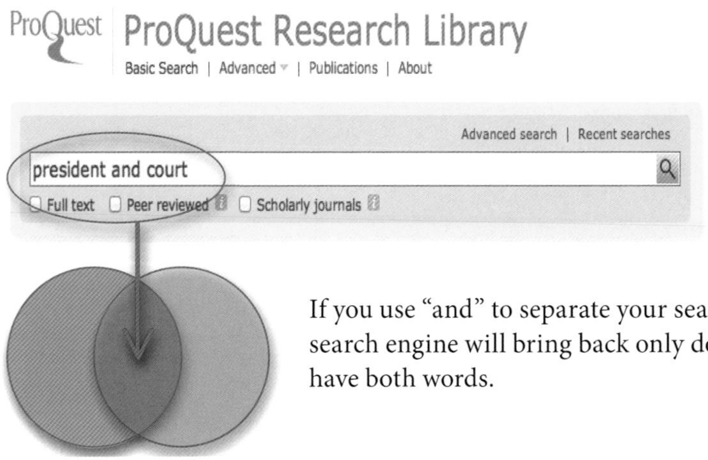

If you use "and" to separate your search terms, a search engine will bring back only documents that have both words.

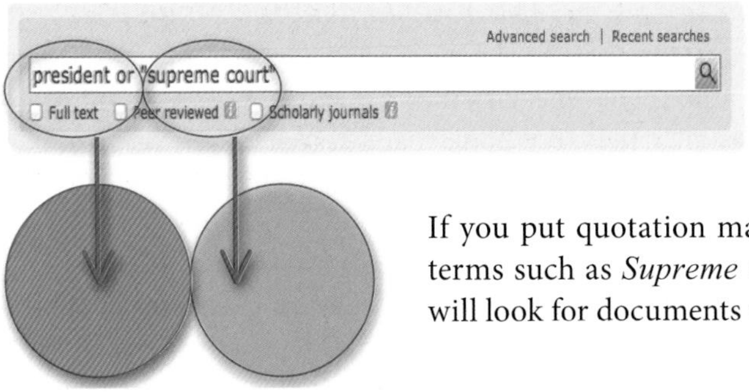

If you put quotation marks around your search terms such as *Supreme Court*, the search engine will look for documents with that exact phrase.

If you place "or" between your search terms, your hits will include a set of documents that have the word *president*, and a set that include the phrase *Supreme Court*.

Placing the word "not" in front of a search term or phrase will exclude all documents that have the term or phrase from the hits returned.

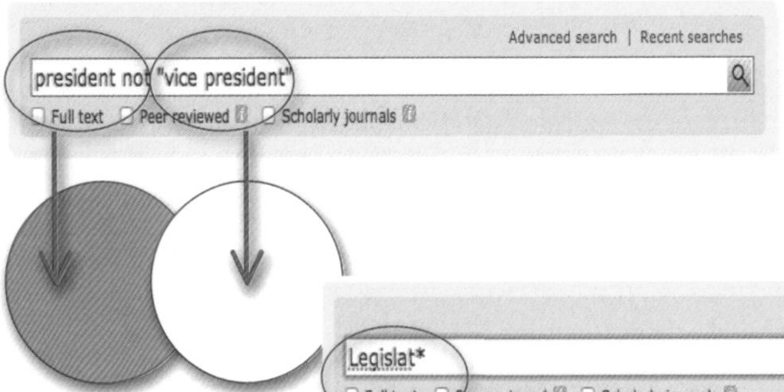

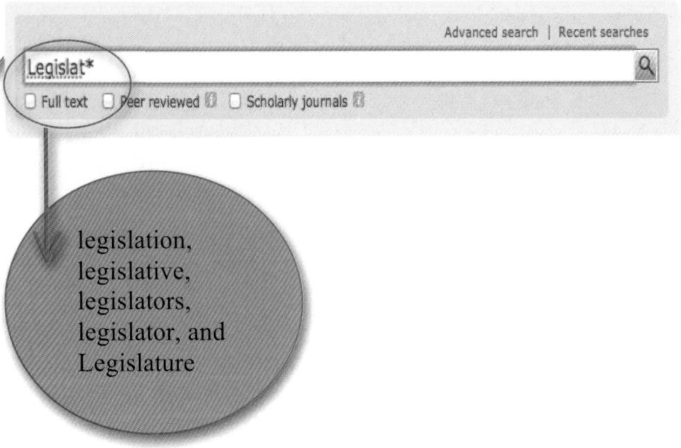

If you do not know how to spell a word, don't know how it begins or ends, or if you want to find documents that include all variations of a word, place a "*" at the front or end of your search term. As the example above shows, a search of "Legislat*" will bring back documents that include the words *legislation*, *legislative*, *legislators*, *legislator*, and *Legislature*.

Each search engine is a little different, but most offer tips in the support or help pages. Below is a list of the most common tips and tricks.

Use keyword combinations. The goal of any search is to return the most relevant, most useful, and most authoritative hits. If your search returns thousands of hits, the scope is too large. If your search returns fewer than three hits, and these hits are not helpful, it is too tightly focused.

Ideally, you want as many hits as you can reasonably review and evaluate. To make a precise search, you need to search within a subject and use keywords to zero in on specific information. A **keyword** is a significant word used to index or reference information.

When you are doing research to gather or develop your ideas during the early stages of writing, prepare and use a brief list of keywords in different combinations. For example, if you are interested in the qualities of our most effective presidents, typing "effective AND president" into a search box will bring up an overwhelming number of hits.

Instead, first create a list of potential search words. Then do a series of searches using different combinations of *three* of these terms. A student searching within the subject of political science might try the following strings of keywords linked by "and":

1. President	Leadership	Qualities
2. President	Excellent	Vision

As you search in this way, you are likely to discover very long and very brief lists of entries. If your list is more than 100 entries, a different, more focused, list of keywords will help you narrow down your results. Whenever you discover a manageable list of entries, save your hit list and highlight the search terms used to generate each hit list. Chapter 20 will give you the tools to review your hit list and identify the sources best suited to your audience and your argument.

MODULE IV-3

ORGANIZING YOUR RESEARCH

Excellent research is part searching and part record keeping. The best, most exhaustive research plan and schedule are of little value if you cannot retrieve and use the data, information, and documents you discovered during research. Your research will yield a treasure trove of great ideas, and you must be able to record them as you discover them.

Over time, successful students, professional researchers, and scholars have developed tricks of the trade that make researching, organizing findings, and integrating sources easier and quicker.

- **Search, retrieve, and then read**. You should first search for data, information, and documents, and then review and read your discoveries, keeping the two activities separate. Resist the temptation to stop and read an article you have found while doing your initial search.
- **Keep track of your search history**. Repeating a search you have already done is time consuming. Most database search engines allow you to export your search history and the hits for each search. If not, print out or save each search results page, and mark each search with the terms you used to find the results.
- **Get hard copies, or complete electronic copies**. If you download an article from a database, make sure your copy includes all the documentation information you will need to write a works-cited or references entry or a bibliography. Chapter 22 details the essential information you will need.
- **Take notes in the same way and same place**. Hard copies make it easy to take notes on the data set or document as you read. Note taking on electronic documents, however, allows you to search your notes with your computer's search function.

  However, your notes should include the following information:
  - all of the information needed to document the source.
  - the quotation, paraphrase, or summary you find relevant.
  - the page number of the quotation, paraphrase, or summary.
  - your thoughts, such as why you found the source important and relevant to your argument.
- **Keep a Dialectical Notebook**. While you are reviewing and reading your research, you are engaged in a conversation. Ideas will flow as they do in a real conversation. To keep track of the ideas and information you discover and the questions it inspires in your thinking, jot down your thoughts as you read. A **dialectal notebook** (Figure 19.8) makes it easy. On a blank page, draw a line down the center or create two columns on your screen. On the left side, write or type in quotations, summaries, and paraphrases form the source you are reading. Don't forget to include page numbers. On the right side, write down the questions and insights that occur to you. Often, these notes will become paragraphs in your final paper.

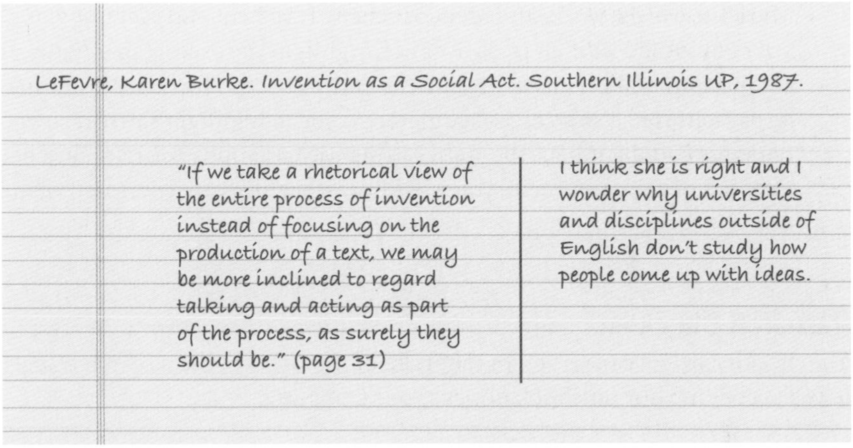

LeFevre, Karen Burke. Invention as a Social Act. Southern Illinois UP, 1987.
"If we take a rhetorical view of the entire process of invention instead of focusing on the production of a text, we may be more inclined to regard talking and acting as part of the process, as surely they should be." (page 31)
I think she is right and I wonder why universities and disciplines outside of English don't study how people come up with ideas.

Figure 19.8 Dialectical Notes record your conversation with the text.

- **Keep all your research, notes, and drafts together**. If you cannot pick up a single bag or box or open a single electronic folder that holds all your work on a project or assignment, you risk losing important work. Keep everything in one place so that you will not misplace or overlook anything. That does not mean having only one copy, however. Read on.
- **Maintain three points of contact**. As climbers move up a rock face, they try to maintain three points of contact, three holds, in order to hang on. Likewise, you need to have three points of contact for your research notes and drafts, such as your laptop hard drive or a thumb drive, a print copy, and a file on a cloud storage service such as Dropbox or Google Drive. Having three copies of your research files on the same computer gives you only one point of contact; lose or crash your computer and you lose your research.
- **Save different versions of your research notes and drafts**. Each time you add a note or citation or make even a small revision on a draft, save it as a different version of the same document. You can identify each version by adding the current date to the file name, or you can simply add a number each time you save:

  Dropbox/History 404/ResearchNotes 4
  Dropbox/History 404/ResearchNotes 5

- **Use Track Changes**. Any time you add to or edit your notes, turn on the Track Changes option. By doing so, you will build a record of your thoughts as they evolve, and you will be able to recover cuts you might later regret. In addition, many portfolio-based assignments ask you to draft a reflection essay describing the development of a project. If you do not track your changes, you will have to rely on your memory to recall them.

- **Mark the words, work, and ideas of others**. If you cut and paste *anything* from *any* source onto a different page or file, highlight the excerpt in a distinct color and place quotation marks around the entire excerpt. If you have summarized or paraphrased a source, use a different color to highlight the text so you will remember to document the source. This way, as your research notes become the draft of your argument, you will know what ideas are yours and what ideas must be cited.

Research Checklist

The checklist below can serve as a reminder of the tricks of the research trade. Copy it and keep it in your notebook or near your computer.

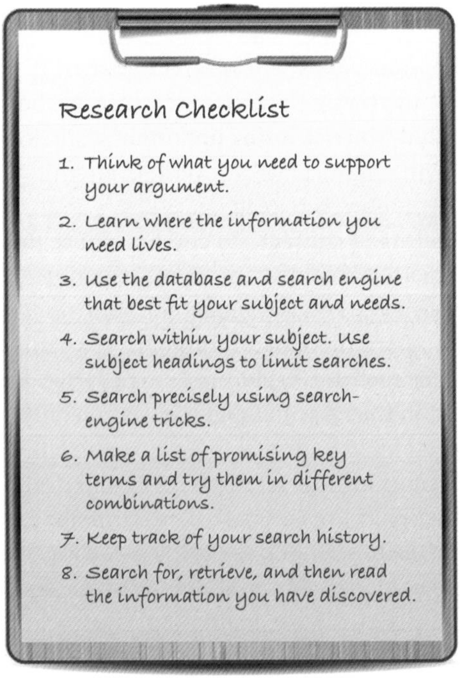
Research Checklist
1. Think of what you need to support your argument.
2. Learn where the information you need lives.
3. Use the database and search engine that best fit your subject and needs.
4. Search within your subject. Use subject headings to limit searches.
5. Search precisely using search-engine tricks.
6. Make a list of promising key terms and try them in different combinations.
7. Keep track of your search history.
8. Search for, retrieve, and then read the information you have discovered.

CHAPTER 20

EVALUATING SOURCES AND DOCUMENTS

> **The Amish In America Commit Their Vote To Donald Trump; Mathematically Guaranteeing Him A Presidential Victory**
>
> By Jimmy Rustling, CNN - October 25, 2016 45 0

No, didn't happen. However, if you Google the headline above you will find several news and social media sites repeating or reposting the same false information as the story above, produced by Paul Horner, who writes fake news stories and even fake Craigslist ads posing as a political party looking to hire people to act like protestors.

Why does he do it? One simple reason: $10,000 per month from sites such as AdSense, Facebook, and Google that pay a small amount per ad impression or click. Other producers of falsifications do it to promote or sabotage a cause or candidate, or for fun. There have always been, and always will be, incentives to produce falsifications, including fabricated scientific research or plagiarized term papers.

Still, you may be thinking, what do you care? You are not gullible, you are not tempted by clickbait, and you know who to trust. In fact, the belief that you can't be fooled and you only trust those who think like you is part of the problem.

Creators of these ads use targeted, values-based appeals and the markers of journalistic authority to mimic the appearance of real news sites or academic research. So if your grandmother is worried about global warming, she is more likely to see and click on a headline that speaks to her concerns. If your uncle is convinced there is a war on Christmas, he is more likely to follow the link to what appears to be a CNN news story that confirms his belief. Even if you ignore these sites, someone you know and trust may mail you a link or post it on Facebook.

How then are you to decide what is real and true and what is fake and false? The fact is, you are on your own. And so is each member of your audience. You have good reason to be skeptical, and so do your readers and listeners. You may be honest, but how does your audience know that? More importantly, how do you move your audience to trust the data, information, and knowledge you discover during research when they are surrounded by false and fake information designed specifically to attract their attention?

MODULE IV-4

WHY DO I NEED TO EVALUATE SOURCES?

There are two reasons you need to evaluate your research sources and cast aside any that are not relevant, not authoritative, or not honest.

First, every bit of information you use to make an argument either contributes to or casts doubt upon your credibility and authority. In short, if you use even one deceptive or questionable source, your whole argument will be seen as deceptive and questionable.

Credibility and believability are critical assets because arguments that are trusted can be persuasive. If your readers or listeners have no reason to believe you, or if they find reason to doubt you, you will not be persuasive. Writers and speakers who have the authority and knowledge to speak about their subject will be heard.

The second reason you need to evaluate your sources is that those who want to pass off questionable data and sketchy information as truth usually hide behind the appearance of trustworthiness. Unfortunately, the most accessible information is sometimes also the least credible, but very few of the dubious sources you will find are going to declare their unreliability.

This chapter defines the qualities of relevant, authoritative, and honest sources and provides a checklist for each. It also provides suggestions for identifying questionable sources.

MODULE IV-5

HOW DO I EVALUATE SOURCES?

If you base your evaluation of sources only on the message and how it fits your argument, you are likely to incorporate some questionable opinions and information, and you may make the serious mistake of discarding credible arguments and evidence simply because they do not agree with your argument. Thus, before you can incorporate sources that support your thesis or deal with those that argue against you, you must evaluate the sources you have discovered.

Responsible Sourcing
How to Evaluate Your Sources

To evaluate your sources, look at each source from three different perspectives:

1. The origin, author, publisher, or container of the source.
2. The elements or components of the source, such as the genre and documentation.
3. The message of the source.

Each perspective in turn allows you to apply three different criteria, or measures, to evaluate the source:

A. Honesty
B. Authority
C. Relevance

Combining the perspectives and the criteria, the three steps of each source evaluation look like this:

1. Where did the source come from, or what is known about its author, publisher, or container?

   A. Is the origin honest? Is the author identified and known? Do you recognize the site or container?
   B. Is the origin of the source authoritative? What makes the author or publisher an expert or reliable?
   C. Is the origin of the source relevant to my argument and my audience?

2. What is the source, or what is known about its genre, documentation, or other elements?

A. Is the source constructed honestly? How is the information verified? Are quotations complete, clipped, or taken out of context?
B. Are the markers of authority valid and will my audience recognize them? Is the construction like other authoritative texts of the same type?
C. Is the type or kind of source relevant to my argument and my audience?

3. What is the message of the source?

A. Will my audience find the argument or expression honest? Does this information appeal to fears or confirm unfounded biases or beliefs?
B. Will my audience find the argument or expression authoritative? Is the source simply opinion or supported by verifiable information?
C. Is the argument or expression relevant to my argument and my audience?

As the "Responsible Sourcing" box indicates, you need to apply the criteria of relevance, authority, and honesty to each source you consider. Let's look more specifically at what each of these qualities means in terms of persuasion. Remember, the goal of a public argument is not to persuade yourself, but to persuade an audience that thinks, believes, and acts differently than you do.

MODULE IV-6

EVALUATING FOR RELEVANCE

A source is **relevant** if it falls within the scope of your argument and contributes to the development of one or more of the assertions you make. You must assess the relevance of a source before you use it in your argument; however, the reader or listener is the final judge of its relevance.

Using Relevance to Guide Your Search

Relevance is the first criterion because it should guide your search for data, information, and documents. In simple terms, a search that gathers irrelevant data, information, and documents has an undefined scope and no focus. (For more on scope and focus, see Chapter 19.) For example, if your research question is "What is in popular protein drinks?" your search should be limited to protein drink labels and perhaps research on protein drinks from the discipline of chemistry, because these sources are relevant to the scope and focus of your subject.

If your research question is more focused, such as "What are the psychological and neuromuscular effects of consistent protein drink intake?," your search should be more focused as well, delving into the disciplines of psychology, nutrition, and kinesiology.

Relevance is also a concern later in the composing process as you incorporate sources into your argument. At that stage, a different set of criteria come into play, as described in Chapter 21.

Considering a Source's Relevance to Your Audience

A reader who finds a source distracting or unnecessary will ignore or discount any support it may give to your argument. For example, imagine you are writing a paper arguing that social media websites that allow the posting or linking of news articles must act like editors who verify the truth and authenticity of posted information. While researching, you discover that when Mark Zuckerberg was attending Harvard, the campus newspaper investigated him twice and wrote critical articles condemning him and his work.

The article seems relevant to you as it may explain Zuckerberg's refusal to replicate the editorial function of traditional journalism on Facebook. But will it be relevant to your reader or listener?

Relevance is tricky, because what may seem obviously relevant to you may not be relevant to your readers or not relevant in the way you think it is. Serious fans of Facebook and Zuckerberg might assume that his experience gives him good reason to be suspicious of journalistic arbiters of truth. By the same measure, those outraged by fake or biased news as you are may see your attempt to link Zuckerberg's college experience to his decisions as a CEO as unfair. Relevance is never obvious. In fact, you must prove relevance in two ways. First, you must prove that a source is relevant to your argument and audience. Second, you must show how a source is supportive of your argument. Until you do, your audience will make what they will of your sources, or ignore them.

Consider what your audience will be thinking before they read or hear your argument. Think about the way they will respond to your source. Chapter 15 can help you understand your audience so you can anticipate and assess their response to your sources. A good rule of thumb is to assume the following:

- ✓ Your reader disagrees with you but is not hostile.
- ✓ Your reader does not know your source.

- ✓Your reader will question your source's credentials, expertise, training, and experience.
- ✓Your reader will be looking for reasons to disregard your sources as irrelevant or not credible.

The Relevance Criteria Checklist in Figure 20.1 will help you determine whether the data, information, and documents you have discovered are relevant to your subject and your audience.

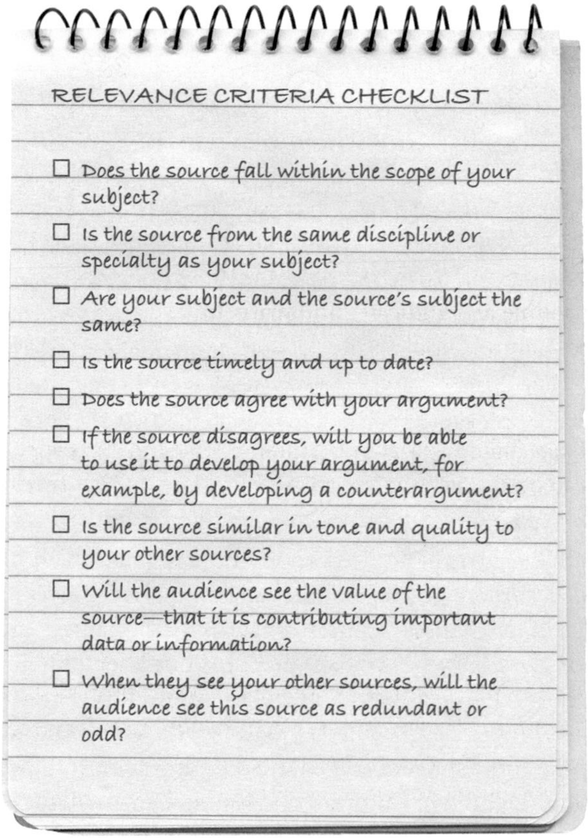
RELEVANCE CRITERIA CHECKLIST
☐ Does the source fall within the scope of your subject?
☐ Is the source from the same discipline or specialty as your subject?
☐ Are your subject and the source's subject the same?
☐ Is the source timely and up to date?
☐ Does the source agree with your argument?
☐ If the source disagrees, will you be able to use it to develop your argument, for example, by developing a counterargument?
☐ Is the source similar in tone and quality to your other sources?
☐ Will the audience see the value of the source—that it is contributing important data or information?
☐ When they see your other sources, will the audience see this source as redundant or odd?

Figure 20.1 Relevance criteria checklist.

MODULE IV-7

EVALUATING FOR AUTHORITY

Authority is the possession of skill, expertise, experience, and knowledge about a specific subject or a range of subjects. We cannot read an author's or speaker's mind to determine if he or she has the necessary knowledge and experience. Instead, we must rely upon **markers of authority**: socially agreed upon, demonstrated signs and symbols of skill, expertise, experience, and knowledge.

If you or a member of your audience passed Nikki Usher Layser on the street, you may think she has nothing special to say about social media or journalism. This is because she, like most scholars, doesn't wear her authority like a badge. Before you can quote Usher Layser's compelling research and findings in your argument, you must persuade your audience to recognize the markers of authority she has earned.

Your audience will evaluate the authority of your sources using many measures. Most people recognize markers such as PhDs, professional experience, and publishing records. Also, readers notice the way the writer or speaker uses the tools, concepts, and language associated with the subject. The depth of study, research, and reasoning of a source also indicates authority. In addition, we see authority in the professionalism and tone of the writer or speaker. Finally, a writer or speaker who speaks with confidence and clearly knows what he or she is talking about conveys authority.

If your audience finds any of these markers of authority lacking, they may remain unconvinced and wonder why you bothered quoting at all. For this reason, you must evaluate your sources' authority before your audience has a chance to ensure the persuasive power of your argument.

Seeing Authority through Your Audience's Eyes

Simply possessing and claiming authority on a subject is not enough. An argument, both yours and those of your sources, must demonstrate authority in the way it presents and deals with data and information.

Some markers of authority are easy to spot, and their absence stands out. If you quote an article or a blog that is poorly written or that has foggy reasoning, odds are that your audience will not find your source authoritative. As another example, if a doctor hands a newborn to the proud parents and then coldly lists all the childhood illnesses that can afflict infants, he is demonstrating a mastery of information. However, the lack of professionalism with which he presents this information, without any thought for the audience, robs him of authority. An argument also lacks authority when the author or speaker uses facts and data to bully or unnecessarily provoke fear, even though the information may be accurate.

Expertise in one subject does not grant expertise in another, no matter how similar or related they are. If you are assembling research for a paper on the psychological and neuromuscular effects of protein drinks, for example, you may consider articles from *Triathlete* magazine and the *American Journal of Clinical Nutrition*. Both the magazine and the journal describe the effects of protein drinks. However, researchers and scholars will put more weight behind the journal, knowing that just because an athlete uses protein drinks, this doesn't mean they are experts in nutrition. Triathletes may also find the academic journal authoritative. However, they are more likely to put faith in the words of other triathletes that have tried different protein drinks and can speak from experience of their effects and benefits. Again, your audience will determine the source that is most relevant and authoritative to the argument you are making.

Seeing Academic Authority through the Eyes of Experts

Peer review, an important marker of academic authority, can help you evaluate academic sources. A peer-reviewed article or book has been examined by several scholars, researchers, and experts in the same field ("peers" of the author). For example, when the *American Journal of Clinical Nutrition* receives an essay from an author, the editors send it to a number of peer reviewers. They in turn review the article, evaluating its relevance to the focus of the journal, the authority of its research, and the honesty of its reasoning and findings. In addition, reviewers determine if the article or book contributes to the discipline or if it merely repeats what is already known. Reviewers then recommend that the journal publish the article, send it back to the author for revision, or reject it.

In addition, an authoritative researcher or scholar will use only authoritative and honest sources. As a result, you can judge the persuasive force and influence of a source based on how many times your source has been quoted and cited by others.

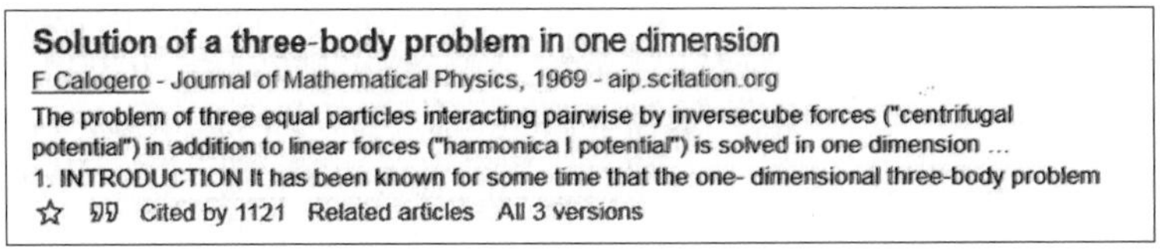
Solution of a three-body problem in one dimension
F Calogero - Journal of Mathematical Physics, 1969 - aip.scitation.org
The problem of three equal particles interacting pairwise by inversecube forces ("centrifugal potential") in addition to linear forces ("harmonica l potential") is solved in one dimension ...
1. INTRODUCTION It has been known for some time that the one- dimensional three-body problem
☆ 99 Cited by 1121 Related articles All 3 versions

For example, the article above, discovered with Google Scholar, has been cited 890 times. You do not have to be a theoretical physicist to know that physicists are unlikely to make a mistake 890 times.

Reference librarians can help you evaluate the reputation of sources such as newspapers, magazines, journals, and book publishers. But you can also do your own investigation. Reference librarians begin by researching the publisher or container of the source. For example, Simon & Shuster has been a reputable publisher since 1924, and this information is easy to find and verified by many reliable sources. PublishAmerica Press, on the other hand, claims to have been around for 20 years and is in "Maryland at the crossroads of I-70 and I-270." Reliable sources describe PublishAmerica as a predator press with no editorial control.

The criteria in the checklist in Figure 20.2 can help you evaluate the authority of data, information, and documents.

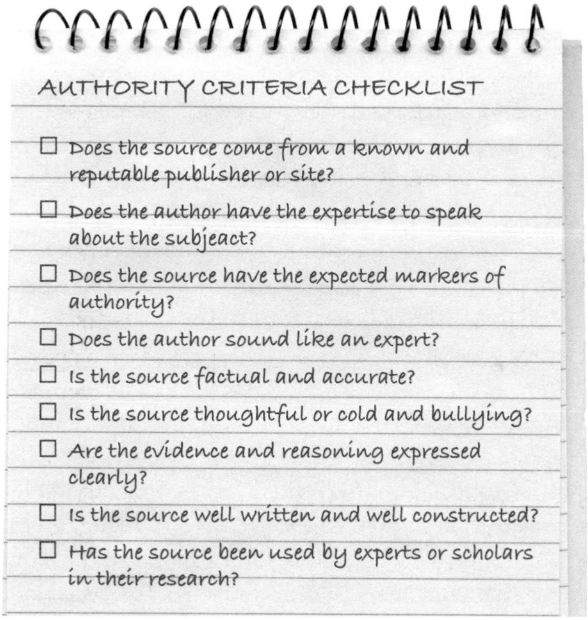
AUTHORITY CRITERIA CHECKLIST
☐ Does the source come from a known and reputable publisher or site?
☐ Does the author have the expertise to speak about the subjeact?
☐ Does the source have the expected markers of authority?
☐ Does the author sound like an expert?
☐ Is the source factual and accurate?
☐ Is the source thoughtful or cold and bullying?
☐ Are the evidence and reasoning expressed clearly?
☐ Is the source well written and well constructed?
☐ Has the source been used by experts or scholars in their research?

Figure 20.2 Authority criteria checklist.

MODULE IV-8

EVALUATING FOR HONESTY

An **honest** source is fair, honorable, and straightforward even about its bias or potential conflicts of interest. A **bias** is a predisposition or prejudice that may affect judgment or opinions. A **conflict of interest** happens when the interests of an individual or group potentially clashes with stated goals, obligations, or positions. Everyone has biases, and conflicts of interest are difficult to avoid. For example, your professor is charged with upholding the academic standards of the college or university. However, professors also want to see you do well and earn high grades. Ignored, denied, or hidden, this potential conflict between the interests of standards/students can cause problems. On the other hand, if biases and potential conflicts of interest are known and understood, you and your audience can use such knowledge to evaluate the honesty of a source.

Editorial Vision Revealed = Good; Bias Hidden = Bad

Rather than trusting claims of objectivity, a more reasonable path is to look for signs of honesty such as an open declaration of editorial vision, policy, or bias. You may not agree with the bias of the source, but at least you know where the author stands.

For example, *Consumer Reports* declares its editorial independence from advertisers as a selling point that makes it a trusted source of product reviews, while *PlayStation: The Official Magazine* wears its bias toward a particular game platform on its cover. Both magazines are honest publishers, however, because the articles they print can be trusted to reflect their stated editorial vision. *The Journal of Technical Physics* is biased toward practical physics, while *The International Journal of Theoretical Physics* proudly declares that it is biased toward the theoretical.

Checking Message Origin

Another indicator of a publication's honesty is the ease with which you can identify the credentials of its editorial board, writers, and contributors. If you can clearly identify everyone who contributed to the creation, writing, and publication of a source, the source is most likely honest. If you cannot find the name of the authors of a research paper that concludes that protein drinks lower blood pressure, you should ask, "Who would benefit from this message, and what purpose is served in keeping the authors anonymous?"

In addition, a database, an article, or a book that clearly identifies its sources and makes it easy for the reader to find and verify them is honest and authoritative. Academic documentation styles such as those offered by the Modern Language Association (MLA) and the American Psychological Association (APA) are a way of formalizing and mandating honest research. Research articles in a peer-reviewed journal or books published by academic publishers such as university presses will almost always cite their sources; an article that didn't do so would be considered suspect, if not dishonest, and would not be published.

Websites also demonstrate honest intentions when they identify their creators, or their sponsoring individuals or organizations, and make it easy to check the sources of information posted on or linked by the site. For example, if you cannot find an "about" or "contacts" link, or if the link is broken or takes you to a blank email form, you have reason to doubt its veracity.

A **spoofed URL** will look like a reputable web address. However, spoofed URLs are designed to mimic other websites and mislead the viewer. Spoofed URLs and domains can be found on authentic, trusted sites, and their links will take you to a fraudulent site. For example, the website for the Amish story at the beginning of the chapter will look like this in the address bar: cnn.com.de. The domain code .de is the domain for Germany. However, if you research the owner of cnn.com.de, you will find it is registered not to the CNN offices in Berlin, but to Paul Horn, who lives in Phoenix, Arizona.

Safe browsing websites such as Google Transparency Report and whois.com allow you to look up a website to determine if a site is flagged as fraudulent and who owns the URL. Fraudulent sites can hide within reputable sites, and spoofed URL links or domains that pose as other, reputable website addresses can be difficult to catch.

Evaluating Internet Domains

An internet domain, such as ".com" or ".edu," identifies a region or area of the Internet and the sponsoring or managing host of that region. A domain can be open, which means that anyone can use that region to locate his or her website, or restricted, which means that a website must meet certain standards to be in that region and be identified with the unique domain name. An example of an open domain is ".org," which is available to anyone who wishes to use it. An example of a restricted domain is ".aero," which is restricted to airports and the aviation industry.

All domains reflect a specific interest or subject. For example, ".com" is open to all commercial or business organizations and activities. On the other hand, ".mil" is a restricted domain for use by the US military.

Figure 20.3 provides a brief list of restricted and open domains. For a complete list of top-level domains and a description of the area of interest and restrictions, follow this link to the Internet Corporation for Assigned Names and numbers: http://www.icann.org/en/resources/registries/listing.

Restricted	Open
.aero	.biz
.edu	.com
.gov	.info
.mil	.name
.coop	.net
.int	.org

Figure 20.3 Restricted and open domains.

It is important to note that individuals and organizations can now register their own domain identifiers. You will soon see identifiers such as ".auto," ".wow," and ".Joe."

Just as the message of articles or books should reflect their origin as a popular or scholarly source, the messages of honest websites should reflect their Internet domain identifier. If you find what appears to be a research paper or what looks like an objective analysis of hotel pricing and airline discounts on a site with the domain ".travel," you should be cautious because this domain was created to host and support the travel and tourism industry. Of course, if you were analyzing advertising strategies of various websites, the research paper format would be an interesting example of one such strategy and therefore a useful bit of evidence.

Authoritative research and logical reasoning drive honest written and spoken arguments, and such arguments are usually convincing. Their tone is honorable and fair, and they avoid extreme or strong language, unsupported claims, and exaggeration.

The criteria in the checklist in Figure 20.4 can help you evaluate the honesty of a source.

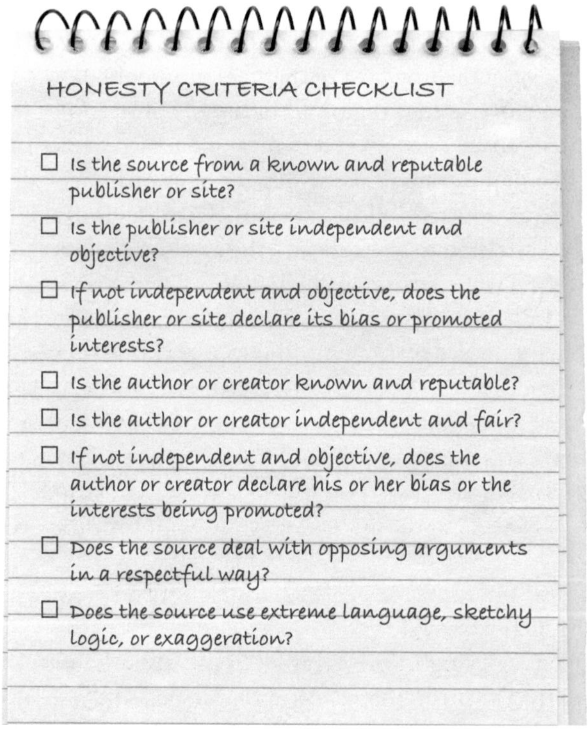
HONESTY CRITERIA CHECKLIST
☐ Is the source from a known and reputable publisher or site?
☐ Is the publisher or site independent and objective?
☐ If not independent and objective, does the publisher or site declare its bias or promoted interests?
☐ Is the author or creator known and reputable?
☐ Is the author or creator independent and fair?
☐ If not independent and objective, does the author or creator declare his or her bias or the interests being promoted?
☐ Does the source deal with opposing arguments in a respectful way?
☐ Does the source use extreme language, sketchy logic, or exaggeration?

Figure 20.4 Honesty criteria checklist.

MODULE IV-9

DETERMINING IF A SOURCE IS QUESTIONABLE

There is no easy way to identify an honest website. However, questionable sources often have one thing in common; they attempt to appear honest. The following tricks of the trade may help you distinguish the honest from the questionable.

Being Contrary Does Not Mean Questionable

A source that takes a position contrary to yours or that argues against your thesis is not by definition a questionable source. Good and thoughtful people will always write honest arguments that agree with, disagree with, or complicate your thinking and beliefs.

Identifying Questionable Sources

It's not difficult to identify the traits of questionable or sketchy sources. We can find them in the origin, in the composition or elements, and in the message of the source. The following red flags should raise questions in your mind about a source and may be reason enough to disregard the information it provides.

Red Flags of Questionable Sources

- You came across the source randomly, such as while reading Twitter feeds from your friends. You didn't discover it during a focused search for information related to your scope and focus.
- The origin of the source is from a questionable Internet domain. For example, .xxx is questionable because it was created for the exchange of pornography. Also, **http://www.**notwhatyouthink.com/**OSU.edu** looks like the web site for Ohio State, but the URL prior to the first slash is actually a redirect that may lead you to places unknown. Finally, the source does not fit the message. For example, the domain is "edu" but the message is commercial in nature.
- The origin of the source provides no way to identify or contact the editor, creator, or Webmaster.
- The source is missing information such as the authors' name, sponsoring organization or institution, date, and funding source.
- The source does not identify the origin of the data, information, and documents it uses and references.

- ⊠ The assertions and arguments made in the source are distinctly different from other research on the same subject.
- ⊠ The logic used in the source is inconsistent and unreliable. Chapter 24 will help you identify unreliable logic.
- ⊠ The conclusions made by the source are not supported by, or go far beyond, the supporting evidence and reasoning.
- ⊠ The source seems extremely opinionated or emotional and uses extreme language and images.
- ⊠ The source does not concede or acknowledge strong and obvious opposing arguments.
- ⊠ The source seems to propose or confirm a hidden conspiracy.
- ⊠ The writing and image reproduction are sloppy, with obvious stylistic problems and grammatical errors.

Remember that one questionable or sketchy bit of data, quotation, or referenced source can cast doubt upon your entire argument. Only arguments that are trusted can be persuasive, and persuasion happens or fails to happen in the mind of your audience.

CHAPTER 21

INTEGRATING RESEARCH AND AVOIDING PLAGIARISM

Plagiarism enrages most professors because it is a corruption of the student–teacher relationship and shows a blatant disregard for the academic values they hold dear. But plagiarism can also be understood as a crisis of authority and voice. Often, students are tempted to plagiarize because they feel they have nothing to say, they do not know how to say what they know, or they do not know how to blend authoritative sources with their own voice.

This chapter will help you understand why professors value intellectual integrity and detest plagiarism. Most importantly, the following four steps to **responsible sourcing** will help you to avoid compromising your voice and to establish your integrity and authority:

1. understand what plagiarism is;
2. understand the causes of plagiarism;
3. quote, paraphrase, and summarize fairly; and
4. integrate sources effectively into the body of your composition.

MODULE IV-10

DEFINING PLAGIARISM AND FAIR USE

An understanding of plagiarism will help you think about how to actively communicate integrity and authority so that you can demonstrate the depth of your understanding. There are two reasons that you need to understand plagiarism.

1. Higher education is built upon the opposite of plagiarism: the ability to trust the integrity of scholars and their research. Therefore, many professors see plagiarism as more serious than simple theft. It is a threat to the values, integrity, and future of scholarship and creative work.
2. The only thing your professors know about you is what you show them. Everything you do in class, and everything you hand in, contributes to or detracts from the authority of your voice.

It has probably never occurred to you to plagiarize. However, there are less extreme, unintentional acts that can also lead to problems. Here are a few examples:

- Misplaced quotation marks, using quotations without quotation marks, and summaries or paraphrases containing sentences from the original are common mistakes. To a professor, these mistakes make it sound as if the voice of an expert unexpectedly interrupted the student's voice. The shift can be startling and may raise suspicions.
- Documentation errors and missing citations suggest that the student's research is sloppy, incomplete, or rushed. In the worst case, the professor may wonder if the student is making up quotations or hiding something.
- Poorly integrated quotations, summaries, and paraphrases signal that the student doesn't really understand the source or how it relates to her or his argument.

Defining Plagiarism

In the academic context, as we have seen, plagiarism is commonly defined as the act of using someone else's work, language, or ideas without identifying the author or acknowledging the origin of a source. Plagiarism is not limited to cutting and pasting paragraphs or sentences from a source, but also includes incorporating the work, data, and ideas of others in paraphrases, summaries, charts, or images without naming the author or source. Plagiarism is a serious academic offense that can result in a failed paper grade, a failed course grade, student judicial action, or dismissal from a college or university.

Definitions of plagiarism do not differentiate between intentional and accidental acts. In simple terms, hiding, obscuring, confusing, or failing to identify the author or origin of a source, on purpose or by accident, is plagiarism. In addition, plagiarism can happen at any stage of composing. For example, a rough draft handed in to a peer-group workshop may be subject to the same rules and policies concerning plagiarism as a research paper turned in to the professor at the end of the semester.

Be aware that different professors may have different expectations and different understandings of what constitutes plagiarism. For example, the 10 common types of plagiarism listed in Figure 21.1 come from an international survey of 879 teachers, instructors, and professors conducted by TurnItIn.com in 2012. The list includes obvious examples such as copying or paraphrasing an entire paper without citation. However, it also includes examples that some students would not consider plagiarism.

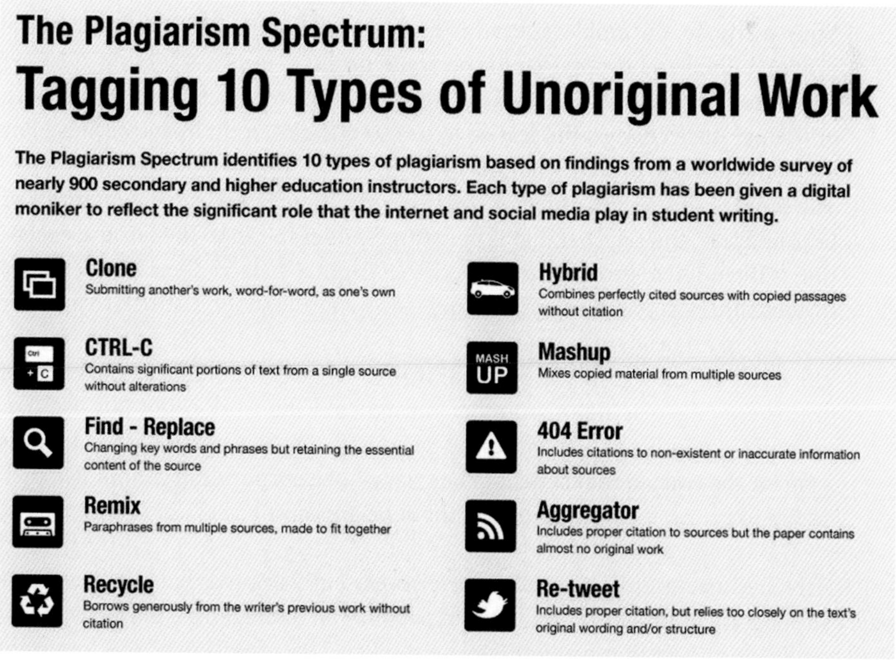

The Plagiarism Spectrum:
Tagging 10 Types of Unoriginal Work
The Plagiarism Spectrum identifies 10 types of plagiarism based on findings from a worldwide survey of nearly 900 secondary and higher education instructors. Each type of plagiarism has been given a digital moniker to reflect the significant role that the internet and social media play in student writing.
Clone
Submitting another's work, word-for-word, as one's own
CTRL-C
Contains significant portions of text from a single source without alterations
Find - Replace
Changing key words and phrases but retaining the essential content of the source
Remix
Paraphrases from multiple sources, made to fit together
Recycle
Borrows generously from the writer's previous work without citation
Hybrid
Combines perfectly cited sources with copied passages without citation
MASH UP
Mashup
Mixes copied material from multiple sources
404 Error
Includes citations to non-existent or inaccurate information about sources
Aggregator
Includes proper citation to sources but the paper contains almost no original work
Re-tweet
Includes proper citation, but relies too closely on the text's original wording and/or structure

Figure 21.1 Types of plagiarism, from a survey of teachers (© 2012 iParadigms, LLC. All rights reserved. Version 0512).

For example, a student who turns in a paper with his or her own ideas and words developed for a different assignment in another class ("Recycle") is plagiarizing according to the survey respondents.

Colleges and universities typically state their definition of plagiarism and related penalties in course catalogues or student handbooks. In addition, professors often include plagiarism policy statements on syllabi. If you have any questions about what constitutes plagiarism at your institution or in your class, be sure to ask right away.

Increasingly, students are required to post their work publicly as blogs, Vimeo videos, or Prezi presentations, for example. If you are required to, or want to, make your work public, you also need to be aware of copyright law and fair use limits.

Defining Fair Use

Fair use is a legal exception to copyright laws that permits limited or educational use of selected portions of another's original work, language, or ideas with attribution. Fair use allows scholars to use words, sound clips, and images created by others. However, fair use is not a license to use the work, language, or ideas of others without acknowledgment.

If your use of someone else's original material complies with all four of the following principles, you may claim fair use.

1. **Your purpose**: Original material is fairly used if it educates or enriches the general public and is not used for personal profit.
2. **The nature or type of the original work**: It is fair to use data about car sales or temperature change, but less so to use song lyrics or an image because fair use is intended to protect imaginative work.
3. **The length and significance of the excerpt**: There is no specific quantity or percentage of the original that is permitted under fair use. The fair use exception is intended to protect the value of the original source. Therefore, it is wise to use as little as possible and to avoid using significant or distinctive parts or excerpts of an original.
4. **The effect of the use of the original work**: Any use that reduces the value of or prevents the originator from benefiting from the work is not fair use. For example, a professor does not need permission to use an Imagine Dragons song for the educational benefit of her class, but a corporation cannot use such a song to promote their product without permission.

WARNING: Music licensing agencies have consistently argued that any use of any part of a song, including its lyrics, without permission damages the market value of the song. It is unlikely that you will violate the Fair Use provision of the copyright act in your typical course work. However, defending against such charges can be extremely expensive. Be very careful if you are planning to publish your work.

MODULE IV-11

AVOIDING PLAGIARISM

To avoid plagiarism, you need to know what causes it, how to accurately cite your sources, and how to fairly reproduce or represent the work, language, or ideas you are using.

Understanding Its Causes

It is impossible to list all the causes and motivations that lead to an act of plagiarism. However, there are a few recurring situations that contribute to plagiarism.

First, intentional plagiarism usually happens the night before a paper is due. At 4:00 a.m., a desperate student will find information, paragraphs, and even complete papers that can be downloaded, disguised, and handed in the next morning. Second, the pressure to turn something in, especially if you have never missed a deadline, can overwhelm your better judgment. This explains why most students found plagiarizing are usually capable people who have never plagiarized before but were worried the professor would think them lazy or incapable if they did not turn in a paper on time.

The third cause of plagiarism is a disregard for academic conventions. It is not uncommon to discover a plagiarized paper that also contains significant research. If the writer had only taken the time to identify and integrate source material and document it according to the expected conventions, the result would have been a strong research paper. Finally, some students simply refuse to do the work. Such students are probably not reading this book. Still, it is worth pointing out that higher education is about mastering material *and* developing abilities and competencies like good work habits and disciplined concentration. In college, plagiarism can lead to a failed class. After college, it can lead to much worse. As a recent *US News* story entitled "10 High-Profile People Whose Degrees Were Revoked" shows, plagiarism can have profound consequences. See the full story at, http://www.usnews.com/education/top-world-universities/articles/2012/05/02/10-high-profile-people-whose-degrees-were-revoked.

Now you know the situations you should avoid. Next, what *should* you do? What steps will help you actively avoid plagiarism?

Knowing What to Cite

Responsible sourcing is not difficult. You need to know what you must cite and what you do not have to cite. You need to keep track of what you have discovered. And you need to be sure that your reader knows what data, information, and ideas came from which sources, and make clear which ideas are your own.

You *do* need to cite any source you quote directly, but also any work, language, or ideas that you use in summaries or paraphrases or as images. Even if you only mention or reference an idea, you must cite it.

You do not have to cite common knowledge. **Common knowledge** includes the following:

- **well known** data, information, and ideas such as that Notre Dame is a Catholic university;
- data, information, and ideas **commonly known by the audience** you intend to persuade, for example the fact that Notre Dame students know that their kilt-wearing cheerleaders are called the Irish Guard;
- **widely available and not controversial** data, information, and ideas such as the fact that the artist Millard Sheets created the mural often referred to as "Touchdown Jesus" on the Notre Dame campus.

However, if your research leads you to assert that the modernist style of the Touchdown Jesus mural was a response to the reforms of the second Vatican Council, this assertion is not common knowledge. Therefore, you need to quote, summarize, or paraphrase this information and cite the article that informed your opinion.

If you are not sure if the information you want to use is common knowledge, play it safe. Document any information that may be questioned by or unknown to a reasonable member of your audience.

Responsible Sourcing
Track Sources during Research

Often, plagiarism happens because students simply lose track of who said what in their research notes. You need to mark ideas that came from your research so you know what to cite. Here are some tricks of the trade to help you keep track of the ideas you discover during research.

- During the initial stages of research, whether you work on screen or on paper, make sure the source material is visibly distinct from your own writing. Use highlighting, bold, or italics. For example, highlight in yellow every phrase, line, or paragraph you copy from a source. Highlight in orange any summary or paraphrase you write based on what you read in a source. Visual cues such as highlighting will remind you of what you need to cite.
- As you integrate source material into your own writing, first add the citation to the "Works Cited," "References," or "Bibliography" page.

Then place the quotation, paraphrase, or summary in your text (Module IV-12 shows you how to use quotations and to write paraphrases and summaries). Be sure to use quotation marks when you use the source's exact words and include page numbers and other in-text information required of the documentation style you are using.

- Finally, make sure each quotation, paraphrase, and summary is paired with its full citation on the "Works Cited," "References," or "Bibliography" page. After you double-check each source and citation, remove the highlighting, bold type, or italics you used to differentiate source material. Chapter 22 will help you understand how citations work.

MODULE IV-12

INTEGRATING SOURCES AUTHORITATIVELY

Thorough research will yield pages of notes and documentation information, as well as pages of the work, language, and ideas of others copied from the sources you have read and researched. Since you cannot use it all, you have to think about how to use the sources fairly and persuasively to support your argument.

There are four common ways of using sources within the body of your argument: (1) brief quotations, (2) lengthy block quotations, (3) paraphrases, and (4) summaries.

These four methods of integrating sources are explained below. In addition, it's important to know how and when to use each method in order to achieve your purpose and persuade your audience. Finally, it's also important to integrate your sources into your argument smoothly.

Using Brief Quotations

A **quotation** is a phrase, sentence, or passage taken from an original source and reproduced word for word. Quotations are used for any of the following reasons:

- Your audience must see and understand the exact wording of the original.
- You are analyzing the wording, phrasing, or meaning of the original.
- The words of the original source are significantly distinct or so profoundly constructed that a summary or paraphrase would alter the meaning.
- You want to emphasize a point made by the author or emphasize the relationship of the author and his or her words.

Enclose a quotation in quotation marks and do not indent it or set it off from the text unless it is longer than four lines (MLA style) or more than forty words (APA style). In the excerpt shown in Figure 21.2, the brief quotation is highlighted in bold.

You may abbreviate or shorten a quotation as long as you do not change the intent or meaning of the words you use as it was commonly understood in its original context. To abbreviate a long quotation, use three periods, to make an **ellipsis** (...) marking where text has been left out of a quotation.

Different documentary style manuals have different rules for ellipses. For example, if you are using MLA style and you want to cut text from the end of a quotation, you still use three periods to make an ellipsis; however, you must also include the period, or question mark or exclamation mark, that ends the sentence. In Figure 21.3, you can see two different ellipses indicating text cut from the long block quotation. The first occurs in the middle of a sentence and the second occurs at the end followed by the period that ends the sentence.

Brackets [ ] are used to insert essential information that may be missing from a quotation because it has been abbreviated or because contextual information is absent, as in the underlined part of Figure 21.2.

> For example, Bradford describes the skill and courage of one member of the ship's crew during the initial attempt to find safe harbor during the storm: "**So he <u>[the seaman steering]</u> bid them be of good cheer and row lustily, for there was a fair sound before them, and he doubted not but they should find one place or other where they might ride in safety**" (72).

Figure 21.2
The sentence before the quotation included the phrase "a lusty seaman which steered." Without the bracketed information, the reader would be confused.

Using Block Quotations

A **block quotation** is typically more than four lines (MLA style) or more than forty words (APA style). Block quotations should be used even more sparingly than brief quotations. Use a block quotation for any of the following reasons:

- Your audience must see and understand the exact wording of a large part of the original.
- You are analyzing the wording, meaning, or argument of a large part of the original.
- The words of the author or original source are so significantly distinct or profoundly constructed that a brief quotation would not capture these qualities of the original, and a summary or paraphrase would alter the meaning.

- You want to highlight an argument or points made by the author or emphasize the relationship of the author and his or her argument.

Block quotations get their name because the entire block of quoted text is indented from the left margin. Check your documentation style manual for the depth of the

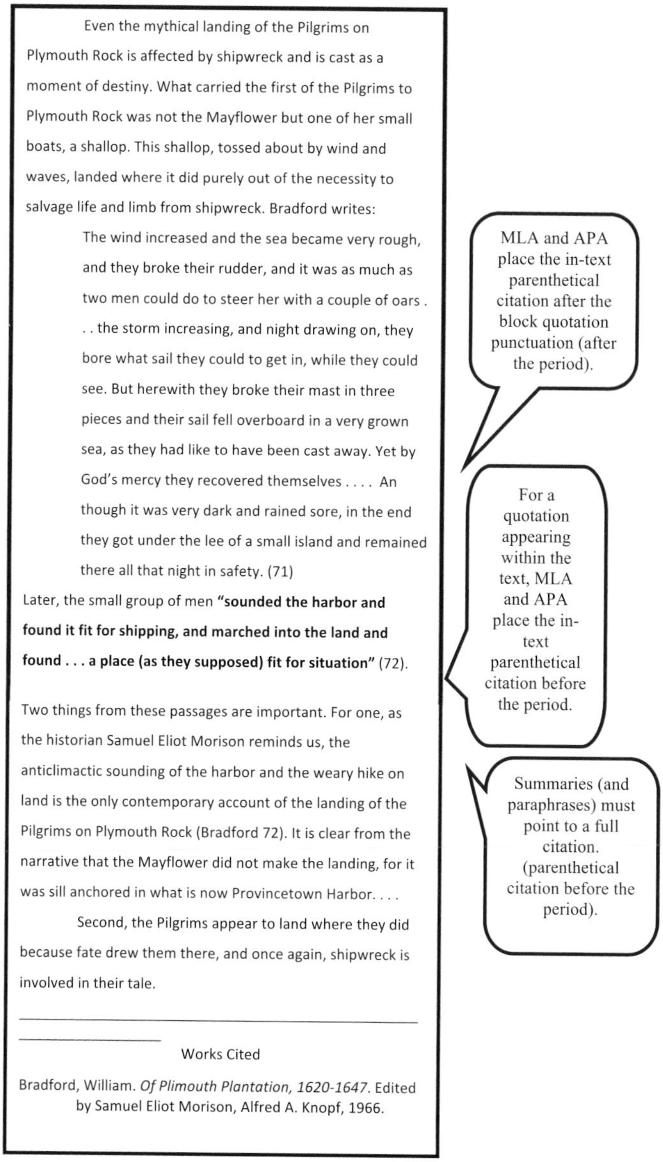

Even the mythical landing of the Pilgrims on Plymouth Rock is affected by shipwreck and is cast as a moment of destiny. What carried the first of the Pilgrims to Plymouth Rock was not the Mayflower but one of her small boats, a shallop. This shallop, tossed about by wind and waves, landed where it did purely out of the necessity to salvage life and limb from shipwreck. Bradford writes:

> The wind increased and the sea became very rough, and they broke their rudder, and it was as much as two men could do to steer her with a couple of oars . . . the storm increasing, and night drawing on, they bore what sail they could to get in, while they could see. But herewith they broke their mast in three pieces and their sail fell overboard in a very grown sea, as they had like to have been cast away. Yet by God's mercy they recovered themselves . . . . An though it was very dark and rained sore, in the end they got under the lee of a small island and remained there all that night in safety. (71)

Later, the small group of men **"sounded the harbor and found it fit for shipping, and marched into the land and found . . . a place (as they supposed) fit for situation"** (72).

Two things from these passages are important. For one, as the historian Samuel Eliot Morison reminds us, the anticlimactic sounding of the harbor and the weary hike on land is the only contemporary account of the landing of the Pilgrims on Plymouth Rock (Bradford 72). It is clear from the narrative that the Mayflower did not make the landing, for it was sill anchored in what is now Provincetown Harbor. . . .

Second, the Pilgrims appear to land where they did because fate drew them there, and once again, shipwreck is involved in their tale.

Works Cited

Bradford, William. *Of Plimouth Plantation, 1620-1647*. Edited by Samuel Eliot Morison, Alfred A. Knopf, 1966.

MLA and APA place the in-text parenthetical citation after the block quotation punctuation (after the period).
For a quotation appearing within the text, MLA and APA place the in-text parenthetical citation before the period.
Summaries (and paraphrases) must point to a full citation. (parenthetical citation before the period).

Figure 21.3 A sample page from a student's paper showing a block quotation and an in-text quotation.

indentation and for proper line spacing. The block quotation is indented, rather than enclosed in quotation marks, because a reader moving through such a large excerpt is apt to lose track of the beginning and end of the quotation and confuse the source with the surrounding text.

Too many quotations, quotations that are too long, and quotations that seem irrelevant can look like padding or filler to a professor. Be sure you link each quotation to your argument with an appropriate verb so the reason you have included it is clear. And check with your professor before using block quotations longer than half a page.

Using Paraphrases

A **paraphrase** is a detailed rewrite of a part of an original source in your own words. Use a paraphrase for any of the following reasons:

- To help your audience understand a source that uses words that are specialized, outdated, or simply unfamiliar.
- To help your audience understand a source that is highly technical or extremely detailed.
- To help your audience understand ideas or concepts that are confusing or less than clear in the original source.
- To help your audience focus on an aspect or feature of an idea found in a source.

A paraphrase typically is about as long as, and sometimes slightly longer than, the original source. A paraphrase must accurately represent the data, information, and ideas of the original without adding comments, opinions, or indications of bias that were not in the original source. A paraphrase must be expressed in your own words and manner of expression. Mimicking the sentence structure of the original or using too many distinctive words from the original may be considered plagiarism.

Original	Paraphrase
The wind increased and the sea became very rough, and they broke their rudder, and it was as much as two men could do to steer her with a couple of oars . . . the storm increasing, and night drawing on, they bore what sail they could to get in, while they could see. But herewith they broke their mast in three pieces and their sail fell overboard in a very grown sea, as they had like to have been cast away.	Bradford recounts that because the rudder broke in high winds and rough seas, two men in the boat struggled to steer using oars. The people in the boat tried to make landfall under sail, but the increasingly stormy sea made progress difficult. Then, the mast broke, dropping the sail overboard, and endangering all onboard (71).

Figure 21.4
A sample paraphrase.

In the left box of Figure 21.4 is the paragraph written by William Bradford that is used as part of the block quotation. In the box on the right is a paraphrase of the Bradford paragraph. You will note that the paraphrase does not replicate Bradford's style or tone but is in the paraphraser's own words and sentence structure. It accurately represents the ideas in the original. By contrast, a faulty paraphrase of this passage might look like the one shown in Figure 21.5.

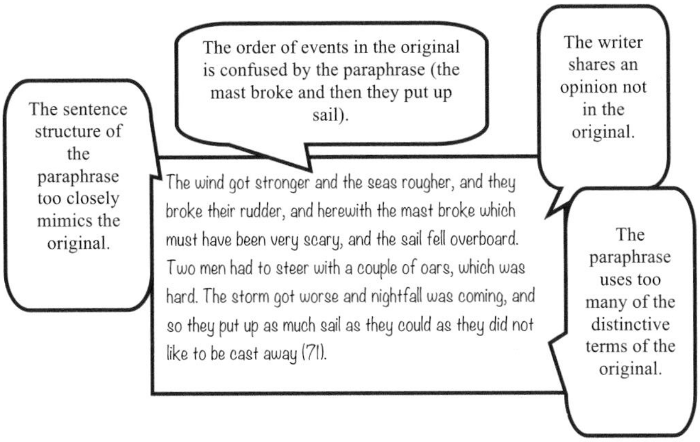

The sentence structure of the paraphrase too closely mimics the original.
The order of events in the original is confused by the paraphrase (the mast broke and then they put up sail).
The writer shares an opinion not in the original.
The wind got stronger and the seas rougher, and they broke their rudder, and herewith the mast broke which must have been very scary, and the sail fell overboard. Two men had to steer with a couple of oars, which was hard. The storm got worse and nightfall was coming, and so they put up as much sail as they could as they did not like to be cast away (71).
The paraphrase uses too many of the distinctive terms of the original.

Figure 21.5 A faulty paraphrase of the passage in Figure 21.4.

Using Summaries

A **summary** is a significant reduction of a large part of a source to its main points and ideas in your own words. Similar to a paraphrase, a summary must accurately represent the data, information, and ideas of the original without adding comments, opinions, or indications of bias that were not in the original source. You would use a summary for the following reasons:

- To help your reader understand complex ideas, a multi-point argument, or a passage that is less than clear in the original source.
- To help your reader understand and focus on the gist, or central point, of a complex idea or argument.
- To help your reader quickly connect ideas or arguments that may be spread out in long text.
- To help your reader move through your argument quickly and smoothly, with brief summaries in your own words as opposed to large block quotations of another's voice and a different manner of speaking.

In the boxed excerpt in Figure 21.6, a page-long paragraph of seventeenth-century English is summarized in two brief, easy-to-read sentences. A summary must accurately represent the original. However, you may leave out points and ideas if they are not essential to the meaning of the original and not relevant to your argument. As you read the examples of an appropriate and an inappropriate summary in Figures 21.6 and 21.7, keep in mind that the student is arguing that shipwrecks have shaped much of our understanding of America's founding.

Original	Summary
The wind increased and the sea became very rough, and they broke their rudder, and it was as much as two men could do to steer her with a couple of oars . . . the storm increasing, and night drawing on, they bore what sail they could to get in, while they could see. But herewith they broke their mast in three pieces and their sail fell overboard in a very grown sea, as they had like to have been cast away. Yet by God's mercy they recovered themselves . . . An though it was very dark and rained sore, in the end they got under the lee of a small island and remained there all that night in safety.	Bradford describes a difficult voyage that nearly ended in shipwreck for the passengers of the boat that suffered a broken rudder and broken mast. However, all aboard survived the night protected somewhat from the storm by a small island (71).

Figure 21.6
An effective summary.

A poor summary can look like a poor paraphrase if it is too long and mimics the wording and sentence structure of the original. Or, a poor summary can look like the example in Figure 21.7. The example in Figure 21.7 is a summary of the weather conditions, but it is not a good summary of the main points of the Bradford excerpt.

Bradford recounts that the storm and wind increased and it began to get dark, but luckily a small island provided protection from the wind but not the rain (71).

Figure 21.7
An ineffective summary focusing on information that is irrelevant to the main point of the original.

A good summary is an accurate representation of the original. It represents the data, information, and ideas in the original without bias, and it does not include any opinions that were not in the original.

Choosing Quotations, Paraphrases, or Summaries

Each of the methods of incorporating sources has its own benefits, and each is used for different reasons. For example, quotations provide a sense of the quoted author's voice, tone, and language in a way that summaries cannot. On the other hand, a summary can help a reader quickly process an idea that was developed at length in the original source. To choose the best way of integrating your source, consider how the source can best support the point you are trying to make.

If . . . your argument or analysis depends upon the reader seeing and understanding the exact wording of the original.	**Then . . .** use a quotation
If . . . your argument depends upon your reader seeing and understanding the exact wording, and your excerpt is more than four lines or forty words.	**Then . . .** use a block quotation
If . . . you need to explain or break down complex ideas or concepts in terms your audience can easily understand.	**Then . . .** paraphrase
If . . . you want to emphasize or examine the gist of the source's ideas, and the exact wording is not important.	**Then . . .** paraphrase
If . . . you want to describe a lengthy work, or you want to emphasize a long work's central idea or main points.	**Then . . .** summarize

Keep in mind that the purpose of using sources is to support your argument. However, altering or misrepresenting a source not only will rob your argument of persuasive power, but can also turn your reader against you and may result in charges of plagiarism. If you are not sure you are representing a source fairly or wonder if your interpretation of a source is accurate, visit your professor with the original source in hand and explain how you hope to use it.

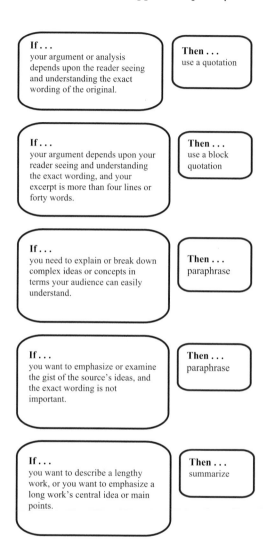

Responsible Sourcing
Using Images and Sound

Using non-textual source material such as images and sounds is similar to quoting or summarizing a sentence or paragraph. Non-textual sources must be cited. In addition, there are three ways of quoting images and sounds.

1. When you reproduce an image or sound, you are trying to provide the most accurate representation of the original. A reproduced image or sound is similar to a block quotation of text. Reproducing an accurate, detailed image or sound allows you to examine the entirety of a work in detail and allows your audience to examine the parts and the whole of the work as your argument or analysis progresses. When you reproduce an image or sound, try to use the highest quality image or sound sample available.
2. You highlight a part of an image or sound to focus your audience's attention on one element or aspect. A highlight is similar to a quotation. A highlighted use does not necessarily reproduce a large portion or the entirety of an image or sound, but presents merely part of the original. When you highlight an element of a large work or sound, be sure to introduce the source and give your audience the necessary background or context for understanding the highlighted excerpt.
3. You reference, or name, an image or sound when you merely want to draw attention to its existence or its relationship to other concepts or ideas. Similar to a summary or paraphrase, when you reference, a detailed reproduction is unnecessary.

Integrating Sources

When you have spent a great deal of time writing and building your argument, it is easy for you to see the connections between your thesis and the support provided by your sources. Your audience, however, is encountering your argument and your sources for the first time and may read your work only once. What is obvious to you is what you must try to make obvious to your audience. It is up to you to explain the significance of the sources you choose.

When you bring scholars and experts into your argument, you need to do three things:

- introduce the new voice,
- let the expert speak, and
- blend his or her words with your argument.

You choose your sources based on their authority, honesty, and relevance to your argument and your audience (see Chapter 20 for tips on evaluating potential sources). Having done that, you can introduce the source into your argument by explaining the following:

- **Who the source is and what their credentials are**: the name of the author and what authorizes the source as an expert and ensures his or her intellectual integrity. You may need to include the relevant degrees, specialties, accomplishments, publications, or offices held by the source. Scholars and experts with a great many publications have more authority than those with few publications. In addition, providing context—such as the title of the book, article, or speech from which the material comes—will help your reader understand who the source is. Remember that authority, like persuasion, happens in the mind of your audience. Research your readers' expectations and whom they respect and listen to.
- **How the source is related to your argument.** You need to help your readers understand how the source supports or contributes to your argument. This may mean breaking down or explaining a complex idea presented in the source, analyzing the information provided by the source, or synthesizing the ideas in the source with your own ideas. Before you explain, analyze, or synthesize, make sure your reader knows who is talking, why, and how the source is related to your argument, as well as what is coming.

Signal words and phrases link a source with the writer's argument. Think of signal words and phrases as road signs that alert your reader to what is next, how the next voice is related to your argument, and where the next voice is going. In the following example, a student introduces a source and signals how the reader should understand the source:

> In their article "Pursuing happiness: The architecture of sustainable change," Lyubomirsky, Sheldon, and Schkade describe the factors that determine happiness, as seen in the pie chart in Figure 1.

Sources can support your argument in many ways including the following:

- supporting your position
    - asserts, claims, comments, concurs, confirms, goes further, suggests (signal words)
- conceding or granting a contrary point
    - agrees, accepts, acknowledges, allows, concedes, grants, permits
- denying or disputing a fact
    - counters, denies, doubts, disagrees, disputes, opposes, quarrels with, rejects, responds
- describing and explaining a difficult concept
    - adds, contributes, expands, enhances, concludes, defines, depicts

MODULE IV-13

INTEGRATING SOURCES INTO AN ARGUMENT: AN EXAMPLE

Cedar Smith was working on a research paper, trying to figure out how some people seem to will themselves to be happy. She found an article by three recognized scholars, copied the following quotation, and wrote down her notes.

> "**Drawing on the past well-being literature, we propose that a person's chronic happiness level is governed by three major factors: a genetically-determined set point for happiness, happiness-relevant circumstantial factors, and happiness-relevant activities and practices**" (111). Sonja Lyubomirsky, Kennon M. Sheldon, David Schkade in Pursuing happiness: The architecture of sustainable change. *Review of General Psychology*, Vol 9, No 2, pages 111–131. 2005. Includes a helpful pie chart.

As Cedar began to draft, she summarized the quotation from her notes and the information provided by a pie chart from the original article in a bold font to keep the author's ideas distinct from hers. She then added the full citation to her "References" page (see Figures 21.8 and 21.9).

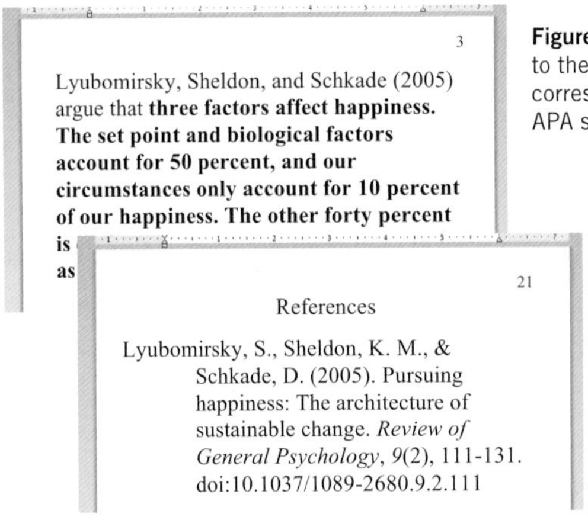

3

Lyubomirsky, Sheldon, and Schkade (2005) argue that **three factors affect happiness. The set point and biological factors account for 50 percent, and our circumstances only account for 10 percent of our happiness. The other forty percent is**
as

21

References

Lyubomirsky, S., Sheldon, K. M., & Schkade, D. (2005). Pursuing happiness: The architecture of sustainable change. *Review of General Psychology*, *9*(2), 111-131. doi:10.1037/1089-2680.9.2.111

Figure 21.8 The in-text reference to the source material and the corresponding reference-page entry, in APA style.

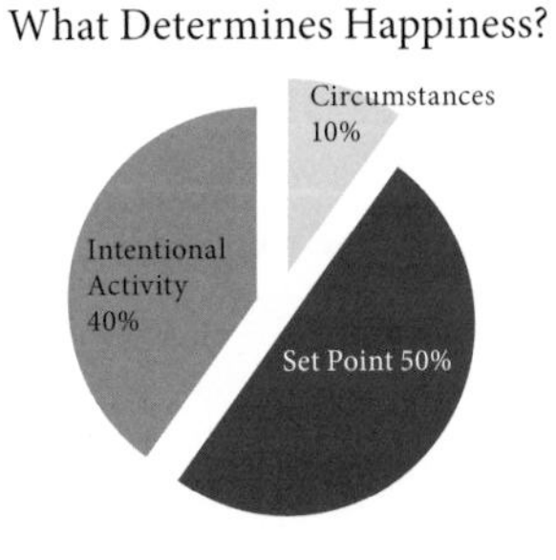

Figure 21.9 The original black-and-white pie chart.

After talking with her professor and getting advice from her peer group, she decided to include the pie chart image from the original. Unfortunately, the original image was black and white, and when she copied it, she could barely read the small print. Using the data from the chart, she created a pie chart that was easier to read.

Cedar added a caption with the correct citation for the pie chart and then integrated the summary into her argument. Notice how her introduction of the authors at the beginning of her argument (reproduced here) builds authority and persuasive power.

An Ever-Changing State: What the Science of Happiness Can Teach Us about Our Moods

The science of happiness is a focus on positive psychology, exploring how to become happier, what influences our happiness, and the influences of our internal activities, genetics, and happiness set point. **Sonja Lyubomirsky, a nationally renowned professor of social psychology at the University of California, Kennon M. Sheldon, a professor of personality at the University of Missouri Columbia, and David Schkade, a professor at the University of California San Diego specializing in the psychology of judgment and decision-making, have all spent years exploring human happiness**. In their article "Pursuing happiness: The architecture of sustainable change," the authors **describe** the factors that determine happiness, as seen in the pie chart in Figure 1.

Introducing three new voices

Our set point, or beginning state, and biological factors account for 50 percent, and our circumstances only account for 10 percent of our happiness. The other 40 percent is decided by our intentional activity such as our mood (Lyubomirsky, Sheldon, & Schkade 2005). Expanding upon their work, I will argue that because individuals can alter their mood, mood must be considered one of the intentional activities that determine our happiness. If we can change our mood, we can improve our likelihood of achieving happiness and perhaps even redefine our set point and the way we respond to circumstances.

Summary of quotation found on p. 115-116 of original article

Blending source and argument

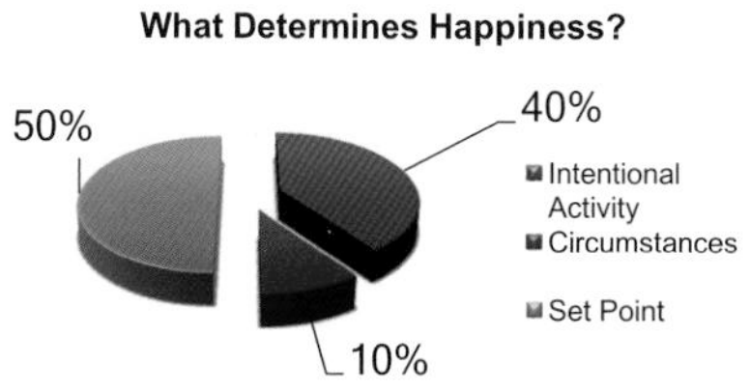

Figure 1. Adapted from "Pursuing happiness: The architecture of sustainable change," by S. Lyubomirsky, K.M. Sheldon and D. Schkade, 2005, *Review of General Psychology*, 9(2), p. 116.

Source accurately represented

APA Style Caption Figure

Cedar followed two rules of thumb that help her integrate information from the source into her argument:

1. She preceded the information from the source by introducing its authors and avoided starting a paragraph with information from the source, in effect leaving the source to introduce itself. Instead, she used signal words ("describe" and "expanding") to show readers how to understand the information and how she will connect it to her argument.
2. She did not end a paragraph with information from the source, in effect giving the source the last word. Persuasive writers understand it is their argument to make, and the sources merely provide support. It is the writer's responsibility to conclude the point or argument with a summary, analysis, and synthesis of the source in his or her own words.

CHAPTER 22

CITING AND DOCUMENTING SOURCES

Google has 15 server farms scattered all over the globe holding an estimated 900,000 individual computers, or servers, that search, scan, index, and store information about web pages, allowing Google to process an estimated 100 billion searches a month. It is one thing to scan 30 trillion web pages, but it is a technical miracle to index and store what is known about each web page so anyone can conduct a Google search and find a website. If Google should ever lose its index to a massive hack, the sites you search for might as well not exist, because the Google search engine uses the index to find and retrieve the webpages you are looking for.

Keeping track of information, as well as the sources of that information, is also important to scholars, researchers, and students. Instead of keeping index information on a gigantic server, though, you will need to organize information about your sources on the last page of an essay or a research paper. Just as the index is essential to Google's search engine, citing and documenting sources is essential to scholarship. Without information about the origin and quality of a writer's sources, potentially useful knowledge becomes useless rambling. A list of references also provides clues about the quality or authority of your sources. If you are in the business of discovering and contributing to the world's knowledge, backing up your contribution with solid, accurately documented sources is essential.

MODULE IV-14

HOW DOCUMENTATION STYLES EXPRESS AUTHORITY

Writers in academic situations establish authority by linking their argument to the chain of thinkers and scholars whose discoveries and ideas have shaped their discipline. For example, in rhetoric, the chain begins with Aspasia, the Greek woman who taught rhetoric to Socrates. Socrates is linked to Cicero, who explored the ethics of rhetoric, and continues on to the contemporary rhetorician Stephen Toulmin, who is discussed in chapter 18, and ends when you use him as a source.

An argument that is linked to authoritative sources shares in the authority of the entire chain, but an untrustworthy link can damage a writer's credibility. But to whom and what do you link your argument to?

Identifying the best sources may sound like a challenge, but it is really no different from figuring out the best source of a great cheesesteak if you use the *who, what, when*, and *where* questions.

Suppose you are visiting Philadelphia, and you want to try a cheesesteak. How do you decide where to get a great sandwich in a city crowded with options? You decide by asking *who, what, when*, and *where* questions. *Who* sells Cheesesteaks on Wharton Street? "Pat's King of Steaks" and the "This and That Convenience Store."

What Pat's offers is a sliced rib-eye sandwich smothered in Cheese Whiz, with or without onions. The convenience store has pre-packaged, microwave steak sandwiches. Pat's makes each sandwich *when* you order it, but it is hard to tell *when* the sandwiches in the store cooler were made, though they don't expire for another three days. As for *where* they were made, the package doesn't say. By contrast, Pat's sandwiches have been made on the same corner since the very first one was assembled in 1930.

The same *who, what, when*, and *where* questions also help scholars and researchers sift through the many available sources and determine the most reliable and authoritative. It should come as no surprise that the most common documentation styles answer the same set of questions so that the reader can determine who is trustworthy and what sources have the most authority.

Responsible Sourcing
Three Steps to Building an Authoritative Link

Each discipline uses an established style of documentation to build links to the chain of discovery and knowledge. If you are using one of the two common styles covered in this chapter—the one recommended by the Modern Language Association (MLA) and the one recommended by the American Psychological Association (APA)—you must always follow these three steps:

1. **Integrate** the ideas and research of others into your argument. Chapter 21 explains how to introduce, quote, paraphrase, or summarize information from sources fairly, and to use transitions to integrate sources.
2. **Connect** the ideas and research of others that you quote, paraphrase, and summarize to the list of works cited or references at the end of your text using in-text citations.
3. **Document** every source you have used in your text by supplying complete answers to the *who, what, when,* and *where* questions about each source in the format that is appropriate for the academic context and discipline. An entry in the list of works cited or references allows your reader to locate and retrieve the same information you consulted.

No one—not even your professors—memorizes the proper format for all the different types of citations and works-cited entries that make up a documentary style. There are simply too many. However, if you know the three steps to follow (integrate, connect, and document), have the source information (answers to the four *w* questions), and can access the proper style manual, you have everything you need to document your sources and demonstrate your authority.

MODULE IV-15

MLA STYLE FOR IN-TEXT CITATIONS

The documentation style recommended by the Modern Language Association, called **MLA style,** is used by disciplines in the humanities and liberal arts. MLA provides the definitive, or official, guidelines for this style in the *MLA Handbook, 8th edition,* published in 2016.

As with any documentation system, the purpose of following the MLA style is to link the words, work, or ideas of others that you use in your argument to the original sources. The MLA style is composed of brief citations within the text that point to a list of works cited with full bibliographic information.

In-text citations, sometimes referred to as *parenthetical citations* because they are often enclosed in parentheses, appear in the body of an essay, immediately after or before material from a source that has been integrated into the text. In-text citations provide just enough information for a reader to find the source in the works-cited list, as shown in Figure 22.1. The list of **works cited** is arranged in alphabetical order at the end of an essay. Each entry provides the who, what, where, and when information needed to find a source using any library, search engine, or database.

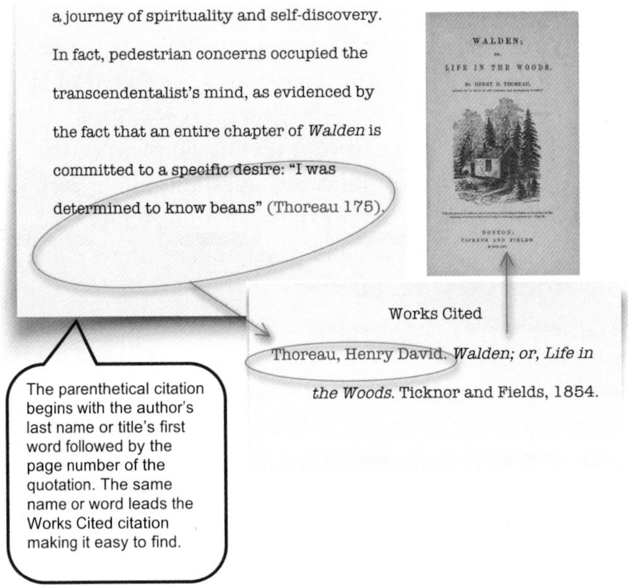

Figure 22.1
An in-text citation, and a works-cited entry, for a book by Henry David Thoreau.

In-Text Citations Focus on Who and Where

In-text citations are composed of the answer to the *who* question and a small bit of *where* information, such as page numbers, so that the reader can find where a quotation or piece of information is located within a source.

Identifying the author in an integrating phrase or sentence is the method of in-text citation preferred by most instructors and is a more effective way to incorporate information from a source than placing an author's name in the parenthetical citation. Examples 1, 3, and 5 below show how to integrate an author or authors in the text using signal phrases. If the author is not identified in the sentence that introduces or includes the information from the source, a parenthetical citation that includes the author's name is necessary. Examples 2, 4, and 6 place the author information in the parenthetical citation. Naming the author in the parenthetical citation may also help the reader when you are referring to more than one source in a single paragraph. (See Chapter 21 for more on integrating sources into your text.)

Page numbers are uncommon in many electronic formats such as web pages. If you can find page numbers, use them in the parenthetical reference, following the author's or authors' name(s). If the author's or authors' name(s) appear in the integrating phrase or sentence, only the page number appears in parentheses. Think of the page number like a red pin on a Google map: they make things easier to find. Here are some simple tricks of the trade for using page and other numbers in parenthetical citations.

- When you are citing multiple pages, use only the last two digits of the second, or ending number. For example, (Faulkner 571–78) actually means pages 571 to 578.
- If you are citing a work with many volumes or organized by parts and sections, that kind of additional information makes it easier to track down your source and can demonstrate your authority. For example, a parenthetical citation of *Robert's Rules of Order* that uses parts and articles might look like this: (Robert 185; pt. 2, art. 4).
- Many novels, poems, and plays are available in multiple editions, so other types of location information, such as book, chapter, act, scene, canto, line, or part, can be added to the page number or be used instead of page numbers:

    > Lena does not resist her suitors, but suggests she is helpless against their interests when she says, "I can't order him off. It ain't my prairie" (Cather 94; bk. 2, ch. 4).

    If you are using line numbers, do not include page numbers. Use line numbers only if provided by the source.

    > And I a smiling woman.
    > I am only thirty.
    > And like the cat I have nine times to die. (Plath, lines 19–21)

- If you are referring to an entire work, such as a book or an article, you do not need to use page numbers.

Example In-Text Citations

1. One author identified in an integrating sentence

Introducing a source and a brief explanation of its relevance to your argument is essential to building an authoritative voice. When you introduce the author of a source in your text, there is no need to repeat his or her name in parentheses. The page number, if it is available, is sufficient. If a page number is not available, the parenthetical citation is omitted.

> Willa Cather's sense of the lives of Nebraska farmers and the power of the land is captured by the narrator of *My Ántonia* when he thinks, "At any rate, that is happiness; to be dissolved into something complete and great" (14).

2. One author in a parenthetical citation

If you do not identify the author or authors in the integrating phrase or sentence, you must do so in the parenthetical citation. For individuals, use the last name only followed by the page number, with no intervening comma.

> "At any rate, that is happiness; to be dissolved into something complete and great" (Cather 14).

3. Two authors identified in an integrating sentence

Name both authors, connecting them with "and." The title of a work you are citing can also appear in the in-text reference, as shown here.

> James Watson and Francis Crick's article "A Structure for Deoxyribose Nucleic Acid" is renowned for first describing DNA as we know it today. It should also be celebrated for its humble tone—"It has not escaped our notice that the specific pairing we have postulated immediately suggests a possible copying mechanism for the genetic material" (737)—as well as its brevity.

4. Two authors in a parenthetical citation

The last name of both authors must be in the same order as listed in the original text.

> The essay that first described DNA as we know it today (Watson and Crick) is only 15 paragraphs long.

5. Three or more authors identified in an integrating sentence

When your source has three or more authors, use the last name of the first author listed and the abbreviation "et al.," which means "and others."

> In their study of predictive coding, Saygin et al. trace human responses to humanoid movement, and as they do so they appear to treat the humans they study as robots (413–16).

Whether you list all the names or use "et al.," the in-text citation must match the *who* information that begins the works-cited citation, or the reader will have difficulty finding it.

6. Three or more authors in a parenthetical citation

If your source is authored by three or more people, begin the citation with the first author's last name and the abbreviation "et al."

> Some cognitive researchers of human responses to robots treat humans as robots (Saygin et al. 413–16).

The name in the parenthetical citation must match the *who* information that begins the works-cited citation so that readers can make the connection to the works-cited list.

7. Group author identified in an integrating sentence

If a source produced by a group, such as a corporation or an organization, does not name individual authors, the group name appears in the in-text citation, following the pattern of example 1 (one author). Note that this citation does not include a page number because it is from a website.

> The California Dry Bean Advisory Board argues that it is almost impossible to meet the USDA's inspection standards for "insect webs and filth" in beans sold for human consumption.

8. Anonymous author in an integrating sentence

If a document, text, or work has no identifiable author, use the *what*—the title of the document, text, or work—to identify the source and connect it to the list of works cited.

> In "One More Punch," we are reminded that Ivermectin has been around since the 1980s (76).

9. Group author in a parenthetical citation

If a group or organization produced your source, use the first distinctive word or words in the group name to connect the source to the works-cited list. Since the following is a web-based source without numbered pages, page numbers are not included in the parenthetical reference.

> It is almost impossible to meet the USDA's inspection standards for "insect webs and filth" (California Dry Bean Advisory Board).

10. Anonymous author in a parenthetical citation

If the *who*, or author, information is not available or is listed as anonymous on the original source, then the *what* information—usually the title—will help your reader connect your source to the works-cited citation. If the title is brief, you may use it all. If the title is more than three words, use the first few distinct words of the title (not *a*, *an*, or *the*).

> As the November edition of *The Economist* points out, Ivermectin is powerful: "It has been known since the 1980s that the drug kills arthropods (ticks, mites, insects and so on) foolish enough to bite someone treated with it" ("One More" 76).

If, however, you happen to use two sources with similar titles, such as "One More Punch" and "One More Job for the CFO," then you need to use enough words from the titles to make it clear which you are referring to.

("One More Punch" 76).
("One More Job" 12).

MODULE IV-16

MLA LIST OF WORKS CITED

In MLA style, the list of works cited includes a single entry for each source cited within the text. Each entry provides detailed answers to the *who*, *what*, *where*, and *when* questions, allowing the reader to search for and locate the exact source you used.

Elements of Style for Works-Cited Citations

Works-cited page format. The works-cited list starts a new page with "Works Cited" as the centered title. Double-space each citation, and alphabetize each entry using the first important word of the citation (last name of the author or first-named author, group name, or title).

Sequence of elements. In the MLA style, the elements that answer the *who*, *what*, *where*, and *when* questions are always the same and almost always in the same order:

Author. Title of source. Title of the container, other contributors, version, number, publisher's name, date of publication, location.

The concept of **containers**—simply where your source is found—is new to the eighth edition of the *MLA Handbook*. For example, if you are citing a poem in a collection such as an anthology, the anthology is the container. If you are citing a data set from a database or an article from a website, the database or website is the container for your source.

Different types of citations will use different elements. For example, the basic citation for a book uses only four elements:

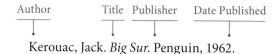

Author Title Publisher Date Published

Kerouac, Jack. *Big Sur.* Penguin, 1962.

Hanging indent. A hanging indent is the reverse of a normal indent. The first line begins at the margin, and all following lines of the same entry are indented one-half inch (about five spaces):

Brassett, James. "British Irony, Global Justice: A Pragmatic Reading of Chris Brown, Banksy and Ricky Gervais." *Review of International Studies*, vol. 35, no. 1, 2009, pp. 219–45.

The author, authors, or authoring group begins the citation, if there is a named author, and the *who* information for each citation must connect to the name or names in the integrating phrase or sentence or be identical to the name or names in the parenthetical reference. The MLA lists names, groups, or the titles of anonymous texts in the same way for all types of documents, texts, and works, as shown in examples 1–6 below.

Example Works-Cited Citations for Different Types of Authorship

1. One author

Put the family name first, followed by first name and then any middle name or initial, as shown in the original source. Note that in the example below, "UP" is the standard and acceptable abbreviation for "University Press."

Cather, Willa. *My Ántonia*. Oxford UP, 2009.

2. Two authors

Reverse the first author's name and list the second author as her or his name appears in the source: Last, First, First Last, and First Last, etc.

Watson, James, and Francis Crick. "A Structure for Deoxyribose Nucleic Acid." *Nature*, vol. 171, 1953, pp. 737–38.

3. Three or more authors

In the same way in which three or more names are cited parenthetically in the text, use the abbreviation "et al."

Saygin, Ayse Pinar, et al. "The Thing That Should Not be: Predictive Coding and the Uncanny Valley in Perceiving Human and Humanoid Robot Actions." *Social Cognitive and Affective Neuroscience*, vol. 7, no. 4, 2012, pp. 413–22.

4. A group author

Government documents and reports put out by corporations and other groups often list the group name, such as the Rand Corporation or the National Geospatial-Intelligence Agency, as the author. In such cases, the full name of the group is used and alphabetized based on the first important word in the name (not *a*, *an*, or *the*).

United States Department of Agriculture. "United States Standards for Beans." Federal Grain Inspection Service, 2005, p. 5. http://www.usdrybeans.com/wp-content/files/2011/08/US-Dry-Bean-Grading-Standards.pdf.

5. Anonymous author

If no author, of any kind, is identified by the source, skip the *who* information and begin the entry with the answer to *what*, that is, the title.

Diary of an Oxygen Thief. 2nd ed., V Publishing, 2009.

6. Two or more works by the same author

If you are citing two or more works by the same author, alphabetize the works using the first important word in each of the titles. The citation of the first book will invert the full name of the author as described in examples 1–3 above. The second and any subsequent works by the same author will begin with three hyphens and a period to indicate that the work is also produced by the same author.

Kerouac, Jack. *Big Sur.* Penguin Books, 1962.

———. On the Road: The Original Scroll. Edited by Howard Cunnell, Penguin Books, 2007.

Example Work-Cited Citations for Different Types of Sources

Works-cited citations vary greatly depending upon the *what* information they include, in part because documents, texts, and other works are available in so many different genres and media.

Below, you will find documentation models for the following broad types of sources:

- books
- periodicals, or sources published regularly

- interviews
- visuals
- audio, video, and broadcast sources
- online sources
- other digital sources.

Always cite the sources that you summarized, paraphrased, or quoted. Sometimes, you may lose the original documentation information and think that any version or edition of the source will do. However, such switches can only lead to trouble. Books or articles that have the same author and title can be very different in terms of editing and page numbers. For example, the Knopf edition of Toni Morrison's novel *The Bluest Eye* is 215 pages long, but the Vintage reprint is 224 pages long.

Books

7. Print book

The print citation sets the pattern for all citations of books.

> Kerouac, Jack. *Big Sur.* Penguin, 1962.

8. Book downloaded from an e-book publisher

Indicate the version and digital publisher, if any.

> Kerouac, Jack. *Big Sur.* Kindle version, Devault-Graves Digital Editions, 2012.

Some digitally distributed books are read using your browser, so you do not need to download a copy. The following is an example from Google Play Books.

> Dickens, Charles. *Great Expectations.* Boston, 1881. Google Books, 2017, play.google.com/books/reader?printsec=frontcover&output=reader&id=fhUXAAAAYAAJ&pg=GBS.PA527.

9. An introduction, foreword, or afterword of a book

Begin the citation with the name of the person who wrote the introduction, foreword, or afterword. The full name of author of the book follows the title of the book and the word "by," and the page number or numbers follows the date of publication. If the author wrote the element you are citing, include only the author's last name after "By." If no name is given, then you may assume the author of the book is also the author of the introduction, foreword, or afterword.

Fussell, Paul. Introduction. *The Road to Oxiana*, by Robert Byron, Oxford UP, 2007, pp. 9–16.

10. Book with an editor and/or translator

The names of an editor and or a translator are considered part of the *what* information and follow the title.

Kolmogorov, A.N. *Foundations of the Theory of Probability.* Translated and edited by Nathan Morrison, Chelsea Publishing, 1950.

11. A book with a volume or an edition number

A. A book with a volume number is one of a set of books that have the same title. Use "Vol." for the word "Volume."

Freud, Sigmund. *The Standard Edition of the Complete Psychological Works of Sigmund Freud.* Vol. 7, edited by James Strachey, Vintage, 2001.

B. An edition is a version of a book or one of many printings of a book. Use "ed." for the word "edition."

Diary of an Oxygen Thief. 2nd ed., V Publishing, 2009.

12. A work in an anthology or collection

Though anthologies or collections may have many contributors, such as the translator of a specific work or a general editor, the citation always begins with the author of the particular work you are citing.

De Man, Paul. "Semiology and Rhetoric." *Critical Theory: A Reader for Literary and Cultural Studies*, edited by Robert Dale Parker, Oxford UP, 2012, pp. 133–45.

Periodicals or Sources Published Regularly

13. An article in a scholarly journal

The articles in a scholarly journal are written by experts and scholars for the purpose of sharing experimental findings and the results of their research. Some journals are published monthly or quarterly; others are published every six months or every year. As a result, citations for articles in scholarly journals include more specific *where* information than books do, including the journal name, volume number, issue number, and inclusive page numbers for the article.

A. An article from a printed scholarly journal

Author — Title

Mortenson, Erik. "Capturing the Fleeting Moment: Photography in the Work of Allen Ginsberg." *Chicago Review*, vol. 51, no.1–2, 2005, pp. 215–31.

Journal Title
Volume
Issue — Date Published — Page numbers

B. An article in an online scholarly journal is similar to a print article. However, online articles often do not include page numbers. After giving the basic citation information, include the DOI. A **DOI**, or digital object identifier, is a specific code that provides an enduring link to a work that will not change or get lost. If you can't find a DOI, use the URL web address (omitting the http://).

Lippit, Akira Mizuta. "David Lynch's Wholes." *Flow*, vol. 15, no. 3, 2011, www.flowjournal.org/2011/11/david-lynchs-wholes/.

C. An article from an online database such as *JSTOR* or *ProQuest* must include the name of the database and the DOI or URL of the article.

Jauss, Hans Robert. "Literary History as a Challenge to Literary Theory." *A Symposium on Literary History*, vol. 2, no. 1, 1970, pp. 7–37. *JSTOR*, doi:10.2307/468585.

14. Magazine

Magazine citations are similar to scholarly journal citations, but they lack volume and issue numbers. Note the specific month or date of publication.

A. An article in a magazine published monthly

Mathews, Dana. "It's Austin Mahone's World and We're All Just Living in It." *TeenVogue*, Dec. 2014/Jan. 2015, pp. 53–56.

B. An article in a magazine published weekly

Foroohar, Raina. "Starbucks for America." *Time*, 5 Feb. 2015, pp. 23–27.

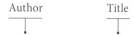

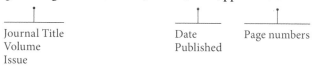

C. An article from a magazine's online edition

Peters, Mark. "*Felgercarb*: An Underused, Sci-Fi Word for BS." *Slate*, 5 Nov. 2015, www.slate.com/blogs/lexicon_valley/2015/11/05/mark_peters_bullshit_word_of_the_day_felgercarb_is_a_sci_fi_word_for_bs.html.

15. Newspaper
An article in a newspaper must indicate the edition and section and page numbers if they are available.

A. An article in a newspaper

Musetto, Vincent. "Headless Body in Topless Bar." *New York Post*, final ed., 15 Apr. 1983, p. A1.

B. An article from a newspaper's online edition

Many newspapers have online editions. Include the date when the article was posted and its DOI or URL.

Rocha, Veronica. "Arrest Made in Death of Transgender Woman after O.C. Silicone Party." *Los Angeles Times*, 9 Feb. 2015, www.latimes.com/local/lanow/la-me-ln-transgender-silicone-party-death-20150209-story.html.

C. A review of a book or work

Russo, Maria. "A Book That Started with Its Pictures: Ransom Riggs Is Inspired by Vintage Snapshots." Review of *Miss Peregrine's Home for Peculiar Children*, by Ransom Riggs. *The New York Times*, 30 Dec. 2013, p. C1.

Government-Sponsored or Related Document

16. Government documents
A government document may have an individual author, or it may have authors affiliated with corporations or research centers. Or such documents may list only the government agency as the author. Also, it is possible for the publisher to be the same as the author, as in example A below. In that case, start with the title and list the organization as the publisher.

A. A printed government document

Report to the President. Presidential Commission on the Space Shuttle Challenger Accident, 6 June 1986. 5 vols.

It is not unusual to find a source with **no date of publication.** If you cannot find a date, use the available evidence to make an informed guess and indicate your estimate with a question mark, (for example 2009? or 18th century?).

B. A government document published online

Daues, Jessica. "Lunar Maps Paved Way for Moon Exploration." *NGA Historical Collection.* National Geospatial-Intelligence Agency, 2009? www.nga.mil/About/History/Apollo%2011/Pages/default.aspx.

Interviews

Interview citations always begin with the name of the person answering the questions: the interviewee.

17. Interviews

A. A printed interview

Derrida, Jacques. "'Eating Well,' or the Calculation of the Subject." *Points...: Interviews, 1974–1994*, edited by Werner Hamacher and David E. Wellbery, translated by Peter Connor and Avital Ronell, Stanford UP, 1995, pp. 255–77.

B. An interview from an online source

Crumb, Robert. "R. Crumb: The Art of Comics No. 1." Interview with Robert Crumb. *The Paris Review*, no. 193, 2010, www.theparisreview.org/interviews/6017/the-art-of-comics-no-1-r-crumb.

C. A personal interview

If you interviewed someone, use "Personal interview" and include the date of the interview.

Ryan, Dermot. Personal interview. 14 Apr. 2017.

Visuals

18. Map or chart

Maps can be individual sheets but are commonly part of a book or atlas, such as example A below. A map citation provides the name of the creator or mapmaker and name of the map in the usual sequence. If no name is provided, give the map a title that would make it easy to identify and fits the context in which it was found. In addition, include the word "map" or "chart."

A. Print map

Paullin, Charles O. "Settled Area 1760 and Population 1750." Map. *Atlas of the Historical Geography of the United States*, edited by John K. Wright, Greenwood, 1975, p. 60.

B. Online chart

Federal Aviation Administration. "Omaha SOMA." Sectional aviation chart. FAA FFR Charts, 20 July 2017. aeronav.faa.gov/content/aeronav/tac_files/PDFs/Kansas_City_TAC_84_P.pdf. Accessed 28 Feb. 2018.

19. Work of art

A citation for a work of art such as a painting or sculpture begins with the creator and the title of the work. Then include the date it was created, the institution or collection where the work is housed, and the city. If the date is approximate, use "circa" (for example, circa 1450).

Caravaggio, Michelangelo Merisi da. *The Conversion of St. Paul*. 1601, Odescalchi Balbi Collection, Rome.

20. Image or screenshot

Any image, such as a screenshot from a computer game or instant messaging text discussion, requires the *who, what, where,* and *when* information. If the screenshot or image has no title, you may need to give the source a title to help the reader understand and locate the source if possible.

Associated Press. *Cassius Clay Malcolm X*. 1964. AP Images, www.apimages.com/metadata/Index/Associated-Press-Domestic-News-New-York-United-/62c2ee253ae5da11af9f0014c2589dfb/15/1.

Audio, Video, and Broadcast Sources

21. Television or radio

Television and radio broadcasts use the same sequence of information; however, the *where* information is the title of the program or series, such as *Nightly News with Lester Holt*, the name of the broadcasting network, such as NBC, and the call letters of the broadcasting station, such as WMAQ Chicago.

"La Mancha Screwjob." *Radiolab*, narrated by Jad Abumrad and Robert Krulwich. National Public Radio. KBSX, Boise, 24 Dec. 2017.

22. Sound recording

A published sound recording is often the product of a number of artists, such as lead soloist, ensemble, composer, and conductor. Often, the name you discovered during the research that led you to the sound recording should be the same name you use to begin your citation. Your citation should begin with the name you use in your argument or the name used in the parenthetical citation.

A. Recording in physical format

Adler, Richard, and Jerry Ross. *Damn Yankees: Original Broadway Cast Recording*. Performances by Gwen Verdon, Stephen Douglass, and Ray Walston, directed by Hal Hastings, BMG Music, 1988.

B. Recording downloaded

Wilco. "Random Name Generator." *Star Wars*, by Jeff Tweedy, dBpm Records, 2015, wilcoworld.net/music/star-wars/.

23. Lecture or performance

A live lecture or a play, dance, or other performance will be cited in a similar way. The primary difference is that citations for performances typically begin with the title of the work performed.

A. Lecture or reading

Lythcott-Haims, Julie. "How to Raise an Adult." 92nd Street Y, New York, 16 July 2015. Address.

B. Performance

Hamlet. By William Shakespeare, directed by Austin Pendleton, performance by Peter Sarsgaard, Classic Stage Company, New York, 27 Mar. 2015.

Online Sources

24. Website

Websites can be a challenge to document simply because there is no standard place to find publication information, as there is on the title and copyright pages of a book, for example. Still, answers to the *who*, *what*, *where*, and *when* questions should be available at the bottom of the home page or on the "About Us" page. Because websites are revised and change often, provide your reader with the date when you accessed the source, unless the citation is for a dated entry such as a blog post.

LHCb—Large Hadron Collider Beauty Experiment. CERN, lhcb-public.web.cern.ch/lhcb-public/. Accessed 11 Jan. 2017.

25. Wiki entry

There are many types of wikis, including some built by enthusiasts who are not experts and some that are built by and for experts and scholars to share information. Because wikis are developed collaboratively, authors' names are rarely cited. Obviously, you should examine any wiki carefully to determine its authority before using it as a source.

"Mammalian Bites." *WikEM, The Global Emergency Medicine Wiki*, OpenEM Foundation, 15 June 2015, wikem.org/wiki/Mammalian_bites. Accessed 1 Aug. 2017.

26. Social network

Savage, Doug. "How to Train Your Cat." *Savage Chickens. Facebook*, 2 Feb. 2017, www.savagechickens.com/wp-content/uploads/chickentrainyourcat9.jpg. Accessed 23 May 2017.

A tweet is so brief that the entire tweet is used as the *what* information. The container is identified as "*Twitter*," and the local time when the message was sent is enough information for the reader to locate this type of source.

@DeptofDefense. "From 1 SecDef to another: Hagel calls @timhowardgk to say thanks for defending USA. We (USA) are proud of @ussoccer!" *Twitter*, 2 July 2014, 4:46 p.m., twitter.com/deptofdefense/status/484438026152460288.

27. News group, discussion board, blog

Kiko, Jennifer. "Night Light." *Farmgirl Follies*, 9 July 2015, www.farmgirlfollies.com/2015/07/night-light-20024.html.

28. Email

Peters, K.J. "Re: Avoid the Turtles." Received by Alex Neel, 25 Dec. 2017.

29. Online video and audio

A. Streamed movie or TV

Movies and television shows may have several creators and contributors. You should begin your citation with the name of the individual that is the focus of your discussion, and the reason you are using the source. For example, if you want to examine the editing of a movie, begin with the name of the editor. If you are examining an actor's performance in a television show, begin with that actor's name. You are free to add other significant contributors if it will help the audience locate the source.

Bathurst, Otto, Director. "National Anthem." *Black Mirror*, season 1, episode 1, Netflix, 4 Dec. 2011, www.netflix.com/title/70264888.

B. YouTube video

An online video must cite the website, such as YouTube, as the container and identify the uploader as another contributor. However, you do not need to repeat the name of the uploader if they are also the creator.

Film Theorists. "Harry Potter, More Voldemort Than Voldemort!" *YouTube*, 17 Jan. 2017, www.youtube.com/watch?v=mbC-sDMHypU.

C. Podcasts

Abumrad, Jade. "Stranger in Paradise." *Radiolab*, 27 Jan. 2017, www.radiolab.org/story/stanger-paradise/.

Other Digital Sources

30. PDF

Ramist, Leonard, Charles Lewis, and Laura McCamley. "Student Group Differences in Predicting College Grades: Sex, Language, and Ethnic Groups." *ETS Research Report Series*, vol. 1994, no. 1, 1994, pp. 1–41. File last modified on 8 Aug. 2014, research.collegeboard.org/sites/default/files/publications/2012/7/researchreport-1993-1-student-group-differences-predicting-college-grades.pdf.

31. DVD or film

"Christmas at Downton Abbey." *Downton Abbey*, written by Julian Fellowes, directed by Brian Percival, season 2, episode 9, PBS, 2012.

The Great Gatsby. Directed by Baz Luhrmann, performances by Leonardo DiCaprio, Tobey Maguire, Carey Mulligan, and Joel Edgerton, Warner Bros., 2013.

32. An app

The citation of computer software or apps is very similar to online or downloaded books. Apps have titles, containers such G Suite or the Apple App Store, publishers, and dates of publication. The author can be the creator or the copyright holder of the app.

Aspyr Media. "Sim City: Complete Edition." Computer Software, version 1.0.2, Apple App Store. Aspyr Media, Inc., 30 Mar. 2015.

Excerpts from a Student Paper in MLA Style

The MLA style includes formatting expectations for margins, line spacing, and captions. The first page and works-cited page from a paper formatted in MLA style are presented below.

Adonis Williams wrote the paper for his Irish literature course, in which the professor expected students to use MLA style.

This is the order of identifying info that MLA recommends, but your professor may have a different preference.

The last name and page number appear on every page, top right.

Williams 1

Adonis Williams

Professor O'Keeffe

Irish Literature

29 April 2015

Center the title.

A New World

The MLA does not require title pages, though if your professor asks for one, follow the format he or she recommends.

Use a common font like Arial or Times New Roman. Use 12 point font size and doublespacing

In the very beginning of *A Portrait of the Artist as a Young Man,* James Joyce foreshadows the artistic development of his protagonist, providing the conditions that will, unfortunately, alienate Stephen. Taking readers into the mind of his young protagonist, Joyce offers for the first time instances when Stephen gravitates towards a budding interest in language, coupled with a growing separation from his classmates, some of whom are shown in fig. 1.

Fig. 1. James Joyce, front center, with classmates at Clongowes School. Boardinghouseblog 1888. Photograph.

Number and name all images as "Fig." Also, refer to figures within the text.

While in class, Stephen writes on his page, "Stephen Dedalus is my name, Ireland is my nation. Clongowes is my dwelling place. And heaven is my dwelling place" (Joyce 255). The conflict between Stephen's nation, home town, and the heaven in which he dwells reflects changes in the political and religious atmosphere of 20th century Ireland. As my analysis will show, Stephen's development as an artist is informed by these changes and an increasing disillusionment with the religion of his family, as represented by his Uncle, and his own desire

One inch margins top, both sides, and bottom

Williams 9

MLA uses the phrase "Works Cited." It should be centered.

Works Cited

Alphabetize by the first letter of the first important word of every citation.

Double space the page with no special spacing between entries.

Akoi, Mohammed. "Stephen and the Technique of Symbol-Switching in Joyce's *A Portrait of the Artist as a Young Man* and *Ulysses*." *Language in India*, vol. 13, no. 10, 2013, pp. 294–307. *Communication & Mass Media Complete*, www.languageinindia.com/oct2013/mohammedulysses.pdf.

Buttigieg, Joseph A. "Aesthetics and Religion in *A Portrait of the Artist as a Young Man*." *Christianity and Literature*, vol. 28, no. 4, 1979, pp. 44–56. *ATLA Religion Database with ATLASerials*.

Farrell, Kevin. "The Reverend Stephen Dedalus, S. J.: Sacramental Structure in *A Portrait of the Artist as a Young Man*." *James Joyce Quarterly*, vol. 49, no. 1, 2011, pp. 27–40. *MLA International Bibliography*. doi:10.1353/jjq.2011.0102.

Joyce, James. *A Portrait of the Artist as a Young Man. The Portable James Joyce*, edited by Harry Levin, Penguin, 1976, pp. 243–526.

A hanging indent is the opposite of a normal indent. Everything after first line is indented five spaces.

Many professors read the Works Cited first to evaluate depth of research and attention to detail.

MODULE IV-17

APA STYLE FOR IN-TEXT CITATIONS

The documentation style recommended by the American Psychological Association, or the **APA style**, is used by disciplines in the social sciences such as psychology, linguistics, economics, and political science. The following guidelines are based on the 6th edition of the *Publication Manual of the American Psychological Association* (2010) and the *APA Style Guide to Electronic References* (2012).

As with any documentation style, the purpose of the APA style is to give your reader the information necessary to link a source you use in your argument to the original source as efficiently as possible. The APA style is composed of brief citations in the text of your argument that point to the list of references with full bibliographic information at the end.

In-text citations have three parts: the family name of the author, the year of publication, and for quotations and specific information the page number. In-text citations appear in the body of an essay, immediately after or before material from a source that has been integrated into the text.

The list of **references** is arranged in alphabetical order at the end of the text. Each entry provides the answers to the *who*, *what*, *when*, and *where* information needed to find a source using any library, search engine, or database (Figure 22.2).

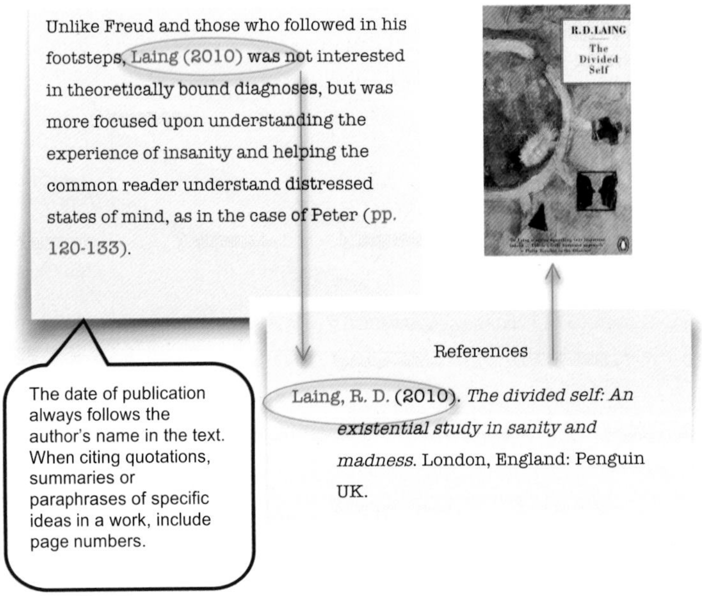

Unlike Freud and those who followed in his footsteps, Laing (2010) was not interested in theoretically bound diagnoses, but was more focused upon understanding the experience of insanity and helping the common reader understand distressed states of mind, as in the case of Peter (pp. 120-133).
R.D. LAING
The Divided Self
References
Laing, R. D. (2010). *The divided self: An existential study in sanity and madness.* London, England: Penguin UK.
The date of publication always follows the author's name in the text. When citing quotations, summaries or paraphrases of specific ideas in a work, include page numbers.

Figure 22.2 An in-text citation, and a reference entry, for a book by R.D. Laing.

In-Text Citations Focus on Who, When, and Where

In-text citations answer *who* (the author or authors), *when* (the year a work was published), and, for quotations and specific information, a small part of *where* (page numbers where the quotation can be found within a source).

Identifying an author in an integrating phrase or sentence is the method that writing instructors and other professors generally prefer and is a more effective way to incorporate information from a source than placing all the information in a parenthetical citation. When identifying the author or authors of a work for the first time, use each author's family name only.

Date of publication is of special importance to all types of scientists, including those in the social sciences. In fact, the APA calls its method of in-text citation "the author-date method." The sciences progress quickly, and recent discoveries and recent revisions of findings and theories drive these disciplines forward. As a result, a student or researcher who is aware of the most recent peer-reviewed research coming out of the Large Hadron Collider speaks with greater authority than someone citing data from the Relativistic Heavy Ion Collider, which was a predecessor to the Hadron Collider and seems like an antique now. Therefore, in-text citations always include the year of publication in parentheses.

Page numbers, when available, are a useful tool for locating cited sources. In APA style, page numbers are required for quotations and specific information. Many contemporary sources do not use page numbers, however. The following practices will help you deal with page numbers:

- If you are referring to an entire book or summarizing an entire work, page numbers are not necessary in the in-text citation.
- If you can find page numbers, use them in the parenthetical reference.
- Place a comma after the year if you are including a page number, and use "p." as an abbreviation for "page" or "pp." for "pages."
- If paragraph numbers are available instead of page numbers, use "para." as the abbreviation for "paragraph."
- If there are no page or paragraph numbers, use the first few distinctive words of a heading within quotation marks, followed by the number of the paragraph in which the quotation appears: "Final Thoughts," para. 3. If the heading is too long, abbreviate it.
- If none of the above is available, the date within parentheses is sufficient.

Example In-Text Citations

1. One author identified in an integrating sentence
When you introduce the author of a source in the sentence that includes the parentheses, there is no need to repeat his or her name in parentheses. The year and, if needed, the page number, are sufficient.

> Laing (2010) was focused upon understanding the experience of going insane and helping the common reader understand distressed states of mind.

A direct quotation of an author's specific idea requires a page number. A summary or paraphrase of an author's ideas does not require page numbers according to the APA; however, you may provide page numbers if you think it will help your reader or affirm your authority.

> Cather's (1918) sense of the lives of Nebraska farmers and the power of the land is captured by the narrator of *My Ántonia* when he thinks, "At any rate, that is happiness; to be dissolved into something complete and great" (p. 14).

2. One author in a parenthetical citation
Note that a comma separates the author from the year of publication.

> Unlike Freud and those who followed in his footsteps, other therapists were more focused upon understanding the experience of insanity (Laing, 2010).

3. Two authors identified in an integrating sentence
Cite the names of both authors each time you refer to their work.

> Watson and Crick's (1953) article "A structure for deoxyribose nucleic acid" is renowned for first describing DNA as we know it today, but it should also be celebrated for doing so in 15 brief paragraphs.

4. Two authors in a parenthetical citation
If you do not identify the author or authors in the integrating sentence, use the family name of each in parentheses, separated by an ampersand (&).

> The essay that first described DNA as we know it today (Watson & Crick, 1953) is only 15 paragraphs long.

5. Three or more authors identified in an integrating sentence
The first time you use a source with three or more authors, include all the named authors.

In their study entitled "The thing that should not be: Predictive coding and the uncanny valley in perceiving human and humanoid robot actions," Saygin, Chaminade, Ishiguro, Driver, and Frith (2011) trace human responses to humanoid movement, and as they do so they appear to treat the humans they study as robots.

The second time you use the source and every time afterward, use only the family name of the first author followed by "et al." The abbreviation "et al." always includes a period.

There is no doubt designers and programmers can resolve the uncanny valley. However, it should be noted that Saygin et al. (2011) end their study by suggesting we may not want robots to look anything like us (p. 420).

6. Three or more authors in a parenthetical citation

The first time you use a source with three or more authors, include all the named authors in the parenthetical citation.

Some cognitive researchers studying human responses to robots treat humans as robots (Saygin, Chaminade, Ishiguro, Driver, & Frith, 2011).

All subsequent references will include only the first author's family name and "et al."

Not surprisingly, cognitive research confirms Freud's theory of the "uncanny" (Saygin et al., 2011, p. 420).

7. Group author identified in an integrating sentence

For the citation of a source produced by a group such as a corporation or organization, the group's name is included in full in the text. If the name is long, it may be abbreviated after the first use of the source.

The US Dry Bean Council (2015) argues that it is almost impossible to meet the USDA's inspection standards for "insect webs and filth."

8. Group author in a parenthetical citation

If a group has authored your source, use the full name of the group in the first parenthetical citation.

The President's Executive Order 12333 prevents the US government and its agencies from using satellites and other methods of intelligence collection against US citizens on US soil (National Geospatial-Intelligence Agency).

In subsequent references to the same source, you may use the first few distinctive words of long group names.

> US citizens overseas may be subject to the collection of intelligence information by way of satellite-based communication or observation monitoring (National Geospatial).

9. Anonymous author in an integrating sentence

If the information about who authored a document, text, or work is not available, the *what*—that is, the title—is the means of identifying the source and connecting it to the list of references. The first time you use a source in your argument, state the full title. Thereafter you may use the first few distinct words of a title if it is long.

> In "One More Punch" (2015), we are reminded that Ivermectin has been around since the 1980s (p. 76).

10. Anonymous author in a parenthetical citation

If a source lists an author as "anonymous," use the same word in the parenthetical citation.

> Of course, identity is never a sure thing (Anonymous, 1912, p. 238).

If there is no indication of an author, use the title of the work in the parenthetical citation. If the title is long, use the first few distinct words of the title.

> The coywolf, half coyote and half wolf, numbers in the millions ("Evolution: Greater than," 2015).

11. Personal communication

Emails and other personal communication such as interviews, memos, letters, and conversations are cited in the text but are not included in the list of references. Since these citations do not provide information that would help a reader locate the original, APA considers it unnecessary to include them in the list of references. Identify the person you spoke with by initials and include the date.

> D. Ryan was insistent that this is Everton's century (personal communication, April 14, 2015).

> This is Everton's century (D. Ryan, personal communication, April 14, 2015).

MODULE IV-18

APA LIST OF REFERENCES

In the APA style, the references list at the end of your argument includes a single entry for each source you cite within the text. Each entry provides detailed answers to the *who, what, when,* and *where* questions, allowing the reader to locate the exact source you used.

Elements of Style for References Citations

References page format. The references page begins with the word "References" as the centered title. Double space each citation, and alphabetize each entry using the first word of the in-text citation (name, group, or title).

Sequence. In the APA style, the answers to *who, what, when,* and *where* are consistently in the same order, with few exceptions. The location of the publication must include a state, province, or country. After the location information, APA style may include information such as a digital object identifier, or DOI, or the uniform resource locator, or URL, for documents retrieved from online sources. Pages numbers always include all digits.

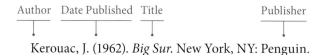

Author | Date Published | Title | Publisher

Kerouac, J. (1962). *Big Sur.* New York, NY: Penguin.

Hanging indent. A hanging indent is the reverse of a normal indent. The first line begins at the margin and all following lines of the same entry are indented one-half inch or five spaces.

Family name and initial only | No quotation marks for article titles

Brassett, J. (2009). British irony, global justice: A pragmatic reading of Chris Brown, Banksy and Ricky Gervais. *Review of International Studies, 35*(1), 219–245.

Hanging indent

Volume number (issue number) | Page numbers | Book and journal titles are italicized

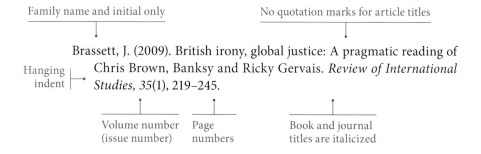

The references are alphabetized by the family name, group name, or the first important word of the title that starts the citation.

Capitalization rules for journals are not the same as the rules for other sources. All significant words in journal titles are capitalized. However, only the first word of a book title, book chapter title, or website is capitalized, along with the first word after a colon.

The **author, authors, authoring group, or title** leads the citation. If there is an author, the *who* information in the citation must connect to the name or names that appear in the text, either in the integrating sentence or in parentheses. The APA lists names, groups, and titles in the same way for all types of documents, texts, and works.

Example References Citations for Different Types of Authorship

1. One author
Use the author's family name followed by the first initial of the first name and middle name, if any.

> Cather, W. (2009). *My Ántonia*. Oxford, England: Oxford University Press.

2. Two to six authors
For all authors, use the family name followed by first initial of the first name and middle name if any, and separate all names with a comma. Prior to the last name, use "&" in place of "and."

> Saygin, A.P., Chaminade, T., Ishiguro, H., Driver, J., & Frith, C. (2012). The thing that should not be: Predictive coding and the uncanny valley in perceiving human and humanoid robot actions. *Social Cognitive and Affective Neuroscience*, *7*(4), 413–422. doi:10.1093/scan/nsr025

3. Seven or more authors
List the first six authors, then use three ellipses to indicate names missing, and then add the last of the author's names.

> Aad, G., Abajyan, T., Abbott, B., Abdallah, J., Khalek, S.A., Abdelalim, A.A., . . . & AbouZeid, O.S. (2012). Observation of a new particle in the search for the Standard Model Higgs boson with the ATLAS detector at the LHC. *Physics Letters B*, *716*(1), 1–29. doi:10.1016/j.physletb.2012.08.020

4. A group, organization, or corporate author

Government documents and reports put out by corporations and other groups often list a group name, such as the Rand Corporation or the National Geospatial-Intelligence Agency, as the author. In such cases, the full name of the group is used and alphabetized based on the first important word in the name (not *a*, *an*, or *the*).

National Research Council: Committee on the Biological Effects of Ionizing Radiations, & United States. Environmental Protection Agency. (1980). *The effects on populations of exposure to low levels of ionizing radiation, 1980* (vol. 3095). National Academy Press.

5. Anonymous documents, texts, and works

If no author of any kind is identified by the source, move the title, or *what* information, to the beginning of the citation.

One more punch. (2015, October 31). *The Economist, 417*(8962), 76.

6. Two or more documents, texts, or works by the same author

If you are citing two or more books by the same author, list the earliest publication date first.

Kerouac, J. (1962). *Big Sur.* New York, NY: Penguin.

Kerouac, J. (2007). *On the road: The original scroll.* New York, NY: Penguin.

If you are citing one work by a single author and another work where the author was the lead author of a work with multiple authors, the single-author citation should come first.

Saygin, A.P. (2007). Superior temporal and premotor brain areas necessary for biological motion perception. *Brain, 130*(9), 2452–2461.

Saygin, A.P., Chaminade, T., Ishiguro, H., Driver, J., & Frith, C. (2012). The thing that should not be: Predictive coding and the uncanny valley in perceiving human and humanoid robot actions. *Social Cognitive and Affective Neuroscience, 7*(4), 413–422. doi:10.1093/scan/nsr025

Responsible Sourcing
APA Abbreviations

The APA, like many style manuals and handbooks, uses its own set of abbreviations. The following are used in references.

doi:—digital object identifier
ed.—edition
Ed.—Editor
n.d.—no date
n.p.—no place
n.p.—no publisher
n. pag.—no page
No.—number
p.—page
pp.—pages
Pt.—Part
Trans.—Translator
Vol.—volume

Example Reference Citations for Different Types of Sources

The listing of author's or authoring group's names is the same no matter what kind of source is being documented. And the sequence of the *who*, *what*, *when*, and *where* information will also be consistent. However, the *where* information may include different types of information, such as a DOI number or URL.

Make sure you have one reference citation for each source you use in the text of your argument. Always cite the same version of a source you consulted when you did your research. Books or articles with the same author and title can differ from each other in terms of editing and page numbers. For example, the Knopf edition of Toni Morrison's *The Bluest Eye* is 215 pages long, but the Vintage reprint is 224 pages long. In addition, different editors working with the same text can make different edits, cuts, and revisions.

Below, you will find documentation models for the following broad types of sources:

- books
- periodicals or sources published regularly
- visuals

- broadcast, audio, and video sources
- online sources
- other digital sources

Books

1. Print or digital book

A. The **print** citation sets the pattern for all book citations.

Kerouac, J. (1962). *Big Sur.* New York, NY: Penguin.

B. For an **electronic book** that must be purchased from an e-book publisher, indicate the version and replace publisher information with "Available from" and the Internet address. Include the format version of the book in brackets. If the book is freely available from an online source, use the phrase retrieved from.

Kerouac, J. (2012). *Big Sur* [Kindle version]. Available from http://www.amazon.com

2. An Introduction, foreword, or afterword of a book

Begin the citation with the name of the person who wrote the introduction, foreword, or afterword. Use the title or word that best describes your source, such as "Introduction" or "Foreword."

Slethaug, G.E. (2014). Introduction. In *Adaptation theory and criticism: Postmodern literature and cinema in the USA* (pp. 1–12). New York, NY: Bloomsbury.

If the author of the introduction, foreward, or afterword is different from the author of the book, the author of the work being cited begins the citation. The name of the book author appears after "In."

Sharistanian, J. (2008). Introduction. In Cather, W., *My Antonia* (vii-xxiv). Oxford, England: Oxford University Press.

3. A selection or part of a book or anthology

For any selection that appears within another book, such as an essay or a short story in an anthology, remember the larger book or anthology is where the selection is located. The citation begins with the author of the selection, followed by the title of the selection, with no quotation marks. The title of the book or anthology is italicized and the page numbers are in parentheses.

Derrida, J. (1995). Between brackets. (P. Kamuf, Trans.) In W. Hamacher & D. Wellbery (Eds.), *Points...: Interviews, 1974–1994* (pp. 5–29). Stanford, CA: Stanford University Press.

4. Book with an editor or translator

The names of an editor or a translator are placed in parentheses and follow the title. For an editor use "Ed." and for a translator use "Trans."

Kolmogorov, A. (1950). *Foundations of the theory of probability.* (N. Morrison, Ed. & Trans.). New York, NY: Chelsea.

5. Book with a volume or an edition number

A. A book with a volume number is one of a set of books that have the same title. The volume number is part of the title. Use "Vol." for "Volume."

Freud, S. (2001). *The standard edition of the complete psychological works of Sigmund Freud* (Vol. 7). (J. Strachey, Ed.). London, England: Vintage.

B. An edition is a version of a book or one of many printings of a book. Place the edition number in parentheses following the title and use "ed." for "edition."

Meier, P., & Zünd, R. (2000). *Statistics for analytical chemistry* (2nd ed.). New York, NY: Wiley.

Periodicals or Sources Published Regularly

6. An Article in a Scholarly Journal

Articles in scholarly journals are written for and read by experts, scholars, professors, or others who seek information about current research in a specific discipline. Journals can be published monthly, every six months, or once a year, for example. As a result, citations for articles in scholarly journals provide more specific *where* information by including the volume number and issue number in addition to page numbers.

Citations for both print articles and those published electronically should include the DOI (digital object identifier) if one is available. A DOI is a specific code that provides an enduring link to a work that will not change or get lost. DOIs will be found on the first page of an electronically published article, next to the copyright notice, or on the web page that contains the article. If a DOI number is not available, use the URL (uniform resource locator) of the journal's home page. The DOI or URL is not followed by a period.

A. An article from a **print scholarly journal**

Who When What

Mortenson, E. (2005). Capturing the fleeting moment: Photography in the work of Allen Ginsberg. *Chicago Review, 51*(1/2), 215–231.

Where—journal title volume (issue)

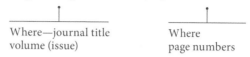

Where page numbers

B. An article from an **online scholarly journal** is cited like a print article

Maia, C., Aparecido, J., & Milanez, L. (2004). Thermally developing forced convection of non-Newtonian fluids inside elliptical ducts. *Heat Transfer Engineering, 25*(7), 13–22. doi:10.1080/01457630490495805

Lippit, A.M. (2011). David Lynch's wholes. *Flow, 15*(3). http://www.flowjournal.org/2011/11/david-lynchs-wholes/

C. An article from an **online database** is cited slightly differently than an online journal. There is no need to identify the database name, such as EBSCO or JSTOR. However, the database name can be provided if it adds useful information such as context. The DOI number is preferred, but if one is not available use the phrase "Retrieved from" followed by the URL.

Grahn, H., von Schoenberg, P. & Brännström, N. (2015 Mar. 18). Who farted? Hydrogen sulphide transport from Bardarbunga to Scandinavia. *arXiv preprint.* doi: arXiv:1503.05327

7. Magazines

Magazine citations are similar to scholarly journal citations. However, because magazines may be published monthly or weekly, the citation needs to include the specific month or day of publication.

A. An article in a magazine published monthly

Mathews, D. (2014, December/2015, January). It's Austin Mahone's world and we're all just living in It. *TeenVogue*, 53–56.

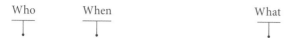

B. An article in a magazine published weekly

Foroohar, R. (2015, February 5). Starbucks for America. *Time, 185*(5), 23–27.

C. An online magazine article

Griswold, A. (2015, March 23). The world's taxi unions may have just convinced the U.N. to stop working with Uber. *Slate*. Retrieved from http://www.slate.com/

8. Newspaper
An article in a newspaper must indicate the page and section number of the newspaper, if they are available.

A. An article in a newspaper

Musetto, V. (1983, April 15). Headless body in topless bar. *New York Post*, p. A1.

B. An article from a newspaper online edition

Rocha, V. (2015, February 9). Arrest made in death of transgender woman after O.C. silicone party. *Los Angeles Times*. Retrieved from http://www.latimes.com/

C. A review of a book or other type of work

If the author and book reviewed are not named in the title of the review, use "Review of" and name the title and author in brackets following the title.

Cisneros, S. (2015, October 18). Sandra Cisneros' 6 favorite restorative books [Review of the book *Teresita*, by W.C. Holden]. *The Week*. Retrieved from http://theweek.com/

King, S. (2013, October 10). Flights of fancy: Donna Tartt's *Goldfinch*. *The New York Times Book Review*, p. 1.

Government-Sponsored or Related Document

9. Government documents
Government documents and government-sponsored documents may list only the government or specific agency as the author. Also, it is possible that the publisher is the same as the author.

A. A printed government document

Presidential Commission on the Space Shuttle Challenger Accident. (1986). *Report to the President.* 5 vols. (US Government Printing Office. 62-885 0). Washington, DC: Government Printing Office.

B. A government document published online

Many government agencies issue reports by the same name periodically. After the title of the work, state the report number or date of issuance in parentheses to help identify which report you are citing.

Office of Naval Intelligence. (2008, April 23). *World wide threat to shipping (WTS) report.* Retrieved from http://msi.nga.mil/MSISiteContent/StaticFiles/MISC/wwtts/wwtts_20080423100000.txt

Office of Naval Intelligence. (2017, February 1). *World wide threat to shipping (WTS) report.* Retrieved from http://msi.nga.mil/MSISiteContent/StaticFiles/MISC/wwtts/wwtts_20170202100000.txt

Interviews

Interviews appear in almost any genre or format and may also be unpublished, as in a phone interview. APA interview citations always begin with the name of the interviewer. If you conducted the interview yourself, cite the interview in the text but do not include an entry in the list of references (see p. 434).

10. Interviews

A. A printed interview

Nancy, J. (1995). "Eating well," or the calculation of the subject. In *Points...: Interviews, 1974–1994* (pp. 255–277). Stanford, CA: Stanford University Press.

B. Interview from an online source

Widmer, T. (2010, summer). R. Crumb, The art of comics no. 1. Interview. *The Paris Review, 193.* Retrieved from http://www.theparisreview.org/

Visuals

11. Map or chart

Maps are commonly part of a book or atlas, such as in example A below. They can also be available as individual sheets. A map citation provides the name of the creator, or cartographer, and the name of the map in the usual sequence. If no name is provided, give the map a title that would make it easy to identify and fits the context in which it was found. In addition, include a brief description of the type of map or chart in brackets following the map title.

A. Print map

Paullin, C. (Cartographer). (1975). Settled area 1760 and population 1750 [Demographic map]. In J. Wright (Ed.), *Atlas of the historical geography of the United States* (p. 60). Westport, CT: Greenwood Press.

B. Downloaded chart

Federal Aviation Administration. (2015). Omaha SEC 92. *Sectional raster aeronautical chart*. Retrieved from http://www.faa.gov/air_traffic/flight_info/aeronav/digital_products/vfr/

12. Image or screenshot

Any screenshot, such as an image from a computer game or instant messaging text discussion, requires the *who*, *what*, *when*, and *where* information. You may need to give the source a descriptive title and in brackets provide a brief description of the format.

Cassius Clay Malcolm X. [Photograph]. (1 Mar. 1964). AP Images. Retrieved from www.apimages.com/metadata/Index/Associated-Press-Domestic-News-New-York-United-/62c2ee253ae5da11af9f0014c2589dfb/15/1. (Originally photographed 1964)

Broadcast, Audio, and Video Sources

13. Television or radio broadcast or podcast

Television and radio broadcasts are similar to a citation for a selection from a book. Begin the citation with the scriptwriter and director as the *who* information, if available. Producers can be listed in the same way as editors.

Abumrad, J. (Producer). (2015, February 24). La Mancha screwjob. *Radio-lab* [Audio podcast]. Retrieved from https://www.wnyc.org/radio/#/ondemand/433231

14. Sound recording
A published sound recording is often the product of a number of creators, such as lead soloist, ensemble, composer, and conductor. Your citation should begin with the name you cite in your argument. List the manner of each artist's contribution in parentheses. Often, the name you discovered during the research that led you to the sound recording should be the same name you use to begin your citation.

A. Recording in physical format

Adler, R. (writer and composer), & Ross, J. (composer and lyricist). (1988). *Damn Yankees: Original Broadway cast recording* [CD]. New York, NY: BMG Music.

B. Recording downloaded

Wilco. (2015). Random name generator. On *Star Wars*. Retrieved from http://wilcoworld.net/splash-star-wars-links/

Online Sources

15. Website
Websites can be a challenge to document simply because there is no standard place to find publication information, as there is on the title and copyright pages of a book, for example. Still, answers to the *who*, *what*, *when*, and *where* questions should be available at the bottom of the home page or on the "About Us" page. If not, you can use the APA abbreviations (see box above, p. 438) to indicate the missing information.

A. A selection from a website

CERN. (2015). First LHC run2 physics results. *Large Hadron Collider beauty experiment*. Retrieved from http://lhcb.web.cern.ch/lhcb/

B. Wiki entry

The APA manual warns against using wikis as authoritative sources. There are many types of wikis, including some built by enthusiasts who are not experts and some that are built by and for experts and scholars to share information. Because wikis are developed collaboratively, authors of entries are rarely cited. Obviously, you should evaluate a wiki in terms of its authority before citing it in an argument.

Mammalian Bites. In *WikEM, The Global Emergency Medicine Wiki.* Retrieved March 20, 2017, from https://www.wikem.org/wiki/Mammalian_bites

C. Social network

Savage, Doug. (2017, February 2). How to Train Your Cat [Facebook posting]. Retrieved from www.savagechickens.com/wp-content/uploads/chickentrainyourcat9.jpg

A tweet is so brief that the entire tweet may be used as the *what* information. Provide the name of the page or the content or caption of the post (up to the first 40 words) as the title. The format is identified as "Tweet" in brackets. When listing the "retrieved from" information, provide a reliable URL address.

Hagel, C. [SecDef]. (2014, July 2). From 1 SecDef to another: Hagel calls @timhowardgk to say thanks for defending USA. We (USA) are proud of @ussoccer! [Tweet]. Retrieved from https://twitter.com/deptofdefense/status/484438026152460288

D. Newsgroup, discussion board, blog

Kiko, J. (2015, September 23). Night light [Blog comment]. Retrieved from http://www.farmgirlfollies.com/2015/07/night-light-20024.html

16. Online video and audio

A. Streamed movie or TV

Movies and television shows may have several creators and contributors. In APA style, you begin your citation with the name of the most immediate creator of the work you are citing. For example, if you are citing an entire series of streamed episodes, you would begin your citation with the name of the producer. If you are citing a specific episode, cite the writer and director first, and then include the name of the producer after the title.

Brooker, C. (Writer), Bathurst, O. (Director). (2011, December 4). National Anthem [Television series episode]. In *Black Mirror.* U.S. Netflix. Retrieved from http://www.netflix.com/title/70264888

B. YouTube video

A YouTube video citation begins with the creator's name, typically the username, followed by the date uploaded, name of the video, and a description of the source in brackets.

Film Theorists. (2017). Harry Potter, More Voldemort Than Voldemort! [YouTube Channel]. Retrieved from www.youtube.com/watch?v=mbC-sDMHypU

C. Podcasts

Abumrad, J. (2017, January 27). Stranger in Paradise [Podcast]. *Radiolab.* Retrieved from http://www.radiolab.org/story/stanger-paradise/

Other Digital Sources

17. PDF

Ramist, L., Lewis, C., & McCamley, L. (1994). Student group differences in predicting college grades: Sex, language, and ethnic groups. *ETS Research Report Series, 1994*(1), pp. 1–41. Retrieved from https://research.collegeboard.org/sites/default/files/publications/2012/7/researchreport-1993-1-student-group-differences-predicting-college-grades.pdf

18. DVD or film

Fellowes, J. (Writer), & Percival, B. (Director). (2012). Christmas at Downton Abbey [Television series episode]. In J. Fellowes & G. Neames (Producers), *Downton Abbey: Season 2* [DVD]. New York, NY: PBS.

Luhrmann, B. (Director). (2013). *The Great Gatsby* [Motion picture]. United States: Warner Bros.

Excerpts from a Student Paper in APA Style

APA style includes formatting expectations for margins, line spacing, and captions. The first page and References page from a paper formatted in APA style are presented below. Hannah Gioia wrote the following paper for her First Year Seminar.

Running Head: LIKENING DOUBLE-TAP DRONE STRIKES 1

If It Looks Like a Duck and Acts Like a Duck, It's a

Duck: Likening Double-Tap Drone Strikes to Terror

Tactics Hannah Gioia

Loyola Marymount University

The header for the entire paper includes the title in capital letters on the left and page number on the right. On the first page, the title is preceded by "Running head" and a colon.

Center, up and down and left and right, the title, your name, and college or university name.

APA suggests Times Roman font at 12 point size.

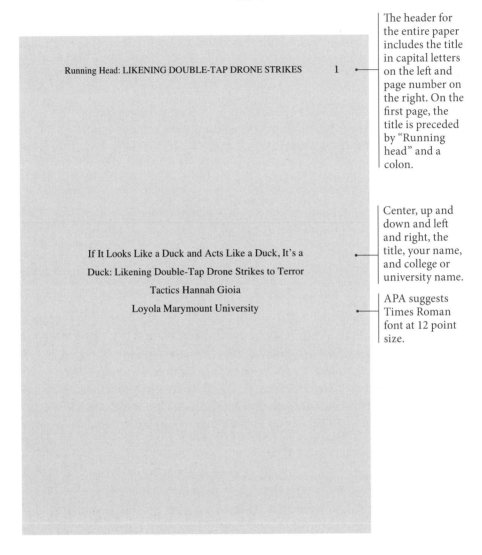

Center the title.

If It Looks Like a Duck and Acts Like a Duck, It's a Duck: Likening Double-Tap Drone Strikes to Terror Tactics

Are U.S. double-tap drone strikes a form of terrorism? The first obvious obstacle to answering this question is the lack of consensus among scholars, states, and international organizations as to what, exactly, terrorism is in a definitional sense. While this paper does not attempt to discern the elusive definition of terrorism, it will adopt common criteria found in many pre-existing, scholarly definitions and test double-tap drone strikes against those sets of standards. The second obstacle to addressing this question is the disagreement among scholars of whether or not "state terrorism" is even a legitimate distinction to make since non-state terrorism is a more accepted field of study.

One inch margins at the top, both sides, and bottom.

The idea that states cannot, themselves, commit acts of terror can be traced back to Max Weber's claim that states enjoy "the monopoly of the legitimate use of physical force within a given territory" (Weber 1965). Countries have a vested interest in maintaining the idea that they enjoy a certain legitimacy, a privilege of power, when it comes to the use of violence, intrastate or interstate. For example, the U.S. Department of State defines terrorism as "politically motivated violence perpetrated against noncombatant targets by subnational groups or clandestine agents, usually intended to influence an audience" (U.S. Code). Noticeably missing is the possibility of a state actor committing an act of terror. They, the states, benefit from distancing their forms of violence from the

The References list always starts a new page.

LIKENING DOUBLE-TAP DRONE STRIKES 14

APA uses the word "References." Other styles use other titles.

References

Alphabetize by the first letter of the first important word of every citation.

Double space page with no extra spacing between entries.

A hanging indent is the opposite of a normal indent. Everything after first line is indented one-half inch or five spaces.

Many professors read the References page first to evaluate depth of research and attention to detail.

Armborst, A. (2010). Modelling terrorism and political violence. *International Relations*, *24*(4), 414–432.

Broomhall, B. (2004). State actors in an international definition of terrorism from a human rights perspective. *Case Western Reserve Journal of International Law*, *36*, 421.

Crenshaw, M. (1987). Theories of terrorism: Instrumental and organizational approaches. *Journal of Strategic Studies*, *10*(4), 13–31.

Friedrichs, J. (2006). Defining the international public enemy: The political struggle behind the legal debate on international terrorism. *Leiden Journal of International Law*, *19*(1), 69.

Ganor, B. (2002). Defining terrorism: Is one man's terrorist another man's freedom fighter? *Police Practice and Research*, *3*(4), 287–304.

Walsh, J. I. (2013). The effectiveness of drone strikes in counterinsurgency and counterterrorism campaigns. Army War College, Carlisle Barracks Pa. Strategic Studies Institute.

Walter, E. V. (1969). *Terror and Resistance*. Oxford, England: Oxford University Press.

Weber, M. (1965). *Politics as a vocation*. Philadelphia, PA: Fortress Press.

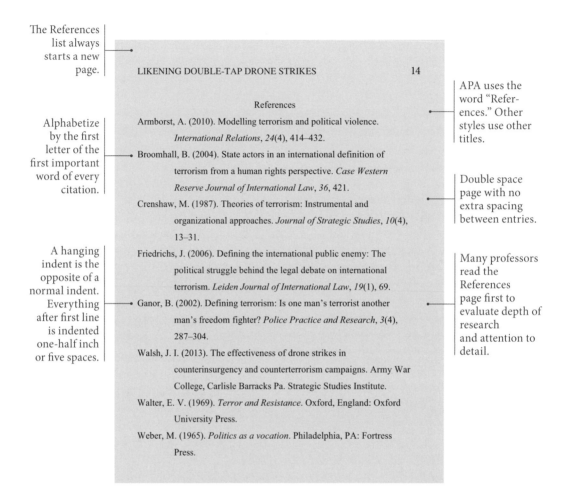

PART V

PROJECTING AUTHORITY

CHAPTER 23

CRAFTING STYLE, VOICE, AND PRESENCE

Few have the presence of Ellen DeGeneres. Her talk show has won 27 Emmys, and her fans see her as fun, honest, authentic, and generous. As a result, International Game Technology developed a line of slot machines based on Ellen and her show. Liam Neeson also has a well-defined media presence. However, it is unlikely you would be drawn to a Liam Neeson slot machine or imagine that such a machine would be generous. After all, a slot machine with *Taken* in lights across the top and a picture of Neeson with a gun suggests a very different experience.

As DeGeneres and Neeson show, it is possible to create and communicate presence—a combination of style and voice—in many different ways. In an academic setting, an authoritative presence or *ethos* leads your audience to believe that what you say is trustworthy and accept your arguments. As you can imagine, the *ethos* that is most appealing to an audience of professors and instructors is that of an honest, well-read, and insightful student who is sensitive to nuance and willing to work for an education. You communicate presence with your style and voice.

Voice, style, and presence are the building blocks of *ethos*. Style makes the flow of ideas understandable and irresistible. A distinctive voice keeps the reader's or listener's attention and makes a writer's or speaker's words, ideas, and arguments memorable. When style and voice work together, for example when you connect the right words with an appropriate tone and tenor, you create a coherent, authoritative presence. A complex argument that is put together thoughtfully has this kind of presence.

And yet, when asked to write with your own style or develop your own voice, you may wonder what this involves. You are not alone in wondering. Even professional writers struggle with establishing their voice, style, and presence because there are so many options to choose from. No list of words or phrases automatically results in a strong voice. No specific sentence structure or way of shaping ideas is always stylistically memorable or inevitably results in an authoritative presence. To develop an authoritative voice, style, and presence, you need to consider the audience for your argument.

MODULE V-1

BUILDING AUTHORITY WITH STYLE

Style is the shape and flow of an argument and is often a reflection of the rhetorical situation. For example, the style of *The New York Times* is very different from the style of the *Nashville Scene* because the messages, audiences, and settings of the two publications are different.

Style can attach the weight of authority to otherwise doubtable statements. It can shape dry information into irresistibly moving appeals, and it can breathe life into stiff genres. For example, if you have ever drafted a Wikipedia entry, you know the list of things to avoid is very strict (see *Wikipedia: Manual of Style*, https://en.wikipedia.org/wiki/Wikipedia:Manual_of_Style). With that in mind, read this introductory paragraph from a Wikipedia article about a British military officer.

> Lieutenant General Sir Adrian Paul Ghislain Carton de Wiart... (5 May 1880–5 June 1963) was a British Army officer and recipient of the Victoria Cross, the highest military decoration awarded for valor "in the face of the enemy" in various Commonwealth countries. He served in the Boer War, First World War, and Second World War; was shot in the face, head, stomach, ankle, leg, hip, and ear; survived two plane crashes; tunneled out of a prisoner-of-war camp; and bit off his own fingers when a doctor refused to amputate them. Describing his experiences in the First World War, he wrote, "Frankly I had enjoyed the war."

If you are like most readers, this paragraph will make you want to read more about this weirdly heroic general. The entry for General Carton de Wiart is compelling because it makes the most of the five elements of style: clarity, word choice or diction, appropriateness, evidence, and sentence structure.

Clarity

Clarity is the experience of reading or hearing a clear, unambiguous, and easy-to-understand expression. For example, read the following paragraph from a "Motor Grader Operator's Handbook" produced by the Montana Association of Country Road Supervisors for people who are planning to take their motor grader exam:

> A windrow of excess material that is left on one or both shoulders can create a dam and cause water to stand on the road. This windrow can also become a traffic hazard and a nuisance for mowers or snow plows. "Curbing" can have the same effect as leaving a windrow of excess material on the shoulder. Curbing is caused by making a deep cut in the shoulders inside the actual shoulder line.

If you were studying for the motor grader exam, you might find the paragraph clear and informative despite its jargon and repetitious sentence structure. If you are not the intended audience, though, you might have found the passage confusing and difficult to read.

Clarity is not simply a matter of using concrete terms and simple sentences, though such terms and sentences can help create the experience of clarity. Because clarity is experienced, the audience determines whether a text has clarity or not. Clarity is the impression that the author is speaking directly to the reader, with ideas flowing easily from the page and the reader understanding exactly what the author means. Readers value clarity and will stop reading if a text is ambiguous or confusing.

To write clearly for an audience, then, you need to know what readers or listeners expect, what they already know, and why they are reading or listening. If your purpose is to tell people what they need to know to pass the road grader certification exam in Montana, you probably don't need to begin by defining a road grader.

Word Choice or Diction

Word choice or **diction** concerns the words and phrases you use to communicate. The words you choose can help your reader understand, or they can act as a barrier between your reader and your ideas. To help your reader, pay attention to word choice and make sure you are aware of jargon, slang, connotations, and abstract words and phrases.

Jargon and Slang. Have you ever wondered why we need so many words for the same thing? For example, "pile," "mound," and "heap" are all useful synonyms. However, none of these accurately describes the long, raised bank of dirt and gravel that a road grader leaves as it levels an undeveloped country road. Road graders need the word "windrow," but few others do.

"Windrow" is an example of **jargon**, a specialized term used by professionals in their work or by people with focused interests and hobbies. When deciding whether to use jargon, consider whether your audience will understand and even expect it. All specialized conversations and academic fields use jargon, and using it correctly can contribute to your authority.

Whereas jargon is specialized language used in formal, professional situations, **slang** is specialized language that occurs in informal, often spoken situations. For example, when expectant parents visit an obstetrician, they will probably hear jargon like "epidural anesthesia." However, expectant parents are unlikely to hear the slang phrase an exhausted obstetrician might use in the doctor's lounge to describe her last shift: I was on duty all night "catching babies."

Properly used, jargon can add to your authority by demonstrating your specialized knowledge and your ability to speak as an authority on a particular subject. However, it can also be off-putting to an audience not familiar with it. The use of slang can diminish your authority with some audiences while establishing a common bond with others.

When deciding whether to use jargon or slang, answer these questions with your audience in mind:

- Does your audience know the word or phrase?
- Do the members of your audience need to know the word or phrase? Will it benefit them?
- Does your audience expect the word or phrase?
- Will you use the word or phrase only once?
- Does the word or phrase refer to a complex idea that would be difficult or awkward to repeat each time you refer to it?
- Will use of the word or phrase annoy your audience?
- Will use of the word or phrase demonstrate your authority?

Connotation

A **connotation** is the implied or commonly understood meaning of a word. A word's connotation differs from its **denotation**, which is the basic, historic, or dictionary definition of a word. Think of connotation as the associated meanings that people link to a word or as a word's baggage.

Used and controlled carefully, connotation can help you drive home a point or add subtleties and nuance to your writing. For example, read these three descriptions of playing in a fantasy sports leagues such as FanDuel:

> *[FanDuel] is like the best adrenaline rush ever*—Arman K.
>
> *After I played FanDuel the first time, I was hooked*—Zack Poff
>
> *Daily fantasy sports, the most addictive thing you can do on your phone other than perhaps cocaine*—John Oliver

The first two quotations come from commercials promoting FanDuel. In that context, "adrenaline rush" and "hooked" connote excitement and fascination. However, when placed next to Oliver's quotation, which compares daily fantasy sports play to cocaine addiction, the words of Arman K. and Zack Poff take on a darker connotation.

Connotations are determined by the audience and context. The more positive connotation of "hooked" (I'm a huge fan) and the darker connotation (I'm addicted) were in your mind before you read Oliver's joke. The words and phrases have not changed, but as the context changes, so too do the connotations.

Concrete and Abstract Terms

Concrete and abstract terms are useful in different situations. Typically, readers prefer concrete words and phrases to abstract ones. However, general rules of thumb do not take into account different situations and different audiences. You should.

In an academic setting, many abstract terms are shorthand for complex, intangible ideas. In psychology, for example, the term "transference" refers to Sigmund Freud's description of the repetition and projection of repressed childhood emotions upon authority figures. When you use words like "transference" accurately, you demonstrate that you know the discipline and can participate in discussions as a psychologist would. In other words, you communicate authority.

You also demonstrate authority when you use abstract terms to help your audience understand your argument. In the excerpt below, for example, author Laurel Braitman blends concrete words, abstract terms, and connotations to introduce her subject and move quickly through complex ideas:

> For almost all of his life, Sigmund Freud wasn't into dogs. Unless they appeared in his patients' dreams where they crouched in trees, bushy-tailed and menacing, or nipped and wriggled as the embodiment of difficult relatives or past sexual trauma.
>
> Then in the mid 1920s, he met Wolf, an Alsatian shepherd with a wide grin and bat-like ears and just like that, dogs went from being Freudian symbols to

> being Freudian friends and officemates. The analyst had purchased Wolf for his daughter Anna sometime around 1925 as protection for her on her evening walks through Vienna. However, Freud fell so in love with the dog that Anna joked to a friend that there was some transference at play—her father had shifted all of his interest in her onto the shepherd.

In the first paragraph, Braitman could have used the abstract psychological phrase "ideogenic object-relation" instead of the concrete phrase "the embodiment of difficult relatives or past sexual trauma." However, readers of *Fast Company*, a popular business magazine in which the article appeared, would probably be baffled or annoyed by it. In a paragraph intended to spark interest, Braitman went for easily understandable, concrete words. However, in the second paragraph, she uses the abstract term "transference," followed by a definition as Anna Freud meant it. In this context, the abstract term works. It is the word Anna Freud used, it is an important concept repeated throughout the article, and its more common connotation, meaning "shifting or moving to," is all that is necessary to understand Freud's relationship to dogs in Braitman's article.

Concrete, specific terms can help your reader follow your reasoning and argument, while vague words like "this," "that," "thing," and "they" force the reader to guess your meaning. On the other hand, the appropriate use of concrete and abstract words can help you and your reader move though complex ideas and arguments efficiently.

Appropriateness

The words, language practices, and attitude you use to communicate are **appropriate** when they are acceptable, effective, and persuasive in the minds of your audience. Traditionally, there are three levels to choose from:

- **Low style or very informal language** ranges from the casual language practices of small groups and specific settings, to slang and nicknames. For example, some twins have their own private words and expressions. Social media like Twitter have their own language practices that would be odd in other settings. And at some worksites you may hear crude language that would provoke stares in more public settings.
- **High style or formal language** ranges from ceremonial language like a presidential oath of office to words and expressions used in solemn public speeches, such as an argument made before the Supreme Court. Formal style can be marked by terms and concepts that sound academic or intellectual, such as the word "perspicacious" used instead of the less formal "insightful."
- **Medium style or common language** is typically heard in public settings such as when a flight attendant gives pre-flight safety instructions or a store clerk

> answers a question. It is the language of common everyday life, which is why it is the language of TV news and newspaper journalists.

Donald Trump's level of formality during his campaign was unlike that of any other candidate and proved to be appropriate for his intended audience, as the opinion polls of the time proved. Trump's style of speaking and his use of terms like "stupid" to describe his opponents and members of the media proved appropriate because he knew his intended audience and wanted to distance himself from candidates who seem too polished and guarded in what they say in public. By the same measure, many people found his casual style off-putting. However, it is safe to assume that Trump wasn't talking to people who were turned off by his style of speaking.

A style is appropriate if your audience finds it authoritative and persuasive. Sounding too formal when your audience expects a casual style is as inappropriate as using an informal style while officiating at a wedding where the guests are wearing gowns and tuxes.

Evidence

When we think of **evidence** stylistically, we are talking about how evidence is presented to and understood by the audience. Evidence such as facts or expert testimony rarely speaks for itself. You first must persuade your audience to read and consider the evidence by making it interesting and showing its relevance. Usually a number of isolated facts can say and prove much more if they are organized and contextualized well.

A simple fact can be presented in many different ways. As an example, consider the following description:

> The subject served with distinction as an officer and describes his military experience in positive terms. Combat injuries include wounds to the ear, hip, leg, ankle, stomach, head, face, and the amputation of two fingers. The subject was also held as a prisoner of war.

This excerpt presents the same facts as the Wikipedia entry about General Carton de Wiart. However, unless you were the general's physician, you probably would not care if the information were true or not.

The author of the Wikipedia bio doesn't simply list the general's injuries or achievements chronologically. Rather, the facts are carefully organized, moving from noteworthy, to impressive, to astonishing. Then the author contextualizes all the facts with the general's own surprising words, which show that in spite of all his hardships he maintained a proper, British, stiff-upper-lip attitude. A list of injuries simply proves that the general was injured, but his Wikipedia bio shows him to be a serious snake eater, militarily speaking, with a never-say-die attitude.

Attention to *ethos* can also help you shape the persuasive power of your evidence and reasoning. Recall that *ethos* is the way in which an author or a speaker moves the audience to believe that the source of the message is trustworthy and authoritative.

For example, in the public service poster produced by the federal Office of Human Rights (see Figure 23.1), the speaker appears to be just another person you might meet on the street. His statement, "I'm a transgender man and I'm part of DC" and his request to be treated with courtesy are hard to dispute or disregard because his reasonable character, and by extension his average guy *ethos*, has already been established by his appearance.

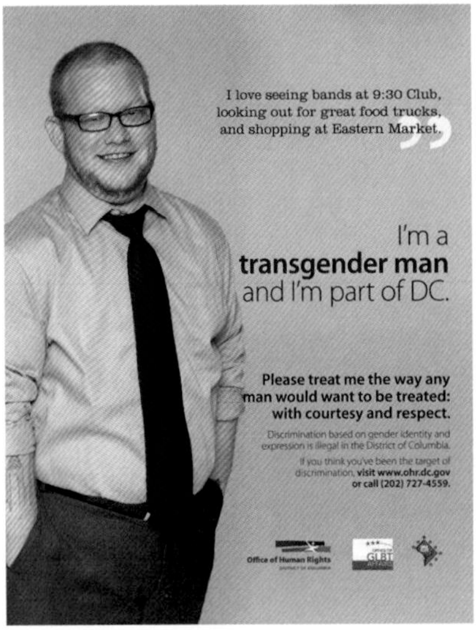

Figure 23.1
A poster from the Office of Human Rights.

Sentence Structure

If style is the shape and flow of an argument, sentences are the structures that create shape and the experience of flow. Consider this list of reasons for setting a goal of walking on the moon, which someone may have compiled in the early 1960s:

Reasons to Go to the Moon

- It is a hazardous challenge only the best can face.
- Facing challenges may lead to international cooperation.
- The effort will test our energies and skills.
- We like a good challenge.
- We want to win, now.

A list such as this one can be recast as a paragraph, but to do so you need to construct sentences that provoke and maintain the audience's interest. Look at how President John F. Kennedy shaped the same simple points into his famous "Moon Speech," delivered in 1962 as he tried to persuade the American public to support a moon shot.

> There is no strife, no prejudice, no national conflict in outer space as yet. Its hazards are hostile to us all. Its conquest deserves the best of all mankind, and its opportunity for peaceful cooperation may never come again. But why, some say, the moon? Why choose this as our goal? And they may well ask why climb the highest mountain? Why, 35 years ago, fly the Atlantic? Why does Rice play Texas?
>
> We choose to go to the moon. We choose to go to the moon in this decade and do the other things, not because they are easy, but because they are hard, because that goal will serve to organize and measure the best of our energies and skills, because that challenge is one that we are willing to accept, one we are unwilling to postpone, and one which we intend to win, and the others, too.

Why a shout out to Rice football? Because he was at Rice University in Texas

In these two brief paragraphs, Kennedy uses short, long, and medium-length sentences, parallel sentences, and rhetorical questions to fire up his audience. As the Kennedy quotation shows, sentences are not simply boxes into which you put information. How a sentence is structured, the relationship between the verb and the subject and any modifiers, turns raw data and isolated facts into compelling questions, provocative ideas, and persuasive appeals.

Types of Sentences

You can use several sentence structures to make your argument provocative and persuasive.

Simple sentences are composed of a noun and verb and may include a modifier. Modifiers can be adjectives that modify or change the meaning of the noun, or they can be adverbs that modify the meaning of the verb or other elements. Or you could say that a simple sentence is composed of only one **independent clause**, a clause whose full meaning does not depend upon any other sentence. For example:

> We choose to go to the moon.

Compound sentences may be composed by combining two simple sentences, or independent clauses, with a conjunction such as "and" or "but":

> I'm a transgender man and I'm part of DC.

Complex sentences are made of an independent clause and at least one **dependent clause**, which is a group of words with a subject and verb that cannot stand alone as a sentence:

> After I played FanDuel the first time, I was hooked.

In the sentence above, the dependent clause beginning with the conjunction "after" cannot be a sentence, but the independent clause "I was hooked" can stand alone as a sentence. The introductory words add information that shapes the meaning of the independent clause that follows the comma.

Compound-complex sentences are composed of at least two independent clauses and at least one dependent clause:

> Though NASA was first, budget cuts have crippled our nation's exploration of the moon and Mars, and yet private space flight and exploration are now a real possibility.

Broken down to its most basic structure, this compound-complex sentence could have been written as three shorter sentences:

> NASA was the first to travel to and explore the moon. Budget cuts have crippled our nation's exploration of the moon and Mars. Private space flight and exploration of the moon and Mars are now a real possibility.

The declarative sentences above are clear, but they do not flow (Chapter 24 has more about flow) and are repetitive. Complicated ideas often require a mixture of simple, compound, complex, and compound-complex sentences.

- **Sentence Length**. All four sentence types can be seen in short, medium-length, or long sentences. Using different sentence types and varying sentence length can add different qualities to your writing.
- **Short sentences** can add punch or speed up the pace of your argument. Used to state a fact or declare a position, short sentences suggest clarity of vision, thinking, or purpose. "We choose to go to the moon," for example, is definite, with no qualifications. Short sentences also move the reader along more quickly than longer sentences. Short sentences emphasize a single idea, which is why they rarely work as transitional sentences linking two ideas or paragraphs. For that kind of work, you need a longer sentence.
- **Medium-length sentences** do the heavy lifting in paragraphs and are the most common sentences in written arguments. In fact, medium-length sentences are the measure of shorter or longer sentences and serve as a text's metronome

or pacesetter. For example, if the average sentence in an essay has 22 words, then 22 is the length of a medium-length sentence in that text. A reader of such a text would experience longer sentences as slowing the pace and sentences of 18 words or less as quickening the pace. If, on the other hand, you are reading Hemingway's *Old Man and the Sea*, with an average of 14 words per sentence, then a 20-word sentence would seem to slow the pace of reading.

- **Long sentences** are used to develop, link, and modify ideas. Sentences that define, as an example, are often long because defining is a multi-step process. In the same way that paragraphs that state, develop, and modify a single idea can be long, a sentence that shapes, develops, and modifies a subject will be longer than one that states a fact.

Sentence Variety

Your reader will assume you are using different sentence types and lengths for a reason. For example, you would use longer sentences to explain a detailed accounting process or analyze an intricate weather pattern. Therefore, think of different types of sentences as tools or apps to be used for specific reasons.

Varying sentence length adds variety to your paragraphs. You need to vary sentence length for three reasons:

1. Working with ideas, introducing them, developing them, and comparing or contrasting them with other ideas requires many different types of sentences.
2. Readers find paragraphs composed of a single type of sentence monotonous and dull.
3. The pace or reading speed communicates meaning. Short quick statements can express certainty, and longer sentences can demonstrate careful analysis and critical skill.

Varying sentence openings and first words of paragraphs is another technique. When brainstorming or inventing, you might write a number of sentences that begin with the same word. When developing an idea in the body of an argument, you might start each paragraph in the same way. Repeating openings is not a problem when drafting, but revising to address both problems will prevent readers from perceiving your argument as mechanical or rigid.

Sometimes repetition can be effective, however. For example, **parallel constructions** link different words, phrases, or ideas using the same structure. In the sentence below from Kennedy's speech, the absence of strife, prejudice, and national conflict is reflected in parallel phrases:

> There is no strife, no prejudice, no national conflict in outer space as yet.

Making "no strife," "no prejudice," and "no national conflict" part of a parallel construction not only links them to the condition of space at the time but also makes all three issues equal in importance. Use parallel structures to emphasize the similarities between things and ideas, to link different things and ideas, and to emphasize relationships.

MODULE V-2

BUILDING AUTHORITY WITH VOICE

If style reflects your analysis of the rhetorical situation and audience expectations, voice reflects your individual perspective. We express our emotions, attitudes, moods, and even ideas through the sound of our voice. When you write, you can think of your **voice** as the sound that arises from the page in the mind of your reader. How, you may be asking, does a distinctive voice arise from a silent page?

Think about it this way. In an academic context and beyond, most of your readers do not know you and may never meet you. As a result, everything your reader learns about you—your reasoning, perspective, temperament, disposition, ideas, and views—is communicated through your writing.

Many types of writing intentionally hide the personality and perspective of the author, with **passive sentences** in which the subject does not perform the action, and **objective, impersonal language** where the ideas on the page are cast as separate from the author. In academic settings, such as in the sciences, you will be asked to write with an objective voice. However, in such cases the voice that arises from the page and communicates your ideas is still under your control. You determine if you want to sound like an objective scientist with professional disinterest, a passionate art history scholar tracing a surprising theme in two very different paintings, or a quirky fan of history.

For example, imagine you asked 10 writers to draft a paragraph about Abraham Lincoln's Gettysburg Address. Although each paragraph would be different, many of them would stick to the facts about the circumstances of the address or go in a different direction and evoke the great speech with soaring imagery and profound statements. However, the following paragraph by Sarah Vowell would stand out from the others:

> The Gettysburg Address is more than a eulogy. It's a soybean, a versatile little problem solver that can be processed into seemingly infinite, ingenious products. In this speech, besides cleaning up the founding fathers' slavery mess by calling for a "new birth of freedom," Lincoln comforted grieving mothers

> who would never bounce grandchildren on their knees and ran for reelection at the same time.

It is unlikely that you have ever heard America's greatest speech compared to a soybean. You may also have been surprised to learn that the Gettysburg Address served so many different purposes at the time it was delivered. The facts Vowell relays are not new, but her voice sets her paragraph apart.

As a writer, you have as many ways of shaping and controlling your voice as an actor or even a singer does. Here we will focus on three elements of voice: tone and tenor, vivid words and figurative language, and the distinctive qualities that emerge from who you are.

Tone and Tenor

Writers use **tone** and **tenor to** link their emotions with their ideas and express their attitude.

> **tone**—your attitude toward your subject
> **tenor**—your attitude toward your audience

Let's look at the tone and tenor of an exchange between two people attempting to be persuasive about a serious issue.

After the police shootings of unarmed Cleveland residents Tamir Rice and John Crawford III in 2014, during a pre-game warm-up Andrew Hawkins of the Cleveland Browns wore a T-shirt calling for justice. After the game, Jeffrey Follmer, the president of the Cleveland Police Patrolmen's Association, demanded an apology.

> It's pretty pathetic when athletes think they know the law. They should stick to what they know best on the field. The Cleveland Police protect and serve the Browns stadium and the Browns organization owes us an apology.

The following Monday after practice, surrounded by journalists in his locker-room, Hawkins responded to Follmer's demand:

> I was taught that justice is a right that every American should have. Also justice should be the goal of every American. I think that's what makes this country. To me, justice means the innocent should be found innocent. It means that those who do wrong should get their due punishment. Ultimately, it means fair treatment. So a call for justice shouldn't offend or disrespect anybody. A call for justice shouldn't warrant an apology.

Follmer's words expressed contempt for Hawkins's protest, and his tone came across as aggressive and angry. The question then is whether Follmer's tone and tenor suited his audience and added persuasive power.

Hawkins, on the other hand, addressed Follmer's words with a calm, measured tone that indicated he had carefully considered the protest his shirt represented and that he had thought long and hard about the concept of justice for the families of those killed and for everyone. Hawkins's tenor also demonstrates a concern for his audience. He does not disregard those who question why he wore the shirt but tries to address the questions that those who disagree with him might have. As a result, his tenor draws the audience in closer with the intention of helping his listeners understand his decision to wear the shirt.

Those who routinely speak in public forums constantly need to consider their tone and tenor.

In an academic setting, you also need to control and shape your tone and tenor. For example, if a chemistry assignment includes instructions on how to write a lab report, but you don't follow them carefully when writing your own report, you may give your professor the impression that you don't care. If your research paper includes language that you and your friends use when texting, you may unintentionally suggest you don't really value the more formal conversation with a professor that a research paper requires. You will no doubt be given assignments and subjects you don't really care about. By actively shaping and controlling your tone and tenor, you can prevent these attitudes from creeping into your writing.

Learning the appropriate academic tone and tenor to use will help you share your distinctive insights and ideas in an authoritative manner. A course syllabus will give you important information about the tone and tenor you will be expected to use. Textbooks, class handouts, and class discussion also provide clues, as does the way in which the professor talks.

Vivid Words and Figurative Language

Effective writers use vivid words and figurative language to give their ideas impact and make their voice memorable. Unfortunately, there is no master list of **vivid words** or words that are automatically read as clear, precise, provocative, and ripe with meaning. However, we can say that a vivid word provokes a specific image or a significant emotion. At first glance, this line from T.S. Eliot's "The Love Song of J. Alfred Prufrock" may not seem too vivid:

> When the evening is spread out against the sky

Then again, give it a shot: try to express the same perspective, sense of smallness, and grandeur as twilight sweeps across the horizon, with fewer or more precise words.

Vivid expressions and figurative language are not simply composed of fancy words or high style. In fact, you use figurative language every day. **Figurative language** is the use of images, turns of phrase, and relationships between words and ideas to say more or say something different from the literal meaning of the words that make up the figure. Five figures that are useful in academic settings and beyond are metaphors, similes, analogies, irony, and rhetorical questions.

Metaphors at their heart are comparisons that reveal a more profound truth or insight than is possible when just considering the subject by itself. A metaphor is a figure of speech where two subjects that are not actually similar are compared, with one being described as the other. For example, when Sarah Vowell says that the Gettysburg address "is more than a eulogy. It's a soybean," she isn't being flippant but is instead setting readers up for a reconsideration of Lincoln's speech.

Similes compare something to a similar thing, idea, or event to make a description or an analysis of the subject memorable and to create a new understanding. A simile typically uses the words "like" or "as" to show that two things, ideas, or events have common qualities. For example, when astrophysicist Neil DeGrasse Tyson was asked if someone would be torn into little pieces if they fell into a black hole, Tyson responded,

> It's worse than that because the very fabric of space... in the vicinity of a black hole is like a funnel and so in fact as you fall toward a black hole, you're being funneled through the fabric of space. So you're not only being stretched, you're being extruded like toothpaste through a tube.

Similes have great explanatory power, which is why they are often found in academic writing.

Analogy links two subjects to make a statement about a relationship or shared qualities and characteristics. Whereas a metaphor or a simile is suggestive, an analogy is a logical claim of a relationship or a claim of significant commonalities between two things, ideas, or events. Kennedy used an analogy in his moon speech when he described the role that Houston, Texas, would play in space exploration.

> What was once the furthest outpost on the old frontier of the West will be the furthest outpost on the new frontier of science and space.

Analogies are common in academic debates and beyond, in part because they rely upon accurate analysis and logical links.

Irony is used when authors mean something very different, and sometimes the opposite, of what the words they use literally mean. Importantly, irony only works if the audience understands the ironic intent of the words. Irony can be used to highlight a specific idea, and it can also be used to show the absurdity or ignorance of common thinking and expressions. *The Onion* headline "Housing Prices Spike as Tech Employee Takes Stroll Through Neighborhood" makes the reader stop and think about fears of gentrification, or the renewal of older communities by newly arrived rich people.

Your professor may use irony in class. However, irony is rare in academic genres and should be avoided as your ironic intentions may not be recognized.

Rhetorical questions are posed by an author or a speaker who does not expect the audience to answer aloud. However, if an obvious response does not immediately leap to the audience's mind, the question isn't really a rhetorical question. When Ellen DeGeneres, in discussing the many benefits of her slot machines, asked, "I mean, honestly, what more do you want from me?," her intent was not to provoke a reply. But the response that should have jumped to mind is something like "we could not ask for more." Rhetorical questions can be annoying if they are used too often or are too obvious. They can be useful in academic presentations and speeches, but they are uncommon in written academic arguments.

Vivid words and figurative language are persuasive only if your audience can understand your intended meaning. For example, an ironic statement that misses the mark may in fact say exactly the opposite of what you intend. A turn of phrase or an analogy may work in your head, but if it does not persuade a skeptical audience, it does not work in your argument.

Your Distinctive Qualities

A voice with **distinctive qualities** rises above the average and the noise. When a speaker or writer has distinctive qualities, you recognize the individual behind the words. You can see that someone with a specific perspective and individual life experiences is sharing ideas that could come only from that person's mind. Read the following brief article from the *Los Angeles Times* and imagine the person behind the words:

> *Earthquake aftershock: 2.7 quake strikes near Westwood*
> A shallow magnitude 2.7 earthquake aftershock was reported Monday morning four miles from Westwood, according to the U.S. Geological Survey. The temblor occurred at 7:23 a.m. Pacific time at a depth of 4.3 miles. A magnitude 4.4 earthquake was reported at 6.25 a.m. and was felt over a large swath of Southern California. According to the USGS, the epicenter of the aftershock was five miles from Beverly Hills, six miles from Santa Monica and six miles from West Hollywood. In the last 10 days, there has been one earthquake of magnitude 3.0 or greater centered nearby.

If you think it sounds as if anyone and no one is behind these words, you are right. An algorithm generated this article. A newspaper can employ an algorithm in this situation because the genre expectations for weather forecasts and initial earthquake reports are very simple—just the facts, please. More nuanced stories require a human perspective. Consider John McPhee's description of the 1989 Loma Prieta earthquake that devastated San Francisco:

> The Interstate 80 tunnel through Yerba Buena Island moves like a slightly writhing hose. Linda Lamb, in a sailboat below the Bay Bridge, feels as though something had grabbed her keel. Cars on the bridge are sliding. The entire superstructure is moving, first to the west about a foot, and then back east, bending the steel, sending large concentric ripples out from the towers, and shearing through bolts thicker than cucumbers. This is the moment in which a five-hundred-ton road section at one tower comes loose and hinges downward, causing one fatality, and breaking open the lower deck, so that space gapes to the bay.

Though the paragraph recounts facts, clearly a person selected the vivid words, chose the testimonials, constructed the similes, and arranged the evidence. You can argue with McPhee's perspective because there *is* one. Impressive feats of engineering and construction, and the normalcy they bring to everyday life, can be quickly disassembled by natural forces. On the other hand, it is hard to critique the perspective of the *Times* earthquake story, because the algorithm is built to play it safe by sticking to the genre form and the facts.

In an academic context, your first instinct will be to play it safe by doing exactly what you think your instructor expects and avoiding perspectives or ideas that could be criticized. Such choices will probably result in "safe" grades. Allowing your distinctive perspective and individual ideas into your arguments may not be as safe a strategy, but it will catch your reader's attention. Notice how after pages of reading you can connect the elements of the two lists in Figure 23.2 because the authors' distinctive qualities create memorable, individual ideas.

Match the parts to form a complete, distinctive idea.

The Gettysburg address	No apology needed
Ellen's presence	Like a soybean
A call for justice	Generous and authentic

Figure 23.2 Connecting the subjects on the left to the way they are described on the right is easy because distinct perspectives and figurative language make these ideas memorable.

In fact, if your research paper is going to be one in a stack of 25 or more, you'll want your voice to leap off the page and your perspective and ideas to be remembered by your professor. You do not want your paper to read as if an algorithm wrote it. Furthermore, you don't have to fake an authoritative voice, as the Conventions in Context box entitled "Do You Want Me to Fake My Voice and Who I Am?" explains.

Conventions in Context
Do You Want Me to Fake My Voice and Who I Am?

Code switching is the ability to shift between different languages, ways of speaking, and sets of terminology when the need arises. For example, you switch codes when you change from speaking Spanish to English, from the somber tenor of a funeral service to the more playful tone of a conversation with friends at a party, or from the specialized terminology of a materials science lab to Pittsburghese at a football game.

When it comes to your style and how to present yourself, you have a range of voices and unlimited opportunities to be creative. You make such adjustments every day because you know who you are, why you are talking, and to whom you are talking. In other words, you are aware of and can adapt to the rhetorical situation.

Transferring that same code-switching ability to an academic setting is easier than you might think. Admittedly, moving from how your 10:00 am logic professor speaks to the terminology your 12:00 pm materials science professor expects you to use can seem overwhelming. Just remember: moving between these groups is about adjusting your voice (diction, tone and tenor, and distinctive qualities) to your audience. By the time you graduate you will be a master of code switching.

MODULE V-3

BUILDING AUTHORITATIVE PRESENCE

When a judge or magistrate steps into the courtroom or a member of the highway patrol or mounted police walks up to your car window, the mood changes. Even without the uniform, some individuals naturally seem to command attention. In fact it is not natural. Police and military academies teach command presence. For the officer, commanding presence is a combination of posture, movement, and eye contact. For a judge it is tone, procedural knowledge, and eye contact. You may not be required to control a chaotic situation with just your voice and posture. However, as a speaker or writer your presence can draw attention, make others focus on your expressions, and give your audience confidence in your knowledge and words. Consider the alternative. Why do you sometimes turn away from a speaker or scroll past an article or essay you just started?

Presence is a combination of style and voice: the contemporary version of *ethos*. Presence is how the reader or viewer imagines you, your personality, and your authority. As they read your argument or hear you speak, do they think of you as a trustworthy, thoughtful person, someone parroting known information, or merely a spouting know-it-all with little understanding?

A coherent presence that connects the elements of voice and style is powerful. The power of his coherent, authoritative presence is why Morgan Freeman plays such roles as a high-school principal, Batman's right-hand man, a chief justice, Nelson Mandela, the President, and God.

Just as Freeman builds a presence from a screenwriter's words, choices about tone and tenor, and how he speaks, you can use the strategies and devices described in this chapter to put forward an authoritative presence in an academic setting. If you can coherently connect the voice and style commonly used by the experts and scholars in a discipline and the content of the course with your own distinctive perspective and ideas, your professor will perceive the presence of a student who is building authority in the discipline.

Remember: you have a great deal of control over how your audience thinks about you and your ideas. It would be nice if this chapter could give you a list of 10 things to do to establish an authoritative presence. However, it is not that simple, and either your authority and your presence—like your persuasiveness—are experienced in the mind of your audience or they are not.

CHAPTER 24

CHECKING FOR LOGICAL FALLACIES AND FLOW

MODULE V-4 LOGICAL FALLACIES DEFINED
MODULE V-5 AWKWARDNESS AND FLOW DEFINED

Search for a list of things everyone does but nobody admits and you are likely to discover a number of private, icky, and surprising—or perhaps not so surprising—acts. For example, some freak out if a friend doesn't text back quickly, some eat an entire bag of chips in one sitting, and some snoop in other people's medicine cabinets.

People are unlikely to admit that they do any of these things, even when they are caught, because they do not want to be known as rude, ill mannered, or inconsiderate. And yet people freak out, binge, and snoop because they are stuck in their own heads and not thinking about how others will understand their actions.

The same is true of logical fallacies, paragraphs that do not flow, and awkward sentences. Although people believe they have reasons for using logical fallacies and almost everyone uses awkward constructions, an audience will see such reasoning and writing as unthoughtful, undisciplined, and untrue.

Once you learn to recognize logical fallacies, you will find them everywhere. Advertisers, your parents, the media, your boss, politicians, and your friends—in short, everyone—uses logically fallacious thinking. You might ask, then, if fallacies are so common, why are they so bad? In fact, why shouldn't I use them since they seem to get the job done?

Yes, everyone uses fallacies, but when we catch others using them we tend to judge them harshly, with good reason. Using logical fallacies is like snooping in other people's medicine cabinets: eventually you will get busted, and it will lead people to question your integrity.

Although awkward sentences and a lack of flow are not usually intentional, they can be as off-putting as logical fallacies and lead your audience to question your reasoning ability. And all these things have the same cause: a failure to consider how your audience will read and evaluate your argument.

The following modules will help you understand and identify logical fallacies so you can find and fix them. They will also help you think about flow as an audience's experience of an authoritative voice.

MODULE V-4

LOGICAL FALLACIES DEFINED

A **logical fallacy** is an error or breakdown in an argument's reasoning. One way to classify logical fallacies is by the type of logic that breaks down:

- A **formal fallacy** is a breakdown in the structure and reasoning of a deductive argument. (Chapter 17 describes the structure of deductive arguments.)
- An **informal fallacy**, on the other hand, is caused by a breakdown in the meaning, language, and expression of an inductive argument.

Because inductive arguments do not depend upon a rigid form, they can fail, mislead, confuse, or deceive in many different ways. The logical fallacies that follow are all informal fallacies.

Misleading Readers: Fallacies of Relevance

When an argument wanders away from its original subject, it leads the audience away from the central claim or to a conclusion that is not supported by the evidence. Fallacies of relevance can happen when writers are careless or make mistakes of scope and focus. They can also be intentional. Here is a list of the most common fallacies of relevance.

1. Appeal to false authority

You would be lucky to get acting advice from a star like Gwyneth Paltrow. However, she is not an authority on menopause or vitamin and supplement protocols such as the "Goop Wellness Madame Ovary" that her company Goop sells and she promotes as providing "support for thyroid health as well as things like mild hot flashes, mood shifts, and stress-related fatigue." Audiences fall for the **appeal to false authority** fallacy if they are distracted by the fame or impressive-sounding title of the person being cited. If someone claims that an authority or expert supports his or her argument, check the expert's credentials and note whether he or she actually is a recognized expert on the subject of the argument.

Figure 24.1
Gwyneth Paltrow is the founder and CEO of Goop, a lifestyle company.

2. Appeal to ignorance

An **appeal to ignorance** states that a position must be correct because no one has proven it wrong. Someone who uses this fallacy distracts the audience by pointing out a lack of contrary evidence. For example, if someone were to argue that the bright spots on the dwarf planet Ceres, discovered by the Dawn spacecraft in 2015, are probably examples of alien technology because no one has proven otherwise, the argument would be a fallacy. A lack of contrary evidence does not mean that aliens are on Ceres or predict what evidence yet to be discovered will prove. Audiences that accept the true vs. false thinking do not consider other possible explanations that may be discovered in the future.

3. Appeal to fear

A person whose argument tries to make you afraid of the people holding opposing views, or tries to prejudice you against an alternative position by making you fear what will happen if you do not agree with a claim, is using an **appeal to fear**. For example, people wanting to gain your support for blocking the arrival of immigrants from a specific part of the world might say that if we let those immigrants in there will be terrorist attacks in America, just like those in Europe. Terrorism is a serious concern, but stoking fears of violence and then linking that fear to an entire group is simply unjust and irrational. An audience persuaded by fear is convinced only as long as the fear remains, because real conviction comes from critical thinking, reasoning, and evidence.

4. Appeal to tradition

A person who ignores your proposal for change by saying we have always done it this way is using an **appeal to tradition**, diverting attention from the merits of your proposal to look instead at the past or at a tradition. For example, when grandpa says, it is tradition that the eldest son takes over the family business, he is not considering the talents and preferences of the eldest son or of others in the family. What was or has been may have merits. However, simply pointing to tradition is not an argument based on the merits of tradition, nor is it a rational evaluation of an alternative way of doing things.

5. Bandwagon fallacy

The pressure of **groupthink**, the tendency of people to agree with other members of their group, makes the **bandwagon fallacy** difficult to recognize and hard to resist, especially if the group consists of your friends or a crowd you want to be a part of. For example, if your friends say everyone will think you're lame if you don't do shots with us, they are not making a claim for the benefits of shots. They are simply applying pressure. Audience members fall for this fallacy if they base the truth or value of an argument on the number of people who accept it or on a fear of being left out (Figure 24.2).

Figure 24.2 The bandwagon fallacy.

6. Personal attack or *ad hominem*

If someone disagrees with your argument by calling you names, criticizing your appearance, or attacking other personal qualities, that person is leading you and the audience away from the subject—your argument—by using an ***ad hominem* fallacy**. For example, when someone running for office says that his opponent isn't ready to lead because, after all, he has had only one job his entire life, and that's as a farmer, the speaker is distracting the audience from important issues such as the candidate's qualifications and policies. If you or an audience responds to such an attack by denying the insults, being defensive, or hollering names back, you have fallen for this fallacy.

7. Faulty analogy

An **analogy** links two subjects to make a statement about a common relationship or shared qualities and characteristics. For example, comparing how the brain stores information to how a computer stores data can be helpful. However, a **faulty analogy** draws attention away from the subject of an argument to a thing, idea, or event that is not comparable. For example, the claim that a brain retains memory the way a sponge holds water is a faulty analogy: water is a substance held in a sponge's cells by surface tension, while a memory is information encoded as electrical impulses and stored in the mind's neural net. An audience is distracted by a faulty analogy when they accept the mischaracterization of a thing, idea, or event.

Confusing Readers: Fallacies of Ambiguity

A vague, poorly worded, or disorganized argument can lead the audience to accept conclusions that have not been proven or supported by the evidence. Fallacies of ambiguity may be intentional, but they are more often caused by a failure to consider how the audience will understand the words, sentences, and organization of an argument. Though such mistakes often merely confuse readers or listeners, the following fallacies can also lead to false conclusions.

8. Equivocation fallacy

Words are slippery because most of them have multiple meanings. Speakers use the **equivocation fallacy** when they use two different meanings of a word in their argument. For example, the following is an equivocation fallacy: "Yes, a liberal arts college is an option, but I want my daughter to see both sides of politics and not just learn liberal ideas." "Liberal" in the phrase "liberal arts" means a broad range of subjects suited to a free society. However, the author shifts the meaning of the word "liberal" to mean a political ideology in opposition to conservative ideas. An audience that does not notice the shift in meaning or accepts it is duped by an equivocation fallacy.

9. Straw man

A person who falsely claims that you hold a dubious position on an issue and then easily disproves the position is using a **straw man fallacy** to confuse the audience. In the following example, the straw man appears when the author summarizes the opposing argument: "My opponent says he wants to give illegal immigrants, who are all lawbreakers, a path to citizenship. In essence, he wants to let criminals go free and only enforce the laws he likes. But we don't have a choice. We can't let criminals walk free." The claim that serious crimes should be prosecuted is an easy debate to win, which is why this argument is set up as a straw man so that it can be easily knocked down. The actual immigration debate is far more complex, however. Just as it is easier to knock down a straw-filled scarecrow than a real person, an audience that falls for this fallacy mistakes the weak argument for the opposition's real argument.

Deceiving Readers: Fallacies of Presumption

A **presumption** is a belief that is not supported by evidence. If a presumption informs or is part of an argument yet remains unseen or unstated, it can result in a deceptive conclusion that appears true but has no real support in reason or evidence.

10. Begging the question/circular reasoning

Begging the question begins where it ends. The **begging the question fallacy** assumes the conclusion is true and uses the conclusion as evidence to support the argument. In a valid argument, reasoning links claims that are supported by evidence to a logical conclusion (Figure 24.3).

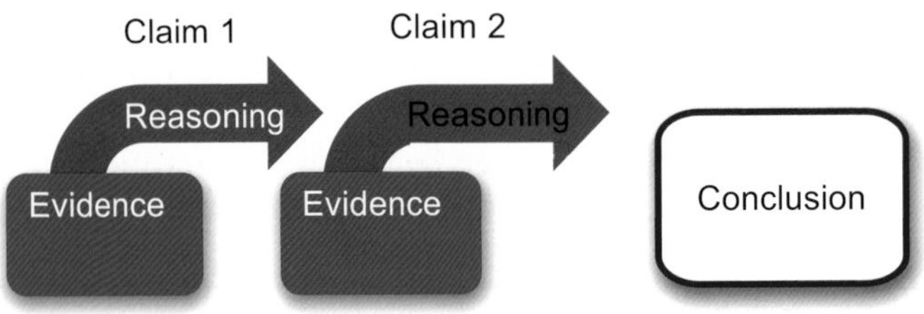

Figure 24.3 The structure of a valid argument.

In an argument that begs the question, however, the conclusion circles back to replace evidence or a claim, leading to a circular argument (Figure 24.4).

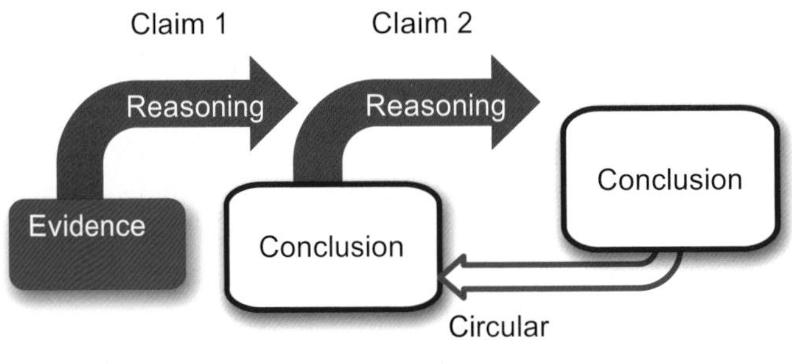

Figure 24.4 The structure of an argument that begs the question.

An argument that begs the question sounds like this: "Candidate X was a great governor and is the best presidential candidate because all the other candidates are inferior." An audience may not recognize circular reasoning if the conclusion is rephrased when it is used as evidence, as in the example above.

11. False dilemma/either-or fallacy

In a debate, if your opponent tries to force you to choose between only two options, she has placed you in a **false dilemma**, sometimes called the **either-or fallacy**. For example, the argument that either we send all the illegal immigrants back or we grant them all amnesty reduces a complex issue with many possible responses to an either-or decision. The deception here is that there are actually more than two responses to the issue of illegal immigration. If audience members resist this fallacy by failing to choose between the two options, they can be portrayed as avoiding the problem or being indecisive.

12. Hasty generalization fallacy

Suppose a friend mentioned to you that Nebraskans always wear red, claiming she knows this because she walked down O Street on Saturday and every person she saw was wearing something red. It is true that red is a popular color in Nebraska, but a different sample of Nebraskans on a different day would prove that the closets in Nebraska hold a rainbow of colors. Audiences fall for the **hasty generalization fallacy** when they are directed away from considering additional observations, or accept a small sample size (Nebraskans on O Street in Lincoln on football Saturday) as large enough—and representative enough—to make a more general statement.

13. *Post hoc ergo propter hoc* fallacy

It's often tempting to conclude that one event caused another because the first event immediately preceded the second one. This reasoning—known as *post hoc, ergo propter hoc* or "after this, therefore, because of this"—is a fallacy. Closeness in time, or correlation, does not by itself prove that a cause-effect relationship exists between the two events. For example, imagine you said the following to your sister: "It seems that since you started cheering for the Crunch, they haven't won a soccer game. Before you became a fan, they were in the running for the MLS championship. Clearly, you are bad luck." Your belief that your sister caused the slump is fallacious. You can watch out for this fallacy in your own arguments or those of others by considering other possible causes or simply by refusing to accept a causal claim without evidence.

14. Slippery slope/camel's nose fallacy

A **slippery slope fallacy**, also called a **camel's nose fallacy**, suggests that one thing will inevitably lead to another. For example, if you slip on a slope, you will slide all the way to the bottom. Or if you let a camel stick its nose inside your tent, soon the whole animal will be sitting inside. Or a professor may say that if she allows you to hand in your paper late, soon everyone in class will be late with their papers. People who use this fallacy are trying to persuade you to accept a chain of events leading to an undesirable consequence, without offering evidence that these events will actually happen. Valid cause-effect arguments provide evidence for each causal relationship in a chain and acknowledge alternative causes and other possible effects.

15. Sweeping generalization fallacy

When people apply a general rule to all situations, they are making a **sweeping generalization**. For example, people who say that everyone must avoid sugar are speaking too broadly, because the best way to treat sudden hypoglycemia is to eat raw sugar or a candy bar. A person who passes out because of low blood sugar is an exception, of course, but just such an exception proves that you cannot sweep all situations under a single general rule. An audience may fall for this fallacy if an argument hides exceptions or neglects to consider them (Figure 24.5).

Figure 24.5 Mother Chicken's statement may make sense, but it is a sweeping generalization.

Conventions in Context
Logical Fallacies and Moral Choices

Logical fallacies occur because they are part of everyday thinking and grow out of common activities like trying to make sense of the world and protect ourselves or those we love. Or they are simply the result of human error. However, if we consciously choose to use logical fallacies in our writing and public arguments, or if we decide not to fix the accidental fallacies we discover, we are no longer making a common error. Instead, we are making a moral decision.

Speakers or writers who deliberately use fallacies are choosing to mislead, confuse, or deceive their audience. That kind of choice will affect how others see them and how they can or are allowed to engage the world. In short, people are known by their words, and authority in academic settings is based upon honest and valid reasoning.

It is true that some public figures and writers are intentionally provocative and use fallacies all the time with little negative effect. Then again, such figures and writers are typically preaching to the choir: their supporters have no reason to check the logic of arguments they agree with. In an academic setting, you will typically be making arguments to people who don't agree with you but may do so if you appear reasoned and authoritative. Again, it comes down to a choice. How do you want to be known, and what do you want to be able to do?

Types of Appeals in Logical Fallacies

Logical fallacies can also be categorized by the type of appeals (*pathos*, *ethos*, and *logos*) that characterizes them. For example, a hasty generalization such as, a survey of 20 college students indicates that most college students are unhappy with their major, sounds like it is based on evidence and solid reasoning, or a *logos* appeal. Below you will find the most common fallacies organized by appeal type.

Pathos Appeals	**Example**
Appeal to False Authority	Champion soccer player Kathy Johnson recommends Vitafresh granola bars.
Appeal to Ignorance	No one has complained about Professor Snape, so he must be a good teacher.
Appeal to Tradition	My grandparents, parents, and siblings were all business majors, so I can't major in English.
Personal Attack / *Ad Hominem*	My opponent is just a lonely, frustrated woman. That's why she's advocating ending the football program at our high school.
Straw Man	My opponent says we must enforce immigration laws. He wants to rip families apart, but that is not who we are.

Logos Appeals	**Example**
Faulty Analogy	Taking my ear buds without asking me is like what the big banks did to the economy in 2008.
Equivocation Fallacy	Being kind is the right thing to do, which is why I have a right to be treated with kindness.
Begging the Question / Circular Reasoning	Clearly, the first ranked Cougar football team is the best in the nation—just look at the polls.
Hasty Generalization Fallacy	These two apples are bad; better throw out the whole barrel of apples.
Post Hoc Ergo Propter Hoc Fallacy	Every time I wear my blue suit I get bumped to first class. Clearly the gate agents appreciate fine tailoring.
Slippery Slope / Camel's Nose Fallacy	If you skip a workout today, it will be easier to skip a workout next week. Then you will just give up and never work out again.
Sweeping Generalization Fallacy	Fifty percent of people who start a Ph.D. program drop out, so I am not going to grad school because I want a better than 50 / 50 chance of success.

Ethos Appeals	**Example**
Bandwagon Fallacy	Everyone is voting for Katherine. If you don't what does that say about you?
Appeal to Fear	We don't know who is entering our country, but we do know terrorists want to hurt us.
False Dilemma / Either-Or Fallacy	It's simple: either you support the Patriot Act or you let the terrorists win.

MODULE V-5

AWKWARDNESS AND FLOW DEFINED

If you were asked to name the smoothest dancer or athlete you have ever seen, you might think of someone like the ballet dancer Misty Copeland or the basketball star Stephen Curry. You recognize brilliant dancers or basketball players by the flow and accuracy of their movements. But if you had to teach your cousin, who moves like a baby giraffe on ice, how to dance like Copeland or drive like Curry, you might be at a loss.

You know smoothness, elegant movement, and flow when you see them, and you can detect awkwardness just as easily. But trying to define which moves are smooth and which are awkward is difficult. In fact, no movement of a leg or hand is inherently awkward or smooth. Your perception of them depends on the situation. If you were to put Curry on a dance floor or Copeland on a basketball court, their physical talents would probably still be apparent, but they would seem out of place and wrong.

What is true on the dance floor or the basketball court is also true of writing: the audience and their expectations shape how a sentence is perceived. An awkward sentence isn't simply a mishmash of jittery punctuation, sloppy subject-verb agreement, or confusing sentence structure, though such things can lead to a breakdown in flow. Instead, readers experience jitteriness and confusion when they read a sentence that is structured in an unexpected way, given the situation.

For example, read the following opening sentence to *Signatures of the Visible*, written by Fredric Jameson, a renowned, award-winning professor of comparative literature. How do you experience this passage as you read?

> The visual is essentially pornographic, which is to say that it has its end in rapt, mindless fascination; thinking about its attributes becomes an adjunct to that, if it is unwilling to betray its object; while the most austere films necessarily draw their energy from the attempt to repress their own excess (rather than from the more thankless effort to discipline the viewer).

Readers who are unfamiliar with Jameson's writing are likely to be disturbed by the style and abstract reasoning in this passage. However, readers who know Jameson's work recognize the excerpt above as an example of his "dialectical prose"—a style of writing that forces the reader to experience the contradictions and discontinuities that Jameson finds in the texts and images he critiques. Not only does Jameson's intended audience expect his convoluted sentences and ambiguity, but readers who seek out Jameson's writing may also find his very long, complicated sentences and reasoning to be as elegant as a complex ballet jump executed by Misty Copeland.

On the other hand, imagine you were asked to write a review of *Signatures of the Visible* for the campus newspaper. Your readers would expect clear writing with standard sentences and specific words and phrases that avoid unnecessary abstractness. Unfair? Not exactly.

Jameson's intentionally awkward constructions and reasoning mean that his book is accessible to a very small, specialized audience: Marxist literary critics or scholars of postmodernism. When you write using easily accessible sentences and phrases, a large, broad audience can understand your argument and potentially be persuaded by your reasoning.

Written work is considered **awkward** when it is difficult for readers to process and frustrates their ability to perceive meaning. Think of awkwardness as speed bumps, your writing as a road, and your reader as a driver. Any time drivers have to slow down for a speed bump, they will become frustrated.

For most readers, including professors reading student work, spelling errors, grammar errors, and sentences that are too short or too long are awkward speed bumps. In addition, words or phrases that the reader does not know can bring that reader to a dead stop.

The opposite of a bumpy road is a highway that flows. When writing **flows** it is easy for readers to understand, and they can effortlessly follow the development of an idea in a paragraph or passage. Writers achieve flow when they understand what the audience expects in a sentence, paragraph, or longer piece of writing. Writers can also achieve flow by appealing to readers' unconscious preferences or by using tricks of the trade that make reading easier. For example, alternating sentence length and using graphics effectively can result in a sense of flow.

Awkward writing has these common causes:

- Staying in your head, or not getting peer reviews or other opinions about your writing, when you are composing a public argument.
- Not knowing or not considering your audience members' perspective, thoughts, or knowledge.
- Not revising and proofreading, or ignoring the traits and qualities your audience looks for in authoritative texts and voices.

During the invention stage, first and early drafts will always seem awkward to others, because they are your unpolished thoughts and ideas. However, a thoughtful invention stage will set you up well for the revision stage. Necessarily, the revision stage of your writing process is the crucial step in crafting your private thoughts for public consideration. The revision and proofreading stages are also where you craft your authoritative voice and style.

Flow Checklist

The following checklist will help you work with awkward sentences to create an experience of flow for your audience.

- Invention

✓ Generate a great deal of support for your argument through invention and research so that you will have plenty to say, and your argument will move easily from point to point. In addition, it is always easier to refine and cut information as you move toward your final draft than to add information and sources.

✓ Concentrate on putting your ideas on the page during your first few drafts. Don't worry about punctuation and grammar. In later stages you can look for the kind of sentence-level errors that lead to awkwardness.

- Audience

✓ Research your audience's expectations so that you can deal with them effectively. If your professor is an electrical engineer, she may expect you to think and write like an electrical engineer. If you are writing a lab report, you should use the passive voice ("the beakers were filled" instead of "I filled the beakers") when describing the methods and materials used during an experiment because the doer of the action is not the primary focus. Professors from other disciplines, such as literature, will find the passive voice awkward.

✓ Assume that your audience members are expert detectors of logical fallacies as well as professional proofreaders. Of course, most of your readers will not be either of these things, but by taking a rigorous approach to editing and proofreading, you will be able to focus on the kinds of problems that lead to an awkward reading experience.

✓ Use transitions such as "in addition," "consequently," and "nevertheless" to smooth your readers' way. Remember, your audience members are reading or hearing your argument for the first time. Transitions will help them see how your ideas are connected and will make your argument flow. For example, in the following review of *Star Wars: The Force Awakens*, Stephen Marche explains how the movie is connected to previous episodes. Then he uses the transition "more importantly" to emphasize what sets the new episode apart from the others.

> There are whole chunks of the movie which are direct inheritances from the first trilogy: ice worlds, desert planets, and, not to give too much away, something like a death star, only bigger.

> More importantly, Abrams and the rest haven't forgotten what was so lacking from the prequel trilogy: a mythic substructure to the narrative.

The best transition not only says what is coming next but also indicates *why* the next subject or new idea is being introduced. Again, you know why, but your readers need to know, so tell them in a transition.

✓ Research your audience's thinking, beliefs, and behaviors just as you research your subject and counter-arguments. An understanding of your audience will help you make editorial decisions during the revision stage that convey a sense of authority in the mind of your audience.

- Authority

✓ Use what you know of your audience. Writers who successfully pitch screenplay ideas to studio executives make the types of editorial decisions that come from researching their audience. Though a writer may be excited to talk about her creative project, the studio exec is more interested in its financial potential. If a writer can frame the pitch in a way that indicates the potential profit of the screenplay, her audience will experience the kind of flow that comes from someone who knows how to make pitches—in other words, an authoritative voice.

✓ As you draft, have a friend, peer, classmate, or your professor read your draft, and ask your reader to identify places that are awkward or difficult to follow.

✓ Record yourself reading your draft aloud, or ask a friend to read it to you. Anytime there is a pause during reading, something does not sound right, or the paragraph leaves you hanging with more questions, odds are that is where you should begin to look for errors or better ways of expressing your ideas.

✓ Plan for thorough editing and proofreading. Editorial choices and errors such as the following can result in awkward writing that can lead a reader to question a writer's authority:
  - errors in spelling
  - odd word choice
  - too many words (wordiness)
  - punctuation errors
  - grammar errors
  - breakdowns in sentence structure
  - repetitive sentence structures
  - repetitive sentence length
  - breakdowns in paragraph structure
  - paragraphs that are too long or too short
  - logical fallacies

When audiences read or listen to public arguments, they expect correctness, and professors of any discipline will expect you to be as attentive to details like spelling and sentence structure as they are.

✓ If your writing seems wordy or the structure of a sentence seems wrong or hard to follow, find the skeletal sentence—the basic subject-verb structure—and then determine if you need fewer or additional words to modify or expand the idea in the sentence.

For example, an early draft of a Jameson book review may include the following wordy, hard-to-follow paragraph:

> Jameson begins with the idea that visual images are pornographic in his introduction. The goal, in other words, of visual images like photos and films, which is a recent focus of Jameson's work, is to provoke fascination and, if you think about how a visual image works instead of what an image shows, you are caught in the fascination of a visual image. In fact, films that are more abstract, such as black and white films like *Ballast* about the Mississippi Delta or Pixar's *Wall-E* are more about what they do not show or tell.

Highlighting the skeletal sentences, though, reveals the most basic meaning:

> **Jameson begins with the idea that visual images are pornographic** in his introduction. The goal, in other words, of **visual images** like photos and films, which is a recent focus of Jameson's work, is to **provoke fascination** and, **if you think about how a visual image works** instead of what an image shows, **you are caught in the fascination of a visual image**. In fact, **films that are** more **abstract**, such as black and white films like *Ballast* about the Mississippi Delta or Pixar's *Wall-E* **are** more **about what they do not show or tell**.

Once you have the skeletal sentence, you can decide on what additional information your audience will need to understand your meaning, and what you can leave out. For example, a revision of the skeletal meaning above may look like this:

> Visual images, for Jameson, are pornographic because they provoke fascination. Wondering how an image works as opposed to what an image shows and thinking about what is not shown are examples of the ways images fascinate.

✓ Look for sentences that begin with the same introductory clause or word. Repetition may sometimes be necessary and effective, but it can also lead to an experience of awkwardness. For example, the Declaration of Independence has 17 paragraphs that begin with "He has...." The 17 paragraphs are intended to demonstrate "repeated injuries and usurpations" by King George and provide overwhelming evidence supporting the decision to declare independence. However, in a research paper, such repetition can be tiresome to read, can diminish the impact of the points that follow, and can be an indication of an overly simple argument.

✓ Pay attention to sentence variety. As you develop your ideas, you may find yourself varying the lengths of your sentences without even thinking about it. When you review your work, though, look for and revise passages with a number of sentences of the same length or structure, which can be mind-numbing. For more on sentence variety, see Chapter 23.

✓ Use appropriate sentence lengths to add authority to your argument. A long sentence can help you focus on the parts of a big or complex idea. You may have noticed that the definitions that follow a bold term in these chapters are often quite long. A medium-length sentence is the workhorse of a paragraph, but it can also be a counterpoint to longer or shorter sentences. A short sentence can emphasize a point, add dramatic effect, or indicate speed.

✓ Focus on a busy reader who is skeptical. What would make such a person slow down or stop reading? Sometimes making sure your writing has authority is as simple as remembering that even though your argument makes sense to you, you are not your audience. And never assume that your audience will be able to guess what you are thinking.

- What is overly complicated that needs to be defined, explained, or put in context so the reader can understand?
- What more needs to be said before you can move to your next point?
- Does the reader know why you are using a source and how the source supports or is related to the argument?
- Does the reader know why you think the source is authoritative? Should you add information about a source's credentials?

✓ Do not fall in love with any of your sentences or think that any sentence is too perfect to be cut.

CHAPTER 25

USING CONVENTIONS PERSUASIVELY

In comic book and film-hero Tony Stark's lab, the screens in the background are constantly in motion. Even the screens that moviegoers can't see display graphics such as an exploded view of Iron Man's leg armor or the data feed as Jarvis performs an articulated joint stress test. All the while, the action of the movie plays in the foreground.

Why would the artists and programmers who developed the background imagery for the *Iron Man* films study advanced robotics and military heads-up displays and then write millions of lines of code for visuals that viewers will hardly see, or won't see at all? It would have been easier and cheaper just to draw futuristic images that would scroll on monitors using an off-the-shelf program like PowerPoint. After all, the audience can't really tell if the images are real—most audience members wouldn't recognize a computer-simulated metal alloy tensile stress test if the 3D infographic display fell on their foot.

David Sheldon-Hicks, who founded the company that created every computer screen and interface in *Avengers: Age of Ultron*, explains that the purpose of this meticulous work is to show genius Tony Stark at work, back-engineering to improve his own designs. To create a believable superhero genius who has mastered futuristic technology, Sheldon-Hicks and his production designers needed to make Stark and his technology realistic, which meant getting the details and conventions of advanced computer interfaces right.

It had to be right, not just for the character's ordinary fans, but also for fans such as robotics engineers, AI professors, and rocket scientists. After all, tech heads are an important part of the audience for the *Iron Man* movies. If they do not believe the character and the source of his power, who will?

Building a successful persuasive argument also means getting the details right. However, instead of building a believable character, you must build an authoritative voice, presence, and argument. In other words, you need to be the Sheldon-Hicks of persuasion.

The following modules will first introduce principles for producing and using effective visuals. Then we will look at design conventions and techniques to build a persuasive argument, before bringing it all together to show how to shape effective presentations such as a PowerPoint slideshow or a Prezi canvas. Finally, we will focus on how to polish your argument by proofreading carefully and effectively. Attention to these details will help you convey your message to your audience and convince them to agree with your claim.

MODULE V-6

USING VISUALS IN YOUR ARGUMENT

A **visual** is an image, illustration, display, or graph used to communicate data, ideas, or emotions. **Visual conventions** are the elements of a visual that an audience expects in a given situation. These elements make communicating with a visual efficient and the data, ideas, or emotions more appealing or useful.

Visuals are effective. A study in the journal *Public Understanding of Science* found that readers are more likely to be persuaded by visual images such as graphs than by text or speech alone. Why? Visuals communicate a sense of authority, a connection to science, or an urgency that captures audience members' attention. Visuals catch a reader's eye, and if they are well designed and based on solid research, they can have the persuasive power of a longer written argument.

You can use visuals to create *logos*, *pathos*, and *ethos* appeals.

- *Logos* appeal. Graphs and charts give the impression of logical reasoning and can persuade your audience of the logic of your argument.
- *Pathos* appeal. Moving pictures and images, such as a hungry child or a soldier in the middle of a firefight, can provoke and link strong emotions to your argument.
- *Ethos* appeal. Framing and point of view can suggest or emphasize authority, wisdom, or leadership (Figure 25.1).

Chapter 17 explains appeals in detail, and the Conventions in Context box entitled "Use Images and Rhythm to Make *Logos*, and *Pathos* Appeals" (p. 507) gives an example of these appeals in a PowerPoint presentation.

Figure 25.1
Statues of our nations' leaders are typically larger than life, forcing the viewer to look up. Such an ethos appeal is created by perspective rather than by words.

Creating Effective Visuals: General Guidelines

An argument can be composed primarily of visuals, like the visual argument for Women's Equality Day created by Heather Jones for *Time* magazine (Figure 25.2). Or writers or speakers can use visuals such as line graphs or pie charts to support a claim in a text or as part of a speech. Photographers, graphic designers, painters, and information designers keep the following guidelines in mind as they create effective persuasive visuals.

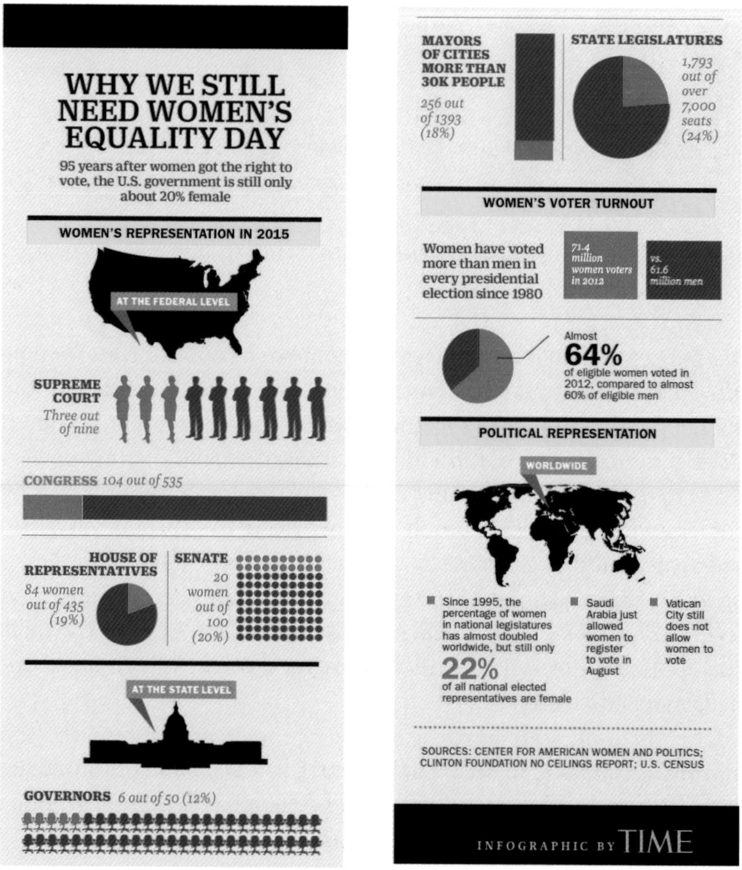

Figure 25.2
Heather Jones's argument is composed of 10 visual panels.

Keep it easy to understand. Whether you are using a graph or an image, simple is best, especially if your visual will be incorporated in a written text. For example, which is easier to understand in Figure 25.3, **A** or **B**?

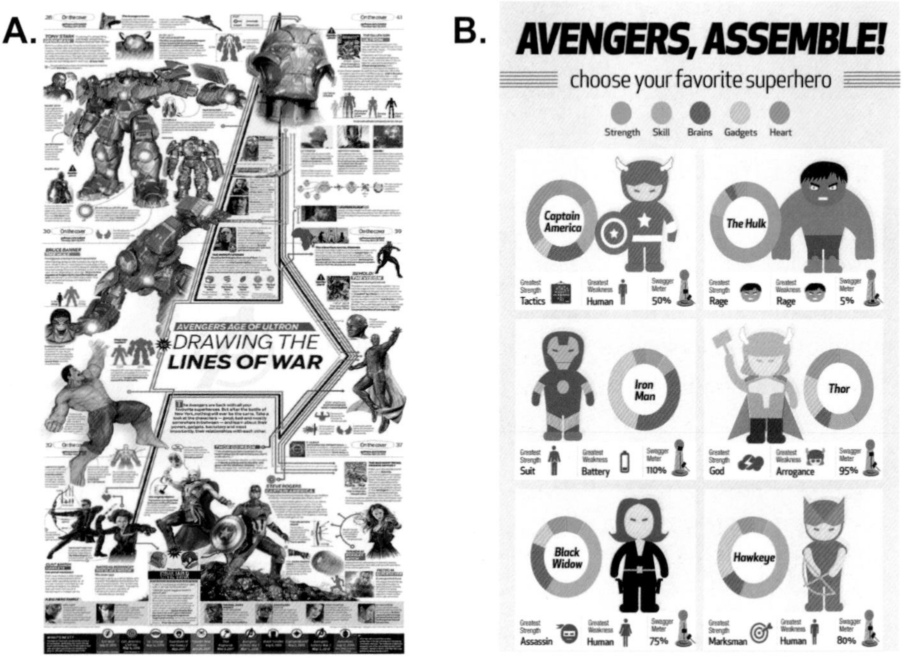

Figure 25.3 Visually, A. is more exciting, but B. organizes textual and visual information in an easy to understand format.

A visual that is part of a written or spoken argument must communicate a single idea or point. The idea or point may be complex, but it must hold together in the same way in which a paragraph is held together by a single idea or point. Visual B shows that the Avengers are a group of individuals with remarkable, distinct powers that come together to do more than anyone could. This idea is communicated by organizing the diverse characteristics of each Avenger using five specific **variables** (qualities, numbers, or values) as criteria.

When composing a chart, you need to shape your visual for your purpose and avoid overloading your reader's ability to process information. For example, Visuals A and B in Figure 25.4 illustrate social media sharing on the web. Which one communicates its ideas more efficiently?

The answer depends upon your purpose. If you are focusing on how the top four social media sites compare, Visual A is better. If you want to communicate the complexity of social media sharing—a single idea—then B is the better graphic.

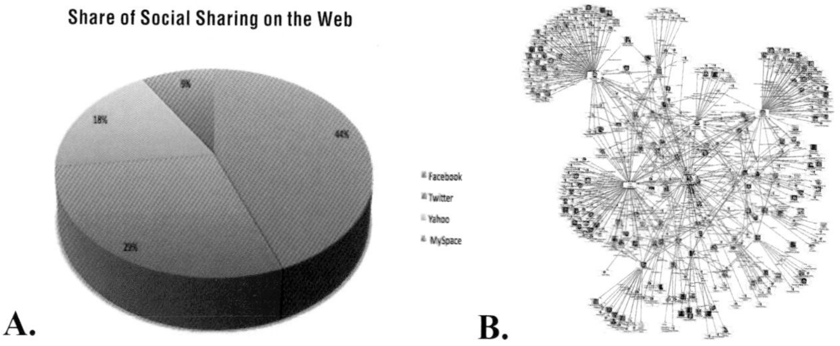

Figure 25.4 The pie chart (Visual A) and the node-link chart (Visual B) both provide information about sharing patterns in social media.

However, keep in mind that while the variables in Visual A are easy to understand quickly, the massive number of variables in Visual B may not be understood fully unless the reader stops to study the chart.

Use the composition of the image to convey meaning. Lines have traditionally been used to communicate different meanings and sensations within images. Your audience may expect you to use these same conventions.

- Diagonal lines convey speed, movement, and dynamic scenes.
- Horizontal lines suggest quiet, calm, pastoral scenes.
- Vertical lines convey a sense of tradition, permanence, upward movement, and optimism in a scene.

The arrows in the images in Figure 25.5 show the dominant direction and movement of each image. Effective visual arguments use direction and movement to communicate meaning and direct the viewers' eyes, so pick images that express the effect and meaning you intend.

Figure 25.5 The arrows have been added to highlight the graphic direction and movement within each image.

Use colors to convey meaning. Like composition, colors also communicate emotions, ideas, and sensations:

- Red suggests strong emotions: passion, energy, and violence.
- Blue offers a sense of calm, stability, faith, and purity.
- Green conveys power, ambition, security, and growth.

Authoritative groups and websites, such as the Graphic Artist Guild, can help you explore the meanings of colors and shapes.

Like rhetorical conventions, the conventional connotations of colors are reflected in our expectations and in how we read images. Specific audiences will read specific colors and color combinations in predictable ways. For example, royal purple and old gold means just one thing in Baton Rouge: Louisiana State University. For city dwellers, bright red and blue can bring to mind an emergency or crisis, but if you are a plumber, these colors mean hot and cold.

Black and white images can also communicate distinct meanings. Because a lack of color removes some context, black and white may give the impression of timelessness or endurance. A color image, on the other hand, is more engaging and easier to understand because most people see in color, color images capture context, and color suggests a contemporary setting. As a result, black and white images have a distant, objective feel, while color images seem more vibrant and immediate.

Frame your visuals to direct your reader. Scope is the context of your argument, such as an academic discipline. Within that scope, you have a **focus**, the position or specific proposition you want your reader or listener to accept and adopt.

When you are creating a visual to support your argument, you can use scope and focus to direct your readers' or viewers' eyes to important information, while providing the context that helps them understand what you want them to see. For example, in the original info graphic in Figure 25.6, data journalist David McCandeless used bright red to direct the viewer to look first at the center of his Venn diagram. He used less vibrant colors to encourage the viewer to move out and around the diagram to consider the scope of elements and strategies that make for successful information design.

Adjust the frame of your visual to reflect your purpose. Visuals can be shaped to direct the reader's or viewer's eye just as a paragraph or essay directs the reader's thinking. For example, both Visual A and Visual B in Figure 25.7 represent the same information—the appearance of the words "manifest destiny" and "exceptionalism" in English language literature scanned by Google Books. If you wanted readers or

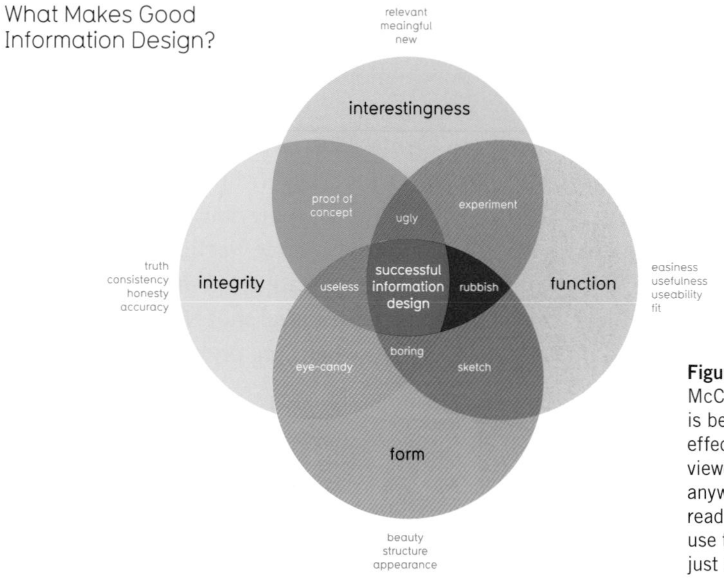

Figure 25.6
McCandeless's image is beautiful, and it is effective because the viewer can begin reading anywhere, take in and read the entire image, or use the information from just a few parts.

viewers to compare the lack of these two words in literature from the seventeenth to the eighteenth centuries to their increasing presence in the nineteenth and twentieth centuries, Visual A would be a better choice. If your focus was the nineteenth and twentieth centuries alone, Visual B would be better because it directs the viewer's focus to the appearance of these words during that time.

Keep in mind that dishonest writers can manipulate visuals and graphs to distract or deceive. Chapter 20 shows you how to check a source for its honesty. You can use the same principles to determine if you have misrepresented or unfairly manipulated the information and sources you use in a visual.

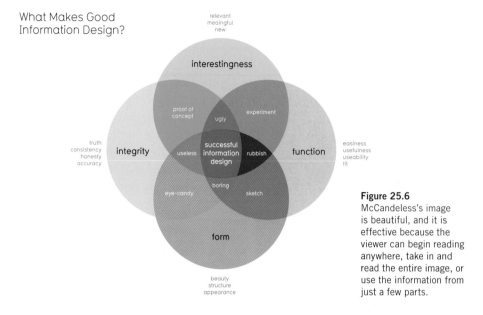

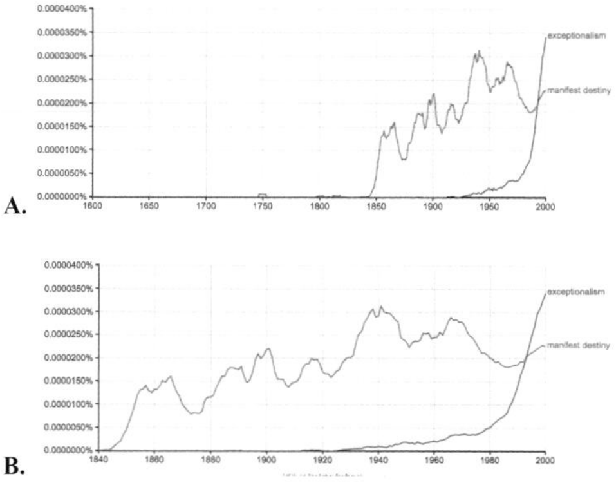

Figure 25.7
Two visuals tracking the appearance of "manifest destiny" and "exceptionalism" in English language literature.

Use point of view to highlight your focus. Your perspective, or the position from which you view an object, is your **point of view.**

Point of view can be created with the shot angle, lighting, framing, and positioning of elements within an image. For example, notice how the lighting and positioning directs your eye in the two images in Figure 25.8. In Image A, Aung San Suu Kyi, chairperson of the National League for Democracy in Burma, is highlighted and centered in a down shot, giving the appearance of separation, if not isolation, in a crowd as she prepares to cast a vote in Myanmar's first free election. Unlike Image A. in which the photographer's perspective appears distant from the subject, Image B is taken in the midst of Black Friday shopping with a level shot. The image centers on the chaotic pile of boxes, making them an overwhelming presence in the image.

Figure 25.8 Point of view in a photograph is determined by the location of the camera lens as well as the lighting and framing.

You can also create point of view in graphics. For example, it is almost impossible to ignore the center of the Venn diagram in Figure 25.6 because the compelling red color and the arrangement of the circles creates a central focal point. In addition, you can use **negative space**, or the space surrounding the subject of the visual, to shape how an audience sees and understands information. Notice how framing creates empty or negative space in the graph in Figure 25.10 and how this space affects the way you understand the graph's information. How a graph is structured can shape an audience's understanding. Figure 25.2 is composed of many different graphs, but the up-and-down organization moves the reader to consider the first point in the visual argument before moving down to the next.

How you create and use an image will reflect a point of view that your reader will attach to you and your argument. Like any rhetorical device or strategy, you must be careful to use images in a way that contributes to your authority. Though it is easy to manipulate images and graphs, as the Responsible Sourcing box entitled "Honesty Is Authoritative" shows, your audience measures your authority based on how you use textual and visual sources.

Responsible Sourcing
Honesty Is Authoritative

In September 2009, *Newsweek* published this image of former Vice President Dick Cheney stabbing a bloody piece of meat. The image was cropped from a larger photo that showed his family clearing away dishes after a meal. Cropping provides a different, and possibly menacing, view of Cheney, whereas the fuller image portrays him as a family man.

In 2010, an *Economist* cover appeared to show a lonely President Barack Obama considering the damage to the Gulf of Mexico caused by the BP oil spill. However, the original image showed Obama being briefed by a Coast Guard admiral and a parish president on a much sunnier day than the cropped, darkened, and scrubbed image portrays.

As these two examples demonstrate, data and images are easily misrepresented when you change the scale of a graph, crop an image, or use tools like Photoshop. Prior to digital photography, dimming and scrubbing a photo would have taken a darkroom full of equipment, extensive expertise, and hours of work. As a result, there was time to consider whether altering a photo was worth the effort and expense and whether such changes were ethical. Now images can be altered on a smart phone with a few swipes. However, keep in mind that the ability to change the composition of a photo does not mean that it is ethical to do so.

The same principles that guide you when you are quoting, summarizing, or paraphrasing a source also apply to the visuals you use. If you use only a portion of a photo or, for example, one panel from Heather Jones's visual argument (Figure 25.2), don't manipulate it in a way that alters its intended meaning. Always provide context and background that will help the reader understand the original circumstances in which the photo was taken or the graphic was presented. Make sure your documentation is accurate, and assume your audience will check to determine if you were responsible when documenting your source.

Types of Visuals

Different types of visuals communicate different messages in different ways. A photo can tell a story at a glance, and a graph can break down massive amounts of complex data into a simple presentation. The type of visual you use must deliver your message effectively for your intended audience so you can achieve your purpose.

Images. Images are representations of people, places, or items in the form of photos, drawings, or cartoons. Images typically portray a scene and can include individuals or items. As a result, they are especially effective at communicating narratives. For example, documentary images made by photojournalists, such as those in the Responsible Sourcing box, portray an occurrence or event. A landscape can tell the story of a location and impart a sense of what it is like to be there. A portrait can connect a face with a name, or it can function as a character study, revealing moods and dispositions.

Charts. A **chart** is a visual representation of data, data sets, or data trends. Timelines, bar graphs, line graphs, and pie charts are the most common types of charts. Each presents relationships among data in a different way.

- **Timelines** sequence information chronologically to highlight influences, effects, and events over time (Figure 25.9).
- **Bar graphs** portray significant differences in subjects that are being compared (Figure 25.10).
- **Line graphs** portray small changes over time, and they are most effective when portraying one trend (Figure 25.11) or at most a few trends over time.
- **Pie charts** are useful when you are comparing parts of a whole or elements within a single data set (Figure 25.12).

Figure 25.9
The history of hip-hop artists and musical styles is portrayed in this vertical time line.

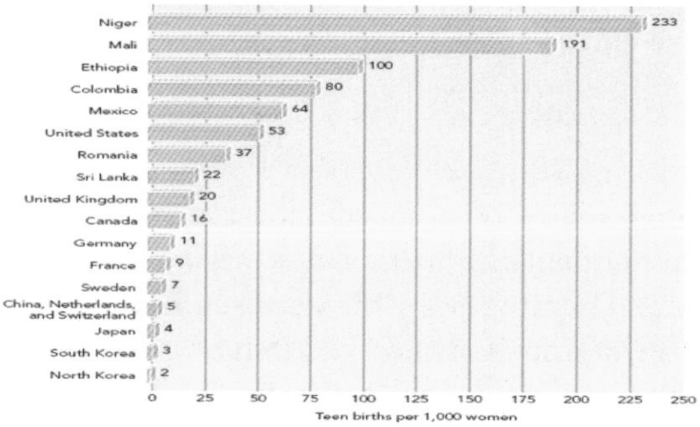

Figure 25.10
The bar graph compares birth rates in different countries.

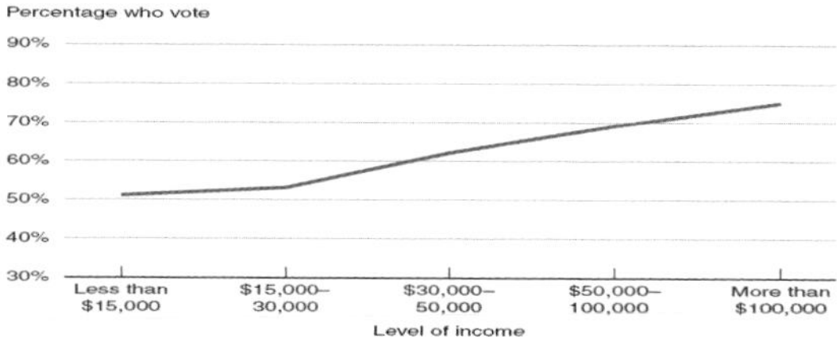

Figure 25.11
Probability of voting is graphed against income in this line graph.

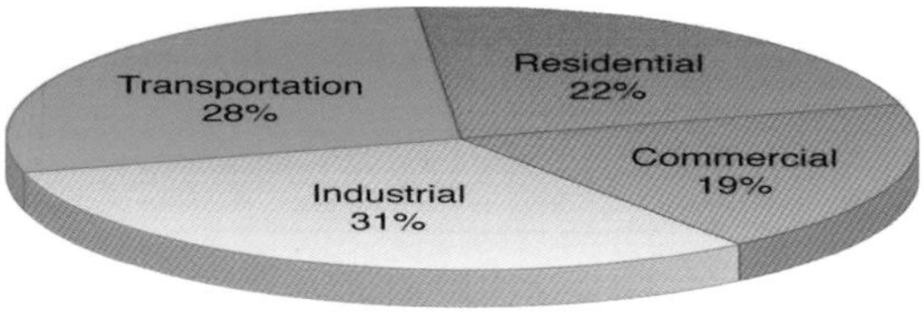

Figure 25.12
The energy use of four sectors is shown in this pie chart.

There are many other ways to tell the story of relationships found in data, including Venn diagrams (Figure 25.6), node link charts (Figure 25.4B), and **word clouds** (Figure 25.13). These options can help an audience understand data trends and comparisons. Chart templates can be downloaded from sites such as Tableau Public and developed using software provided by TimeFlow, Protovis, and Excel. Word clouds can be produced on sites such as WordItOut.com and Wordle.com.

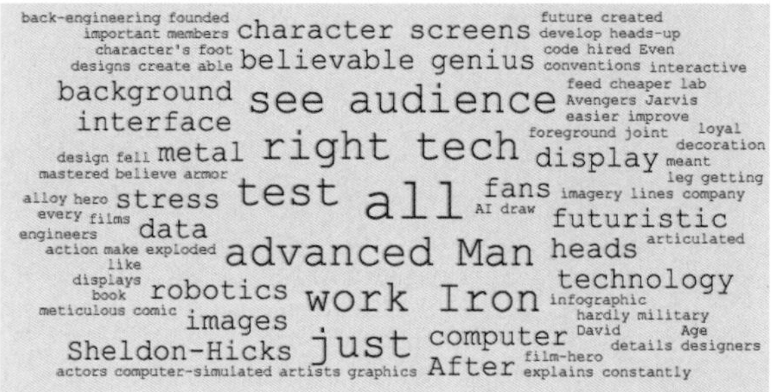

Figure 25.13
The most frequently used words in the introduction to this chapter (p. 489) are larger in this word cloud.

Information graphics. Information graphics, often called infographics, are composed of images, graphs, and text that communicate brief, coherent arguments, assertions, or facts in an easily accessible and beautiful way. The visuals in Figures 25.2, 25.3, 25.6, and 25.9 are infographics. You can easily find all kinds of infographics on the web, and the site Information Is Beautiful is an excellent source of compelling infographics. (Images you find, especially infographics, must be documented, as the Responsible Sourcing box entitled "Visuals Have Sources" explains.) You can also make your own infographics using software provided by sites such as Easelly, Google Developers, or Piktochart. Infographics are most effective when dealing with data that require a number of graphs or charts to illustrate. In addition, infographics that describe a process or hierarchy, like a flowchart, can also be useful. When deciding whether to use an infographic, consider your audience's expectations and the common practices of the situation you are in.

Maps. Maps organize information geographically. For example, a topographical map locates, names, and shows relationships between elevation changes, geological formations like hills and canyons, and built places like towns. There are many types of maps. A dot distribution map places dots on a geographic map to represent data, numbers, or values (Figure 25.14). Maps of all types can be downloaded from sources such as GeoCommons or produced using software suites such as Google Maps API.

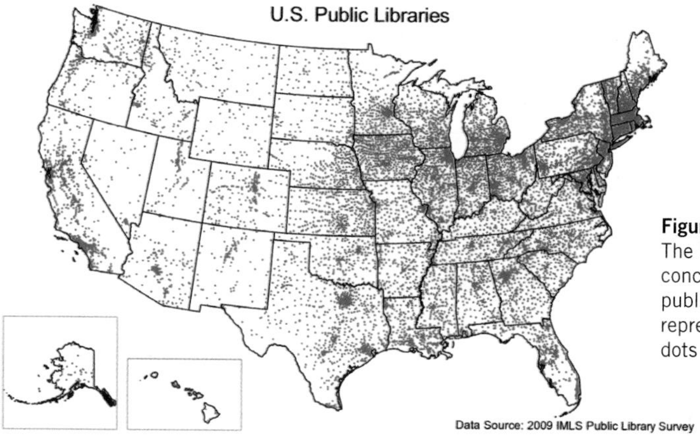

Figure 25.14
The location and concentration of public libraries are represented using dots in this map.

Responsible Sourcing
Visuals Have Sources

Visuals that are presented without a source are suspicious, while visuals that include information about a source trusted by your audience are persuasive. Not only does a source note—presented and formatted in a style expected by your audience—have persuasive power, but the authority of that source also contributes to the authority of your argument.

In an academic setting, when your audience is a professor or fellow classmates, you must include the source of any visual you use. In addition, if you are using a visual found online, you must acknowledge the copyright of the author or creator of the visual.

For more information on why citing sources is necessary and how accurate in-text citations, bibliographies, and works-cited pages contribute to your authority, see Chapter 21. That chapter also explains copyright laws and the fair-use exceptions to those laws that permit limited or educational use of selected portions of another person's original work. Fair use allows scholars to use words, sound clips, and images created by others for academic purposes without formally requesting permission. However, fair use is not a license to use another person's work without properly acknowledging the source. For help with documenting sources, including visuals, by correctly using MLA or APA style, see Chapter 22.

Use Relevant Visuals

To be effective, visuals should be relevant, enhance your authority, and support the appeals of your argument. You know what the image you are using portrays and why it is in your text, but will your audience know? When selecting or creating images, keep these guidelines in mind.

- Charts and other visuals communicate authority only if they are directly related to your argument and the source of the data portrayed is easily understood. The meaning of a complex graphic may be clear to you, but what matters is whether your audience understands it.
- Images can help you describe a scene or an object or to analyze or compare objects with small, subtle, or nuanced qualities or differences. For example, an effective screen shot can supplement, or even replace, a detailed description in the text.
- Avoid cliché images, and do not use images as filler to meet a page minimum: both options are obvious and undercut your authority. For example, clip art, emoticons, and images of sunsets or animal gifs may be fun, but they distract from your subject and authority.
- Used strategically, an image or a graph can also create a pause in a text or a transition from one point to the next. For example, let's say you were writing a research paper on the evolution of rap music. After a discussion of bling rap of the late 1990s, you are ready to move on to part two of your analysis, the emerging hipster hop movement. Visualizing the transition between the two subjects in some way could help your audience follow your argument.

MODULE V-7

USING DESIGN CONVENTIONS IN YOUR ARGUMENT

Back when newspapers, magazines, and books were the primary media, accepted ways of using texts and visuals were determined by professional editors and designers. Times have changed: third graders can now use Evernote, Photoshop, and Google Docs to produce slick-looking class journals. Multimedia chapbooks and PowerPoint or Prezi presentations are common assignments in universities and colleges. Still, many of the conventions that audiences expect and find helpful have remained relatively constant. In fact, when readers move through a traditional print or digital presentation, they have similar expectations for the use of text, space, and images.

Textual Conventions

Textual conventions are language and formatting practices that writers, speakers, and their intended audiences have agreed upon and accepted. Some groups, such as the Associated Press, Wikipedia, and American Horse Publications, formalize their conventions in stylebooks. Even Badoo and Twitter have informal, accepted language practices. On most social networks, you learn the accepted style by watching how people successfully engage one another and by their mistakes.

In an academic setting, conventions may include expectations about margin width, the content of headers and footers, the use and placement of visuals, in-text source citations and lists of sources, footnotes or endnotes, spelling and punctuation, and fonts. Imagine the one research paper in a stack of forty that has different margins than all the rest. Such a paper will stand out, and probably not in a good way.

If you are composing an argument outside of college, following the textual conventions your audience expects will contribute to your authority. Your readers or listeners may not even be aware of the conventions they use as markers of authority, but they can recognize when something is off. Imagine THE WALL STREET JOURNAL. banner in a different font. Imagine *Time* magazine without its signature red border. Conventions can help you recognize authority, and playing with conventions can help your work stand out.

Some conventions, like those for spelling and punctuation, are consistent across most writing situations. Other textual conventions—such as margin width, the use of personal pronouns, and the correct placement of visuals—can vary depending on the audience or the academic discipline.

Many professors give detailed descriptions of the conventions they expect you to follow in writing prompts or assignment sheets, or they may indicate that you should follow the conventions explained in the handbook they require you to buy. If your professor does not tell you the conventions to use in your writing, ask which standard style, such as that recommended by the Modern Language Association (MLA) or the American Psychological Association (APA), they prefer. Most academic style manuals also include detailed instructions concerning margin width, documentation, spelling and punctuation, and even the best fonts to use. (For more on MLA and APA style, see Chapter 22.)

Everything you read either upholds conventions or breaks them, either intentionally or unintentionally. Writers who make the most effective use of visuals and text do so by making their choices about conventions, techniques, and visuals both effective and invisible to the reader. For example, most readers won't know which font a writer is using, but a font that is difficult to read can affect the writer's authority nevertheless.

Fonts or **typefaces** are styles or designs of letters. Some fonts are designed to be easy to read and some are designed to provoke an emotion or send a message, such as the constancy, power, and authority expressed by the *Wall Street Journal*'s banner font. On paper, serif fonts, with tiny tails at the ends of certain letters, appear to aid readers' comprehension more than sans serif fonts, which do not have tails. Most electronic texts are sans serif because making the little tails and feet legible on all screens with different resolution rates is difficult.

Serif
Courier
Times New Roman
Andale Mono

San Serif
Arial
Calibri
Verdana

Your professor may indicate a preferred font. If not, use the simplest font, keeping in mind that all editorial choices, including which font to use, can enhance or damage your authority.

Spatial Conventions

Though the term "spatial conventions" may sound theoretical, in fact you encounter these conventions every day. For example, we expect rooms to be furnished and hallways to be plain. A hallway cluttered with chairs and bookcases would seem as odd as an office with no desk or chair. Spatial conventions for texts involve the way in which linear text, like the lines of words in this paragraph, is organized and presented, the composition of an image, or the ways in which a graph and written text are arranged.

Layout refers to how you place images and texts on a page, poster, or slide. Good layout helps the audience move smoothly through your pages and slides and contributes to the persuasive power of your argument, whereas poor layout is confusing or leads to questions such as "What is that graph supposed to mean?"

Think about how audiences move through your text. Each genre is shaped differently, depending on readers' expectations and the medium in which it appears. If your argument is a web page, composed of text and visuals, for example, think about how your audience will move through such a text.

Research that tracks readers' eye movements shows that people typically move through a web page in an F pattern. Readers typically start at the top left of a page or section reading from left to right and work their way down. However, the further down a page they go, the more likely they are to skip words or images on the right side. As Figure 25.15 shows, those reading web pages with narrow columns (left image) of text have narrow F patterns compared to pages where the text runs from the left edge to the right edge (right image). Also, web pages with visuals (center image) show the same F pattern as pages of text alone. All three eye-tracking maps of the different web pages show that the text or images at the bottom right received almost no attention.

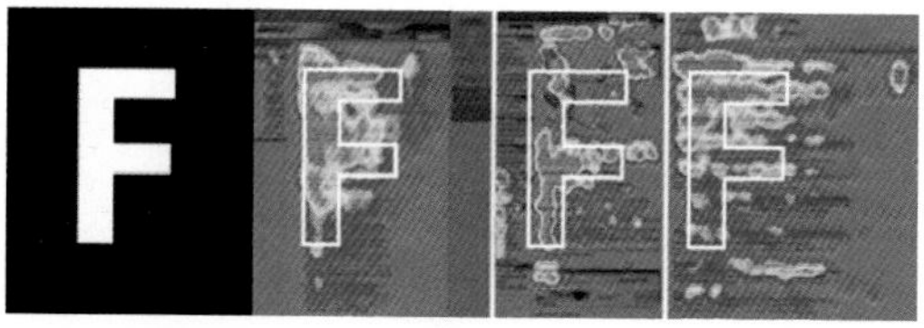

Figure 25.15 Areas where a viewer's eyes were focused for the longest time or most frequently are framed by the letter F. Areas outside the F are rarely noticed by the reader.

Layout techniques are based on how audiences move through documents, pages, websites, and presentation slides. Web usability consultant Jakob Nielsen tells his clients to build their web pages with the most important images and information in the top left, and always to assume that the first few lines of a section or paragraph will have the most impact. Readers place less value on information and images farther down or farther to the right of the screen.

The following techniques will help you lay out the visuals and text of your argument:

- **Determine the types of layouts your audience expects**. For example, if you have to give a class presentation in a business class, you might ask your professor for examples from previous classes so you can see how those students laid out their argument efficiently.
- **Use the layout templates that PowerPoint and Prezi provide**. Microsoft and Prezi both provide video tutorials that show you how to lay out slides and build presentations.
- **Incorporate visuals at points where they can be useful**. Include your visuals when you outline a multimedia argument. In this way, you can see where you may need visuals and where you have too many.
- **Be consistent**. If all your graphs are in rich colors except for one, your audience will wonder why. Such inconsistencies should be avoided if possible, or explained.
- **Indicate importance by size**. If all your visuals are equally important or of the same type, they should be the same size. If your argument ends with a passionate call to action, a tiny motivating image would work against the mood or need you are trying to establish.

Tie visuals to your text. Your audience will not make the connection between your argument and a visual that supports it if you don't, or they will make a connection that is different from what you intended. When you use images or graphs in your argument, therefore, you need to do the following:

- Introduce each visual individually.
- Discuss the relevance of the visual to your immediate point and your overall argument.
- Duplicate or represent the data and image honestly.
- Locate your image or graph above or just after the point you are trying to illustrate, unless the style you are using requires a different placement.
- Avoid separating images and the text that discusses them. For example, if a graph is on page 10, the analysis of the graph's data should not be on page 9 or 11.
- Include a caption to help readers know what they are looking at in an image.

Captions are brief titles or descriptions of a visual located immediately below the visual. Your caption should provide enough information for your audience to understand the image or graph. In addition, your caption should be in the same style as the text, it should be brief, and it should support your argument. Ideally, a caption identifies relevant individuals, activities, processes, or items in the image. If you have multiple visuals or refer to the same visual at different times during your argument, your caption should include a number, like the figure numbers in this chapter.

MODULE V-8

CREATING EFFECTIVE PRESENTATIONS

When your argument takes the form of a presentation, you have many options. You can create a video combining slides, action shots, and prerecorded narration, or you can create an online slideshow. You can use slides to illustrate your talk before a live audience or simply talk to your audience while illustrating your ideas with a poster board or a white board. Whether you are drafting an argument that uses a single poster board or a multimedia presentation with multiple slides, attention to your audience's expectations will help you use visuals effectively and persuasively.

Use Design and Visuals to Enhance Your Authority

Well-designed slides and effective visuals not only persuade but can also make an impression on your audience that is hard to forget. Poor use of design and visuals during a presentation can annoy your audience and diminish your voice and authority. Here are some suggestions for designing effective slides.

- **Make the slides readable at a distance.** If you are speaking before an audience, make sure the type and images in your slides are as clear and easy to read in the back of the room as they are in the front. If possible, experiment with different font sizes and the projection equipment you will be using. Use at least 14-point type for regular text and 26-point type for primary titles.
- **Use slides to create flow.** Use slides to indicate the narrative of your argument and the sequence of points you will make, as well as to drive points home as you conclude your talk.
- **Avoid slide lock.** "Slide lock" happens when your talk is locked to the content of each slide and you pause in your delivery each time you move to a new slide. To avoid slide lock, remember that you don't need a slide for each point you make.
- **Use each visual for a specific purpose.** To check, ask peers to watch you give your presentation. Then ask them to name the purpose of each visual. Was the visual used to clarify, explain, summarize, or portray, or was its purpose unclear?
- **Use two to four bullet points on a slide.** If a slide has more than five points or large sections of text, your audience may be distracted from what you say as they try to read.
- **Control the quality of images.** Visual resolution and image quality get worse as a picture or graph gets bigger. Also, some colors like bright red may overwhelm other colors or cause "color bleed"—when a color appears to change differently colored images or objects nearby.

Conventions in Context
Using Images and Rhythm to Make *Logos*, and *Pathos* Appeals

The web offers many examples of the effective use of slides during a presentation. In LZ Granderson's TEDx talk entitled *The Myth of the Gay Agenda*, which is available on YouTube, Granderson uses slides to surprise his audience and add humor to his presentation. In addition, he uses simple slides to make the traditional rhetorical appeals.

He begins his talk by stating that as a gay man, he is going to explain the gay lifestyle and gay agenda so no one will ever have to wonder what these gays are up to. In appealing to his own life, and joking that he has finally discovered the gay agenda document, Granderson appeals to the audience's sense of authority and establishes himself as an authentic voice of gay experience.

To explain the gay lifestyle, he describes typical gay activities like being stuck in traffic, cooking dinner, and being in love. The slides projected as he talks portray the mundane activities of daily life. These slides complement his talk, as he appeals to audience members' emotions and their sense of empathy because most people have been stuck in traffic, have cooked a meal, and have experienced love—a *pathos* appeal.

When, midway through his talk, he says he is ready to reveal the gay agenda, the *Star Wars* "Imperial March" song starts playing, he walks off stage, and six slides of the original Constitution of the United States are projected. When he returns, he explains that the gay agenda is the simple pursuit of equality before the law. He then shows two slides portraying states where it is legal to discriminate against gay people by, for example, kicking someone out of a rented apartment because that person is gay.

Based on simple reasoning, common values of equality as defined by the Constitution, and evidence of legal discrimination, Granderson's final slides compose an effective *logos* argument.

Use Your Voice to Express Your Authority

Presentation slides, with or without visuals, do not speak for themselves. Without your voice and your concern for the audience's understanding, persuasion is not possible. Necessarily, the link between your talk and the visuals you present must be smooth and practiced, invisible and obvious, and easy to understand and insightful. The following points can help.

- **Practice, practice, practice**. Going over your presentation in your head is not practice. Practice by delivering your talk to a live audience. If you can practice in the room with the equipment you will use for your talk, the environment will be familiar and surprises unlikely. The more at home you are with your presentation, the more comfortable you will appear to your audience.
- **Control your pacing and voice**. Slower is almost always better than faster. Simple is often better than complex. Walk your audience through your argument slowly so they can catch up to your thinking. If you are in a crowded room, you may need to speak louder than you normally do. Finally, the rise and fall of your voice should reflect genuine interest in your subject and the points you are making.
- **Look at your audience**. If you are shy or have difficulty looking at individuals in a large crowd, look at their hairlines. Remember to look around the room to give all listeners a sense of inclusion.
- **Ask a trusted friend to advance the slides for you**. Your friend will need your written presentation with cues for advancing the slides. In this way, your slide presentation will appear more practiced, you are less likely to turn and look at

your slides or get stuck in slide lock, and you can use your hands more freely.

- **Focus on the audience, not your nerves**. If you really believe what you have to say and really believe the audience will benefit from your insights, you won't have time to worry about mistakes. And even if you make a mistake, your passion and concern will be what your audience remembers.

MODULE V-9

PROOFREADING YOUR ARGUMENT

Proofreading should be your final step before turning in any type of assignment. Once you have made larger editorial decisions and are satisfied with how your text flows and that your visuals are working, you should proofread for mechanical errors. It may seem unfair or petty, but audiences judge the intellect and competency of authors or speakers by their accuracy, polish, and attention to detail. For professors and other readers, a five-page paper with no errors may have more persuasive power than a carefully researched 10-page paper with mistakes on every page. Because readers of all types put such value on correctness, and a flawless paper or talk enhances authority, writers and public speakers turn to professional proofreaders like Naomi Long Eagleson.

Long Eagleson has four rules that she keeps in mind when proofreading:

1. Work from a printed text on paper to see small punctuation marks and letters more clearly.
2. Temporarily change the font type, type size, and/or color you are using. Seeing your work anew will give you fresh eyes to spot the hidden errors.
3. Focus like a ninja by using a ruler to cover the line below the one you are scanning for errors.
4. You will rarely go wrong with using the Oxford comma. An **Oxford comma** is the second comma in a sequence of three words or phrases, or the comma before the word "and" that leads to the final element of a longer series:

    I traveled to Maine, Georgia**,** and Florida during the summer.

    Journalists, however, do not use the Oxford comma.

The following checklist will also help you build and protect your authoritative voice as you proofread.

- Schedule time for proofreading

✓ Just as you set aside time to write, set aside time to proofread.
✓ Proofread each page at least three times, including cover pages and lists of works cited or references. For example, if it takes you five minutes to proofread a single page carefully and you are planning to proofread three different times, you should be prepared to set aside 1 hour and 15 minutes for proofreading a five-page paper.
✓ Take a break between proofreading sessions. Careful proofreading requires concentration, and the longer you do it the less able you will be to focus.

- Get help

✓ Peers, friends, and classmates can help you proofread. You don't have to be a professional like Long Eagleson to find errors. All you or your reviewers need is time to read and a sense of what doesn't sound right and what seems wrong.
✓ Don't assume that your readers have caught everything or that their advice is always correct. Even if you have run spell check and grammar check three times and had four friends read and correct your errors, *you* still need to go through it and make the decisions to revise sentences or fix typos yourself. If you don't understand an error that a peer reviewer has pointed out, don't make a change until you understand how to correct it.
✓ Most campus writing centers, learning centers, or tutors will not proofread your paper for you. However, they will work with you on your text, explaining why a word, sentence, or paragraph needs your attention. In this way, they are teaching you how to proofread: skills that will help you in all your classes and in the other types of writing you will do.

- Develop and stick to a proofreading strategy

✓ Always start with major problems and work your way to smaller issues. For example, the first time you proofread, you might focus only on transitions between paragraphs and captions beneath images. The second time you might decide to focus only on punctuation and word choice or usage. Finally, for your last reading you would focus only on spelling. In addition, if in the past you have had trouble with transitions and using commas in a series of three, you should prioritize those types of errors.
✓ Trick your mind into seeing your paper anew. You may have noticed that it is easier to find errors in someone else's paper than in your own. Because you have worked on your paper so long and read it so many times, you will tend to correct your mistakes automatically while reading it. You can trick your brain

with this simple process:

- Start reading at the last sentence, and read it for a specific error type, like punctuation mistakes.
- Go to the second to the last sentence, and read it for the same type of mistakes.

Reading in this way will help you focus on mechanical errors like sentence problems and incorrect or missing commas.

PERMISSIONS ACKNOWLEDGMENTS

Page 23: Figure 1.2: Savage, Doug. "The Argument." *Savage Chickens.* Reproduced with permission of Doug Savage.

Page 104: Figure 7.2: Nebraska Tourism advertisement.

Page 100: Savage, Doug. "You're Fired." *Savage Chickens.* Reproduced with permission of Doug Savage.

Page 121: Figure 8.1: Amazon. Logo. Reproduced with permission of Amazon, Inc. Amazon and the Amazon Logo are trademarks of Amazon.com, Inc. or its affiliates.

Page 125: Figure 8.2: Jurvetson, Steve. Elon Musk oveseeing the construction of Gigafactory. Image courtesy of Wikimedia Commons. This image is licensed under the Creative Commons Attribution-Share Alike 2.0 Generic license.

Page 128: Bachman, Jonathan. "Protestor Ieshia Evans is approached by law enforcement near the headquarters of the Baton Rouge Police Department in Baton Rouge, Louisiana, U.S. July 9, 2016." Reproduced with permission of REUTERS.

Page 183: Figure 10.4: Always. "Like a Girl" ad campaign. Used courtesy and with permission of Always.

Page 242: Figure 13.1: Zyglis, Adam. "Drone Strikes." *The Buffalo News*, 29 December 2013. Reproduced with permission of Adam Zyglis.
Page 338: Figure 18.1: Häggström, Mikael. X-ray of normal hand by dorsoplantar projection. Image courtesy of Wikimedia Commons.

Page 348: Savage, Doug. "Understanding." *Savage Chickens.* Reproduced with permission of Doug Savage.

Page 393: Figure 21.1: Turnitin. "The Plagiarism Spectrum: Tagging 10 Types of Unoriginal Work." Reproduced with permission of Turnitin. www.turnitin.com.

Page 475: Figure 24.1: Raffin, Andrea. Gwyneth Paltrow, 2011. Image courtesy of Wikimedia Commons. This image is licensed under the Creative Commons Attribution-Share Alike 3.0 Unported license.

Page 476: Figure 24.2: Savage, Doug. "New Evidence." *Savage Chickens.* Reproduced with permission of Doug Savage.

Page 478: Savage, Doug. "In Moderation." *Savage Chickens.* Reproduced with permission of Doug Savage.

Page 491: Figure 25.2: "Canadians on Citizenship." Reproduced courtesy of Environics Institute, Institute for Canadian Citizenship, Maytree foundation, CBC News, and RBC Royal Bank.

Page 492: Figure 25.3a: Sanchez, Hugo. "Drawing the Lines of War: *Avengers Age of Ultron.*"

Page 492: Figure 25.3b: Lemonly. "Avengers, Assemble!" Reproduced with permission of Lemonly - www.lemonly.com.

Page 495: Figure 25.7: McCandless, David. "What Makes Good Information Design?" Reproduced with permission of David McCandless@informationisbeautiful.net.

Page 496: Figure 25.8 A: Elections In Myanmar (Photo by Lam Yik Fei/Getty Images).

Page 496: Figure 25.8 B: Eager Retailers Greet Crowds Of Shoppers On 'Black Friday' (Photo by Tom Pennington/Getty Images).

Page 499: Figure 25.9: SoJones. "The History of Hip Hop" from "#AMAs The Ultimate History of Hip Hop." *SoJones.* https://sojones.com/news/105761-amas-the-ultimate-history-of-hip-hop-sojones-infographic.

Page 501: Figure 25.14: Donnelly, Frank. "Distribution of US Public Libraries" from "Average Distance to Public Libraries in the US." *At These Coordinates*. https://atcoordinates.info/2016/02/22/average-distance-to-public-libraries-in-the-us. Reproduced with permission of Frank Donnelly.

Page 505: Figure 25.15: Nielsen, Jakob. Image from *F-Shaped Pattern For Reading Web Content* (2006). https://www.nngroup.com/articles/f-shaped-pattern-reading-web-content-discovered. Reproduced with permission of Nielsen Norman Group.

INDEX

From the Publisher

A name never says it all, but the word "Broadview" expresses a good deal of the philosophy behind our company. We are open to a broad range of academic approaches and political viewpoints. We pay attention to the broad impact book publishing and book printing has in the wider world; for some years now we have used 100% recycled paper for most titles. Our publishing program is internationally oriented and broad-ranging. Our individual titles often appeal to a broad readership too; many are of interest as much to general readers as to academics and students.

Founded in 1985, Broadview remains a fully independent company owned by its shareholders—not an imprint or subsidiary of a larger multinational.

For the most accurate information on our books (including information on pricing, editions, and formats) please visit our website at www.broadviewpress.com. Our print books and ebooks are also available for sale on our site.

broadview press
www.broadviewpress.com